Advanced Praise for

Education as Transformation

"With the increased dominance of specialized knowledge and technical process, all in higher education—students, faculty, and administrators alike—are searching for new sources of meaning and coherence in their lives. *Education as Transformation* is a landmark response to this pressing need. The authors in this volume are the key leaders of what has become a major movement aimed at cultivating substantive engagement and a vigorous dialogue on these critical issues. This book should be read widely throughout higher education."

R. Eugene Rice, Scholar in Residence and Director
of the Forum on Faculty Roles and Rewards
of the American Association for Higher Education

"This valuable collection draws fresh and useful insights on the current state of American university culture from the worlds of religion and spirituality. The voices encountered here, both new and established, will surprise the academy with their humanity and utility. The reflections about campus community building and the promise and challenge of values, spirituality, and religious diversity, are new, useful, and long overdue."

E. Gordon Gee, Chancellor of Vanderbilt University

"Education at its best is always about transformation. The contributors to this book come from diverse traditions, but they share at least one deep conviction: when we reduce education to the mere transmission of data and techniques, we rip the heart out of the enterprise. This book, and the wisdom traditions that inform it, offer both encouragement and guidance as we educators pursue our life-giving vocation."

Parker J. Palmer, Author of The Courage to Teach:
Exploring the Inner Landscape of a Teacher's Life

"The higher I went in my formal education, the more my intellectual work was valued and my spirit devalued. After completing a doctoral degree, I felt a great need to resurrect my soul. The Education as Transformation Project seeks to turn around this alienating process and in compiling this resource, the project seeks ways toward an education that is integrative and unitive."

Patricia M. Mische, Co-Founder and President Emerita
of Global Education Associates; Lloyd Professor
of Peace Studies and World Law at Antioch College

"One of the happiest conjunctions of my life was my service on the Board of Trustees of Wellesley College at the time Victor H. Kazanjian, Jr. became our first Dean of Religious and Spiritual Life. The vitally new concept of campus ministry that he brought to Wellesley is now shared with an increasingly appreciative audience across the country and beyond. This collection puts the vision of a new relationship between higher education and the religious dimension at the forefront of our public discourse where it belongs."

The Reverend Peter J. Gomes, Plummer Professor of Christian Morals and
Pusey Minister in the Memorial Church, Harvard University;
Author of The Good Book: Reading the Bible with Mind and Heart

Education as Transformation

PETER LANG
New York • Washington, D.C./Baltimore • Boston • Bern
Frankfurt am Main • Berlin • Brussels • Vienna • Oxford

Education as Transformation

Religious Pluralism, Spirituality,
and a New Vision
for Higher Education
in America

Edited by
Victor H. Kazanjian, Jr.
and Peter L. Laurence

PETER LANG
New York • Washington, D.C./Baltimore • Boston • Bern
Frankfurt am Main • Berlin • Brussels • Vienna • Oxford

Library of Congress Cataloging-in-Publication Data

Education as transformation: religious pluralism, spirituality,
and a new vision for higher education in America /
edited by Victor H. Kazanjian, Jr. and Peter L. Laurence.
p. cm.
Includes bibliographical references.
1. Education, Higher—Aims and objectives—United States. 2. Religious pluralism—
United States. 3. Spiritual life. 4. Religion—Study and teaching (Higher)—
United States. I. Kazanjian, Victor H. II. Laurence, Peter L.
LB2324.E36   378'.01—dc21   99-089365
ISBN 0-8204-4546-0

Die Deutsche Bibliothek-CIP-Einheitsaufnahme

Education as transformation: religious pluralism, spirituality,
and a new vision for higher education in America /
ed. by Victor H. Kazanjian, Jr. and Peter L. Laurence.
–New York; Washington, D.C./Baltimore; Boston; Bern;
Frankfurt am Main; Berlin; Brussels; Vienna; Oxford: Lang.
ISBN 0-8204-4546-0

Quote on front cover reprinted by permission of the publishers from
The Letters of Emily Dickinson edited by Thomas H. Johnson, Cambridge, Mass.:
The Belknap Press of Harvard University Press, Copyright © 1958, 1986
by the President and Fellows of Harvard College.
Excerpt from "Knowledge...Shall Vanish Away" in *For the Inward Journey:
The Writings of Howard Thurman*, copyright © 1984 by Sue Bailey Thurman,
reprinted by permission of Harcourt, Inc.

Cover design by Nona Reuter

Contents

Preface

VICTOR H. KAZANJIAN, JR. AND PETER L. LAURENCE

Reflecting on the teachings of twelfth-century Jewish mystics, Kaballistic scholar Gershom Scholem writes, "The tree of knowledge and the tree of life are fundamentally one: they grow from a common root...the giving and the receiving, the creative and the reflective, are one. Life and knowledge are not to be torn asunder from one another: they must be seen and realized in their unity."[1] Sholem's words illustrate the historic ideals of education as a holistic process where life and knowledge are inextricably linked in the pursuit of understanding and engaging self, other, and the world.

Such a calling taps into our deepest hopes, dreams, and aspirations for the role that educational communities might play in moving us toward a more peaceful, just, beloved human community and challenges our contemporary educational institutions to draw upon ancient roots and create new ways of teaching and learning that awaken a desire for wholeness within every human heart. Howard Thurman, former dean of Marsh Chapel at Boston University, speaks of this sense of wholeness in a poem entitled *Knowledge...Shall Vanish Away*. The portion of the poem below appears as it was written at a time before our language became more gender inclusive, but certainly Dr. Thurman's intention was to include all of humanity in its sentiments.

> There is a sense of wholeness at the core of man
> that must abound in all he does;
> that marks with reverence his ev'ry step,
> that has its sway when all else fails;
> that wearies out all evil things;
> that warms the depths of frozen fears
> making friend of foe;
> and lasts beyond the living and the dead,
> beyond the goals of peace, the ends of war!
> This man seeks through all his years;
> to be complete and of one piece, within and without. [2]

In the face of this ideal there is much to suggest that, even with all of the accumulated knowledge of the centuries which has led to extraordinary advancement in industry and technology, we remain a deeply troubled, divided people, flirting with a fragmentation that threatens to shatter both the world around us and the world within us. It was Dr. Thurman's conviction that people of all religious beliefs and spiritual perspectives would discover in the course of our shared lives the essential elements of our humanness which bind us one to another in a web of interdependence. For Dr. Thurman this was the essential task of all spirituality and religion, and also the essential task of education, as student and teacher are useful for the academic community as it searches for ways to incorporate spirituality into curricular and co-curricular activities. **Arthur Zajonc**, professor of physics at Amherst College, deals with the relationship between science and spirituality, objectivity and subjectivity. Regarding that apparent duality he says, "When we have re-grounded both science and spirituality in the soil of experience, we will find ways of establishing a fruitful relationship between our intellectual and moral lives and appreciate the common cognitive source for both." **Patrick Morton**, professor of mathematics at Wellesley College, was a participant in the a program on spirituality an education at Wellesley called "Moments of Meaning in the Classroom." From this experience, he writes about his own encounters with "subjectivity" and how he tries to provide elements of meaning and purpose for his students. Finally, **Beverly Daniel Tatum**, dean of the college at Mt. Holyoke, offers reflections on her work with racial identity development and brings an essential perspective to the search for spirituality in education and the transforming potential of religious pluralism. As a psychologist and a college administrator, she looks at the process of transformation from both the individual and institutional points of view.

The second major section of the book, **From Religious Diversity to Religious Pluralism: New Possibilities for Global Learning Communities**, provides a series of insights into the ways in which several major religious traditions view the existence of religious diversity and the strategy of religious pluralism. While religious diversity is simply a fact, the attitude of pluralism is defined by Diana Eck in the following way.

> Truth is not the exclusive or inclusive possession of any one tradition or
> community. Therefore the diversity of communities, traditions, understandings
> of the truth, and visions of God is not an obstacle for us to overcome, but an
> opportunity for our energetic engagement and dialogue with one another. It
> does not mean giving up our commitments; rather, it means opening up those
> commitments to the give-and-take of mutual discovery, understanding, and
> indeed, transformation.[5]

It is not surprising that many of these essays refer to Eck's writing. Her groundbreaking work that has opened the way for major advances in inter-religious understanding has inspired many of us who are part of this movement. The essays in this section are arranged alphabetically by the primary author's last name so that no particular weight is given to any one tradition. We begin, then, with **Suheil Badi Bushrui**, professor at the University of Maryland, and **James Malarkey**, professor at Antioch College, presenting "A Baha'i Model of Education for Unity," which affirms the critical importance of education for the Bahá'í faith and describes the Bahá'í attitude towards other religions as "unequivocally conciliatory and appreciative." The Bahá'í "Education for Unity" model has been tested by the authors in their team-taught World Order Studies program over a period of nine consecutive summers in Switzerland.

Brad DrowningBear, former spiritual life coordinator at Haskell Indian Nations University, talks of his own transformation within the context of his Native American roots and Christian training. Religious diversity is seen through the image of the unity and oneness of all things, as represented by the Sacred Circle of Life and symbolized by the medicine wheel. **Arthur Green**, professor of Jewish Thought at Brandeis University leads us through the history of Jewish involvement in the academy and in American society, focusing on the differences between two specific schools of thought within the Jewish community and, finally, on Jewish views regarding religious pluralism.

Roman Catholicism's experience with religious pluralism as both challenge and opportunity is thoughtfully presented by **John W. Healey**, Director of the Archbishop Hughes Institute on Religion and Culture at Fordham University, who asserts, "Interreligious dialogue has not, however, had the impact one might expect on the American Catholic college campus." The search for identity at Catholic-affiliated colleges and universities is being actively pursued in light of growing religious diversity among students at these institutions. **Ji Hyang Sunim**, a Buddhist nun and Abbot of the Cambridge Zen Center, begins with a discourse on Buddhism as a pluralistic tradition and then moves on to talk about pluralism in higher education in general, and finally about her experiences at Wellesley College.

Gurucharan Singh Khalsa, psychotherapist, author and educator guides us through an extensive exploration of how the mind may work to promote or inhibit a sense of pluralism. Drawing on Sikh tradition, he suggests that higher education must consider new ways of viewing the functions of the mind in order to provide an education that can keep pace with our rapidly changing contemporary society. **Sulayman Nyang**, professor of African Studies at Howard University, presents a broad view of American pluralism from an Islamic perspective. He identifies elements of diversity within the Islamic community that result in different attitudes toward American culture and makes specific recommendations about ways in which colleges and universities might better address the needs of Muslim students.

A Hindu view of religious pluralism is developed by **Anantanand Rambachan**, professor of Religion and Asian Studies at St. Olaf College, who brings us into contact with Hindu literature and speaks of a modern world "which is radically and self-consciously plural and, for all that we can see, determined to stay so." Finally, **Krister Stendahl**, professor of divinity emeritus at Harvard University and former Bishop of Stockholm, Sweden, explores "claims to uniqueness" from a Christian perspective, in the light of religious diversity. He describes the practice of "Holy Envy," meaning "the capacity of finding in other faiths some things that are meaningful, beautiful and which tell me something important about God."

The last section of this book, **Taking It Home: The Transformational Process in Action**, offers help in taking these important ideas about religious pluralism and spirituality back to your colleges, universities, communities and institutions. The stories are told by people who have worked to develop structures, processes, and programs on these themes. **Douglas C. Bennett**, president of Earlham College, begins with an account of Earlham's attempts to become hospitable to all faiths while maintaining its identity as a Quaker institution. Contrary to the general trend toward secularism experienced by many colleges and universities, Earlham has remained true to its Quaker roots and has fashioned its approach to pluralism from that foundation. **Shirley Hershey Showalter**, president of Goshen College, uses the imagery of three rivers to convey the story of her own life and that of Goshen College. As an institution strongly based in the Mennonite tradition, Goshen has developed programs that exemplify "some of the distinctive elements of Mennonite theology: peace, service, community, nonconformity, and discipleship."

James P. Keen, professor at Antioch College, refers to the research that led to the publication of _Common Fire: Leading Lives of Commitment in a Complex World_ as resulting in the conviction that "promoting encounters that help people learn to sustain relationships which reach across boundaries of irreducible differences should be among the most important aims of contemporary higher education." He describes in detail the E Pluribus Unum conferences as a way of "bringing together Catholics, Protestants and Jews to explore how their own traditions can support collaboration on issues of social justice and prospects of community service."

Victor Kazanjian, dean of religious and spiritual life and director of the Peace and Justice Studies Program at Wellesley College, along with **the students of the Multi-faith Council at Wellesley College**, have crafted an essay which explores the process that Wellesley went through in transforming itself from a mono-religious to a multi-religious institution. It expresses the joys and tensions experienced by the Wellesley students who prepared one of the most striking and popular presentations at the national gathering—the staged version of _Beyond Tolerance_— an artistic rendering of the encounter between students of different religious traditions. **Donna Bivens**, co-director of the Women's Theological Center, draws on her background as a Wellesley College alumnae and as the director of a community-based social change center to reflect on how the EDUCATION as _Transformation_ national gathering provided a context for her to make the connections between her own experiences as an undergraduate at Wellesley College and issues of transformation in the context of cultural diversity, particularly race. **Janet Cooper Nelson**, faculty member and university chaplain at Brown University, writes out of her deep religious roots, her experience at Brown, and as a national leader in issues of religious life on college and university campuses, about bringing the spiritual dimension back into higher education. She beautifully suggests that EDU-

CATION as *Transformation* should best be understood as art, "whose mythic sources and design specifications continue to be articulated as it is being produced."

Robert M. Randolph, senior associate dean in the Office of the Dean of Students and Undergraduate Education at the Massachusetts Institute of Technology, has been a primary force in the creation of the Religious Activities Center at MIT. Bringing together the various religious communities of the Institute in one space has been an experiment in building understanding across religious boundaries and, as Dean Randolph indicates, "those involved in developing shared space must understand at the outset that they might be learning as much as they are teaching." This story can serve as an inspiration and a model for any institution contemplating a similar change process. **Susan Laemmle** recounts her experiences as a rabbi and as the current dean of religious life at the University of Southern California. Her story provides a fascinating case study of a unique religious life program, elements of which might be modeled elsewhere. Of this work she says, "Being dean of religious life or university chaplain at a secular university means walking a delicate line between personal religious commitment and religious neutrality. Maintaining balance when crossing a mountain stream or a even a bridge makes me nervous, but it turns out that performing the religious balancing act has not been as difficult for me as anticipated."

Frederic Bradford Burnham, director of the Trinity Institute, describes a collaborative project involving the Episcopal Church Foundation and the Trinity Institute in partnership with the EDUCATION as *Transformation* Project. *LINKS: Connecting Head and Heart on Campus* is an attempt "to use the interactive capabilities of Internet and satellite communications to establish intergenerational, interdisciplinary, interfaith communities of dialogue on college campuses across the country." His essay also provides a scholarly treatment of the two distinct ways of knowing represented by "head" and heart."

Sally Z. Hare, a professor at Coastal Carolina University, along with **Marcy and Rick Jackson**, co-directors of the Center for Teacher Formation, talk about the *Courage to Teach* program that has grown out of the seminal work of Parker J. Palmer and the Fetzer Institute. While this program has been designed to serve teachers in K-12 schools, there are important implications for higher education that need to be further examined. **Carol L. Flake**, professor at the University of South Carolina, asks, "What can teacher education institutions do to recruit and nurture the development of teachers who can and will create classroom environments that are sites for spiritual transformation?" and goes on to address that question by offering a number of concepts and recommendations. Included is a vision statement from the Global Alliance for Transforming Education, which contains ten principles of holistic education.

And finally, **Claudia Horwitz**, founder and director of stone circles, an organizations that integrates faith, spiritual practice and social justice, provides us with some very practical ways of working with groups to develop a vision for interfaith work. Quoting a colleague, she reminds us that "Martin Luther King did not stand up in front of throngs of people gathered in Washington, D.C., and preach, 'I have a strategic plan.' It was about a dream, and all truly powerful efforts begin with the seed of a dream."

We wish to offer our deepest appreciation to all of the authors who have contributed to this book. Their courage to pursue these issues as scholars and teachers has helped break through the fear that has paralyzed this discourse in higher education for too long. We also want to thank several people whose spirit and energy are reflected in this book: to Helen Marie Casey and Kali Saposnick, whose insights and gifts for editing have given shape and form to this publication; to Diane Dana, Margaret Kowalsky and Kathe Lewis, without whose work the EDUCATION as *Transformation* Project would not be possible; to Diana Chapman Walsh, for her ongoing leadership, inspiration and support; to Wellesley College for making a home for this movement; to all those who donated time, effort and financial support toward making the national gathering in 1998 possible, especially the Laurance S. Rockefeller Fund, the Boston Research Center for the 21st Century and the Episcopal Church Foundation; and to those participants in the EDUCATION as *Transformation* Project from more than 300 colleges, universities and related institutions across the country and around the world who have initiated a movement which seeks to create a new vision for higher education in America and beyond.

ENDNOTES

1. Gershom Sholem, *On the Mystical Shape of the Godhead* (New York: Schocken Books, 1991), 70.
2. Howard Thurman, *For the Inward Journey: The Writings of Howard Thurman* (New York: Harcourt Brace Jovanovich, 1984), 11.
3. Parker J. Palmer, *The Courage to Teach: Exploring the Inner Landscape of a Teacher's Life* (San Francisco: Jossey-Bass Publishers, 1998).
4. Laurent A. Parks Daloz, Cheryl H. Keen, James P. Keen, and Sharon Daloz Parks, *Common Fire: Lives of Commitment in a Complex World* (Boston: Beacon Press, 1996).
5. Diana L. Eck, *Encountering God: A Spiritual Journey from Bozeman to Banaras* (Boston: Beacon Press, 1993).

Introduction

Transforming Education: An Overview

DIANA CHAPMAN WALSH

We seek to envision a whole new place—and space and role—for spirituality in higher education, not as an isolated enterprise on the margins of the academy, not as a new form of institutional repression and social control, but as an essential element of the larger task of reorienting our institutions to respond more adequately to the challenges the world presents us now: challenges to our teaching, to our learning, to our leading, to our lives.

On September 27, 1998, I spoke those words in opening remarks at a national gathering entitled "EDUCATION as *Transformation*: Religious Pluralism, Spirituality and Higher Education." Held on the Wellesley College campus, the conference brought to the foreground a movement already well under way. The movement has accelerated in subsequent months.

Hundreds of people from scores of institutions across the country came to the Wellesley campus for the national gathering and have since been congregating and coalescing across many lines—institutional lines, professional lines, disciplinary lines, lines of individual identity and personal commitment—to explore the place of religious pluralism and spirituality in the academy.

Their conversations are, more consciously, bringing into awareness those aspects of our work as educators that occasion the greatest fulfillment and deepest satisfaction, those aspects that, to us and to our students, are most meaningful and inspiring, most life-giving and life-affirming. Lines of demarcation are gradually being redrawn through this work into circles of inclusion. A broader, deeper, and more daring form of intellectual discourse is taking shape in these academic circles. "All serious daring," Eudora Welty writes at the end of her elegant memoir, "starts from within."[1]

From Richard Tarnas's 1991 history of Western thought I drew an image with which I suggested the gathering might fruitfully begin. Having transported his reader up to, then into the postmodern mind, having traced and described our contemporary predicament of "extraordinary differentiation, dogmatic relativism, fragmenting skepticism," Tarnas offers the provocative and hopeful hunch that humanity may be: "gathering now on the intellectual stage as if for some kind of climactic synthesis—a potential emergence of a fundamentally new form of intellectual vision, one that might both preserve and transcend the current state of extraordinary differentiation."[2]

It is not too great a stretch, I believe, to suggest as a metaphor for the work of bringing more of the spirit back into higher education the image of the academy reside somewhere between us and our imperfect understandings of one another. The Earlham College statement on religious life (described in the chapter by President Douglas C. Bennett) walks this tightrope beautifully, carving out spaces within which groups can experience their own commitments as the norm, avoiding the imposition of one group's values on another group, and yet welcoming friends and visitors to all activities.

What we can hope is that the young people who do this hard work of differentiation and integration in the safe spaces we hold open for them on our college campuses will go out into the world and work to transform it in important ways. They will take responsibility for the contexts in which they find themselves—in workplaces, families, communities. They will continue to confront their own blind spots and to grapple with their internal contradictions, and they will act with integrity, courage, and conviction in the world.

To support our students in this process of transformational growth, we need learning environments that integrate into the educational process all of student experience: curricular, extracurricular, residential, social, inter and intrapersonal. And we must address the central question of how to find greater coherence, meaning, and purpose in academic life. This brings us to the second domain of work in which our questions of spirituality and religion are embedded, the many questions relating to pedagogy, broadly defined, a massive topic on which we can merely scratch the surface.

How We Learn and How We Teach

The ideals of higher education, going back to the Greeks, and the values to which we subscribe in our rhetoric even now, have everything to do with taking time to foster the critical abilities of students, to guide them in developing not only knowledge and skill but also qualities of mind and spirit that will carry them through their lives: wide-ranging curiosity; a taste for scholarship, for ideas, for intellectual challenge and exchange; a willingness to take responsibility for what they count as truth, and why; an openness to multiple viewpoints; and a commitment to self-critique.

And never have these qualities been more vital than they are in the current climate. Public debate is increasingly superficial and shrill, attention spans are shortening, civic life is deteriorating,[15] and the half-life of usable knowledge is rapidly being compressed. At such a time, a liberal education is more essential than ever, for individual learners and for the larger society.

At Wellesley we often say we exist "to provide an excellent liberal arts education for women who will make a difference in a world." And if we were to do a content analysis of mission statements of colleges and universities across the country, we would find different wording but claims in many of them, I suspect, that what we in higher education are about is providing education for citizenship, for leadership, for stewardship—education that will inspire our students to work to create a sustainable, equitable, and hopeful future. Less evident in those same materials is any kind of cogent description of how any of us actually purports to implement that vision. Is it nothing more than lip service then?

From one perspective, higher education right now is rife with fragmentation, relativism, skepticism, hollow rhetoric, disillusionment, and confusion. From another, though, I think we can see the contours of a new and creative synthesis that goes beyond chaos to a fundamental reordering of priorities and preoccupations.

Indeed, some of the most exciting contemporary writings on higher education are forging new, higher-order syntheses. Examples include: Ronald Barnett's elegant philosophical essay on the idea of higher education;[16] Robert Orrill's edited collections, for the College Board, on education and democracy;[17] Bruce Kimball's distinction between orators and philosophers;[18] Donald Kennedy's writings on academic duty;[19] Lawrence Levine's spirited defense of multiculturalism;[20] Charles Anderson's case for what he calls "practical reason;"[21] Bliss Carnochan's historical grounding of contemporary curricular debates;[22] Stephen Brookfield's lessons in how to become a "critically-reflective" teacher.[23] Martha Nussbaum's book, *Cultivating Humanity*,[24] is a thoughtful overview of the classical roots of liberal education and a review of some contemporary experiments that she sees as faithful to those early principles. Thomas Pangle, a political philosopher, analyzes the impact of postmodernist thought on Plato's idea of a liberal education, namely: "the education from childhood in virtue, that makes one desire and love to become a perfect citizen who knows how to rule and be ruled with justice."[25]

Each of these works is a very different analysis; each has its own distinct perspective and point of departure, each sets its own intellectual task. Yet, when they are taken together, it is striking that each, in its own way, is arguing back to first principles—digging under the surface of convocation rhetoric to deeper questions of the purpose and meaning of a liberal education—and moving beyond critique to creative new perspectives on the enterprise of higher education and its obligations in the contemporary context. Several hint at how profoundly the professor's inner life—the professor's identity, integrity, and engagement—color and shape the learning encounter

We know intuitively that disaffected, dispirited, and alienated faculty are unlikely to be teaching well, unlikely to be providing their students the inspiration and guidance they need at a time when we need students to be inspired. If the task of a college or university professor is, as I think we can agree, to inspire students with a love of learning that will companion them throughout their lives, if we subscribe to Yeats's oft-quoted insight that true education is not the filling of a pail but the igniting of a flame, then surely we want faculty who are themselves on fire with a passion for their work.

This is because, as Csikszentmihalyi has posited, the main purpose of higher education is distinct from lower-level schooling. The act of professing—with its root sense of being bound by a vow, or expressing faith or allegiance to a subject matter—has the special significance that the success of higher education involves motivation, not cognitive transfer of information.

Although such a goal runs counter to today's strong tides of vocationalism, value for money, and higher education for instrumental gain—the student's or the society's—most would accept the premise that one desired result of higher education is an intrinsically-motivated learner. From this it should follow that the person producing that result—the professor—ought her or himself to be palpably and fiercely an intrinsically-motivated learner in the search for knowledge, and also in the classroom for the joy of it. Just as John Dewey believed that education for democracy ought itself to be democratically organized,[26] so it seems obvious that education for intrinsic motivation ought to be embedded therein, and spring therefrom.

Helen Vendler, as quoted in *Habits of the Heart*,[27] captured eloquently from the professor's vantage point the sanctity of this professor-to-student transmission of passion for a subject:

> "We owe it to ourselves to show our students, when they first meet us, what we are; we owe their dormant appetites, thwarted for so long in their previous schooling, that deep sustenance that will make them realize that they too, having been taught, love what we love."[28]

Faculty owe it to themselves to teach what they love, and in so doing they nourish their students. They owe it to themselves to show their students what they are. And they need to know what they love, and what they are—not a simple task, but surely an anchor without which they will drift.

Parker Palmer writes about what he calls "the teaching self." He asks, "How does the quality of my selfhood form—and deform—the way I relate to my students, my subject, my colleagues, my world?... How can educational institutions sustain and deepen the selfhood from which good teaching comes?"[29] There, at the heart of the enterprise, is the love of subject from which Helen Vendler suggests we owe it to ourselves to begin.

Great professors, Parker Palmer writes, are the ones who weave webs of connection for their students. The current preoccupations of educational reform—proficiency with technology, tightly-framed learning outcomes, even multicultural awareness—are secondary to the passion professors bring to their subject matter, the compassion, awe, and joy they embody and communicate. Great teaching comes from spirit, not from technique, a truth we are rediscovering as we sense that our center is ceasing to hold.

The freedoms from institutional religious constraint we scholars treasure need not be threatened by opening ourselves to the spiritual dimensions of teaching, learning, and knowing: we need not deny the possibility of a kind of knowing that comes from the heart and soul—in addition to the intellect. We can sense when we are helping students discover places of deep knowing within themselves. We are alert to their intellectual travails and attuned to their inner conditions. We listen intently for what is being said, and for what is still unsayable. We ask gently probing questions that open avenues to self-awareness. We strike a careful balance between nurturing and challenging. We encourage and support thoughtful reflection on experience. I am suggesting, in addition, that we can make an effort to create opportunities—and a cultural ethos—to be those kinds of good teachers to ourselves and to one another within the academy.

For if those of us who are called to be educators in these times of great ferment and change can support one another in our efforts to cultivate our own inner resources, then we can create healthy learning environments. Our students will benefit in two ways: (1) directly from the effects of the healthier environments we create; and (2) indirectly from the influence of the healthier, more balanced, role models we project. Our students desperately want to believe that there are adults who have their priorities straight, who know who they are and what they love, and who find the deep meaning that animates their work.

Inspired faculty are indispensable in that meaning making. They can build the relationships, forge the connections, and bind the pluralistic global learning communities that will provide undergraduates with models to carry through their lives, models of communities that inspire purpose and commitment to causes larger than themselves. This brings us to the third of our broader themes.

THE QUALITY OF CAMPUS INTELLECTUAL LIFE

The success of our educational efforts depends, too, on the quality of the residential learning communities we can sustain. At the threshold of the twenty-first century, American colleges and universities face no more crucial challenge than how to conserve a spirit of community, how to sustain the struggles for collaboration, participation, and inclusiveness as national debates continue to polarize our society and as wide gaps separate rich and poor.

An excellent liberal arts education should foster flexible intellectual skills, critical habits of mind, respect for history, and appreciation of beauty, tolerance, civility and empathy, and a spirit of responsible stewardship for future generations. Students who go to college for individual advancement should find themselves immersed in a learning community in which knowledge is acquired as part of a deeper process of assuming a mantle of maturity and social efficacy.

Garry Wills's elegant study, *Lincoln at Gettysburg,* bears witness to the power of words in forging community and unity of purpose:

> It would have been hard to predict that Gettysburg... would become a symbol of national purpose, pride and ideals. Abraham Lincoln transformed the ugly reality into something rich and strange—and he did it with 272 words. The power of words has rarely been given a more compelling demonstration.[30]

We academic leaders worry quite lot about how we converse with each other and the choices we make in the ways we engage our differences. We sense that those choices do reflect and shape institutional purpose, pride, and ideals. Residential colleges work hard to be special places of refuge for people committed to the life of the mind, spaces in which scholars can reason well together, respect-fully, mindfully, responsibly, and with the eros or love of truth that animated the Greeks. Some are more successful than others at integrating individualism and interdependence, at promoting a communal spirit and a sense of common purpose, at fostering and valuing the contributions of everyone, at addressing human needs for both solitude and support. We are more and less attentive, in the words of Jane Tompkins, to "social excellence as well as personal achievement."[31]

But we hold a common ideal, even knowing that our campuses are never quite all that we wish them to be, not all of the time for anyone; not any of the time for some. We grant that a scholarly community can be a lonely place, but we often conceive of the challenges students face as largely interpersonal, or social, or de-velopmental. Martha Nussbaum identifies, importantly, the intellectual roots of a sense of isolation in the academy. She describes the essential task of a liberal edu-cation as "becoming a citizen of the world." This is "a lonely business," she ob-serves:

> It is, in effect, a kind of exile—from the comfort of assured truths, from the warm nestling feeling of being surrounded by people who share one's convictions and passions. In the writings of Marcus Aurelius (as in those of his American followers Emerson and Thoreau) one sometimes feels a boundless loneliness, as if the removal of the props of habit and convention, the decision to trust no authority but moral reasoning, had left life bereft of a certain sort of warmth and security.[32]

So, warmth and security are not the desiderata of the ideal community called college that we hold in common. Rather, we are reaching toward this notion of world citizenship, this act of "cultivating humanity," the title of Nussbaum's book, which she traces to the Roman Stoic philosopher, Seneca the Younger, tutor to the young emperor Nero: "Soon we shall breathe our last," Seneca wrote at the end of his treatise on the destructive effects of anger and hatred. "Meanwhile, while we live, while we are among human beings, let us cultivate our humanity."[33]

Cultivating our humanity as informed and ethical citizens, not of some paro-chial and exclusive identity group, but of the human race: this lies at the heart of the liberal arts ideal, the ideal of the kind of community we aspire to be. We hold this ideal collectively, and it matters very much. Generations of students, faculty, and staff on campuses across the country have held this ideal sometimes against powerful counter forces. And much has been at stake: not only civility and peace of mind, or collegiality and a spirit of collective purpose that can inspire and ener-gize their work, as important as those leanings are. At stake has been the deepest meaning of a liberal education.

The challenge Lincoln faced at Gettysburg, as Wills tells the story, is that the founding fathers "did not accomplish the political equality they professed. They did not end slavery. They did not make self-government stable and enduring. They could not do that. The ideal is not captured at once in the real."[34] And so it is with the ideal college community—not captured at once in the real—nor indeed likely ever to be, any more than will our national dream of radical equality. But new generations can reclaim the ideal, as Lincoln did—and later Martin Luther King —can reshape and reaffirm it, infuse it with fresh meaning, draw new inspiration from it, make it their own.

The vision of a community that can reason well together speaks to the fundamental purpose of a liberal education, and is essential for its realization. From the beginning, liberal arts colleges were organized around the notion, going back to Plato and Aristotle, that we humans can free—can liberate—our minds if we can develop the discipline of accepting only those beliefs that stand a test of reason: systematic tests of consistency and thoughtful justification.

Education for critical thinking, then, for freedom from prejudice and blind ignorance, is what we are all about, education involving a special kind of human interaction, a constant testing of our most cherished convictions—the ones we most take for granted—against serious and disturbing challenges, that binds together members of an intellectual community united in a common enterprise. Its members are committed to learning from one another everything they can about how a different experience or perspective—how a new insight, argument, or data point—might fundamentally alter their own tentative and provisional notions of what is true. "No experiment can ever prove me right," Einstein said, "a single experiment can always prove me wrong."

Such are the obligations and duties of a community of reason, holding as a collective project the ideal of a liberal education. Ultimately, these same obligations are the demands of citizenship in a democracy, "the great task remaining before us," in Lincoln's immortal words. And these are the practices that provide opportunities for students to learn, in a safe and accepting space, how to take up and defend informed positions of their own, how to know, to the extent possible, what they know and how they know it.

What We Know and How We Know It

Because our national gathering attracted many more people than originally anticipated, we met under a big white tent on the lawn beside the chapel, adjacent to the library, at the busiest intersection on the campus. The sense of fellowship and community under that tent was palpable and added to the pleasure of the gathering. At the closing session, Vincent Harding, as is his custom, felt we needed some music and invited participants to join him in singing "We are Building up a New World" to the tune of "Rise, Shine, Give God Glory." As the hundreds of voices rose in a resonant chorus, the playful thought ran through my mind that faculty walking to the library would hear the music and conclude that their worst fears were being confirmed, that we had installed a revival tent right in the heart of the campus.

When we talk of "alternative ways of knowing," as Parker Palmer did in his keynote address and does in his chapter for this book, we begin to sound to at least some faculty like tent revivalists. Ideas about "alternative epistemologies" can

making dimension of their teaching and learning and of their perceptions of the spiritual aspects of their work, what had drawn them to it, their sense of vocation, as Frederick Buechner defines it: the place where the heart's deep gladness and the world's deep hunger meet.[40]

And we *are* speaking of hunger. For a very long time, our institutions of higher learning, many of which grew from religious and spiritual beginnings, have been disconnected from the sustenance of those roots because of the twin fear of imposing received wisdom on the pure pursuit of knowledge, and monoreligious traditions on our increasingly multireligious communities. Our secularism has confused freedom *of* religion with freedom *from* religion.

As we are gradually coming to appreciate the importance of viewpoint diversity in the academy and of an integrated, holistic educational experience to prepare today's students for the world they will encounter, it is becoming clear that religious diversity is an integral part of the story. Creating a new vision for spirituality in higher education is only one component, but an essential one, of the effort to invent a new educational process that will respond more fully to the challenges the world is calling us to confront with all the honesty, integrity, and intelligence we can muster. I hope you, too, will find in the essays, ideas, and stories in this collection, the moments of inspiration, wonder, and awe that gladden your heart and enable you to do what you can to meet the needs of the world.

ENDNOTES

1. Eudora Welty, *One Writer's Beginnings* (Cambridge: Harvard University Press, 1984).
2. Richard Tarnas, *The Passion of the Western Mind* (New York: Ballantine 1981).
3. Paul Rogat Loeb, *Soul of a Citizen: Living with Conviction in a Cynical Time* (New York: St. Martins, 1999).
4. Jedediah Purdy, *For Common Things: Irony, Trust, and Commitment in America Today* (New York: Alfred A. Knopf, 1999).
5. Anne Colby and William Damon, *Some Do Care: Contemporary Lives of Moral Commitment* (New York: Free Press, 1992).
6. Arthur W. Chickering and Linda Reisser, *Education and Identity* (San Francisco: Jossey-Bass, 1993).
7. Alexander W. Astin, *What Matters in College? Four Critical Years Revisited* (San Francisco: Jossey-Bass, 1993).
8. Howard Gardner, *The Disciplined Mind* (New York: Simon and Schuster, 1999); Howard Gardner, *Frames of Mind* (New York: Basic Books, 1983).
9. Laurent A. Parks Daloz, Cheryl H. Keen, James P. Keen, Sharon Daloz Parks, *Common Fire: Leading Lives of Commitment in a Complex World* (Boston: Beacon Press, 1996).
10. See J. Walker Smith and Ann Clurman, *Rocking the Ages: The Yankelovich Report on Generational Marketing* (New York: Harper Business, 1997).

11. Neil Howe and William Strauss. *Generations* (New York: William Morrow, 1991); Neil Howe and William Strauss, *13th Gen: Abort, Retry, Ignore, Fail?* (New York: Vintage Books, 1993); William Strauss, *The Fourth Turning* (New York: Broadway Books, 1997).
12. Daryl G. Smith and Associates, *Diversity Works: The Emerging Picture of How Students Benefit* (Washington, DC: Association of American Colleges and Universities, 1997).
13. William Bowen and Derek Bok, *The Shape of the River* (Princeton: Princeton University Press, 1998).
14. Diana L. Eck, *Encountering God: A Spiritual Journey from Bozeman to Banaras* (Boston: Beacon Press, 1993).
15. Campus Compact, *President's Declaration on the Civic Responsibility of Higher Education* (Providence: Campus Compact, 1999).
16. Ronald Barnett, *The Idea of Higher Education* (Buckingham, England: The Society for Research into Higher Education, 1990).
17. Robert Orrill, ed. *Education and Democracy: Re-Imagining Liberal Learning in America* (New York: College Board, 1997) and Robert Orrill, ed. *The Condition of American Liberal Education: Pragmatism and a Changing Tradition* (New York, College Board, 1995).
18. Bruce A Kimball, *Orators and Philosophers: A History of the Idea of Liberal Education* (New York: College Board, 1995).
19. Donald Kennedy, *Academic Duty* (Cambridge: Harvard University Press, 1997).
20. Lawrence Levine, *The Opening of the American Mind: Canons, Culture and History* (Boston: Beacon Press, 1996).
21. Charles W. Anderson, *Prescribing the Life of the Mind: An Essay on the Purpose of the University, the Aims of Liberal Education, the Competence of Citizens, and the Cultivation of Practical Reason* (Madison: University of Wisconsin Press, 1993).
22. W. B. Carnochan, *The Battleground of the Curriculum: Liberal Education and American Experience* (Stanford: Stanford University Press, 1993).
23. Stephen Brookfield, *Becoming a Critically-Reflective Teacher* (San Francisco. Jossey Bass, 1995).
24. Martha Nussbaum, *Cultivating Humanity: A Classical Defense of Reform in Higher Education* (Cambridge: Harvard University Press, 1997).
25. From Plato's "Athenian Stranger," quoted in Thomas L. Pangle, *The Enobling of Democracy: The Challenge of the Postmodern Age* (Baltimore: Johns Hopkins University Press, 1992), 164.
26. Alan Ryan, *John Dewey and the High Tide of American Liberalism* (New York: W. W. Norton, 1995).
27. Robert N. Bellah, Richard Madsen, William A. Sullivan, Ann Swidler, Steven M. Tipton, *Habits of the Heart* (Berkeley and Los Angeles: University of California Press, 1985); see also Robert N. Bellah, Richard Madsen, William A.

Sullivan, Ann Swidler, Steven M. Tipton, eds. *The Good Society* (New York: Random House, 1992).

28. Bellah, op cit., 293–294.
29. Parker J. Palmer, *The Courage to Teach* (San Francisco: Jossey-Bass, 1998).
30. Garry Wills, *Lincoln at Gettysburg: The Words that Remade America* (New York: Simon and Schuster, 1992) 20.
31. Jane Tompkins. "The Way We Live Now," *Change*, November-December, 1992: 13–19.
32. Nussbaum, op. cit., 83.
33. Nussbaum, op. cit., 301.
34. Wills. op. cit., 21.
    Note that there is no footnote 37 here. This will have to be fixed.
35. Quoted in George M. Marsden, *The Soul of the American University: From Protestant Establishment to Established Nonbelief* (New York: Oxford, 1994).
36. See Marsden, op. cit.
37. See Marsden, op. cit.
38. David Pillemer, *Momentous Events, Vivid Memories* (Cambridge: Harvard University Press, 1998).
39. Arthur Zajonc, *Catching the Light* (New York: Oxford University Press, 1993).
40. Frederick Buechner, *Wishful Thinking: A Seeker's ABC* (San Francisco: Harper, 1993), 119.

PART ONE

*A New Vision of
Education as Transformation*

1 A Vision of Education as Transformation

PARKER J. PALMER

As I launch into this brief reflection on the relationship between higher education and spirituality, I do not need to belabor the well-known resistance of the
contemporary American academy to all things religious. But I want to take just a
moment to turn the prism on that relationship, to remind us of some of its complexities.

The first turn of the prism reveals how much of American higher education
was set in motion by a religious impulse—an impulse, in part, to understand the
marvels of creation. As I have come to know a variety of traditions—Buddhism,
Judaism, Islam, Christianity, among others—I have seen that each of them has
such a deep desire to understand the reality in which we are embedded that each
has given rise to a system of education that is remarkable in its own right.

But a second turn of the prism reminds us why contemporary education re-
sists any active relationship to religion or spirituality. Just ask Galileo. At the heart
of every religious tradition, right alongside the desire to understand creation, there
is also the potential for a fearful clinging to how *my* tradition understands it, a
desire to limit understanding to *my* version of rigid religious orthodoxy.

The third turn of the prism is the one I'd like to stay with for a while. It
reminds us of the fact that higher education has developed its own orthodoxy, its
own set of blinders through which to view the world that surrounds us. It is an
orthodoxy that can, and does, trammel inquiry as fully as the orthodoxies found in
the world's formal religious traditions.

The orthodoxy I want to focus on for a few moments is the one called objectivism. It is an epistemology, a way of knowing, whose tacit doctrines and creeds
are at the heart of academic practice—at the heart of how we conduct both our
research and our teaching—in exactly the same way that the doctrines and creeds
of any formal religious tradition are at the heart of its practices. On second thought,
there is one difference. The religious community is more straightforward than the
academic community about the fact that it has doctrines and creeds!

As I examine objectivism, I want to be clear from the outset that I am *not*
talking about what I understand as true science. I do not believe that true science is
the enemy in this dialogue—on the contrary, I believe it is an ally and asset in the
conversation we're having here. As I travel the country, I meet many physicists
and chemists and biologists who are themselves reaching for the deeper dimensions of knowing, teaching, and learning—and in their company this becomes an
even more probing and searching conversation.

Objectivism insists that we can know the world only by distancing ourselves
from it, by separating our inner lives from the external objects we want to know.
According to objectivist doctrine, we must safeguard those so-called objects from

what this epistemology perceives as the extreme danger of subjectivity—a subjectivity that, if unleashed, will slop over onto the objects in question and render our knowledge of them inaccurate, impure.

The central doctrine of this orthodoxy is that inside the subjective self are dangerous things—like bias, ignorance, prejudice, error, blinders, limitation—things that would distort our knowledge of the objects of the world if we allow the self into the knowing equation. (It has occurred to me that while the concept of original sin, of the essential untrustworthiness of the human self, is dead or dying in my own liberal Protestant religious tradition, it is alive and well at the heart of academic orthodoxy!) So objectivism, with its distrust of the human self, insists that we can know the world truly and well only by holding the knower at arm's length from the known.

I have only two problems with that notion. One, it is morally deforming. Two, it is an unfaithful rendition of how human beings know the world. (Other than that, I think objectivism is a perfectly splendid epistemology!)

It is a morally deforming way of knowing because it leads us to hold our knowledge in a way that removes us from the world, so that our knowledge can lead neither toward moral engagement with that world nor toward moral responsibility for it. I can illustrate this most clearly, I think, with an example from my own education—one that I have reflected on often and painfully.

I was taught in the objectivist manner about the history of the Holocaust, taught, through abstract words and cold statistics, the history of the Third Reich, whose murderous details are well-known. But because the underlying mode of knowing was so distanced, I ended up somehow imagining—and I've never known quite how to say this—that the Holocaust happened on another planet to another species. My knowledge of those horrors was not "felt" knowledge, not embodied knowledge, not incarnate in my life.

In that distancing, two things happened that were profoundly morally deforming. One, I never learned the truth of my own story. I grew up in a privileged suburb of Chicago called Wilmette. But if you were a Jew living in that area in the 1950s, you didn't live in Wilmette, and you didn't live in Winnetka, and you didn't live in Kenilworth: you lived in Glencoe, because a systemic form of fascism was at work to keep "them" apart from "us." Glencoe was a ghetto, a gilded ghetto, to be sure, but a ghetto formed by a fear of otherness that was a part of my history. The "big story" I was learning should have been taught in a way that illumined my own "little story."

Second, and deeper still, my objectivist education did not teach me that I have within myself a certain "fascism of the heart." It is a shadow force that, when the difference between me and you gets too great, when you threaten my conception of truth, will press me to find some way to kill you off. I will not do it with a gun or a gas chamber but with some sort of categorization or objectification that renders you, for all practical purposes, lifeless, irrelevant to my life: "Oh, you're just a (fill in the blank)."

This is moral deformation that happened not because I lacked courses on ethics but because the very shape of the knowledge in which I was trained contained its own moral—or amoral—trajectory, a distancing of the knower from the known that renders ethical reflection (to say nothing of ethical action) impossible. It is the selfsame deformation that made the German academy complicit in the horrors of the Third Reich because it practiced a studied detachment that kept it above the fray. It is vital that many people in higher education today are working hard to make sure that neither students nor society continue to be deformed in those ways.

My other problem with objectivism is that it does not offer a faithful rendition of how human beings know the world. By way of demonstrating that point, let me briefly rehearse a story many of you know—the story of Barbara McClintock, Nobel prize-winning geneticist, arguably the greatest American scientist of the twentieth century, who died a few years ago in her early nineties.

As a young woman, McClintock began working on the mysteries of genetic transposition, studying the genetic structure of maize, and doing so at a time when the instruments to make direct observation of these phenomena were not available. In addition to her empirical acuity and her powers of logic, she had to use a deep intuitive capacity to understand what was going on within the genes: "I needed," she once said, "to learn to think like an ear of corn." At her funeral, a fellow biologist from the University of Chicago eulogized her with a wonderful phrase, saying, "She was a mystic who did not mystify"—and I would lift that image up as a norm for all inquiries into the relation of education and spirituality.

When McClintock was in her eighties, another scientist named Evelyn Fox Keller came to her and said, "I want to write your intellectual biography. What is at the heart of doing good science?" McClintock reflected for a moment and said, "The best I can tell you is that to do good science you have to have a feeling for the organism." Keller pressed her to say more, so McClintock reflected again and said—in reference to the maize she had worked with all her life—"To do good science you have to learn somehow to lean into the kernel."

Now, McClintock was one of the keenest empirical observers and sharpest logical minds of our century. So it is important to note that, when pressed to talk about the heart of her great knowing, she used images that are both affective ("a feeling for the organism") and relational ("leaning into" the world rather than disconnecting from it.)

In her book about McClintock, *A Feeling for the Organism*, Keller summarizes these insights with a statement I find luminous: McClintock, in her relation to ears of corn, achieved "the highest form of love, love that allows for intimacy without the annihilation of difference." When I read that sentence, I thought, "Barbara McClintock had the kind of relation with ears of corn that I yearn to have with other people!" Such love is at the heart of true science, great science—and "intimacy without the annihilation of difference" is another norm for any exploration of spirituality and education.

When we consider the relation of higher education and spirituality, we certainly do not want to forget Galileo. But neither do we want to forget the complicity of German higher education in the evils of the Third Reich—the complicity of a form of higher education that wanted to stay so detached, so objective, that it refused to engage the messiness of life. That is the deep danger of the disengagement at the heart of this academic orthodoxy that is both ethically deforming and unfaithful to the way real knowing occurs.

One of the most important contributions our spiritual traditions can make to higher education is through the alternative ways of knowing these traditions offer—ways of knowing that counter the deformations of objectivism. It is an oft-neglected but important fact that, before a spiritual or religious tradition can offer a new vision of how to live in the world—a new ethic—it has to offer a new vision of what's real, of what's true, a new way of seeing and of knowing—a new epistemology.

I have noticed that when the media cover the renewal of spirituality in higher education, the headline often reads something like, "Educators Attempt to Revive Morality on Campus." Morality concerns me, but morality is not foundational to what we're trying to do here. There is no way to construct a religious ethic that would be recognizable in any of our traditions without grounding it in a way of knowing that is more capacious, more relational, more responsive than objectivism. If we don't lay that foundation, we're not going to be able to build a structure of life that will stand for long.

So I would like to offer some brief comments about the nature of those alternative epistemologies. I will risk writing in a way that is limited to my own understanding of my own tradition. But I hope I can do this in a way that will reach out to all of you—not proselytizing, but encouraging you to articulate the ways of knowing at the heart of your own traditions. Together, in dialogue, we will discover whether what I am about to say opens the door to that possibility.

There are, I believe, four marks of the alternative epistemology at the heart of my own tradition, four ways of understanding the truth that is the goal of all knowing. First and foremost is the radical notion that truth is much more than propositional—truth is personal.

When I look at "truthing" in the academy, it seems so often to consist of tossing verbal propositions at each other. Words are important because they point us toward something, but what they point us toward is more important than the words. Central to my own religious tradition is the understanding that "the word" can "become flesh and dwell among us." This means that words alone are not enough. What is really important is our own incarnation or embodiment of them, our own capacity to "walk the talk," to reach for authenticity.

The notion that truth is a personal embodiment does not mean that we are required to be perfect—and I personally am very grateful for that! But it does mean that I am required to be honest about what I do and do not embody, about what I can and cannot claim to know experientially. It means understanding that issues I want to approach as abstract and conceptual may well be more personal than theory suggests, may well implicate me and the way I live my life. It means allowing the truth I know to challenge my embodiment, my incarnation.

For example, when I see faculty tossing propositions at each other about different approaches to pedagogy—some emphasizing affect, some emphasizing cognition, with the rift between the two positions growing wider as they throw concepts at each other's heads—I want to cry out: "You're not really having a theoretical debate here. You're telling each other something about who you are as persons, about what gives you life and what gives you pain, about what you can and cannot abide. Please cut to the chase and speak directly about your personhood. This would be a much more fruitful dialogue if you could speak of the needs and struggles of your own hearts rather than masking them in such self-assured theoretical generalizations."

The second dimension of this alternative epistemology is the claim that truth is communal. It is not enough for truth to be personal; taken alone, that notion too easily degenerates into "one truth for you, another truth for me, and never mind the difference." We do and must mind the difference because we live together in the same world. What I take to be true has impact on you, and what you take to be true has impact on me.

Truth is communal—and the nature of community excludes competition, which is a zero-sum game in which there are winners and losers. Instead, community implies something the academic community needs to learn to value, and to practice: creative conflict, a clash of perspectives, of ideas, of experiences that can give rise to larger truth, but a conflict that is conducted compassionately, with forgiveness, and in a generative manner. We too often confuse competition with conflict, but they aren't the same. In competition someone wins and someone loses. In creative conflict we can all win because we can all have our hearts and minds stretched.

A third point in this alternative epistemology is the claim that truth is not inert but alive and interactive. There is an interesting phrase in the catalogues of most colleges and universities: "This institution is dedicated to the pursuit of truth." I love the conceit hidden in that phrase, in which truth is imaged as an evasive fox fleeing from us as fast as it can, tearing across the fields and hiding in the hedgerows, while we—nobly mounted on horses, blowing our horns and urging on our hounds— are passionately trying to track truth down, to capture it, and, of course, to kill it!

It's a very odd image, at best, and every spiritual tradition knows why. Truth is not evasive. We are. We are the ones running across the fields and hunkering down in the hedgerows, fleeing from "the Hound of Heaven." We are the ones who are hiding from truth's claims on our lives, even as truth actively seeks us—and seeks to transform us.

While we must seek truth, to be sure—must move out with our minds and hearts and hands into the mysteries of reality—we must also learn the spiritual countermovement to our frantic truth-seeking. I am referring to contemplation, which is at the heart of all of the great religious traditions, a movement in which (to quote the Desert Fathers and Mothers) you "sit in your cell and it will teach you everything."

Catherine of Sienna offered a wonderful gloss on that image when she said, "My cell is not of stone and wood but one of self-knowledge." Contemplation means: sit in your self-knowledge quietly, receptively, openly, vulnerably, with your defenses down, and you will learn a great deal about the world—as did Einstein when, as he said, "I listened to the universe."

The final point in my brief description of this alternative way of knowing is that truth is transformational. The reason that objectivism has been so popular, despite its moral deformations and its basic infidelity to how we know, is that it is constructed as a tool of control—or, more precisely, as a tool to help us maintain the illusion that we are in control. As long as we can hide away in a form of knowledge which aims at mastery over the world rather than interaction with the world— rather than knowing that this is our planet and our species that we're talking about here, and that our lives are challenged by all we learn about the world—as long as we can maintain that illusion of superiority and distance, we somehow feel safer.

I will leave you with a word from the poet Rilke who said, in one of his poems, "There is no place at all that is not looking at you. You must change your life." That line could and should be carved over the doorway of every academic department. Taken seriously, it would transform academic life.

What if we were to study the peasants of Guatemala not just in a way that allowed us to look at and analyze them, but that allowed them to look back at us and call us to change our lives? What if we were to study ecosystems and their degradation not just in a way that allowed us to look at and analyze them, but allowed them to look back at us and call us to change our lives? What if we studied literature not simply to parse the language and learn what the critics have to say, but to enter into that powerful world of imagination, to allow it to speak back to us, to grab our hearts, to let it look back at us and call us to change our lives?

At the heart of all our spiritual traditions is the conviction that knowledge of reality is a pearl of great price because with that knowledge we come closer to the source of all that is real. The spiritual traditions, at their best, do not dismiss or disavow or dishonor knowledge: they treasure it. By taking those traditions as seriously as we take the mission of higher education, we have a chance to challenge the ways in which the academy at its worst has dishonored the depths and demands of true knowing, a chance to call ourselves and our institutions back to the highest educational purposes.

2.   *Spirituality in an Integrative Age*

David K. Scott

Something we were withholding made us weak,
until we found it was ourselves.

—Robert Frost

As the end of the millennium approaches, there is a growing movement toward transformation in the world, in nations, and institutions. On the one hand there is hope for a new vision, but on the other hand a fear that time is running out with many serious problems unresolved. The solution to the challenges ahead demands collaborative approaches instead of the extreme fragmentation and competition which dominate much thinking today.[1] The ability to adopt a systems approach integrating different perspectives and ideas will be crucial. While the times we live in are often referred to as the Information Age, or the Knowledge Age, I believe that a better description of the spirit of the new millennium will be—and must be—the Integrative Age. Key to our future will be the concept of the complete individual, with a greater sense of wholeness and connectedness. Education must adopt an integrative philosophy of knowledge, including religion and spirituality, which have been largely eliminated from formal education in public institutions for more than a century.

There are many signs that this transformation is under way. Historically, the national mood swings between periods of community caring and periods of individual selfishness. During these oscillations revivals of interest in religion are also common. In *The Cycles of American History*, Arthur M. Schlesinger, Jr. describes this phenomenon as shifts between centralization and diffusion of energy.[2] He was building on an idea of his father in an essay titled "Tides of American Politics."[3] From 1765 onward, there have been periods of community ascendancy, lasting for about 16 years, followed by comparable periods of individual ascendancy. These swings transcend political parties and reflect reactions of society to either extreme. During this century, for example, Roosevelt's accession in 1901 heralded the sweep of reform measures comprising the Progressive Era and the Square Deal. Another two cycles of community ascendancy were the New Deal in the '30s and the New Frontier/Great Society in the '60s. Schlesinger predicted that some time in the '90s another burst of innovation and reform would take place. The rhetoric of reform is certainly present. President Bush called for a "kinder, gentler nation," and Clinton spoke of a "new covenant with society." Today we hear about "compassionate conservatism." Slogans, by themselves, are merely "words marching across the landscape in search of an idea." The idea may be discernible on college campuses, which are often the bellwethers of imminent transformation.

In his book, *Portrait of Today's College Students: When Dreams and Heroes Died*, Arthur Levine also describes periods in universities and colleges of community ascendancy which are future-oriented and ascetic, and periods of individual ascendancy which are more present-oriented and hedonistic, more concerned with duty to self than to others.[4] In a more recent work, Levine and Cureton analyze student activism during the century by using data gathered from measures of organization strength, viability of student publications, and participation in demonstrations.[5] The high points of these movements coincide with the swings in national mood described earlier. These historical cycles predict that we should now be in a period of community ascendancy. But this time a greater transformation may take place. As Tarnas has suggested, humanity may be gathering for a climactic denouement, a unification of knowledge, of cultures, of faith and reason, of matter and spirituality, of art and science and religion, which have been increasingly fragmented and separated for almost three hundred years.[6]

People everywhere are searching for greater meaning, wholeness, and relatedness in their lives and in their interactions with others, and for a more spiritual and religious view. Yet public education continues to chart a world without religion. Throughout history, as pointed out by Nord, nothing has been more stable, less budgeable, than religious belief and practice.[7] Polls consistently show that nine out of 10 Americans believe in the existence of God. More than seven out of 10 believe in life after death. Some 55 percent of Americans say that religion is very important in their lives. Based on decades of polling data, the United States cannot by any stretch of the imagination be described as secular in its core beliefs. The Swiss theologian Hans Kung asks, "Why don't people openly admit the fact that the death of religion expected in late modernity has not taken place?"[8]

A recent survey by Winston found that students on college campuses are exploring new ways of believing and behaving in their search for a richer, more meaningful way of being in the world. She also notes that as Americans have become more racially and ethnically diverse—and more comfortable with cultural expressions of diversity—our understanding of religious pluralism is changing. "It is not unusual these days for a student to describe her religious preference as Methodist, Native American, Taoist, Quaker, Russian Orthodox and Jew. The growth of religious diversity in our society is paralleled by an increased diversity within individual religious practices. Learning, working and, increasingly, living together, Americans of different faiths bump into beliefs and behaviors that once seemed unusual, even exotic."[9] Winston concludes that, rather than dismissing these interests of students, we should attempt to learn along with them.

The Constitution must guide our response to these interests. Although the courts have removed the practice of religion from public education, the constitutional legitimacy of the study of religion has been affirmed, and many universities have departments of religious studies. But the discussion of religion is segregated into these departments so that every other discipline is free to ignore religion. What George Marsden claims for Christianity is probably true of all religions: "It has become not only entirely peripheral to higher education but it has also often come to be considered absolutely alien to whatever is important to the enterprise."[10]

I believe that we need a new epistemology which will be more integrative across all areas of knowledge and which will address the emerging emotional and intellectual needs. But it will also be necessary to respond to a second spiritual movement in the academy dealing with the structural organization as institutions downsize, restructure, and re-engineer. Even the language reflects a philosophy of machines, devoid of any human dimension. William Byron draws attention to the rhetoric we often hear of transforming the workplace, making it more humane and respectful of human diversity. But this will not happen until the people who go to work are transformed.[11]

In considering religion and spirituality in higher education, and in particular in public universities and colleges, this essay deals with these three important challenges: the challenge of the Constitution, the challenge of epistemology, and the challenge of organizational structure. My intention is not to reintroduce into the academy the teaching of morals and religion but rather to open up a dialogue on the interpretation of the Constitution, the relation between different areas of knowledge, the balance between faith, reason, and spirituality, and the harmony between our work and lives. I do not underestimate the difficulty of this undertaking. A word like "spirituality" is, as Lesser points out, laden with contradictory meanings and confusing traditions. "For some the word is connected to their mistrust of religion. For others the word means anti-scientific. Others hear the word and are encouraged by its whispered promises of grace; others are threatened by it, afraid of looking too deeply at their own behavior, the unlived parts of their lives. For most of us, the word spiritual probably activates all of the above associations." [12] A statement read before the United Nations in October 1995 provides a prescription for the challenge ahead. "The crises of our time are challenging the world religions to release a new spiritual force transcending religious, cultural and national boundaries into a new consciousness of the oneness of the human community and so putting into effect a spiritual dynamic towards a solution of the world's problems.... We affirm a new spirituality, divested of insularity and directed towards planetary consciousness."

I have long believed the mission of a university to be the creation of ever more complete and integrative human beings through whom we shall create a better and a wiser world more rapidly. This goal is an essential challenge for the new millennium.

Cᴏɴsᴛɪᴛᴜᴛɪᴏɴᴀʟ Cʜᴀʟʟᴇɴɢᴇs

In order to respond to the growing need for spiritual dimensions in our organizations, the requirements imposed by the Constitution need analysis in public universities and colleges. In the past we have too readily invoked the Constitution as a shield to avoid the discussion. As we shall see in the next section, the epistemological issues pose the greatest challenges and the Constitution does not prohibit a discussion of them. Nord provides a useful perspective: "Public education is obligated to take religion seriously. Judicial conservatives typically argue that the Establishment Clause allows the state to promote non-sectarian religion as long as it does so non-coercively. Liberals argue, rightly, that the state and public education must be neutral both among religions and between religion and non-religion. What liberals seldom acknowledge is that, by ignoring religion and by promoting secular views hostile to religion, public education is effectively taking sides against religion. Therefore, if neutrality is to be restored as the First Amendment requires, religion must be given its voice. It is not the task of public education to promote any particular religion, or religion generally, but it should not ignore or denigrate religion either."[13]

The Supreme Court, more than 50 years ago, agreed that the Establishment Clause was intended to erect a wall of separation between church and state. More recently, as pointed out by David Schimmel,[14] this interpretation has been debated by the Court. However, in a 1992 opinion, Justice Souter emphasized "the settled principle that the Establishment Clause forbids support for religion in general no less than support for one religion or none." He also rejected the notion that public schools could promote a diversity of religious views because such an approach would necessarily compel schools to make wholly inappropriate judgments about the number of religions the state could sponsor and the relative frequency with which it should sponsor each. But it is also true that the nation was much less diverse in the past, with only one or two major religions. Diana Eck has commented on the new pluralism in universities and colleges today: "What has happened at Harvard has happened at major universities throughout the country. In the 1990s universities have become microcosms and laboratories of a new multicultural and multi-religious America. It is not uncommon to have a Hindu and Jew, Muslim and Christian in a single rooming group. These changes in university demographics have come not from abroad, but from the rapidly changing cultural and religious landscape of the United States. Harvard's issues, America's issues, have become increasingly a fresh recasting of India's issues, the world's issues: race, culture, difference, diversity and whether it is possible to move from diversity to pluralism."[15] On this subject, Nord concludes, "Because of the massive importance of religion in human affairs, because public institutions must take seriously the full range of ideas, because the Establishment Clause requires neutrality between religion and non-religion, and because truth has become increasingly elusive even for intellectuals, religion must be taken seriously in public universities."[16]

In the current pluralistic environment, universities need to examine what is permissible, under the complexities of the law, to meet the needs and aspirations of today's students, faculty, and staff, thereby liberating us to address the intellectual and spiritual needs of the community.

THE EPISTEMOLOGICAL CHALLENGE

In his inspiring book, *The Idea of Higher Education*, Ronald Barnett identifies the crises facing universities as the undermining of two axioms: first, the epistemological axiom that there is a realm of objective knowledge and that there are recognized truths is under assault with no apparent substitute in sight; and second, the sociological axiom that objective knowledge is most effectively maintained and disseminated in institutions that are relatively autonomous and in which the academic community enjoys comparative freedom.[17] Both of these axioms have led to a "pain of disconnection," as Parker Palmer has described the current status of our universities.[18] Overcoming this disconnection calls for a deeper engagement of the disciplines with each other and with society about the values and agenda of the university.

In the Western world, universities have existed for close to a thousand years. During this time they have undergone massive transformation. As society changed from an agrarian age to the industrial age and now to the information age, our approaches to knowledge also evolved. For the first five hundred years universities operated in the medieval culture where knowledge was based on faith and religion. Medieval society and learning were all compounded of numerous and diverse elements with scholars pursuing knowledge from a mixture of motives, combining rational and irrational, scholarly and superstitious methods of empiricism and speculation. There were, however, attempts at the integration of knowledge which we lost in the scientific revolution of the seventeenth century and the Enlightenment of the eighteenth century. The so-called Age of Enlightenment also coincided with the onset of the industrial age. Philosophers of the Enlightenment aimed to develop objective science and a universal morality and law. They planned to use the accumulation of specialized culture for the enrichment of everyday life through highly analytical and empirical thinking about a universe that was mechanical and predictable. Although noble in intention, the epistemology has resulted in enormous fragmentation of knowledge with the concomitant loss of a coherent, integrative perspective.[19] In the twentieth century, post-modernist philosophy has challenged the assumption that the intellect can direct human civilization toward the progressive realization of ideal forms of human existence and understandings that are universal, knowable, and achievable through discoveries in science. In this epistemology, objective standards of truth and justice are nothing more than conventions propagated by dominant forces in society. This philosophy has perpetuated a fragmented approach to knowledge so that physics departments in different universities around the world interact more closely with each other than with philosophy departments (and certainly the religious studies department) in the same university. Their approach is that there is no universal truth, but a multiplicity of different truths. This approach to knowledge is also giving rise to dissatisfaction within the academy and in society.

I believe that post-modernism is a transitory phase and that we are on a journey to a transmodern philosophy which will overcome the modern world view—not by eliminating world views as such—but by constructing a new world view through a revision of modern premises and traditional concepts. This constructive trans-modernism demands a new unity of scientific, ethical, aesthetic, and religious intuitions. It rejects not science as such but only that scientism in which the data of the modern natural sciences are alone allowed to contribute to the construction of our world view.[20] In spite of its fragmented approach, the post-modern movement has created the characteristics necessary for a new intellectual vision, which I call transmodernism. In the words of Tarnas: "If the postmodern mind has sometimes been prone to a dogmatic relativism and a compulsively fragmenting skepticism, and if the cultural ethos that has accompanied it has sometimes deteriorated into cynical detachment and spiritless pastiche, it is evident that the most significant characteristics of the larger postmodern intellectual situation—its pluralism, complexity and ambiguity—are precisely the characteristics necessary for the potential emergence of a fundamental new form of intellectual vision, one that might both preserve and transcend the current state of extraordinary differentiation. In the politics of the contemporary Weltanschauung, no perspective—religious, scientific, or philosophical—has the upper hand. Yet that situation has encouraged an almost unprecedented intellectual flexibility and cross-fertilization, reflected in the widespread call for, and practice of, open conversation between different understandings, different vocabularies, different cultural paradigms."[21]

Instead of the information age and the explosion of knowledge, we should speak of the integrative age and the implosion of knowledge. I am not advocating a return to the past with a total rejection of reason and empirical approaches. Rather the possibility now exists for the connection of different knowledge areas in new transdisciplinary ways at a deep level. This connection differs from the traditional interdisciplinary and multidisciplinary approaches common in universities, which really continue to link closely related areas of knowledge. I am advocating exploration of the relationship between religious, spiritual views, and approaches of science, for example. The current debate over evolutionary theory and creationism highlights the poverty of thinking that results when the deeper linkages between different areas of knowledge are ignored. Failure to explore the deeper interconnections drives people into one extreme mode or another, forcing a choice between faith and reason. The university of old—the University of Faith—evolved to the University of Reason. We must now foster the University of Communication, described by Gregory Heath,[22] which will integrate different approaches to knowledge. I call this university of the future the Integrative University for an Integrative Age.

The task ahead relates to Kant's attempts to integrate the "big three" value spheres of art, science, and religion (morals) which, as a result of the Enlightenment, were beginning to fall apart, and which have become even more disassociated in the modern university. Attempts to bring about this integration in the past have failed because they have adopted a rigid stance against rationalism, as in the romantic movement, for example. Wilbur points out that they fell into the "pre-trans" fallacy. "Granted, spirituality is, in some sense, beyond rationality. But there is a trans-rational and a pre-rational. Pre-rationality includes all of the modes leading up to rationality.... Trans-rationality, on the other hand, lies on the other side of reason. Once reason has emerged and consolidated, consciousness can continue to grow and develop and evolve, moving into trans-rational, trans-personal...modes of awareness. Trans-rationality includes pre-rationality, happily incorporates the rational perspective and then adds its own defining characteristics."[23] The exploration of these approaches to knowledge is the responsibility of the modern university, influencing all aspects of education through the curriculum, research, and applications of knowledge.

In achieving this integration, all disciplines, including religion, will have to adopt new ways of thinking. As Ken Wilber points out: "Many of the world's great religions contradict each other, but if we cannot find a common core of the world's great religions, then we will never find an integration of science and religion. Indeed if we cannot find a common core that is generally acceptable to all religions, we would be forced to choose one religion and deny importance to the others; or we would have to pick and choose tenets from among various religions, thus alienating the great religious traditions themselves. We would never arrive at an integration of science and religion that both parties would find acceptable, because most religions would reject what was done to their beliefs in order to force this reconciliation. It will do no good, for example, to claim, as many Christian creationists have, that the Big Bang suggests that the world is the product of a personal creator God, when one of the most profound and influential religions in the world, Buddhism, does not believe in a personal God to begin with. Thus we cannot use the Big Bang in order to integrate science and religion unless we can find a way to reconcile Christianity and Buddhism, and the world's wisdom traditions in general."[24]

It seems to me that the great challenge for universities and colleges is the definition of this common core, this general framework which would be acceptable to most religious traditions at least in the abstract. Students at many institutions recognize this need through the formation of inter-faith councils and dialogues between different religions. This spirit was very much in evidence at the Wellesley Conference,[25] with close to one thousand participants. It is also evident on our own campus where students of many different faiths have proposed that our Old Chapel (which has not been used as a chapel in over a century) should be transformed into a spiritual center for a new community.

An excellent starting point for a dialogue between humanities, sciences, and religion, is David Bohm's work on implicate order.[26] In his theory, which derives from a reformulation of quantum mechanics, the universe is constructed as a hologram with all aspects of the entire universe enfolded into each component, just as a holographic image contains the entire image in each fragment of the hologram, only more blurred as the component selected becomes smaller. Karl Pribram, has also suggested that the hologram is a possible model for how the brain stores memory in a distributed rather than localized fashion.[27] Since holograms are constructed from interference patterns of laser beams reflected from objects, perhaps the brain also deals in interactions, interpreting frequencies of vibration so that what we perceive as reality is in fact isomorphic with the brain processes. I mention this example because the idea of the concrete world as illusion has long been present in various eastern religions. An extraordinary ancient description of a holographic reality is found in a Hindu Sutra, "In the heaven of Indra there is said to be a network of pearls so arranged that if you look at one you see all the others reflected in it. In the same way, each object in the world is not merely itself but involves every other object, and in fact is in every other object."[28] Pribram observed: "It isn't that the world of appearances is wrong; it isn't that there aren't objects out there at one level of reality. It's that if you penetrate through and look at the universe with a holographic system, you arrive at a different reality, one that can explain things that have hitherto remained inexplicable: paranormal phenomena... synchronicities, the apparently meaningful coincidence of events."[29] This example is not meant as "scientific proof" of spiritual dimensions of experience (although there are studies also on this topic)[30] but rather as fertile ground for opening up a dialogue across disciplines which have little contact at present.

After all, our current approach to knowledge evolved over the last five hundred years and is also based on a theory of mind and matter, the relationship between them, and the relationship of human beings to the universe. Following Tarnas, the evolution began from the Copernicus shift of perspective in the mid-sixteenth century, which displaced the human being to a peripheral position in a vast, impersonal universe with the ensuing disenchantment of the natural world. The Copernican revolution constituted the epochal shift to the modern age. Almost a century later, Descartes woke up in the Copernican universe and fully articulated the experience of the emerging, autonomous self as separate from the external world it tries to master. With the human mind distinct from the world, then the apprehended universe was ultimately the mind's interpretation. Another century passed, bringing us to the mid-eighteenth century, before Kant, building on his empiricist predecessor, drew out the epistemological consequences. He deduced that all human knowledge is interpretive, and that the mind can draw no mirror-like knowledge of the objective world. Here was seen emerging the roots of post-modernism. The world is essentially a construct and knowledge is radically interpretive. Every act of perception and cognition is congruent, mediated, situated, contextual, and theory-soaked. Over a period of two hundred years the cosmological estrangement of Copernicus and the ontological estrangement of Descartes were completed by the epistemological estrangement of Kant, a threefold mutually reinforcing prison of modern alienation which has resulted in the fragmentation and relativism of knowledge prevalent today.

Gradually, over the ensuing 250 years the model has permeated thinking in almost every discipline. Another century after Kant, the radical displacement of the human being from the cosmic center was emphatically reinforced by Darwin's relativization of the human being in the flux of evolution—no longer divinely ordained, no longer the favored child of the universe. Tarnas concludes, "The world revealed by modern science is devoid of spiritual purpose, opaque, ruled by chance and necessity, without intrinsic meaning. The human soul has not felt at home in the modern cosmos: the soul can hold dear its poetry and its music, its private metaphysics and religion, but these find no certain foundation in the empirical universe.... But the lesson of Kant is that the locus of the communication problem—the problem of human knowledge in the world—must first be viewed as centering in the human mind. Therefore, it is theoretically possible that the human mind has more cards than it has been playing. The pivot of the modern predicament is epistemological, and it is here that we should look for an opening."[31]

The theory of mind and matter implicit in the holographic model of memory and the universe and of the intimate relation between them differs radically from the theory of Descartes. Instead of estrangement we discover a web of connections which could reverse the fragmentation of knowledge, the separation of reason and emotion, of spirituality and science. Here may lie the opening to greater overlap of the value spheres of art, science, and religion. The times have never been more propitious for such transdisciplinary thinking. A fresh perspective was recently given by Edward Wilson in his book, *Consilience: The Unity of Knowledge*.[32] Once a conversation in universities between the disciplines takes place, the fear of studying deeper connections will dissipate.

An example of this deeper connection is discussed by John Polkinghorne.[33] He points out that mathematics, which is essentially an abstract, free creation of the human mind, repeatedly provides the indispensable clue to the understanding of the universe. For example, abstract theories developed hundreds of years ago by Euler, with no application of any kind imaginable, have recently turned out to provide the theoretical framework for the string theory of the universe. It is as if there is a connection between the structure of the universe and the structure of the human mind. Polkinghorne relates these connections to the logos doctrine of Christianity but they may also be implicit in Pribram's holographic theory of the universe.

We need to unfreeze the boundaries and barriers constructed by the empirical approach to knowledge over the last three hundred years. There are signs that a warming trend is in the making. But it will also be necessary to unfreeze the culture of our academic institutions and make spirituality an integral dimension of the workplace. This topic is the subject of the last section of this paper.

THE ORGANIZATIONAL CHALLENGE

Judging from the plethora of books on spirituality and soul in organizations, it

of the Constitution, the nature of knowledge and epistemology, and the challenge of developing dynamic interactive organizations. Our impression is that we have readily chosen to interpret the Constitution as a convenient barrier to tackling the difficult issues of fragmentation in our educational models and in our organizational structures. But there are signs of a great transformation which will make us more integrative in our world view. I end with a quotation from Tarnas, who sums up the emerging ideas as follows: "More generally, whether in philosophy, religion, or science, the univocal literalism that tended to characterize the modern mind has been increasingly criticized and rejected, and in its place has arisen a greater appreciation of the multidimensional nature of reality, the many-sidedness of the human spirit, and the multivalent, symbolically mediated nature of human knowledge and experience. With that appreciation has also come a growing sense that the postmodern dissolving of old assumptions and categories could permit the emergence of entirely new prospects for conceptual and existential reintegration, with the possibility of richer interpretive vocabularies, more profound narrative coherencies. Under the combined impact of the remarkable changes and self-revisions that have taken place in virtually every contemporary intellectual discipline, the fundamental modern schism between science and religion has been increasingly undermined. In the wake of such developments, the original project of Romanticism—the reconciliation of subject and object, human and nature, spirit and matter, conscious and unconscious, intellect and soul—has reemerged with new vigor."[44]

This vision sets the stage for education in an Integrative Age. It will combine aspects of the University of Faith and the University of Reason into a new Integrative University preparing educated citizens for a new millennium and a new age in which spirituality will be a natural ally rather than an enemy in the education of engaged citizens for an enlightened democracy. The words of Lawrence Durrell in *Justine* from the Alexandria Quartet give a message of hope for the future:

> Somewhere in the heart of experience there is an order and a coherence which we might surprise if we were attentive enough, loving enough, or patient enough. Will there be time?

ENDNOTES

1. David K. Scott and Susan M. Awbrey, *Transforming the University* (Proceedings of the Conference on Women in Science and Engineering, Bloomington, Indiana: Committee on Institutional Cooperation, 1993).

2. Arthur M. Schlesinger, Jr., *The Cycles of American History* (Boston: Houghton Mifflin Company, 1986).

3. Arthur M. Schlesinger, "Tides of American Politics," *The Yale Review* vol. XXIX, no. 2 (December 1939).

4. Arthur Levine, *Portrait of Today's College Student: When Dreams and Heroes Died* (San Francisco: Jossey-Bass, 1980).

5. Arthur Levine and Jeanette S. Cureton, *When Hope and Fear Collide: A Portrait of Today's College Student* (San Francisco: Jossey-Boss, 1998).
6. R. Tarnas, *The Passion of the Western Mind* (New York: Ballantyne Books, 1991).
7. Warren A. Nord, *Religion and American Education: Rethinking a National Dilemma* (n.p.: The University of North Carolina Press, 1995).
8. Hans Kung, *Theology for the Third Millennium* (New York: Anchor Books, 1990).
9. Diane Winston, "Campuses are a Bellwether for Society's Religious Revival," *The Chronicle of Higher Education* (January 16, 1998).
10. George Marsden, *Soul of the American University* (New York: Oxford University Press, 1984).
11. William Byron, "Spirituality in the Workplace," *American Association of Higher Education Bulletin* vol. 51, no. 8 (April 1999).
12. Elizabeth Lesser, *The New American Spirituality* (New York: Random House, 1999).
13. Nord, *op. cit.*
14. David Schimmel private communication, University of Massachusetts, Amherst, 1999.
15. Diana L. Eck, "Neighboring Faiths," *Harvard Magazine* 99 (September–October 1996): 38–44.
16. Nord, *op. cit.*
17. Ronald Barnett, *The Idea of Higher Education* (n.p.: The Society for Research in Higher Education and the Open University Press, 1990).
18. Parker J. Palmer, "Community and Commitment in Higher Education," *American Association of Higher Education Bulletin* (September 1992/1993).
19. See Nicholas Maxwell, *From Knowledge to Wisdom: A Revolution in the Aims and Methods of Science* (London, Basil Blackwell: 1984).
20. See David W. Orr, *Ecological Literacy* (Albany, NY.: State University of New York Press, 1992).
21. Tarnas, *op. cit.*
22. Gregory Heath, *The University as a Communicative Institution,* (Warwick, England: EAIR Forum, University of Warwick, 1997).
23. Kenneth Wilber, *The Marriage of Sense and Soul* (n.p.: Random House, 1998).
24. Wilber,. *op. cit.*
25. Education as Transformation: Religious Pluralism, Spirituality and Higher Education" held at Wellesley College, September 27–28, 1998.
26. See David Bohm, *On Creativity*, ed. Lee Nichal (n.p.: Routledge and Kegan Paul, 1998); David Bohm, *Wholeness and the Implicate Order* (n.p.: Routledge and Kegan Paul, 1980); Kevin J. Sharpe, *David Bohm's World: New Physics and New Religion* (London and Toronto: Bucknell University Press and Associated University Presses, 1993).

27. See Karl Pribram, *Consciousness and the Brain*, ed. Gordon Globus (New York: Plenum Press, 1976), and Karl Pribram, *Perceiving, Acting and Knowing*, ed. R. E. Shaw and J. Bransford (n.p.: Wiley, 1977).

28. Marilyn Ferguson, *The Aquarian Age* (n.p.: Penguin Putnam Inc., 1987).

29. David Peat, *Synchronicity* (n.p.: Bantam Books, 1988).

30. See David A. Ash, *The New Science of the Spirit* (London: The College of Psychic Studies, 1995), and Frank J. Tipler, *The Physics of Immortality* (n.p.: Anchor Books, Doubleday, 1994).

31. R. Tarnas, *op. cit.*

32. Edward O. Wilson, *Consilience: The Unity of Knowledge* (n.p.: Alfred A. Knopf, Inc., 1998).

33. J. C. Polkinghorne, *The Particle Play* (n.p.: W. H. Freeman and Company, 1979).

34. C. William Pollard, *The Soul of the Firm* (n.p.: Harper Business and Zondervan Publishing House, 1996).

35. Lee G. Bohman and Terrance E. Deal, *Leading with Soul* (San Francisco: Jossey-Bass Publishers, 1995).

36. Kay Gilley, *Leading from the Heart: Choosing Courage over Fear in the Workplace* (n.p.: Butterworth-Heinemann, 1997).

37. Charles C. Manz, *The Leadership Wisdom of Jesus* (n.p.: Berrett-Koehler, 1998).

38. Robert Marx, Peter Laurence, Diane Dana, Karen Manz, Charles Manz, and David Schimmel, *Concept Paper on Conference on Going Public: Spirituality and Religion in Higher Education and Workplace* (to be held at the University of Massachusetts, Amherst, June 2000).

39. See Peter M. Senge, *The Fifth Discipline: The Art and Practice of the Learning Organization* (n.p.: Doubleday, 1990); Peter M. Senge, Art Kleiner, Charlotte Roberts, Richard B. Ross and Bryan J. Smith, *The Fifth Discipline Field Book* (Doubleday, 1994); and Peter M. Senge, Art Kleiner, Charlotte Roberts, Richard Ross, George Roth, and Bryan Smith, *The Dance of Change* (Doubleday, 1999).

40. Peter M. Senge, *The Academy as Learning Community: Contradiction in Terms or Realizable Future?*, private communication, to be published in 2000.

41. Susan M. Awbrey, David K. Scott, Peter M. Senge, Ronald Hansen, Phillip DiChiara, Joseph Raelin, and Mark Braun, *Learning to Change: A Proposal to Create the Center for Integrative Studies* (n.p.: Kellogg Foundation, June 1999).

42. Margaret J. Wheatley, *Leadership and the New Science: Learning about Organization from an Orderly Universe* (n.p.: Berrett-Koehler, 1994).

43. Jennie Spencer Green and Page Monahan, *Building Capacity and Resilience for Change: Personal and Organizational Levels* (Professional Development Workshop at American Council on Education Annual Meeting, February 13, 1999).

44. Tarnas, *op. cit.*

3. Spiritual Assumptions Undergird Educational Priorities: A Personal Narrative

CHERYL H. KEEN

As a child, when I saw light streaming down from a break in the clouds I thought it was God reaching down. I can now recognize that the comfort I felt was a sense of connection between the heavens and the earth. Here I am, forty years later, still scanning the horizon for connections that might supplant the void that often lurks in the fragmented hallways of academia.

A STORY ABOUT CONNECTIONS

The "light" that entered my office one school day not that long ago was one of my best students—thoughtful, hardworking, mature beyond her 20 years. Last year she really extended herself for other students when she served under me as a writing tutor. However, this semester she's been impatient because my course examining the high school as an institution, which also serves as a general education course, is required for her major. She feels that some of the other general education students aren't taking it seriously enough. She's been negotiating all along for different and more challenging assignments. Her latest request is that, in lieu of a five-page paper, she further develop her own educational philosophy, which she has to write for another course.

I agree easily, assuming she'll do a very high quality piece of work and that she will be well served by having more time to deeply consider what is essential for her. Three weeks later, she comes into my office and collapses in the chair. "I'm terribly behind in all of my work and this educational philosophy piece is taking much longer than I thought. Can I have more time?" I offer some quick advice, and say "Yes," trustingly. The latest scene in this saga takes place at my kitchen table a week after the end of the semester. The paper is in hand, but to her mind, it is not "finished." There are kernels of ideas, drawn largely from her four months of full-time teaching experience gained during her recent Antioch College co-op experience. Now she's pained, doubting she can be a teacher anyway, because writing the paper has reminded her of how critical she is of the public schooling system.

In the face of her frustration, I can feel myself shift to a deeper plane. I want to be honest, to partner with her as she asks essential questions. She is pulling from me the best I have to offer. I'm surprised it has taken this long for me to share explicitly my own philosophy of education. I tell her, "I try to speak to that of God in every person. I work to make my classrooms, my assignments, and my conversations with students reflect this approach. I trust that our relationships matter a great deal. I worry just as much about the whole learning environment we are working in as I do about my own classroom. This means I want to know people as individuals (which requires small class size); to design assignments that provoke thought and connections between ideas and with the "other" (by means of writing, team teaching, and experiential tasks); and to give the other person the benefit of the doubt, trusting that people are trying to do their best and hoping to give them the space their inner spirit requires. I have to listen closely and pay attention or I may not see the flickering of a hopeful spirit or an awakening mind. Time has taught me to trust my intuitions. I assume that class discussions, conversations, and counseling sessions are ways of making deeper connections with students that help them toward a sense of what really matters and, ultimately toward their vocation." As my student thanked me, I was confirmed in my philosophical and spiritual hunches.

A Faculty Member's Hunger for Authenticity

I've always had trouble with boundaries—I've wanted to resist them and make connections, as I did that day with my student, across what seem to me artificial lines. Toward this end, I pursued an interdisciplinary doctorate. I did years of interdisciplinary teaching with adult students and with many of them crossed the line from teacher to friend. I always seem to want to act on issues in my college outside of my realm of delegated responsibilities. Along the way of knocking down barriers, I've felt a bit lonely. There are so many choices to make as a teacher and not always enough colleagues with whom to talk these choices through, or enough time.

Questions abound: What do you assign? How do you deal with disagreements in the classroom? Did anyone else—inside the classroom or outside it—use the same basis for those decisions I did? Did anyone else call some breakthrough moments "love"?

Sometimes classroom experiences arouse in me a deep and special kind of "warmth." In those moments I feel a resonance with the spirit of the student(s) and a sense of the two of us (or the group of us) as one in a larger whole. I wonder if anyone else feels these moments when boundaries melt away in relationships with students? There is little to read about this. Because these special kinds of classroom moments are so seldom shared, I know I am not the only faculty member who has felt a loneliness among professional colleagues.

In recent research, Helen and Alexander Astin have found that faculty find few opportunities on their campuses to pursue their eagerness to talk about issues of spirituality and meaning, a felt need that is accentuated by the high levels of stress and fragmentation that their respondents report feeling in their personal and professional lives.[1] The Astins' study has contributed to a set of discussions on the need for authenticity, renewal, and wholeness in higher education by a study group convened by the Fetzer Institute. This Fetzer study group has recently led workshops on this question at the annual conferences of many key higher education organizations. All of the workshops were well attended and well received, confirming that the hunger for authentic dialogue is widespread.

Concerns about authenticity, wholeness, and spirituality also surfaced recently at my kitchen table when I was visited by a young graduate student of color, the daughter of friends. Her mom had insisted she come to meet me. She is about to write a dissertation in history and ethnic studies and is teaching two courses at her doctoral institution. She loves to teach. Her undergraduate mentor is trying to save a position for her when she finishes the thesis. How fortunate in this era to have a faculty position waiting for you at your undergraduate alma mater. But so far she hasn't found anyone in graduate school to invite her into conversations that speak to her at a deep, authentic level. Nor has her undergraduate mentor met her at that level, and she is considering not pursuing a faculty position because, in its spiritual voids and seemingly endless demands, such a position in a university presently seems inconsistent with her life values.

What a potentially tragic loss to higher education, all because we haven't made a hospitable place that responds to this woman's spiritual needs. Because of this void we risk losing or marginalizing some part of a generation of people we need in the academy—those whose voices can speak directly to the centrality of spiritual issues in Native American, Hispanic, and African-American cultures.[2]

I've also witnessed this hunger for spiritual dialogue on other campuses. I recently ran an all-day workshop on sustaining commitment to the common good for a group of 18 faculty from a small, public college. The evening before, over dinner, we had a spontaneous and extended "grace," as we invited each person to share a story of some teaching experience from the past semester that had been important for him or her. The stories carried us through the entire dinner and people listened carefully to their colleagues' devotion to students and subject, a devotion that they are rarely invited to witness. The extent to which we were moved and touched by those stories prepared us to get to a level of significant depth together in our workshop experience the next day.

MAKING A PLACE FOR FACULTY AND STAFF'S SPIRITUAL DEVELOPMENT

In leading workshops on college campuses I've learned of other important divides in higher education that need to be crossed. We need, in particular, to bridge the layers of fragmentation between staff and faculty. Recently, I was asked to lead a six-hour workshop at a Catholic college, St. Michael's, near Burlington, Vermont. A steering group of faculty and staff had been seeking to make a place for spirituality in the shared work life at the college and, having sent a team to the Wellesley College "EDUCATION as *Transformation*" conference, came back inspired to move forward on this quest. At monthly lunch gatherings at least 30 people from St. Michael's considered the questions put forth at the Wellesley conference. Faculty of all backgrounds seem to rejoice in teaching there. Their campus seems hospitable to Jewish, non-Catholic Christians, Buddhists, Sufis, and theosophists alike. There is a beautiful sculpture on campus that seems to capture this valuing of connection. Two rough-hewn figures are walking side-by-side. The inscription from Luke reads, "What are you discussing with each other while you walk along?" (Luke 24:17)

In a campus self-study retreat conducted two days before my arrival, agreement had emerged that people truly valued the sense of community at the college. However, communication was apparently not always good. Often people didn't feel "known," judgmental things were said that disrupted connections, and so on. Especially pained were the support staff who felt cut off from and unrecognized by faculty. As an example of the lack of recognition that often occurred, support staff would have had to take a vacation day to attend the retreat I was offering on commitment and the common good. When he learned of it, the president addressed that problem on the spot. As a result, roughly half of the group of 20 I worked with at the *Common Fire* retreat were support staff.[3]

The design for the workshop was simple. In the first half, we paired with someone we didn't know well and explored, through a set of interview questions that I provided, the sources of each other's commitments. Afterwards, the group expressed enthusiasm for this reminder of how much better you can know and appreciate someone by listening carefully for even 30 minutes. The second round of interviewing in pairs focused on times when commitment is strained or worn and on ways in which mixed motivations potentially clutter commitments. We also explored how people sustain themselves and what gives them hope.

When we came together again, we went around the group and each person shared something personally sustaining. Some had been able to bring objects or poems, having been cued to do so at the lecture the night before. Through these beautiful and tender sharings, we were humbled by what it takes for people to sustain commitments to the mission of the college while trying to meet the needs of the wider global commons, all the while coping with ongoing family responsibilities and, in some cases, with wounds suffered earlier in life.

As we closed, we finally introduced ourselves by name and role, having, at the beginning, tried to leave status demarcations at the door. Now, at the conclusion, there was a reason to share information about where each worked at the college so that individuals could collaborate and extend the energy generated by the retreat. Each also shared some way that they hoped to continue this dialogue in the days to come.

In written evaluations, staff and faculty reported: "The workshop helped us find contexts to use our gifts at the college" and "I saw people in a new light through the deep sharing." Another particularly appreciated "the meaningful sharing of experiences through listening and reflection that was not forced, but sincere," saying, "Perhaps I'm not off-base in my dreams after all."

Others said: "This began to teach us how to be together as a group in a personal and unselfconscious way." "Watching others want to change is beautiful." "I learned today (perhaps have always known) that we share a common need for connection and a desire to find meaning our lives. Today was an experience of rejuvenation for me and I received an infusion of new hope and energy." "Renewal of my commitments, 'our' commitments in life, is vital. Unfortunately, opportunities to do so are rare." "For the first time I felt like a person in the eyes of a faculty member. So often staff are simply present to perform the deeds required by faculty members. It was enlightening to share stories with faculty and to also learn of their personal concerns. Because of our discussion, we will always be more than just a face to each other."

If staff sometimes feel that they are treated as if they are not of equal value with faculty, what about our students? I fear that students usually feel that only a narrow part of them is recognized. After being in high schools where the typical teacher works daily with 125 students, some students may not expect much else.

Not making a place for spiritual development can limit the scope of a learning experience at a time when our graduates will need to sustain themselves and their commitments in a world that seems increasingly challenging.

WHAT DO OUR STUDENTS NEED MOST?

When was the last time you—staff, administrators, faculty—asked a student, "Would you like to have a cup of tea with me and we'll talk about your life?" One of my biggest concerns about higher education is that some faculty advisors don't think it is their business to talk with advisees about anything but courses and choice of major. What a lost opportunity, when students are putting their future interests on the table and exploring what courses in the past have resonated with their concerns. So often their choices are clouded with self-doubt from past experiences and puzzlements about the implications of what they learned in courses. Many are striving for something that more authentically integrates what they are learning about themselves and the needs of the world. For many, what has happened during a semester is inextricably linked up with challenging or thought-provoking life experiences. Sometimes these "advising meetings" come with tears and long periods of silence. I try not to be afraid in those times and to trust that my most important role is to listen carefully, valuing the student. If I am afraid that I can't respond adequately to their searching, pain, and uncertainty, I might refer them to a counselor.

In the wake of recent killings in high schools, there is much discussion in the press about the effectiveness of grief counseling. (You'll find consideration of this kind of professional helping in John McKnight's *The Careless Society*.) If we disregard the naturally-established relationships of families, neighbors, teachers, or coaches as places where we can talk about the meaning of life, death, and changes, we are losing an immense resource. Faculty are well aware that many college resources are going into student services and counseling these days, as our students seem to be coming to college in ever more need of support. Despite the availability of more "expert" counseling, faculty need to be aware of the special opportunity they have to help students through tough choices and cluttered pasts while they seek out an increasingly authentic life path. Mentors, including faculty, can support our highest aspirations, challenge us to reach beyond ourselves, and inspire us about important work to do in the world.

SOME RECOMMENDATIONS FOR DEVELOPING MENTORING ENVIRONMENTS FOR STUDENTS

Common Fire: Leading Lives of Commitment in a Complex World is a book that resulted from a decade-long research project I undertook with Laurent Parks Daloz, James Keen, and Sharon Parks. It contains an analysis of interviews conducted with one hundred people who had sustained commitment to working on behalf of the human family in the face of ambiguity, uncertainty, and diversity. These one hundred people could be seen as exemplifying the goals of higher education as put forth by the mission statements of most colleges: "We educate citizens who will respond to the needs of the world." Conclusions drawn from studying these interviews led us to make several recommendations for higher education, many of which speak to the importance of making a place for spirituality in our institutions.[4]

One recommendation addresses a common goal of higher education, that of moving students from naïveté and dualistic thinking to commitment in the face of ambiguity and relativism rather than moving to simplistic relativism with a heavy patina of cynicism. How do we get students to make tentative but wholehearted commitments?

I've already addressed the need for in-depth dialogue with faculty as well as with fellow students. To help students mature in their thinking, some habits of mind are needed. Students must learn to take the perspective of others, to be able to hear out someone else's spiritual concerns.

Recently, in interviewing Trish, a Unitarian student, I learned that the environment of shared governance and engaged dialogue at Antioch College had allowed her for the first time to let down her guard and "hear" a Christian student's fears that Trish would be damned for not believing in Christ. The two were able to sustain a dialogue about their different beliefs.

Students also need to think systemically. Questions of faith and spirit are part of the framework for examining the quality of life on this planet, including issues of ethnic conflict, women's development, human rights, and environmental preservation.

Finally, students need help beginning to develop the ability to think holistically—to intuit life as a whole. We will make progress if we are conscious of the whole campus as a mentoring environment. We should ask: Are there places on campus where it is safe to address one's deepest concerns? Are those known to students? Do our spaces reflect an openness? Do we encourage students to test out their beliefs and values through experiential learning opportunities such as travel, service, co-ops, and internships?

Are we reluctant to include in our syllabi (even in our list of recommended readings) books and articles, fiction and nonfiction, through which students can explore questions that would enhance their most authentic expression of the ideas under exploration? Good reading enabled the people interviewed for *Common Fire* to take the perspective of others different from themselves, folding into the educational mix a crucial emotional and spiritual ingredient. We can facilitate this "felt" connection and help to keep a human face on complex and systemic problems.

SUPPORTING A COMMITMENT TO PUBLIC SERVICE

The busyness of our society that keeps many of us from more fully seeing and responding to the needs of our communities has its equivalent on campuses. Bill Perry, author of *Forms of Moral and Intellectual Growth in the College Years: A Scheme*, was one of my mentors in graduate school. He listened to students explain what stood out for them at the end of each year of their four college years. At some point, these students found themselves pushing at the edges of their chosen mentor's commitments. "Does he/she really care that much?" they asked, almost poking their mentors' shoulders to see if their commitments were sturdy enough to continue standing.

How can we represent our commitments and guide students if we don't have the opportunity to share our whole vision so that students can decide if we really mean it? To start, perhaps we need time to reflect on and remember just what it is that we care about. In-depth conversations with students take time and it is true that so much else is pulling at us to help us maintain our position in the institution.

I was recently the guest respondent at the senior project presentations in a college's new major in public service. Each student had had to create a project working with a local agency. Almost all of the students mentioned in their presentations how hard it was to find a place to be of service because people in agencies didn't have time to return their phone calls. And then, when the students began working, they found their mentors and supervisors often unavailable and always rushed.

It was clearly important for those students to share what they wanted to contribute to the community and to get advice about how to best do that. Here were 20 young people who had chosen to devote their college major to preparing for a life of service. Yet agencies responding to the urgency of community needs could barely take time to prepare the next generation. One student even talked of carrying her bicycle into her mentor's small, cramped office, virtually trapping him in there while she shared her most important questions.

CONCLUSION

The move towards a less fragmented professional life seems to demand more of us: more time with our students and colleagues in dialogue and more time in reflection and renewal of our essential purposes. It can help to take time to attend conferences and workshops where we may find like-minded people to talk to in settings that free us up from the daily grind. We could follow the call to do more spiritual reading so that we can expand our syllabi to include resources that might offer company to students who are also seeking spiritual reflection. Responding to these new demands risks further fragmenting our already divided lives or igniting anxiety that we will neglect other responsibilities critical to our success. We may need to review, sort through, and reassign our priorities.

Out of the gathered silence of a Friends meeting I once heard someone say, "We do the will of God when we do the best we can." As one of the interviewees in the *Common Fire* video says, "We aren't called to do the saintly stuff." The hope is, in our own reflection and in reflection with colleagues, we will be better able to discern those steps that will help us, individually and collectively, to respond more fully to the challenges of educating students for a complex and potentially alienating world.

ENDNOTES

1. Helen and Alexander Astin, internal document (Kalamazoo, Mich.: Fetzer Institute, 1999).
2. See Laurent Parks Daloz, *Mentor: Guiding the Journey of Adult Learners* (San Francisco: Jossey-Bass, 1999).
3. Workshops are based on the book by Laurent Parks Daloz, Cheryl Keen, James Keen, and Sharon Daloz Parks, *Common Fire: Leading Lives of Commitment in a Complex World* (Boston: Beacon Press, 1996).
4. Laurent Parks Daloz, Cheryl Keen, James Keen, and Sharon Daloz Parks, "Lives of Commitment: Higher Education in the Life of the New Commons," in *Change: The Magazine of Higher Learning* 20, no. 3 (May/June 1996): 10–15 and *Common Fire* (Boston: Beacon Press, 1996): 223–227.

4.   *Spiritual Quest Among Young Adults*

Andrés G. Niño

O ne important factor that makes the EDUCATION as *Transformation* Project so compelling is that it focuses on issues encountered by people who spend some of their most critical formative years in the self-contained environment of the academic world. Here, most activities are valued in reference to the absorbing task of learning, and unfold in an apparently coordinated fashion. But that process, rather than being fluent and cohesive, often becomes compartmentalized and overly constricted,[1] partly because of the insidious demand for specialization and the emphasis on the value of practical knowledge and marketable skills. Spiritual life becomes the victim of that compartmentalization, and is not viewed as an integral part of the whole educational program.

The larger socio-political context that has evolved at the end of the twentieth century adds the impact of rapid and profound changes and technological advances that undermine an individual's sense of personal progress and control. As a result, young adults who are simultaneously negotiating important developmental tasks in relationships, career choices, and identity feel overwhelmed and disoriented. This is a common phenomenon that students often describe as the experience of leading "fragmented lives."

Human experience, when it is unified through meaningful engagements, becomes life-enhancing and enduring. Fragmentation, on the other hand, is always a threatening prospect. Today we observe a widespread longing for internal coherence, a sense of purpose, and a desire for greater global harmony expressed openly through recent autobiographies, films, and other forms of public discussion.

As a clinical psychologist and a teacher, I have long felt a great personal investment in this issue. Consequently, a central preoccupation in my work has been to convey the importance of the ways in which a person can function at the highest possible level, and I have explored with many patients and students how that can be done. Along the way I have taken notes in a variety of situations, from the consulting room to the classroom, through informal conversations and through exchanges in workshops and conferences, that spark further interest and mutual learning, all of which is part of real and ordinary life. I have placed my work within the boundaries of a co-exploration with others, and in that manner have learned one important thing: that beyond the complexity of people trying to make sense of their lives and how they express it, there is a common ground of experience that makes the old, venerable concept of spiritual quest a fundamental aspect of our human condition.[2]

TOWARD A COMMON GROUND

One of the most striking challenges of this century has been the negotiation of demands emerging from a wide variety of ideas and practices that affect fundamental areas of living, including religion, politics, and relationships. This is a fact that is even more impressive within the microcosm of college and university campuses, and applies with particular intensity to the concept of the spiritual quest. In my conversations about the spiritual quest with people in various situations, references to specific religious faiths and beliefs are often made as sources of inspiration and nourishment, and rightly so because the spiritual life has often been associated with the message of the great religious traditions. However, it is important to note that there are many people who either have not identified traditional religious sources for the construction of meaning or cannot integrate those sources into their development of a coherent self—yet they may be people with a profound sense of spirituality.

Because this overwhelming reality has to be taken into consideration, new approaches have developed in the last decade for the exploration of spirituality in a broader and more inclusive sense. The perspective presented in this essay is one taken from a common ground of human development, where those with a religious background can recognize and understand the strivings and concerns of those who do not identify with such a background. Acknowledging the historic tensions generated by the force between the sacred and the secular is a position that allows for a respectful dialogue and moves in a direction that facilitates a greater understanding of the total human experience.[3]

From such a common ground we can recognize an individual's spiritual quest in the "process of inquiry and engagement over questions of ultimacy that grows as people bind together experiences and events into an overarching construction of meaning with a sense of transcendence."[4] The developments that result from this activity grow in importance and change as the individual invests meaning and attention to the dominant themes and concerns of the different periods of adulthood. Its underlying dynamic is not a transitional state of doubt or conflict, but a persistent searching that moves forward throughout life.

In my research work I have identified some basic characteristics that have emerged from analysis of narratives. They can be summarized in these terms:

1. The spiritual quest is rooted in a normal developmental process in which a person negotiates questions and concerns regarding personal destiny, happiness, God, the ethical implications of one's behavior, suffering, and death. These are "big questions" in the sense that they carry the potential for meaning-making at a profound level, both personally and communally. From these questions derive, directly or in subtle association, a myriad of reflections that permeate a person's daily life. The whole process is often nourished by a particular religion or faith community that brings into the experience the input of beliefs, motivations, and practices. In those cases, the individual spiritual quest may benefit from the sup-

port and guidance available in the present or historical experience of the community.[5]

2. Many experiences reported and emphasized by people as central to their spiritual life appear to be confined to discrete events or moments, specific rituals, gestures, and exercises designed to enhance and refine the cognitive or emotional response of the individual. Meaningful and valuable as they might be, they cannot reflect the full extent of an individual's important life events.

The significance of a spiritual quest, by contrast, depends on being integrated within the larger pattern of concerns, tasks, and engagements of adulthood. A spiritual quest is a main component of one's overall life structure, requiring various degrees of involvement and attention in order to maintain its vitality, balance, and internal coherence. It becomes a pattern of personal engagement at many levels throughout the course of living.

As a consequence, the spiritual quest can only find adequate expression in a total life narrative. Whether it is verbalized or framed within other forms available to the individual, the narrative allows for an ample margin of vision that reveals the sequence and variety of situations which convey the quality of one's fundamental strivings.[6] In this essay, I will expand upon this central characteristic in order to establish the groundwork for an interdisciplinary approach.

3. Although the process of a spiritual quest takes shape and strength from the individual's own motivation, it is also greatly influenced by the socio-cultural context in which it takes place. Observers from different disciplines have noted the increasing complexity and impact of the interplay between societal transformations and the changing life courses of the individual. Analysis of the so-called postmodern period shows cultural trends that cause confusion and make one's strivings toward "meaning with a sense of transcendence" particularly difficult. For example, we have seen (or at least been made aware of) totalitarianism, ethnic cleansing, and violence in this century, in addition to an overwhelming display of materialism and widespread disruption in families and institutions. Yet, even in the face of these obstacles we find a strong sense of spiritual striving among many individuals.

This fact has a bearing on our understanding of the human condition and the gradual shifts in the thinking and feeling that influence the way individuals and groups of different generations negotiate the spiritual quest. Although ideas and experiences associated with spirituality may suggest a character of permanency, there is, in fact, a great deal of variability within this phenomenon.

4. An active engagement with the concerns and tasks of the spiritual quest builds internal coherence and strength in the individual. Although theoretical perspectives vary on this issue, this finding is consistent across health-related disciplines. Some recent publications have emphasized the importance of the relationship between spirituality and physical, mental, and social health.[7]

Coherence and stability in the course of personal development reflect to a great extent the depth of one's engagement with life experiences and the degree of motivation invested in facing the challenges that unfold at different periods of adulthood. This is particularly relevant to the idea of education as transformation. The best hopes lie with those institutions that promote a dialogue about what is really meaningful to young adults involved in the task of learning, living, and building a future.

A LIFE STRUCTURE PERSPECTIVE

The relevance of a psychological developmental perspective on the dimension of spirituality is based on practical considerations. Although not free from the common difficulties of identifying and characterizing this domain within the whole of human experience, it allows for a focused approach to issues derived from studies of adulthood. The findings bring us as close as can be expected from rigorous but limited explorations to an understanding of major tasks and issues pertinent to various periods of the life cycle. This is actually a significant advantage when we try to establish an interdisciplinary common ground for dialogue.

In the study of adulthood I use the unifying approach to personality offered by contemporary developmentalists and clinicians. Among them, Kohut, one of the most creative and influential in recent years, focuses on the significance of the search for the realization of one's most enduring values and ideas, together with cherished goals, purposes, and ambitions. He also emphasizes the crucial role played by empathic relationships in the psychological well being of the individual and on one's sense of continuity through time.[8]

Expanding on the basis of such core self, Levinson's work explores the life structure of adulthood.[9] His emphasis is on the self in relation to the world, supported by the dynamics of both central and peripheral components such as family, work, and political and social activities, through the various periods of the life cycle. In that manner, one sees the whole person rather than compartmentalized elements.

Levinson spent most of his professional life studying narratives of adult men and women. He saw a continuity through different periods and eras of the life cycle and identified general human characteristics for both genders. He clarified, however, that the genders differ with regard to the kind of life circumstances they encounter and the ways in which they progress through each developmental period. Women, for example, tend to build life structures with "different resources and constraints, external as well as internal."[10]

In this essay I make reference mainly to that large period between late adolescence and the mid-thirties, which essentially corresponds to the formative period encompassing the years that may be spent in higher education. This is a time which produces a fundamental turning point in the life cycle as young adults move away from parental homes and fairly well-defined roles and frames of reference into a rather uncharted territory where they begin to build a provisional life structure through choices in relationships, career orientation and work, organization of their priorities, and even through personal life style. Gradually, as the college years come to an end, those tasks become a definite hallmark of progress. Crises in this developmental context will occur when a person is having great difficulty negotiating the tasks and, due to internal and external factors, cannot build an adequate structure which would facilitate moving ahead. This experience is different in scope and quality from those crises associated with problems related to coping with a particular situation or event.

Researchers of adulthood, however, have not generally considered the role of spirituality per se as a relevant part of the whole. It is necessary to go beyond some traditional concepts of personality structure and function in order to have a larger picture of the total human experience.

FUNDAMENTAL STRIVINGS

Early in my work I emphasized a concept of the self as an open system that includes the capacity for transcendence as a vital element in the process of meaning-making. I raised critical questions regarding the modern self, which appears to suffer from a condition of widespread emptiness and fragmentation that eludes clinical categories. Spiritual quests have emerged from narratives and seem to be a fundamental striving of human beings that ought to be explored and integrated into new, broader treatment considerations. Such striving constitutes a basic dimension of human experience with a potential for creating cohesiveness at various levels of personality function.

In order to develop an idea of what sort of unified experience a person has, I invite individuals to glance at the synopsis of a life structure (see fig. 1) and consider a few questions:

FIGURE 1. PSYCHOSOCIAL DEVELOPMENTAL AXIS
Andrés G. Niño (after Levinson)

	Creative Work	
Learning	Occupation	Political &
Teaching		Social Causes
Friendships	SELF-IN-RELATION-TO-WORLD	Health &
Groups	Fundamental strivings	Lifestyle
	toward meaning/transcendence	
	(spiritual quest)	
Marriage		
Family		Past Experience
	Faith Community	

- What are the most important components of your life (major sources of meaning and satisfaction) at the present time and how are they interrelated?
- Do you reflect on issues of a spiritual nature?
- What particular events or situations have been the most influential in some of your critical decisions, changes, gains, and losses?
- Do you have a sense that the balance of your life structure allows for the expression of your real self?
- What sort of modifications do you think would be needed for you to have a deeper sense of internal coherence, long-term purpose, and meaning?

THE REFLECTIVE STANCE

In my approach, a major emphasis is placed on the relationship between inquiry and engagement as a powerful source of motivation that keeps alive the process of meaning-making through the various periods of adulthood. Primarily, this approach underscores the value of inwardness and its relevance within those contexts of living that promote detrimental forms of dispersion and fragmentation. In order to encourage the development of the self, aided by the wisdom of ancient spiritual writers and modern psychologists and philosophers,[11] it is imperative to create a protective zone of silence and solitude that provides a favorable environment for personal growth, and which, in turn, may improve the quality of relationships with the outside world.

Throughout adulthood an authentic reflective stance produces a realistic and recurrent appraisal of one's life structure, which then allows for modifications upon forms of knowing and relating that regulate a person's ways of being. Such a reflective stance enriches emerging sets of priorities, goals, and ideals, helping to sustain a vital motivation in the face of unavoidable failures and temptations to give up. One's spiritual quest has the potential to sustain the effort to negotiate failures, simultaneously balancing dreams and flights of imagination, and always preserving a sense of coherence against chaos.

The spiritual quest can be considered to be an assertion of one's fundamental strivings. Such an activity provides a thread to keep together the ever-changing views and interpretations of the surrounding world as a person goes through adulthood. I have observed that when this is effectively integrated in one's life structure, the spiritual quest becomes a major determinant of resilience, and of physical and emotional health.

A RELATIONAL WORLD

Relationships are at the center of one's psychological universe. Some intellectual paradigms have focused too closely upon the individual self at the expense of providing a fuller and more enriching vision. Women in general have suffered as a result of such distortion. It is only in the past two decades that the scholarly and consistent work of some female theorists and practitioners has reversed this trend and made a definitive impact. The relational model proposed at the Wellesley Stone Center is a major contribution to progress in this area. It emphasizes "the yearning for connection" in contrast to the limited and fragile model of the independent self.[12]

The process of a spiritual quest, in this perspective, emphasizes the return to the self—to the inmost zone of being, to preserve the self's cohesiveness and continuity while at the same time strengthening the capacity to transcend its own boundaries in relationship. A person's quest is anchored in that perennial tension between inwardness and the search for an empathic other.

In Search of the Unfailing Other

The task that connects the different periods of adulthood is that of transcending oneself, gradually establishing a balance of cognitive and affective investment in response to the other. Everyone experiences the meaning of transcendence through the quality of the exchanges that take place between people. There is a particular process which, despite vicissitudes and unevenness, of course, includes degrees of transformation:

1. There is a long way from the primal centering of the will-to-be and the ability to have a mutuality in relationships. In between, a developmental struggle unfolds, unveiling joy and suffering alike. Young adults become acquainted with many forms of a "craving for others" that generates transient and superficial attachments. All along there is a growing realization and acceptance of the limitations that the other brings to the encounter. It becomes clear that the others are not always available or empathic. Changes and losses occur against the desire for stability and emotional comfort. A measured recognition of the limitations of the other and the negotiation of mutual needs is an important task in life.

2. The experience of the self grows through a process of increasing interdependence that is at the core of our human condition. The role of friendship can only be appreciated within this context. Unfortunately, friendship is rarely mentioned in developmental theories and studies of adulthood, in spite of its enormous motivational power in the process of change and transformation.

There is a text in Augustine's *Confessions* describing an experience of friendship that emphasizes how the difficult balance of interdependence is achieved and maintained.

> Friendship had other charms to captivate my heart. We could talk and laugh together and exchange small acts of kindness. We could join the pleasure that books can give. We could be grave or gay together. If we sometimes disagreed, it was without spite, as a man might differ with himself, and the rare occasions of dispute were the very spice to season our usual accord. Each of us had something to learn from the others and something to teach in return. If any were away, we missed them with regret and gladly welcomed them when they came home.[13]

Friendship is a context of experience which can best highlight the common-alities and differences that significantly affect the lives and narratives of men and women.

3. It is possible that an inquiry into the images and memories active in former periods of one's life cycle may invite us to deepen the meaning that an "Unfailing Other" holds at the present time. At the center of the experience of empathy there is often a discovery or reaffirmation of an Other beyond and above significant others. A personal relationship with God in adulthood may become an important element in the process of the spiritual quest. This experience has the potential to transform the whole relational process.

In the past, most of what we have known about spiritual quests has been based on the dynamics of this relationship with God. Religions have generally provided the central resource of inspiration. However, as various forces within society have defused or even at times eclipsed the influence of religion, we see more individual quests taking place without such attachments to tradition.[14]

BEYOND US AND OUR TIME

From a developmental perspective, the spiritual quest emphasizes a funda-mental engagement in which the individuals extend toward others the significance of their experience. Implied is the adulthood task of reaching out to a larger con-text beyond the boundaries of personal time and space.

It is, of course, important to be aware of both the potential and problems of one's own generation, as Beaudoin has described recently while examining his own spiritual quest.[15] However, it is equally important to stress the fact that each generation's character and journey builds upon the impact of the previous and other generations. A person's life structure is played out in the crossroads of multi-generational realities. This fact demands mutual interest and respect, a willingness to listen, and a steady effort to maintain forms of continuity and mutual enrich-ment.

There are two critical aspects from which this matter takes its relevance and urgency:

1. *Awareness of a global dimension to our individual quest* Parallel to the interdependence that underlies relationships in dyads or small intimate groups, there is a global dimension to the human experience that is especially characteris-tic of the end of the twentieth century. The concept of "globalization," which in the past often had little effect on one's preoccupations, has now become an inescap-able reality. It has become obvious that the self is embedded in more than just a cultural context, but rather in a global context. In this regard it is critical for each of us to increase our individual and communal awareness of the environmental factors that shape people's life experiences.

Recent psychosocial analysis has pointed out the impact of a number of major factors, from massive and accessible forms of communication to applied scientific and technological advances, and from inequality in the distribution of wealth and resources to social problems like crime and substance abuse.[16] All of this occurs at the same time that different cultures interact at close range, bringing their ways of thought, expression, and living into a formidable tug of war. Globalization, more than any other social phenomenon, has compelled, almost suddenly, different generations to look at each other and wonder: How do we respond to this predicament? Küng has offered a response with the "global ethics" project, which stands as one of the most concerted and relevant statements of postmodern time.[17]

2. *The imperative to cultivate an empathic response with regard to the big questions raised by some harsh realities of life.* A genuine spiritual quest will thrive through engagements beyond oneself and one's safe surroundings. Spiritual quests imply movement and transcendence, creating conditions that allow people to build viable life structures on their own. Rather than complacency and isolation, a quest fosters taking a courageous stance vis-à-vis the contrasting realities of wealth and poverty, the massive urgent problems related to ecological exploitation, politics of discrimination, cultural wars, and the impact of violence in the media.

Such an empathic position can be useful for building common ground for an inter-generational experience of spirituality. In some ways it would also resonate with efforts stemming from a theological foundation, such as Hans Küng's work on the concept of "global ethics."

WORKING THROUGH THE TASK

In the past decade there has been an explosion of interest in and a widespread eagerness for spirituality. Ironically, this century, which has seen so much materialism, cruelty, and arrogance on a grand scale, seems to have developed a general concern for things that really matter. A certain eagerness for the spiritual has come to dominate the spirit of this fin de siècle. We have been taken by surprise when writers preoccupied with the big questions of the human condition are included in the best-seller lists of major newspapers. On this side of the Atlantic, authors like Thomas Merton and Henri Nouwen have become a rich source of inspiration to countless people from all walks of life. Narratives of spiritual journeys are published with consistent frequency.

This trend is indicative of the fact that people are willing to engage themselves and others in the process described in this essay. The task is to help people explore and cultivate the potential of their quest in a manner that steadily contributes to the growth of the whole person.

DECIPHERING TRANSCENDENCE

In education, as in therapy, the fundamental task is to work through the issues in a systematic way, building up through exploration, dialogue, confrontation, and review. It is important to note that, from a developmental perspective, the process of a spiritual quest, rather than being offset by intellectual work, is actually nourished by it. Intellectual inquiry is another major engagement of the self that is striving for the realization of the inner development of ideals, ambitions, and values. Reasoning, which is central to the dynamics of all forms of inquiry, plays a crucial role in the gradual testing and correction through which an individual cultivates spiritual concerns. The challenge here resides in a delicate balancing and coordination that permits the transferring and application of findings in different areas of knowledge into a unified understanding of both self and the world.

Every discipline, in its own way, contributes to the noble pursuit of truth and knowledge. As long as a person is directly involved in the discovery, construction, and interpretation of meaning around the subject, there is a potential for raising questions of ultimacy. Didactic work can engage the student in a progressive effort toward deciphering transcendence, that is, searching beyond the accumulation of data or facts, through the important questions put to the mind by each discipline, and integrating the results into an overall meaning-making process that is both relevant to the individual's life and to forming a connection with the world beyond.

The divorce between fact and value has always been an impediment in both education and psychotherapy. The prevailing trend has been an attempt to avoid any potential entanglement with subjectivity, which has been seen as standing outside of the province of the academy. In recent years, however, there has been a shift in this position. A systematic effort is in progress toward working through issues of value in the curriculum. I have been able to integrate questions of ultimacy into my regular courses on "Personality and Psychopathology," as the subject matter leads the students into inquiry beyond the initial proposition: "Why do we behave the way we do?" Stump and Murray have published a series that has taken a similar approach through various disciplines.[18]

A MENTORING ROLE

There is a task that is just as important as the transmission of knowledge about a particular subject. It is to offer support to individuals in pursuing the important task of defining and focusing an early design of their life structure and then to sustain those persons' motivation to give their life structure adequate expression. This is the area in which mentors play a critical role. Mentors are those who can provide guidance and can convey the message that we are all engaged in a quest for the realization of our aspirations while caring for the effects on other people's lives. This basic empathy is essential in the arts of both education and healing.

Mentoring requires a great deal of vision, honesty, and willingness to engage. Mentoring support is optimally offered toward:
- exploring and working through those questions that establish links with contexts of significance and that are responsive to personal and communal concerns, and

- integrating discoveries and progress into a unified concept of a well-func-
tioning personality.

In this manner the individual can reach a realistic measure of success and satisfaction. Mentoring allows us to move from fragmented knowledge to a broader accomplishment, which Wink and Henson call transcendent wisdom.[19]

CONCLUSION AND FUTURE DIRECTIONS

Throughout the years of academic learning, young adults constitute a large group of people who face "a fundamental turning point in the life-cycle."[20] The thesis of this essay is that their central task is to build life structures with a sense of internal coherence, meaning, and purpose. Both spiritual and intellectual inquiry need to be cultivated as a unifying process and an integral part of that task. It is the degree, quality, and balance of activity present in such a process that has the potential for personal transformation and development.

The role that the EDUCATION as *Transformation* Project can play along this line may be critical. The momentum for a national dialogue and a certain urgency to follow that dialogue with practical programs has been created. The goals of the Project will be achieved mainly by developing a sustained interest in the academic community. Elsewhere I have offered guidelines derived from my work that can be adopted for implementation through seminar and workshop formats.[21] As a brief review, I will summarize these guidelines here so that they can be utilized by colleges and universities that wish to integrate them into their programs and structures.

1. A SEMINAR

In a workshop on "A Developmental Perspective on Spirituality" that I presented at the EDUCATION as *Transformation* National Gathering in 1998, participating students emphasized the need for an integration of ongoing discussions about spirituality into the institutional culture within a safe environment. It is, indeed, of critical importance to create a context of reflection, study, and dialogue on the issues related to spiritual quests. I find that the format of a seminar or a course that expands on the basic ideas presented in this essay can be the starting point for a guided personal exploration and exchange.

During my recent two-year appointment as a visiting scholar at the Wellesley Centers for Research, I developed the syllabus for such a seminar. It is designed to offer, in 12 sessions, an understanding of the role of spiritual quests in the process of adult development. It includes an introduction to methods of inquiry typical of the behavioral sciences. Specifically, it involves those methods which emphasize qualitative description and narrative modes of exposition as most adequate for the exploration of subjective phenomena, such as those unfolding in the process of the construction of meaning in adulthood.

Using both theoretical and applied perspectives, the seminar focuses primarily on three areas of activity, which I have defined as inwardness, relatedness, and generativity. Selected readings help the student to gradually deepen her understanding of the spiritual dimension of personality.

Interested faculty may be invited to participate, presenting views on the topic from the perspective of their own discipline. The seminar, in this manner, has the potential to become an inspirational resource, accumulating relevant literature and systematically incorporating issues and themes uncovered through long-term participation in the EDUCATION as *Transformation* Project.

2. A WORKSHOP

In my writing I propose that engagement in the process of a spiritual quest find adequate expression in a life narrative. The format of a workshop is best suited for that purpose. Participants take their own personal experiences as a narrative text. Students who have participated in such workshops have urged others to explore and share ideas and experiences about spirituality that allow a vital involvement in life and education, and serve as a means for support, sustenance and survival, offering a chance for storytelling, connection, and spiritual discovery.

In addition, participants use a questionnaire and other instruments designed to explore spiritual quests. The results can be elaborated further through a personal narrative project as a follow-up. This in-depth working through the issues provides valuable material, not only for the individual but also for continued research.

Good research, which usually facilitates good teaching and practice, takes its vital questions from real life and people. In that regard, the participation from young adults is critical for our understanding of how fundamental strivings and questions associated with spiritual quests are being formulated and negotiated by different generations. Further discussion on this point would go beyond the limitations of this essay, but I would like to stress the fact that understanding and interpreting generational experiences with regard to spiritual quests is vital to the educational enterprise as a whole, as well as to civic and political life.

Finally, these initiatives derive largely from my personal involvement in a professional role. Working through these formats has become a major focus of my career.

ENDNOTES

1. Charlene Spretnak, *Stages of Grace: The Recovery of Meaning in the Postmodern Age* (New York: Harper San Francisco, 1997).
2. Robert M. Torrance, *The Spiritual Quest: Transcendence in Myth, Religion and Science* (Berkeley: University of California Press, 1994).
3. Robert Coles, *The Secular Mind* (Princeton: Princeton University Press, 1999).

4. Andrés G. Niño, "Assessment of Spiritual Quests in Clinical Practice," *International Journal of Psychotherapy* 2, no. 2 (1997): 193–212.

5. C. Jones, G. Wainwright, and E. Yarnold, eds., *The Study of Spirituality* (Oxford/New York: Oxford University Press, 1986).

6. Niño, *op. cit.*

7. D. B. Larson, J. P. Sawyers, and M. E. McCullough, eds., *Scientific Research on Spirituality and Health: A Consensus Report* (Rockville, Md.: National Institute for Healthcare Research, 1998).

8. H. Kohut, *The Restoration of the Self* (New York: International Universities Press, 1977).

9. D. J. Levinson, "A Conception of Adult Development,." *American Psychologist* 41, no.1 (1986): 3–14.

10. D. J. Levinson in collaboration with Judy D. Levinson, *The Seasons of a Woman's Life* (New York: Alfred B. Knopf, 1996), 36.

11. C. Taylor, *Sources of the Self: The Making of the Modern Identity* (Cambridge: Harvard University Press, 1989); and Arnold H. Modell, *The Private Self* (Cambridge: Harvard University Press, 1993).

12. See note 7 above and J. V. Jordan, A. G. Kaplan, J. B. Miller, L. P. Stiver, and J. L. Stiver, eds., *Women's Growth in Connection* (New York: Guilford Press, 1991).

13. Augustine, *Confessions* (New York: Viking Penguin, 1961), 79.

14. Wade Clark Roof, *A Generation of Seekers* (New York: Harper, 1998).

15. Tom Beaudoin, *Virtual Faith: The Irreverent Spiritual Quest of Generation X* (San Francisco: Jossey Bass, 1998).

16. A.J. Marsella, "Toward a Global Community Psychology: Meeting the Needs of a Changing World," *American Psychologist,* 53, no. 12 (1998): 1282–1291.

17. Hans Küng, *Yes to a Global Ethic* (New York: Crossroad, 1995/96).

18. Eleanor Stump and Michael Murray, eds., *Philosophy of Religion: The Big Questions* (Oxford: Blackwell, 1999).

19. P. Wink and R. Henson, "Practical and Transcendent Wisdom: Their Nature and Some Longitudinal Findings," *Journal of Adult Development* vol. 4, no. 1 (1997): 1–15.

20. Levinson, 1996, *op. cit.*

21. Niño, *op. cit.*

5. Molding the Self and the Common Cognitive Sources of Science and Religion

Arthur G. Zajonc

When we consider what religion is for mankind, and what science is, it is no exaggeration to say that the future course of history depends upon the decision of this generation as to the relations between them.

— A. N. Whitehead

An understanding of knowing is the key to seeing education as transformation. From a partial view of knowing stems not only an impoverished imagination of education but also the radical and misguided separation of science and spirituality. This separation has been an important factor in shaping Western culture for centuries, and more recently is reflected in higher education. When we have regrounded both science and spirituality in the soil of experience, we will find ways of establishing a fruitful relationship between our intellectual and moral lives and appreciate the common cognitive source for both.

Epiphanic Knowing

Knowledge is an event not an object. Consider the following two examples:

1. A physics professor stands before his class with a pile of stones at his side. Talking and gesticulating to his students, he is seen to occasionally pick up a stone and throw it through the air. Sometimes he simply drops one to the floor, other times he tosses a stone straight up and catches it again. "Each of these motions is at root the same motion," he is heard saying. "Try to see it as Newton did when, in seeing the apple fall, he also saw the motion of the moon." Faces are blank. The students have perfectly good eyes, but they are not Newton's and do not see what the professor, judging from his enthusiasm, obviously does see and is so excited about. Another stone is selected. "Watch!" he cries, as he throws it high into the air. Then a single student in the back row, as if waking from a dream, yells out, "I saw it!" The professor pauses appreciatively. Now there are two who see.

Externally nothing essential was different in that particular stone's flight, but the student was ready to see something in it that she had not seen before. That moment is a moment of knowing, of cognition. What happened? An epiphany.

2. Some years later one of the students in the above class, one who never did see what the old professor was driving at, joins the Navy. He is assigned to the ship's artillery on a rather outdated vessel and has become an expert gunner's mate. In drills he performs perfectly, with machinelike precision. Before his command console in a darkened room, he sits awaiting his orders. Over his headset the coordinates of the target's position are called to him from a shipmate above deck.

no further, but rather we rest content with the representation instead of using it as a springboard to a personal, epiphanic encounter.

One way to avoid the error of transforming representations into idols is to value phenomena themselves more, and to devalue representations and models. By phenomena I do not mean raw sensation or sensa, but the thoughtful engagement with phenomena that leads to the knowledge-event, the union of percept with concept in the phenomenon (Newton's apple-moon experience is an example). Modern students of Goethe such as Holdrege, Edelglass, and Bortoft have done much to develop a phenomena-based science of this type.[8]

Goethe suggested that certain phenomena were redolent with meaning, crying out to be seen. All the unessential, obscuring, and contradictory elements that normally confuse us have been pared away so the primary phenomenon can appear to us in stark and often beautiful simplicity. In the process the intellect "fixes the empirically variable, excludes the accidental, separates the impure, unravels the tangled, and even discovers the unknown."[9] Goethe called these "archetypal phenomena." In them, phenomenon is theory. The archetypal phenomenon is a symbol in which one can see nature's patterns, her lawfulness. That which can never be truly visible can nonetheless be revealed through the archetypal phenomenon.

MOLDING THE SELF

As any science educator knows, students do not instantly "see" the pattern Galileo and Newton saw in projectile motion or the swinging pendulum. To move, in Goethe's language, from an initial encounter with "empirical phenomena" through experimentation with "scientific phenomena" to the culmination of "archetypal phenomena" requires discipline, and most of all, a cognitive maturation of the student. In one sense, the brute facts of nature are forever the same. But as Goethe rightly remarks, every fact is already theory; that is to say, facts can become theory if seen in the light of understanding. We bring ourselves to every observation and so initially see everything in the light of our habits of cognition. New epiphanies wait on the remolding of our cognitive capacities: we must learn to see anew. This requires patience and an intimacy with the object of study. Active engagement is essential, but also a proper reticence about applying preconceived notions to the novel. This is what Goethe meant by "delicate empiricism." There is a delicate empiricism that makes itself utterly identical with the object, thereby becoming true theory. But this enhancement of our mental powers belongs to a highly evolved age.[10]

The "enhancement of our mental powers" of which Goethe writes is essential to the education of a scientist, and to his or her continued development. Goethe could be describing the marvels of recent research on neuroplasticity when, in a letter to F. H. Jacobi, he writes,

> To grasp the phenomena, to fix them to experiments, to arrange the experiences and know the possible modes of representation of them...demands a molding of

man's poor ego, a transformation so great that I never should have believed it possible.[11]

"Molding of the ego," or, to use the German word, *Bildung*, is central to Goethe's understanding of science. The relationship between the observer and the observed is dynamic and inseparable.[12] For Goethe, every attentive investigation entails the subtle but significant transformation of self. "Every new object, well contemplated, opens up a new organ within us."[13] Scientific discovery presupposes such a transformation of self. Each epiphany waits on the "new organ" required for that specific knowledge. It is this that separates the unseeing novice from the insightful scientist. Goethe's approach to science emphasizes the perceptual encounter with the laws of nature and not their abstract or mechanical representation. Information can be found in books and databases, and the manipulation of equations is an important technical skill better done by software packages these days than by mathematicians. But the ability to "see" a law of nature is reserved for the human scientist. Here lies the thrill that makes it all worthwhile. If pedagogy would recognize the value of this view of science, then education would reconceive itself as transformation.

Once we appreciate knowing as personal epiphany, the way is opened up for a reconciliation between facts and values, between science and spirituality.

FALSE DICHOTOMY

On a train returning from Marburg to Goettingen in January of 1938, a conversation took place between the mathematician Guenter Howe and the physicist Carl Friedrich von Weizsaecker.[14] Seven years earlier, on February 14, 1931, Howe had been "converted to theology" at Karl Barth's Hamburg lecture *Die Not der Evangelischen Kirche*. On the train back from a scientific meeting, Howe and von Weizsaecker hatched an idea that would bear many fruits. It was not, however, until 10 years later, after the Second World War had concluded, and in the shadow of the first use of nuclear weapons, that Howe was able to realize the idea by convening the first of the "Goettingen Conversations" between prominent scientists and theologians. Physicists of the stature of von Weizsaecker, Heisenberg, and Jordan were there, but the theologians Howe most urgently sought to bring into the conversations refused to meet. Ironically, Karl Barth, Howe's "theological father" and the foremost Protestant theologian of the period, declined to attend. Barth and his disciples, ever distrustful of any alliance between secular, scientific knowledge and Protestant theology, consistently shunned the meetings. For 12 years the meetings continued nonetheless, addressing the moral issues raised by modern science and technology. While distrust between religion and science dates to Luther and earlier, Barth's more recent influential stance still largely dominates contemporary attitudes.

In his recent book, *Rocks of Ages*, Stephen Jay Gould reiterates and reworks Barth's so-called "neo-Orthodox" position, renaming it the "Principle of NOMA—

The prophets of the Old Testament, as well as the disciples in the New Testament, speak incessantly of the experience of Jahve or Christ. The root origin of Islam, Buddhism, and all religions is located in religious experience, not theological speculation or blind faith. In our own lives today, I would suggest it is not otherwise. The contemplative tradition is at the heart, not at the margin, of religion. When it is missing, then religion becomes ungrounded dogmatics, just as science becomes untested assertions when sundered from experiment.

Ultimate knowledge of Nature is as impossible as ultimate knowledge of God. Still, a thrown stone can be understood in at least one dimension of its being, its kinematic dimension. Surely the richness and variety of the divine suggest that we may gain a partial view of it as well. This is not to compromise the infinite, but only to suggest that even infinity is approached through the finite.

Paul Tillich, as well as the two Niebuhrs, granted enormous importance to symbol in the practice of religion. In the "two-realm theory of truth" common to neo-Orthodoxy there is no apparent link between human experience and the divine. As Paul Tillich puts it in his article on religious symbol, "Unconditioned transcendence as such is not perceptible. If it is to be perceived—and it must be so in religion—it can be done only in mythical conceptions."[22] The transcendent must be part of human experience, but Tillich recognized the central mediating role played by the symbolic or representational elements of religion. Like archetypal phenomena they can lead to an epiphanic encounter.

In the epiphanic encounter—where knowledge is experienced—we find the common cognitive source for both science and religion. When shaped and used in one way, it becomes science; when taken in another way, it becomes religion.

Already in the early nineteenth century, Ralph Waldo Emerson felt that science was making profound demands on religion. In a manner analogous to my own, Emerson neither rejected science nor even compartmentalized science and religion in "non-overlappiing magisteria." Rather, he sought to spiritualize science and to lead religion back to knowledge or *gnosis*. He felt the world changing.

The venerable and beautiful traditions in which we were educated are losing their hold on human belief, day by day; a restlessness and dissatisfaction in the religious world marks that we are in a moment of transition.... The old forms rattle, and the new delay to appear. We are born too late for the old and too early for the new faith.

What might be the shape and character of the "new faith"? Emerson does not reduce spirit to matter, or religion to conventional science, but quite the contrary. He wishes to so elevate science that it can learn to know, in the sense of epiphanic seeing, in the realm of the moral and spiritual as well as the natural. No wonder that Emerson considered Goethe his model of the poet-savant, and first practitioner of the "new faith." As Emerson asks in the opening lines of his essay "Nature," "Why should not we also enjoy an original relation to the universe? Why should not we have a poetry and philosophy of insight and not of tradition, and a religion by revelation to us, and not the history of theirs?"[23] Elsewhere, Emerson states his view on the future of religion emphatically,

> The religion which is to guide and fulfil the present and coming ages, whatever else it be, must be intellectual. The scientific mind must have a faith which is science....There will be a new church founded on moral science; at first cold and naked, a babe in a manger again, the algebra and mathematics of ethical law, the church of men to come, without shawms, or psaltery, or sackbut; but it will have heaven and earth for its beams and rafters; science for symbol and illustration; it will fast enough gather beauty, music, picture and poetry. Was never stoicism so stern and exigent as this shall be.[24]

The future of religion will, according to Emerson, be asked to re-integrate knowing as an essential part of itself, a knowing based not only in the sacred scriptures of ancient prophets and teachers, but one that is continuously enlivened by the fresh cognitive encounter with the divine. This is, I believe, what Emerson means by a "faith which is science."

The alternative to NOMA that I propose takes experiential knowing as the basis for both scientific and spiritual insight. It views the human being as capable of gradually extending the range of his or her cognitive capacities through a process of self-development—education as transformation. It recognizes the moral dimensions of science and the cognitive sources of religion. The university of the future should embrace this expansive view of learning and knowing, which entails an expansive view of ourselves and our world as well.

ENDNOTES

1. John Searle makes a similar argument against the strong artificial intelligence position that computer programs can think. See his *Minds, Brains, and Science* (Cambridge, Mass.: Harvard University Press, 1984).
2. Johann Wolfgang von Goethe, *Scientific Writings*, ed. and trans. Douglas Miller (Boston: Suhrkampf, 1988). See also David Seamon and Arthur Zajonc, *Goethe's Way of Science, A Phenomenology of Nature* (Albany, N.Y.: SUNY Press, 1998), and Arthur G. Zajonc, "Facts as Theory: Aspects of Goethe's Philosophy of Science," in *Goethe and the Sciences: A Re-Appraisal*, eds. Frederick Amrine, F. J. Zucker, and H. Wheeler (Dordrecht: Reidel, 1987). This volume also contains an excellent bibliography on Goethe's scientific work by F. Amrine.
3. Goethe, quoted in Rike Wankmueller, "*Farbenlehre:* Goethes Methode," *Goethes Werke*, Hamburger Ausgabe vol. 13, (n.d.): 616.
4. Goethe, *Werke*, trans. F. Amrine, vol. 12, no. 488, 432.
5. Rudolf Steiner, *The Philosophy of Freedom: The Basis for a Modern World Conception*, trans. Michael Wilson, 7th English ed. (London: Rudolf Steiner Press, 1970), 70. See also Steiner's *A Theory of Knowledge Implicit in Goethe's World Conception*, 3rd ed. (New York: Anthroposophic Press, 1978).
6. J. P. Eckermann, *Conversations with Goethe*, 18 February 1829, trans. Gisela

One episode in my own learning stands out as being particularly magical. I was in my last year in graduate school. It was February and I was supposed to finish my Ph.D. thesis by summer. The problem I was most interested in had for a year or more resisted all my attempts to unravel it; let's call it "the class number problem." I had a theorem in mind that I wanted to prove, only it was vaguer and subtler than that: I had a feeling of the kind of theorem I wanted to prove. I was working on other problems at the time and had managed to make enough progress that I had begun interviewing for jobs. During one interview I talked to a colleague about the class number problem and it turned out he had a similar picture in mind about what it should be possible to prove. His idea was close enough to my own internal images that it really got me thinking. I went home to my apartment in Chicago with new enthusiasm. After a few days of working on it with small success I was awakened at 2:00 a.m. by a dream.

I dreamed that I am sitting on a couch while my thesis advisor is walking back and forth telling me all about this problem. He says very specifically to "use abelian fields." He says a few other things I couldn't remember on waking, and then we walk over together to a pedestal on which there is a wildly gyrating mass of energy, swirling and congealing, spinning and bright. Suddenly it turns into a human head and says to us: "You've found the answer!"

The dream was so intense that I got up immediately and wrote it down. I was so excited that I couldn't get back to sleep. I didn't sleep for three days because I couldn't stop thinking about the dream and its admonition to use "abelian fields" (an actual concept in the field I was studying). I did not at that point have a conscious understanding of what the dream meant, nor did I by any stretch of the imagination know the answer to my problem, as the dream head claimed, but I had an intense feeling that something was bubbling up inside me. I could feel the energy, like something about to burst forth or waiting to be born, but for three days it just stayed inside. I knew the answer was there and had no idea how to get at it. For three days I lived with a constant feeling of expectancy mixed with frustration, and kept working. By the third day I had found the key, which was to look at a certain equation and interpret it in two very different ways. Once I worked out the details, it turned out that those "abelian fields" the dream mentions did in fact show up in the theorem I proved. And I did finish my thesis by summer.

What is happening in moments such as this? Where do they come from? Why do they have the profound effect that they do? What would happen if we told these parts of our academic stories to others?

THE MOMENTS OF MEANING WORKSHOP

I had the privilege, in the fall of 1997, of taking part in one of Victor Kazanjian's dinners for faculty, staff, and students, which he eventually came to call a "Moments of Meaning" workshop. Several of us pulled our chairs into the middle of the larger group, which was seated in a larger circle of chairs around us. We were the "fishbowl," and we began nervously to each tell a story of some important moment in our work or in our educational experiences that had left an indelible impression on us. Victor had asked us to describe one of these precious moments in which we experienced awe or wonder in the middle of our learning or teaching. After the members of the "fishbowl" told their stories, the whole group broke up into small groups of four or five, and these smaller groups went off on their own to describe similar experiences to each other. Afterwards, the whole group came back, and everyone mentioned an issue or a question they would be interested in pursuing or willing to lead a conversation about.

Some of the stories had to do with amazing coincidences, such as the same ideas cropping up at the same time in classes in different disciplines, forming a whole picture and giving the student a deep feeling of wonder and appreciation. One of the stories was a personal response to the beauty of the Periodic Table a student had studied in a chemistry class. Some stories were about the influence on a class of a teacher's love of her subject or a teacher's wonder and joy over a student's creation. Still other stories were about human interactions and what was created in a long period of collaboration between teacher and student or between colleagues.

Two things struck me about this experience. We all have these experiences, though we might describe them in different ways, but we almost never talk about them with our colleagues. We sometimes, but perhaps rarely, tell these stories to our students or teachers. In a situation in which 40 or more people were simultaneously all telling their stories to each other it was really obvious how unusual it is for us to let these stories see the light of day. The second thing that struck me was how it changed our interactions with each other to tell these stories. We were truly open to each other in a way that I seldom see in daily college life. Masks were gone, pretenses gone; in their place I felt the glow of genuine conversation, people meeting each other and accepting each other at warm and deep levels.

I participated in several of these workshops, including one at the EDUCA-TION as *Transformation* Conference at Wellesley College in September, 1998 and every time the same thing happened. It was very striking what a powerful effect telling simple stories can have. Why? What is this about? What can we learn from it about the teaching and learning experience?

Two initial ideas suggest themselves to me: spontaneity and wholeness. Spontaneity was involved in these conversations to the extent that the participants didn't know ahead of time that they were going to be asked to tell these stories to each other. The fishbowl participants did know, of course, that they were to tell their stories, but in many cases the story they wanted to tell changed at the last minute, or only formulated itself clearly in their minds as they began to speak. For whatever reason, the stories came across as fresh, unplanned, spontaneous. We didn't have to know anything to tell our stories. We just had to remember an experience, a feeling, and be willing to share it. We didn't have to be experts; there was no homework involved. We didn't have to play a role or protect an institution. We were just asked to be.

We were also asked to bring more of our inner selves to these conversations than is normal in college life. Normally, we meet to discuss "issues" or "curricula" or specific, literal things that we have to deal with. It's surprising the extent to which academia, whose purpose is to help foster the life of the mind, has gotten lost in the literalness of education. The inner dimension of mind seems to have been forgotten or relegated to a dark corner as being "unknowable." There are many teachers and learners who step outside of the box into which the educational environment tries to stuff them, but their beautiful experiences are often private ones, shared between the few people who are immediately involved.

Telling our stories to each other in the simple way we did in Victor's workshops allowed us to be whole in front of each other. That wholeness includes the other facets of deep educational and intellectual experience that are seldom talked about: the emotions we feel in the middle of our learning, the surprise and wonder at the miracles we encounter, the sense of mystery that pervades the discovery of new connections and that often lies just below our normal awareness.

In sharing an experience of this nature and the story of our connection to it, we invoke its energy and its power again into the current situation. This power of story to capture magic and meaning lies outside of time, and in telling it again some part of us remembers that we live outside of time as well. I wonder if that might be part of the reason small children love hearing the same stories or singing the same songs over and over again. As adults, we forget that we can stop the linear song of our lives and sing it again or sing it differently. In connecting our inner worlds with others' inner worlds, we begin to connect to a larger reality. We loosen the grip of the hallucination of the literal world and remember that the imagination is real. This awakens the power of the subjective world to re-imagine and reshape the objective world. Isn't this really the fundamental purpose of the educational experience?

This leads me to the idea that these moments of meaning and wonder are nothing less than moments of magical creation. Something comes together for us in these moments that takes us out of our ordinary waking consciousness. We become aware of a bigger picture or a beautiful wholeness. A door or window opens and we see a part of the fabric of creation itself. These are not just moments of "meaning," because we are in fact hard pressed to make any kind of rational meaning out of them. They come and go and leave their mark. But we can't quite fit them into our ordinary world and we don't go around talking about them all the time. If we did, academic papers would tell stories like these routinely. Instead, they are irrational, defying explanation. They bring ideas and feelings and experience together in a way we couldn't have done consciously. They are often moments that happen to us when we think we are doing something else. In such moments we may just be playing or going about our ordinary routines without trying to do anything special, and then in an instant we become witness to the world creating through us and through our own consciousness.

Thus these stories are pointing to the reality of a hidden dimension in our experience. What is beautiful is that the experiences related in stories of magical moments bring the subjective and objective worlds together in striking ways and even question that very distinction. My graduate school dream was certainly a subjective experience, or was it? It was powerful and undeniable, and provided me with the energy, if not the actual idea, for discovering a new theorem in mathematics that is objectively true by the standard methods of proof. The dream even mentions a piece of that proof in the reference to "abelian fields" that my conscious mind didn't initially know what to do with. In other words, something in me knew what was happening, even though I didn't. Which then is the "real" me, the part that is supposedly "conscious," or the inner part that knows what is going on?

This discovery woke me up to the fact that there is an intelligence operating in levels existing underneath ordinary reality. This was a subjective experience that significantly intersected and changed my objective world. That strikes me as a good definition of magic: magic is the power of the subjective world to transform the objective world! As we relate our individual subjective discoveries to each other, there is the same potential for us to collectively open up doors to the hidden worlds where subjective and objective are intertwined and to recreate reality in a more imaginative and loving rendition. In sharing our individual stories of joyous discovery and wonder we are given a glimpse of a new world and a new way of being.

MAGIC IN THE MATHEMATICS CLASSROOM

The experiences I have had as a research mathematician have led me to try to find ways to help students experience the creative process in mathematics for themselves. However, it has definitely been a challenge for me to bring out the creative side of a subject which is usually presented in a strictly linear way. Mathematics teachers are very used to presenting their subject as established fact. The concepts and definitions are very precise, the techniques work, and the theorems follow inexorably one from another, all very clear and structured and rational and understandable. Well, maybe it isn't so understandable to everyone. Why is it that some of us can connect so easily to it and others cannot? To many students, mathematics presents an impenetrable wall of information with no apparent purpose and little meaning.

I believe that many of the difficulties students have with mathematics can be traced to the way the imagination is treated in the classroom. The key to a student's ability to connect to a subject lies in her ability to imagine it, to connect it to her own inner life and her own wholeness. In order to imagine it truly, she needs to be able to see the subject in its wholeness, which includes its stories, its historical wrong turns, its failures and unsolved problems, its humanness. She needs to be given experiences that lead her to see the individual facts, concepts, techniques, and blind alleys as part of an indivisible and miraculous unity. Once she can grasp that unity, she has grasped the essential idea of mathematics, its meaningful essence and its magic.

This feeling for this unity of mathematics, for the miraculous way that it fits together within itself and with our minds, can be evoked in problem-solving experiences, if they are approached in a way which encourages the use of the imagination. For this to work, the student must be acknowledged for her own imaginative abilities. In other words, the teacher needs to step back and allow the student's creative process to take center stage. Open-ended exploration and spontaneity are necessary for wholeness in mathematics because the subject is so structured and rational. This means that the student has to be free to try her own ideas, to make her own choices, to make mistakes, to see for herself what works and what doesn't. She needs to be given a chance to recreate the subject anew.

There are several avenues I've used to do this, though I'm always looking for new approaches. It has been easiest for me to find these avenues with upper level students working on independent study projects or honors theses. The keys are: 1) making sure the student is studying something she has a real hunger to learn, a topic she has consciously chosen herself; 2) making sure she gains suitable background knowledge in her subject of choice through appropriate readings and exercises, which may include simply explaining the readings back to me or practicing the concepts in concrete situations; 3) my finding a suitable problem for her in this subject which is large enough and difficult enough so she has room to explore and engage her imagination but circumscribed enough that she can make progress on it in a year's time (in the case of an honors thesis); 4) allowing the student time to play, to explore, to stumble, to get stuck, to get good and frustrated; 5) meeting regularly with her to answer her questions and engage in a dialogue about the problem; and 6) continuing to plant seeds in these dialogues that are related to the overall problem she is working on, seeds that may be ideas or specific examples or just hints of connections.

This combination of things is an alchemy that helps the student to forge her own desire to understand the problem and to find a solution. You might say that the main problem I face in these situations is the problem of creating desire in the student and helping her engage her imagination. So we're each working on a challenging problem, and these problems are linked to each other. This approach has regularly created opportunities for magic for myself and for the students I have worked with.

I have also managed to use this approach in a 100-level class I have taught several times on problem solving, titled "Introduction to Mathematical Thought." Since there are normally too many students in the class to have the intense one-on-one interaction that I can have in an independent study situation, I have to find other ways to incorporate the above keys. One way I have done this is to give students choices in the problems they solve during the course of the semester, problems they choose from a list I create. My challenge is to make the problems in this list difficult enough that the students have opportunities to explore and get frustrated, as before, but not so difficult that they lose motivation for finding a solution. My goal is for the students to let these problems get under their skin, so to speak, so that they have trouble keeping them out of their minds. Once a student gets hooked on a problem, she is almost sure to solve it. In order to give the students room to maneuver, I allow them to hand in the same problem up to three times. I look at their solution, circle what is incomplete or incorrect, and sometimes give hints, if appropriate, to keep the student on track. In no instance do I explain the whole answer. The student then works on the problem some more and we continue going back and forth in this way. Most students were able to make significant progress with this method. The attempts the students give me and the responses and hints I give them in return form the dialogue that is crucial for creating an opportunity for the student to reach a new level in her understanding, growth, and confidence in herself.

Naturally, there are many types of questions and experiences that make room for the imagination to enter. In some of my classes I have used very challenging recreational puzzles to achieve this end, problems that the student doesn't initially think she can solve. The more she understands the nature of the question and the precise place of difficulty in the problem, the more open she is for the magic of her own imagination to enter and suggest a solution to her. I have often told students in these classes not to try to solve the problem all at once, but to seek only to understand it, in all its details and fullness. If you understand the problem deeply and you are at all open to the suggestions of your own mind, it's practically impossible not to solve it. That's the magic in i-magi-nation. When a student can let the problem get under her skin, then she is alive to the reality of the problem and to the reality of her own imagination. Then the problem becomes a guide helping her to discover something new in her own inner landscape. A poem of Jelaluddin Rumi speaks to this point:

My poems resemble the bed of Egypt.
One night passes over it and
you can't eat it anymore.
So gobble them up now while they're still fresh
before the dust of the world
settles on them.

Where a poem belongs is here,
in the warmth of the chest.
Out in the world it dies of cold.

You've seen a fish.
Put him on dry land.
He quivers for a few moments
and then he's still.
And even if you read my poems
while they're still fresh,

twenty-first century. The challenge I now face is not how to connect the 25 students in my classroom to the subject at hand and to each other, but how to facilitate the growth, development, and interpersonal connection of approximately 1,800 women representing almost every state in the nation and many foreign countries. It is a twenty-first century task of the spirit, which has its roots in the nineteenth century.

Established in 1837, Mount Holyoke is the oldest continuing institution of higher education for women in the United States. Mary Lyon, a woman motivated by a deep sense of Christian calling, worked tirelessly to found Mount Holyoke Female Seminary as a place to train young women as teachers and missionaries. Today we still quote Mary Lyon when we say that Mount Holyoke women "will go where no one else will go and do what no one else will do." In 1837, that phrase meant that our students should be teachers and ambassadors of the Christian faith. Like other nineteenth century women reformers, hers was a "practical Christianity," designed to respond to the call of Jesus to go forth into the world making disciples and transforming the social order.[6] In reference to the creation of Mount Holyoke, Lyon wrote: "another stone in the foundation of our great system of benevolent operations, which are destined, in the hand of God, to convert the world, will then be laid.... Many hearts have been filled with hope, as they have beheld this enterprise go forward in obedience to the great command, Love thy neighbor as thyself."[7]

Today the arenas for women's leadership are no longer limited to the domains of classroom teaching and missionary work. Mount Holyoke is no longer a "Female Seminary," and chapel attendance is not a requirement any more. It is now a thoroughly secular institution, following a pattern mirrored by many other elite colleges with religious roots.[8] Nevertheless, we continue in the Mary Lyon tradition when we say that we are educating our students to be "effective agents of change."

Because we still seek to provide an education which can be transformative and that will move us closer to an equitable and just society for all, we must facilitate the emergence of the spiritual energy I saw released in my classroom. If we are educating students to be agents of change, we must prepare them for the long haul. Change does not come easily or without struggle. How can we sustain ourselves for such a long-term effort? When I look at the lives of change agents, past and present, what I find at the core of what they do is a strong sense of connectedness to the greater good, a strong sense of spirituality. If the development of one's spiritual life is a component of maintaining one's stamina, then as educators concerned about cultivating leadership, we must also cultivate spiritual growth and development, the capacity for connection.

It is often said that colleges are a microcosm of the wider society. The absence of male students notwithstanding, Mount Holyoke certainly represents the increasing diversity of U.S. society at the dawn of the twenty-first century. Not only do we represent almost every state in the nation and many foreign countries, we are also

Christian (of many varieties), Jewish, Muslim, Baha'i, Hindu, Buddhist, Native American, Spiritualist, and more. Some have come to college with a strong system of spiritual beliefs in place. Others have been unschooled in religious practice of any kind. Many may find the college years a period of spiritual seeking. If I believe, as I have said I do, that the development of one's spiritual life is an important educational objective, how do I seek to facilitate that process, recognizing the diversity within our community? If we understand spirituality as the "human quest for connectedness," the challenge is to help our students see themselves connected to not only those like them but those different from them. Defined in that way, the fact that we are a diverse microcosm of society is an asset rather than a liability, but the challenge remains. We seek to create a community where we will affirm and hopefully understand each other, not seek to convert one another. How do we proceed?

This question is not my question alone. The 1965 Immigration Act eliminated national origins quotas and allowed for increased immigration from Asia, the Pacific, and the Middle East. This influx of new Americans has changed the religious profile of the United States dramatically.[9] The Protestantism that so shaped the founding of Mount Holyoke no longer holds the dominance it had even as late as the 1950s, and we are no longer the three-religion country described by Will Herbert's 1955 publication, *Protestant, Catholic, Jew?* In 1993, Diana Eck, director of the Pluralism Project at Harvard University, wrote that "there are more Muslims in the United States today than Episcopalians. According to some estimates, there will soon be more Muslims than Jews."[10] You can find Muslim mosques and Hindu and Buddhist temples in almost every city in the United States. While clearly America of the eighteenth and nineteenth century was fertile soil for many religious innovations, Eck asserts that what was developing was often a "new world" variation on an "old world" theme. However, she writes, "the world of multireligious America in the late twentieth century is truly a new frontier."[11] It is this world in which our students must be prepared to lead.

It is clear to me that in order to develop the skills necessary to function effectively in a religiously as well as ethnically diverse community, practice is required. Opportunities for dialogue are essential. And yet they are few and far between. And, in a context where Christian privilege has been institutionalized in the academic calendar, in the physical presence of a Christian chapel in the center of campus, and in the past and current presence of a Protestant Christian dean of Religious Life, creating a forum for dialogue where all can enter as equal partners is a challenge. Eck writes:

> Dialogue in which we listen as well as speak may seem so commonsensical it is scarcely worth making a fuss over. And yet dialogue, whether between women and men, black and white, Christian and Hindu, has not been our common practice as an approach to bridging differences with understanding. Power and prestige make some voices louder, give some more airtime, and give the powerful the privilege of setting the terms for communication. We have had a long history of monologues. Much of the Christian missionary movement has been based on a

A CASE EXAMPLE: THE TRANSFORMATION OF A CHAPEL

Each of these four components has programmatic implications which faculty and administrators can work to implement. It is clear that creativity will be required. But now is the time for such creative thinking. Creativity was certainly needed on our campus as the diverse faith communities made their needs for worship space known. How could we affirm the identities of all faith groups when they did not see themselves reflected in our physical structures?

At the center of the campus is a large chapel, clearly designed for Christian worship. Adjoining it is a smaller chapel, also originally intended for Christian worship. In the past few years, the large sanctuary had been regularly used for Catholic worship services, alumnae interfaith services, as well as campus-wide ceremonial events. The small sanctuary had been used weekly for Protestant services. The other faith communities on campus typically made use of lounge space in Eliot House, the building which housed the Office of Religious Life. But this secular space served many functions, and the quiet undisturbed atmosphere needed for prayer was hard to find as students and staff members frequently passed in close proximity to the open space. A prayer room had been established for Muslim students in what was formerly a small office in the building, but the Muslim student population was rapidly outgrowing the available space. How could the needs of not only this community but the Buddhists, the Hindu students, the Jewish community, and the other faith groups be met?

Working with an advisory board of faculty and staff and a multi-faith council made up of students, Dean of Religious Life Andrea Ayvazian conceived the idea of using the underutilized small chapel as an interfaith sanctuary that might be used flexibly by many groups. It seemed like a good idea, but the structure of the sanctuary did not lend itself to that purpose. There was the cross, a symbol of Christianity, engraved in the large wooden pulpit at the front of the chapel. And then there were those traditional wooden pews bolted to the floor. How could Muslims lie prostrate on the floor in prayer in a room free of icons? How could Buddhists sit in a circle on prayer cushions? Where could the Hindu icons be installed without making the space unusable for non-Hindu worshipers?

In fact, the solution was simple. We removed the pews. The cold stone floor that had held the pews was covered with a beautiful Oriental carpet. The open space was perfect for prostrate prayers or neatly arranged chairs, which otherwise lined the walls of the sanctuary. The cross-bearing pulpit was dislodged from its spot and placed on casters so it could be wheeled in and out of the worship space as needed. A wooden cabinet was stationed in a corner of the sanctuary with special shelving built in to permanently hold the Hindu icons to be installed within. The doors could be closed when not in use, thereby maintaining the icon-free space needed by others. Similarly a beautifully finished cabinet held a Torah, ready for use by the Jewish students and their rabbi.

This "simple" solution was not without controversy. Tradition is revered on our campus, and there were those who felt the removal of the old wooden pews would be nothing short of sacrilege. Some Christian students felt the loss of privilege, as "their" space was undergoing change. Yet the choice was clear. All of our students needed to have their identities tangibly affirmed by providing worship space. The campus discussion which ensued in the weeks before the transformation actually took place was an important opportunity for cross-group dialogue, and ultimately led to deeper interfaith understanding in the community as a whole. For those students who participated in the decision-making process, it was an excellent opportunity to experience the kind of leadership needed in a pluralistic community where there are multiple needs and limited resources. We all can learn to share, itself an act of connection. The result is breathtaking, a beautiful and tranquil space where transcendent connection is easily felt alone or with others.

Though the focus of this example is the accommodation of religious pluralism, it is also an example of the power of dialogue to foster a deeper capacity for connection, the spiritual development we seek. This transformation of space is a fitting symbol for the transformation we hope to see in our selves and in our students. It is pluralism that we must achieve in our increasingly diverse society. If we create a climate that supports pluralistic expression and encourages connection during the formative college years, our students will be better prepared to lead us to a more just and peaceful society. May they leave our campuses as they sometimes leave our classes saying, "This experience has changed my life," and ready to change the world.

Endnotes

I would like to gratefully acknowledge the helpful feedback provided by W. Rochelle Calhoun and Stephanie J. Hull.

1. Judith H. Katz, *White Awareness: Handbook for Anti-racism Training* (Norman, Okla.: University of Oklahoma Press, 1978).
2. Parker Palmer, *The Courage to Teach* (San Francisco: Jossey Bass, 1998), 6.
3. Parker Palmer, "Evoking the Spirit of Public Education," *Educational Leadership* 56, no. 4 (December 1998/January 1999): 6.
4. Jean Baker Miller, "Connections, Disconnections and Violations," *Work in Progress*, no. 33 (Wellesley, Mass.: Stone Center Working Paper Series).
5. Beverly Daniel Tatum, "Racial Identity and Relational Theory: The Case of Black Women in White Communities," *Work in Progress*, no. 63 (Wellesley, Mass.: Stone Center Working Paper Series, 1992).
6. Rosemary Radford Reuther and Rosemary Skinner Keller, eds., *In Our Own Voices: Four Centuries of American Women's Religious Writing* (San Francisco: Harper, San Francisco), 254.
7. Ibid, 268–269.

8. G. Neibuhr, "Colleges Setting Moral Compasses," *The New York Times*, 4 August 1996, Education Life Section.

9. Diana Eck, *Encountering God: A Spiritual Journey from Bozeman to Banaras* (Boston: Beacon Press, 1993), 37.

10. Ibid, 39.

11. Ibid, 37.

12. Ibid, 19.

13. Ibid, 168.

14. Diana Eck, "Neighboring Faiths," *Harvard University Magazine* (September 1996), 43.

PART TWO

*From Religious Diversity
to Religious Pluralism:
New Possibilities
for Global Learning Communities*

8. Education as Transformation: A Bahá'í Model of Education for Unity

SUHEIL BADI BUSHRUI AND JAMES MALARKEY

The need for a paradigm shift in educational models to meet the challenges emerging from the transition to a global society must stand out as one of the vital issues for the world community. What such a shift requires is a vision, far-sighted in its scope, and fixed upon the best interests of humanity as a whole. Humankind is, in the words of Shoghi Effendi,[1] "witnessing on the one hand the stupendous advance achieved in the realm of human knowledge, of power, of skill and inventiveness, and viewing on the other the unprecedented character of the sufferings that afflict, and the dangers that beset, present-day society."[2]

The crises that humanity now faces—ethnic cleansing, religious fanaticism, the growing disparity between the rich and the poor, excessive materialism, population explosion, international terrorism, environmental degradation, among others—demand new and inventive approaches in the political realm as well as a profound change in the hearts of people. Education, as propounded in the writings of Bahá'u'lláh,[3] must be a major catalyst for this needed change throughout the world:

> Man is the supreme Talisman. Lack of a proper education hath, however, deprived him of that which he doth inherently possess.... The Great Being saith: Regard man as a mine rich in gems of inestimable value. Education can, alone, cause it to reveal its treasures, and enable mankind to benefit therefrom.[4]

(The authors are fully aware of current sensitivities towards the use of masculine gender and have respected this principle in their writing. It must be noted, however, that the integrity of all quotations, sacred or otherwise, has been preserved.)

This paper explores some conceptual aspects of Bahá'í education by providing a model: Education for Unity. Many of the principles presented in this paper have been tested by the authors in our team-taught World Order Studies program, which was offered for nine consecutive summers in Switzerland (1989-1997). This three-year program included students from over thirty countries with an average number of 75 per summer session. The principles presented here were put into practice, and the profound impact that the course had on all who participated—students, faculty, and staff—has inspired the firm belief that this model can provide a valuable alternative in the field of education.

In presenting this Bahá'í model of education, we readily acknowledge the existence of similar and compatible models which derive from other historical circumstances and religious traditions. Indeed, we are comforted by the prospect of such a convergence. Although our particular model is inspired by writings considered sacred in the Bahá'í faith, we have no doubt that our experience and prospectus is adaptable to a wide range of educational settings, whether religious or secular.

The Education for Unity model derives its inspiration from and is firmly established upon the principle of the Oneness of Humankind. This principle can in no way be aligned with a deadening, difference-suppressing conformism, for it prescribes a unity in diversity. This model and indeed any educational practice animated by this principle, therefore, inculcates a cherishing of the world's myriad cultures and commends the individual's loyalties to family, tribe, country, and nation while, at the same time, generating a wider loyalty to all humanity. It teaches a consciousness of the interrelatedness, interdependence, equal human rights, and basic unity of all the members of the human race who, concomitantly, have the duty of mutual cooperation, respect, and love. The Education for Unity model, furthermore, acknowledges that human beings are spiritual in nature and require education of the heart as much as that of the intellect. In the final analysis, intellectual conviction does not lead to lasting transformation in the world without a necessary transformation that must take place within the hearts of the peoples of the world.

Education for Unity incorporates pluralism into its curriculum. It strives, above all else, to create a global identity, a deep-rooted understanding of the concept of unity in diversity, an awareness of world issues, and a profound sense of obligation to serve the needs of humanity in this momentous age.

This Bahá'í model emerges against the backdrop of two models in the West that make up the foundation of current educational systems. They are here described as the industrial model and the progressive model. The basic premise of the industrial model of education, reshaped in the West after industrialization, is that schools should train people as useful cogs who can be assimilated into the machinery of society. Emphasis is put on teaching skills and facts. Above all, it is—like business—competitive: the best move forward and prosper while others are left behind and languish. Most schools following this model also have a strong national identity aimed at creating solidarity and advancement, possibly for a particular ethnic group or social class.

In the 1920s and 1930s, the progressive movement emerged, of which Stanwood Cobb was a leading figure,[5] along with John Dewey and Arthur Morgan. The general characteristic of this movement is that education should provide meaning for the individual. Under this model, individuals are given a choice in education to study what they find important and valuable to them, rather than what society demands. Furthermore, this model promotes the teaching of values, such as equality and justice. The progressive model utilizes experiential learning, allowing students to be actively involved in the learning process, as opposed to simply being passive recipients of knowledge. Thus, education becomes a cooperative effort, where students learn to work with their teachers and with each other. This educational model, in its more current form, also addresses the need for the appreciation of diversity of cultures, genders, and ethnic groups. The progressive movement is still very powerful today, as is the traditional model. Most institutions draw upon a combination of these two educational models.

While Education for Unity incorporates various elements found in both the industrial and progressive models, its purpose goes far beyond that of either model. Its direction springs from the principle of Unity in Diversity as revealed by Bahá'u'lláh. Distinguishing this approach is the incorporation of a virtue-centered education—a spiritual education—that is a synthesis of those universal principles introduced and renewed by each of the world's great spiritual traditions. Thus, not only are values such as equality and justice promoted and taught; the same is true of virtues such as humility and detachment. The learning process has both a global and a personal dimension. The guiding principles for a Bahá'í model are summarized here in notes from talks given by 'Abdu'l-Bahá[6] during his historic visit to the United States in 1912:

> First: Whole-hearted service to the cause of education, the unfolding of the mysteries of nature, the extension of the boundaries of pure science, the elimination of the causes of ignorance and social evils, a standard universal system of instruction, and the diffusion of the lights of knowledge and reality.

> Second: Service to the cause of morality, raising the moral tone of the students, inspiring them with the sublimest ideals of ethical refinement, teaching them altruism, inculcating in their lives the beauty of holiness and the excellency of virtue and animating them with the excellences and perfections of the religion of God.

> Third: Service to the oneness of the world of humanity; so that each student may consciously realize that he is a brother to all mankind, irrespective of religion or race. The thoughts of universal peace must be instilled into the minds of all the scholars, in order that they may become the armies of peace, the real servants of the body politic—the world. God is the Father of all. Mankind are His children. This globe is one home. Nations are the members of one family. The mothers in their homes, the teachers in the schools, the professors in the college, the presidents in the universities, must teach these ideals to the young from the cradle up to the age of manhood.[7]

This broad vision of education entails cultivation of the full range of human potential: intellectual, through scientific research and application; moral, through community service and inclusive, consultative process; spiritual, through religious study and practice; and, not least, physical, through the promotion of health and healing. These dimensions are complementary, and each is necessary. The creative and performing arts, vital to building community, depend on and, one can argue, achieve excellence in the measure to which they draw upon these dimensions of the whole person in a balanced way.

We will now elaborate on aspects of this Bahá'í vision of education with brief reference to both how it was integrated in the World Order Studies program and how it could be embodied in a more extensive program of study.

The Bahá'í approach to service is the basis of Education for Unity. 'Abdu'l-Bahá describes *service to mankind* as "the paramount motive of all existence."[8]

His purpose, far from belittling the station of the Prophets gone before Him or of whittling down their teachings, is to restate the basic truths which these teachings enshrine in a manner that would conform to the needs, and be in consonance with the capacity, and be applicable to the problems, the ills and perplexities, of the age in which we live.[17]

The emphasis of our approach to education, therefore, is to seek those aspects of religion which inspire people to be better toward one another and which lead to practical solutions. By its nature, religion is subject to a wide and limitless spectrum of interpretations and perceptions. However, its potential to unite and inspire peace is also great. Education is a key to changing perceptions and realigning focus from divisive elements to the unifying potential and the promotion of understanding and harmony.

A holistic model allows time for the balanced development of the whole human being. In the model of the World Order Studies program, which has been effectively applied, the day begins early with a focus on spiritual development and spiritual deepening, which drives the whole organism and influences all other aspects of an individual's life. "Occupy thyself," Bahá'u'lláh writes, "in remembrance of the Beauty of Him Who is the Unconstrained, at early morn and seek communion with Him at the hour of dawn."[18] Meditation and reading of holy texts uplift the spirit and provide a profound sense of meaning and purpose to the student's day. The morning and early afternoon are designated for intellectual development. Prior to the lunch hour, students attend lectures where concepts and ideas are introduced. The afternoon is devoted to the exploration of the ideas presented through the often experiential, diverse learning modes.

Combined with these elements—intellectual and spiritual development—and consonant with the Bahá'í writings on health and nutrition is a physical component that aims to preserve and enhance the sacred vessel of the human body. Students are encouraged, through an understanding and nurtured respect for their own bodies, to exercise, to eat well, and to spend time outdoors in nature. Our model also addresses the social and emotional dimensions of the human being. Here, faculty and staff must be sensitive to the needs and diverse personalities of the student body. No individual is allowed to feel alone or to experience isolation. Attitudes among the students are taught through the example of the faculty and staff and through the virtue-based elements of the program. Furthermore, the encouragement of artistic endeavor and expression as well as the promotion of student gatherings to consult, sing, dance, pray, study, and share help to promote a healthy and uplifting environment. Thus, a Bahá'í model incorporates a balanced development in all areas.

As to the actual contents and curriculum of a Bahá'í program, these are flexible. Education for Unity, as applied in the World Order Studies program, provides a starting point. The core topics of study are three, each of which can be expanded on and developed as the program matures:

1. The State of the World
2. The Cultures of the World
3. The Spiritual Heritage of the Human Race

Among the most important messages to students is that learning is a lifelong endeavor. The state of the world alters constantly. To grasp the movements taking place around the world, students must study the mainstream press as well as the alternative press. Annual publications such as *State of the World,*[19] combined with video series like *Race to Save the Planet,*[20] provide students with in-depth perspectives on global challenges. These works emphasize positive developments but also show where efforts are harmful or ineffective. The Bahá'í publication, *One Country,* describes the activities that Bahá'ís around the world have undertaken in the arenas of social and economic development projects and humanitarian causes.[21]

Studies of the great civilizations of the world—including India, China, and Egypt—are helpful in understanding the cultures of the world. Customs have considerable inertia, far beyond the awareness or control of people. They are transmitted through generations; they may be of help in growth and development in some cases, yet limiting and maladaptive in others. Understanding the logic behind traditions and learning to communicate cross-culturally are critical skills in a Bahá'í education. This effort involves the study of certain branches of anthropology and the humanities.

Furthermore, the ability to be self-reflexive is a skill that students learn on several levels. They learn to analyze their own culture and nationality within the context of the greater world and human history. Through daily meditation and reflection, they learn to revere the nobility of the created world and the evidences of the divine within themselves. They develop an ability to monitor themselves and their actions on a daily level.

A course on the Spiritual Heritage of the Human Race provides a study of the diverse faiths of the world, tracing the history of world religion chronologically through related cultural and geographic regions. The course, unlike comparative religion studies, focuses on the common themes and expressions in religious history. While remaining true to the particular characteristics and qualities of each religion, the Spiritual Heritage course offers a perspective on the underlying unity of faith and religion.

Exploring a host of other themes, Education for Unity, as it expands, can provide tracks of study so that students may specialize and become effective workers for the various aspects that lead to justice, unity, and peace. Consequently, an expanded curriculum would place serious attention on the pervasive and complex problems associated with a history of colonialism and racism. Furthermore, this program, in its attempt to provide exploratory channels for students and to encourage imaginative and creative approaches to current world problems, would incorporate the study of the ancient indigenous cultures into the curriculum. In many cases, these cultures have mastered practices of sustainable development and have also developed remarkable forms of cultural expression.

The study of the environment and the effects of humankind's technological revolution on the natural world is no less critical an issue. The incorporation of the study of this topic combined with the study of sustainable development and agriculture provides students with another piece of the complex web of interconnected processes constituting the world. The question of appropriate technology, an issue of great importance, also arises out of the study of environmental degradation. Here, students learn to use ethical and spiritual principles to direct their understanding of human advancement and progress.

Education for Unity, as it expands its curriculum, will incorporate the study of geography, history, and economics. Within the context of the study of globalization, international economics is among the most important and dynamic topics of study. It is integrally connected to the study of international politics, human rights, and the distribution of wealth, each essential topics of study.

The list of possible subjects for the curriculum is almost endless. Capitalism and socialism, urban renewal, economics, media analysis, ethical theories, management, cross-cultural psychology, anthropology, world literature and poetry, art and music, human development, health and nutrition, and critical thinking are simply some of the broad subjects that an elaborate Bahá'í educational model should incorporate, a model that will have the goal of nurturing knowledgeable and compassionate world citizens.

In conclusion, Education for Unity, founded upon the principle of the Oneness of Humanity, has an underlying mission that addresses the development of the whole human being in the context of the entire human race. At its very core, our Bahá'í model enshrines those sacred and universal principles and virtues that have inspired and elevated humankind throughout the ages; and it strives to translate understanding into action. Commitment to service and cooperation defines community life. Diversity and individual uniqueness are cherished and nurtured.

Although the concepts presented reflect high ideals, it is the firm belief of the authors that this program is effective and practicable. Humanity can no longer afford to ignore the incorporation of spiritual and ethical training in education any more than it can afford to dismiss the diversity of human circumstances, outlooks, and achievements.

The model we have described provides an alternative, which assumes that humanity has arrived at the point of maturity where the divisive doctrines and beliefs that have characterized it in the past must now be replaced by a shift towards unity and oneness. In this vision, diversification, which so invigorates life, may serve as the handmaiden of peace and justice rather than as their assassin. We believe that the future we have envisioned is within our grasp. As educators, it is up to us to open minds and hearts to this millennial opportunity.

ENDNOTES

The authors wish to express their gratitude to Mr. Naisohn Arfai for his generous and invaluable assistance in the preparation of this paper for publication.

1. The Guardian of the Bahá'í Faith from 1921 until the year of his passing, 1957.
2. Shoghi Effendi, *Guidance for Today and Tomorrow* (London: Bahá'í Publishing Trust, n.d.): 127–8.
3. Mirza Husayn 'Ali (1817-1892), who afterwards took the title of Bahá'u'lláh (i.e., Glory of God), was the founder of the Bahá'i faith. He declared his mission in 1863 in Bahgdad, the city to which he was exiled 10 years before.
4. Bahá'u'lláh, *Gleanings from the Writings of Bahá'u'llah*, trans. Shoghi Effendi, rev. ed. (London: Bahá'í Publishing Trust, 1978), 259–260.
5. A distinguished American educator, Stanwood Cobb had the privilege of meeting the head of the Bahá'í Faith at that time, 'Abdu'l-Bahá. When he spoke about his work, 'Abdu'l-Bahá asked him: "Do you teach things of the spirit?" "No, there is not time for that," replied Cobb. Sixty years later, in his book, *Thoughts on Education and Life* (Washington: Avalon Press, 1975), 8, Cobb rued those words, by which he had unwittingly repudiated the spiritual basis of modern education.
6. The eldest son of Bahá'u'lláh, appointed as his successor.
7. 'Abdu'l-Bahá, quoted in: *Star of the West*, vol. IX (1912): 98.
8. 'Abdu'l-Bahá, *The Promulgation of Universal Peace* (Wilmette, Ill,: Bahá'í Publishing Trust, 1982), 369.
9. 'Abdu'l-Bahá, *Selections from the Writings of 'Abdu'l-Bahá* (Haifa: Bahá'í World Centre, 1978), 132–33.
10. R. D. Laing, *The Politics of Experience* (New York: Pantheon Books, 1967), 71
11. 'Abdu'l-Bahá, quoted in John E. Kolstoe, *Consultation: A Universal Lamp of Guidance* (Oxford: George Ronald, 1990), 6.
12. 'Abdu'l-Bahá, *Paris Talks* (London: Bahá'í Publishing Trust, 1961), 143.
13. Ibid.
14. Fritjof Capra, *The Tao of Physics: An Explanation of the Parallels Between Modern Physics and Eastern Mysticism* (Boston: Shambhala Publications, 1983), 307.
15. Bahá'u'lláh, *op. cit.*, 213.
16. Bahá'u'lláh, *Tablets of Bahá'u'lláh Revealed after the Kitáb-i-Aqdas*, (Wilmette, Ill: Bahá'í Publishing Trust, 1988), 169.
17. Shoghi Effendi,. *Call to the Nations* (Haifa: Bahá'í World Centre, 1977), xxi–xxii.
18. Bahá'u'lláh, *A Selection of Bahá'í Prayers and Holy Writings* (Kuala Lampur: Bahá'í Publishing Trust, 1991), 122.

19. *State of the World: A Worldwatch Institute Report on Progress toward a Sustainable Society*, Project Director Lester Brown (New York: W. W. Norton & Company, n.d.)
20. Ten one-hour video programs addressing the world's major environmental problems, and copyrighted by the Annenberg/CPB Projects.
21. Published quarterly by the Office of Information of the Bahá'í International Community.

9.   *The Transformation of DrowningBear*

BRAD DROWNINGBEAR

The Creator's spiritual purposes and gifts are distributed to and through all of creation. I am a mixed-blood American Indian[1] male. Experience and tradition within the context of *community* informs and inspires my faith and my practice of what I call a *transformed* agenda. I believe our Creator has designed humans to live in cooperation with a divine design, giving us the wisdom to make choices for wholeness and well being. I work toward the sacred benefit of the community, for the common good and healing of the global village which all of creation shares. The concept of spiritual formation—which is selfhood and identity transformation—in the context of a local and particular community is vital to human fulfillment in God's purposes. I am empowered to fulfill my vocation by the Spirit of God. I will attempt to show that experience and multifaceted traditions in Indian communities are key factors as I share in ministry with all of creation. I will do this by discussing some of the principal claims of a Native American perspective as well as foundational Christian views.

CONTEXT, PERSPECTIVE, AND EXPERIENCE

Have you ever seen a Cherokee basket woven together from the various strands of buckbrush growing out in the countryside? The plants are observed, selected, and carefully harvested by the maker. Each strand is stripped of its outer coating so that it can be used as a part of the beautiful basket that is used for various purposes. Once it is woven, it is difficult to see the individual strands in the midst of the whole of the circular shape of the basket. Each individual strand has a function in the usefulness of the entire basket that is strategically formed by the Maker. Our individual participation in a sacred way of life is like one of those strands. We each have a part and participate in the whole of the basket or community. We grow in the midst of the world as individuals in different contexts and the Creator strips us of selfish ways through the experience of following wisdom's pathways. We then are prepared by the breath of God to cooperate in the warp and woof of the weaving of our being and becoming in community to participate in life's sacred purposes. Some resist and refuse to cooperate and are alienated or exiled from community. Others are strong and commissioned by the Maker to leadership in the vibrant dance of all of life. Did you know that, in the Yakama tradition, the Great Chief Above gave woman something invisible preserved in a basket through which "first woman taught her daughters and granddaughters the designs and skills which had been taught her?"[2]

My Indian education and identity began with growing up in the Northwest and going to salmon bakes and canoe races on the Quilleute Indian reservation where my grandmother lived in the summertime. We would walk along the beaches and dig clams, collect snails, and catch crabs to eat. The taste of elk, deer, and bear meat was as memorable as the blueberries, blackberries, salmonberries, and many other kinds of berries I ate. Then I lived for periods with my other relatives on the Yakama reservation, on the other side of the Cascade Mountains, riding horses, digging wild onions and roots, pheasant hunting, and eating foods from that side of the mountains. These two kinds of experiences were the roots of my heritage and experience growing up. My makeup is coasts and rivers, woods and mountains, and the eastern plains of Washington, and I don't mean the planes of Boeing although they, too, were a big part of my growing up as an urban Indian in Seattle. Seattle has its own Northwest Indian and international character. After all, I am from my mother's side Yakama, Snohomish, Wanapum, and Nez Perce, as well as a descendant of a Danish riverboat captain and an English trader.

When I went to an Oklahoma College in the 1970s and moved to Oklahoma in the 1980s, I connected with my Cherokee heritage on my Dad's side and became aware of the difficulties and struggles during the Trail of Tears. Though stories of brokenness were predominant and grievous, there were also stories of the great transformation of the people through their experiences in spite of the horrific injustices.

Through the variety of all my experiences, I developed a life full of deep care and respect for all of relationships in life, spiritual as well as physical. Because I grew up in the land of my people's origin and shared the oral community memory of the stories of the way the heavens, earth, mountains, rivers, and sea were formed and of their relationship with the whole of God's creation, I gained deep insight and a coherent perspective, which helped me develop my selfhood and enabled me to launch into the journey where I find myself today, a journey where pluralism is respected.

HISTORY AND MEANING

Because of the trauma caused by the encroachment of foreigners upon this continent's original people, the shock waves of the loss of both individual and communal identities are still reverberating down through the generations. According to materials used by Professor Ines Talamantez in her graduate student programs, removing people from their homeland, "the very matrix of discursive meaning...is to render them speechless—or to render their speech meaningless—to dislodge them from the very ground of coherence. It is, quite simply, to force them out of their mind."[3] I myself call this effect *generational trauma*. This is an entire people going through posttraumatic stress syndrome for generations. The impact of this oppression affects all of life in this hemisphere. God's self-revelation to an oppressed nation or people is vital for individual selfhood and community consciousness. It is particularly important for the American Indian community to hear a relevant and timely communication from God. This community needs to know how it fits in the basket of all nations.

The devastating effect of cultural genocide and hegemony[4] on American Indians has had a personal impact on me. When I consider my vocation and ministry, I find that I cannot embrace Christianity in an uncritical manner because many Christians participated in the American annihilation of Indian peoples. Let me have what we call "a word in season" touching the deeper reaches of the mind, spirit and heart of a people who, after all, are the roots of this continent.[5] Many of the theologies American Indian people adopt offer cursory and imported perspectives and are not rooted in their own geo-historical core.[6] These perspectives often fall short of "good news" in their rigid and legalistic proclamations. Vine Deloria's *Red Earth, White Lies: Native Americans and the Myth of Scientific Fact* does a particularly fine job of contrasting traditional indigenous knowledge with Western scientific ethnocentric notions. The omissions in the Western view include the blind manner of ignoring the great repositories of wisdom in the Native oral histories of the elders concerning this continent.[7] I often wonder why it is that the first nation's resources are not consulted when it comes to researching the original people's history on this landmass.

In my judgment, this country we call the United States of America has run over one people and now attempts to tell the rest of the world how to live. The government of this country is today carrying on policies that are oppressive and limiting to the first peoples and nations. It is hard to want to learn lessons from a materialistic nation that treats the earth as though there is no limit or consequence to its consumption.

The Christian gospel of salvation opened my spiritual eyes to the destructive path I was living in the 1960s, and yet I experienced coldness and shallowness in my first exposure to the Christian way. The history of atrocities and insensitivity to the Native American spiritual and cultural pathways was frightening. The charge to forget or lay aside my heritage, designated as "evil ways of the world, ungodly or pagan," was too painful to ignore. This and the hypocritical lives of some Christians caused my revulsion toward the hubris-centered[8] ways of many Christian peoples. Because of some honest, sincere and respectful followers of the Christian way, however, I kept on hoping for a way to validate the influential Christian tradition as well as other world traditions I was finding so helpful in my spiritual journey. Our way is to always give people the benefit of the doubt. After a significant internal struggle between my own deeply rooted traditions and Christian pathways, I realized that there was no real conflict between the two ways at the core of their spiritual traditions: I could be an Indian *and* a Christian. In fact, I was better prepared for life with two sources of authority and truth.

I carry the multiple perspectives I have explored into the journey of my life. Each way matters and the more I learn and refine my spiritual identity, the more I see that there is also much that is rich beyond these two traditions that can also contribute to my particular vocational development. I have chosen to work with Native Americans. Through personal experience I have concluded that each Native tradition is valid in its own context and each, like other world traditions, has rich contributions to make. No compromise was, in the end, necessary. I had the Peace of God. There was no need to reject my cultural heritage (who I am), and there was no need to avoid participation in others' traditions or systems of belief (who they are). We can share and by being aware of and trying to understand the different traditions, we can achieve a fuller and truer sense of who we are. Many Native Americans have been conspicuous by our absence. We have been cautious about saying anything. It is time to share and thereby to enrich each other with our great contributions of respectful and sensitive observations about our various traditions. We can appropriate the best insights of all our traditions.

When I am driving in an old Indian pickup truck, two headlights are better than one. When I have a clear vision and an uncluttered mind,[9] I am more sensitive to the Spirit's leading and can find my path in life and be a model for others. Sacred stories, scripture and traditions are all of great value and, "the most basic sense of tradition, [is] the continuing activity of God's Spirit transforming human life."[10] The value of a multi-traditional approach is that Christian Scripture and other traditions give me the insights I need to live in today's society and this approach allows the wisdom of my roots, my Native traditions, to shine forth.

All the traditions that have been passed on to me by others assist in forming meaning and coherence for me. When the eagle comes down and swoops over me when I am fasting, praying, and waiting for divine counsel, it is a confirming and affirming sign for me. There is the importance of the eagle in Native American traditions and there are also the Hebrew scriptural passages of Isaiah 40:31 and Exodus 19:4. In my upbringing, the eagle and the eagle feathers are highly respected because they fly closest to God. This is a traditional background that is deeply ingrained in my consciousness. I have even said that partnership and marriage are like an eagle feather, something to be treated with the utmost respect and not to be taken lightly. Loss of an eagle feather in the PowWow arena provides an example of this respect in the common, social dance life of Indian people. Everything comes to a halt for the sacred feather must be handled with care and respect before anything continues.

When the redtail hawk, another of the great hunters of God's creation, flies by when I am looking for some orientation or directional guidance, it is another communication experience for me. The experiences are very real and, in my understanding, designed or intended for me to hone and sharpen my senses and awareness of the messages of the Creator.[11] This is a natural profound communication in light of the immediate circumstances and my open posture and sensitivity to a word from God. Selfhood is being developed and I can begin to find the right path in life and service to others. Even though every day of life is a prayer and sacred, there are pivotal spiritual moments that prepare me, inspire me, and transform my orientation to do sacred work within the pluralistic communities that I encounter. We have our own multi-faith communities because of the many intermarriages between the tribes and nations of First Nations peoples on this continent.

GOD AS CREATOR, CREATION AND REVELATION

When it comes to my understanding and response to the uncreated and eternal God as Creator, I rely on my experience of Creator's self-revelation. This experience and dialogue with tradition play a most important role in the process of developing a concept of the Great Changer or Great Spirit of the universe. My idea of the deity determines how I live my life. It might be said we focus on deeds, not creeds.

The common underlying assumption of many Native American traditions is that "all things in the universe are interconnected and are dependent on one another."[12] The kinship and relatedness stand out in Indian experience and philosophy of creation. Belief and responsibility go hand in hand. Beverly Harrison has expressed it this way, "Where our image of transcendence is represented to us as unrelatedness, as freedom from reciprocity and mutuality, the experience of God as living presence grows cold and unreal."[13] If unbegotten God created the universe (olam)[14] and it was good, and I can experience good things in my life, then I'm going to do my best and have a good time. This does not mean that all in God's world of creation is like paradise, but that it is good. This wholesome understanding guides my understanding of all revelation and theology.

The universe is good and God wants me to experience good things, not shameful or dreadful things. Two experiential suggestions guide my pathway. The first is the advice I was told Rose Kennedy gave to her sons: Follow your heart, ask God for guidance, and sit back and enjoy the adventure. The other came from a speaker at Haskell Indian Nations University. His elder mother's advice was: Whatever you do, make sure you have a good time.

Vital, sensual, agapic, and erotic feelings come from the loving God who created us with the ability to be moved in our emotions and passions. *Law of the Spirit of life, set me free.* I think that the revelation of God is that we are shown who we really are and this realization inspires us to new heights in our spiritual formation. As Karl Rahner has put it, we are spirit beings on account of our metaphysical anthropology and we cannot be indifferent toward God's revelation by "virtue of [our] creaturely ontological constitution." That spirit which is in me is of the Spirit who "discloses."[15] God is welcoming, generous, hospitable and God created a good universe and earth, but not an earth without consequence. We are responsible for the stewardship of God's creation.

Respected traditions of other peoples, often oral and symbolic, carry much weight for their own contextual, cosmological understandings. One of the guiding paradigms of indigenous traditions used to portray the image of the inherent unity and oneness of all things in the universe is through the Sacred Circle of Life.[16] Human existence is always happening in a circular or cyclical fashion, progressing and coming back to its point of origin with a transformed perspective or dimension.[17] (See the diagram of a medicine wheel.)[18] This symbol's simple form of expression offers a source of insight into God's revelation of some of the many relationships concerning God and all of creation. It also affirms that everyday experience can be revealing. Something happens to me in my everyday experience that causes me to be transformed anew with each stage of being that I go through. This sacred space and the progress of human existence along the path of the circle are rich with the basic lessons of life. Black Elk described it this way:

> Everything the Power of the world does is done in a circle. The Sky is round and I have heard that the earth is round like a ball and so are all the stars. The wind, in its greatest power, whirls. Birds make their nests in circles, for theirs is the same religion as ours. The sun comes forth and goes down again in a circle. The moon does the same and both are round. Even the seasons form a great circle in their changing, and always come back to where they were. The life of man is a circle from childhood to childhood and so it is in everything where power moves.[19]

A child is born...a flower blossoms...extraordinary and often phenomenal events happen in our lives frequently enough to be considered routine and common. I feel that I do well to allow the power of God to usher me to the next stage of being and identity in my journey. While all nations and peoples are linked metaphysically by some common characteristics, there are also particular characteristics in that each nation has its own sophisticated and unique authority from its own social location and site-specific community knowledge.[20] This contextual element provides both the unity and diversity of each community of faith. It is for this reason that I believe that indigenous knowledge of Creation—and any theology for that matter— is of dynamic and contextual significance for each people as they direct attention to their authorities for a word from God. The New Testament canon bears this out.[21]

Just as our physical design is for relational experiences with other humans for the purposes of procreation and pleasure, we are designed spiritually to be in communion with God and all of creation. It is in the context of the natural world and in relation with one another that we begin to understand what we are all about. Our spiritual nature is influenced by our past and present experiences and by our expectations of the future. In human community, we have our "origin and orientation toward God."[22] We are relational and transcendent beings. In other words, we are creatures of a spiritual and social nature participating in interactions with God and the world around us. Our very makeup is created with a thirst for God in a way similar to the deer that pants for water in spite of the hunter or the lurking trap. Ultimate value is in our orientation toward God and the resultant relationship with God and all of creation.

Resistance to God and the created order is established by putting self and human intelligence on the top of the scale as the way to control events in the world. This is our "fall to violence."[23] Attempts of the human intellect alone, without spiritual guidance and without honoring and respecting community, lead to futile dead ends. "Community imbalance and disharmony"[24] are sins according to the Native American perspective. Another way of describing this is to say that the communion of God with the human organism has been hindered at the basic level of spiritual relationships. Designed for life, love, and abundant joy in community, the creation experiences moments and periods of resistance, noncooperation, and unhappiness. The results of going our own way instead of God's way are strained relationships, alienation, and immense pain and death.

An Ethic of Respect, Cooperation, Hope and Justice

As our Native faith communities gather for fellowship together, we sense a common strength that we could not have alone. We need each other as we go to the special places and share in the sacred space of the community. We begin to understand, theologically, that we are created deeply connected to all of creation and share worshipful, respectful cooperation with all of life. God will provide all that is necessary for our life on our mother earth; respectful sharing of spiritual and physical resources go hand in hand, and this is our trust and our responsibility. I have what I call an earth ethic and an earth faith[25] and I need the many voices of sisters and brothers of different perspectives. Written beliefs of doctrine and dogma can be helpful to delineate a belief but should not interfere with the dynamic quality of life in which we "live and move and have our being."[26] We also need the guidance of recognized and acknowledged Elders identified and ordained in a manner worthy of the leadership of people, acknowledged and commissioned by the authority of the people, not commissioned only by a degree or license. Chief Joseph of the Nez Perce and Chief Drowningbear of the Cherokee of North Carolina were spiritual leaders and were considered, like the apostle Paul, fathers of faith for many—spiritual progenitors.

Women and men of many faiths guide the individual and communal consciousness and help establish our connectedness and groundedness internally in a praxis as well as a creed. Worship can be defined as *our life lived as prayer in respectful, regular, reflective inner communion with God and self and thus an outer communion with all of Creation.* This organic and earthy paradigm is foundational for truly solid evocative and effective pedagogy and for living a life that goes beyond mere "tolerance" of other faiths and beliefs. Sharing of multiple religious practices is the force that drives transformation in the community where we converge with other paths and peoples. We need to model the community as we know it should be.

Indigenous religion and spirituality have constantly been in tune with local and continental vibrations and energy.[27] Indigenous religion is part of the primal "innate and natural wisdom of the organism" for a specific location.[28] The elements of creation center us in our selfhood and bring us closer to God our creator. The priest or holy person has a prepared and informed ministry. Signs and symbols of divine design and order remind us who we are and facilitate grace, which is the prescription for life increasing our capacity to mobilize our inner resources.

In one Native American tradition, our relationships in worship and practice are often compared to the intersection of the teepee poles. The trees all start in

18.

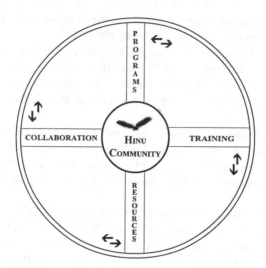

19. John G. Niehardt, *Black Elk Speaks* (Lincoln: University of Nebraska Press, 1961), 194ff.
20. Norbert S. Hill Jr., Oneida, ed. *Words of Power: Voices from Indian America* (Golden: Fulcrum Publishing, 1994), vi.
21. James D. G. Dunn, *Unity and Diversity in the New Testament: An Inquiry into the Character of Earliest Christianity* (Philadelphia: Trinity Press International, 1990), 122, 376ff.
22. Karl Rahner, *idem,* 69.
23. Marjorie Suchocki, *The Fall to Violence: Original Sin in Relational Theology* (New York: Continuum, 1994).
24. James Treat, ed. *Native and Christian: Indigenous voices on Religious Identity in the United States and Canada* (New York: Routledge, 1996), 65.
25. See Larry L. Rasmussen, *Earth Community, Earth Ethics* (New York: Orbis Books, 1996).
26. Acts 17:28.
27. See also Jurgen Moltmann, *The Spirit of Life: A Universal Affirmation* (Minneapolis: Fortress Press, 1993).
28. See Alan W. Watts, *Nature, Man, and Woman* (New York: Vintage Books, 1970), 2.
29. View of Native American Church members.
30. Jace Weaver, *Defending Mother Earth: Native American Perspectives on Environmental Justice* (New York: Orbis Books, 1996), 117.
31. Paul F. Knitter, *Jesus and the Other Names: Christian Mission and Global Responsibility* (Maryknoll: Orbis Books, 1996), 11.

10. Judaism, Religious Diversity, and the American Academy

ARTHUR GREEN

The academic life of North America in the latter twentieth century has been greatly enriched, and in some measure shaped, by the large-scale presence of Jews in the academic community. Ever since the early years of Jewish emancipation in Europe (roughly 1780-1848), the university career has attracted a great number of bright young men (and much later, women) of Jewish descent, who bore with them a wide range of attitudes toward their own Jewish origins. In both European and American universities, generations of Jews had to struggle against *numerus clausus* policies, some formal and others just "gentlemens' agreements," designed to limit their numbers in both faculties and student bodies. These restrictive and discriminatory arrangements, in their last stage in this country described as protecting "geographical diversity," ended only in the 1970s and 1980s. Their final collapse may have had as much to do with the budgetary needs of colleges and the willingness of Jewish parents to pay rising tuition costs as it did with the great decline in the respectability of anti-semitism in the post-holocaust decades.

Despite the odds, and even before the final removal of barriers, Jews played a role in the academy far beyond our numbers in the general population. This is not the place to review well-known statistics to this effect. In claiming, however, that North American academic life has been partly "shaped" by this Jewish presence, a few words need to be added. Two culturally distinct groups of Jews were important presences in the American academy before 1970. The first of these were children of immigrants who came to the United States and Canada from Eastern Europe during the great age of immigration (1900-1924 in the United States; somewhat later in Canada). Raised in Yiddish-speaking homes on New York's Lower East Side and its equivalent in other cities, and forged in the furnace of depression-era poverty within a deeply racist and anti-semitic America, these Jews disproportionately turned toward fields in which a passion for social justice might find expression. Socialism of many varieties played a major role in the "Jewish street" of the post-immigrant years, expressing a dream of a just society that was in some ways continuous with the ancient prophetic traditions of Jewry and that frequently called upon those associations. It was natural that such fields as sociology, economics, history, law, social work, and political science would attract significant numbers of that generation. Their presence undoubtedly lent a leftist edge to the American academy in the wartime and post-war era, something well-perceived by right-wingers and reactionaries from Joe McCarthy to Pat Buchanan. Even those Jews in other fields, such as mathematics and the natural sciences, generally shared the political and social views of their compatriots in the social sciences. The increasing presence of Jews (and other American "outsiders") in the academy also contributed to an atmosphere of no-holds-barred critical inquiry, including a questioning of intellectual, literary, and social conventions long held dear by the Protestant establishment.

A second group of Jews entered the American academy as intellectual refugees from Europe after the beginning of the Hitler era in 1933, some coming as holocaust survivors as late as the 1950s, or even later as emigrés from communist Eastern Europe. More diverse in their political views than their American-born cousins (Hannah Arendt, for example, was not always a darling of the American "old left"), this very impressive cadre of scholars in all fields was forged by a bond of common suffering that also gave birth to great moral passion, as witnessed by such diverse figures as Herbert Marcuse and Elie Wiesel. Middle European Jewish intellectuals occupied distinguished chairs in both sciences and humanities throughout the country and contributed greatly to the early growth of cosmopolitanism in the formerly all-American university community. They virtually created the climate of intellectual seriousness at such young institutions as Brandeis and the New School of Social Research, but the wider echoes of their intellectual and moral commitments, along with their veneration for classical modes of learning in the German university tradition, reverberated throughout American academic life. Their presence served as a challenge to the American academy to meet the standards of those great middle European universities where these immigrant scholars were trained and where many held chairs until the advent of Hitler and his henchmen.

As we reach the millennial marker, it is then fair to say, Jews and the academic community are by no means strangers to one another. Nevertheless, there are some important changes happening in the nature of this relationship. Until recent decades, Jewish academics were the most thoroughly secularized sector of the Jewish community. Synagogue affiliation and religious observance were lowest in this most highly educated (counting only secular education, of course) group of Jews, and intermarriage was more widespread and accepted in the academy than elsewhere on the Jewish map. The small minority of Jewish academics who were religiously observant, most in the New York area, were quite "invisible" as observant Jews when on the campus.

Now I suspect there is a pull in two directions at once. The ongoing process of assimilation, inevitable as the memory of immigration and Jewish foreignness recedes from view, makes for a certain diminishing of recognizable Jewish presence on campus as in the society. Are the children and grandchildren of intermarried families (those raised without Jewish education or commitment) still to be thought of as Jews? How much of the Jewish spirit or tradition may they be said to bear? As the academy becomes increasingly international in make-up, these descendants of assimilating Jews are in fact seen as thoroughly American by their newer Asian and European colleagues, many of whom hardly even recognize certain family names to be distinctively Jewish.

At the same time, however, observant and committed Jews are coming "out of the closet" in the American academy. Sometimes led by those within the field of Jewish Studies, groups of both faculty and students interested in serious Jewish learning and traditional forms of religious expression are appearing publicly on campus. Since the 1970s, and in increasing degrees, it is considered respectable to be visibly and religiously Jewish in the American university. On a few (mostly Eastern) campuses, the concentration of highly observant students—young men with *kippot* or head coverings, women in modest ankle-length skirts—is especially noticeable. But the same phenomenon, in lesser degrees, is present elsewhere as well. Almost for the first time, this generation is bringing an active and committed Judaism with it to the campus, rather than just a Jewish ethnic presence with vague memories of a religious past. Many of these students come to the academy after 12 years of *yeshiva* or Jewish Day School education. Not a few have spent a year or semester studying in Israel before college. Some with little home background wind up spending a year or more at an Israeli *yeshiva* for "returnees" to Judaism during their college years. This minority within the Jewish student and younger faculty population brings to the campus a level of Jewish knowledge and commitment previously quite rare or unnoticed in the American academic community.

There are both traditionalists (those keeping up their parents' ways) and seekers (those experimenting with religious observance, trying on things not done at home) within this cadre of committed Jews on campus. These groups share a dedication to a personal quest for greater religious knowledge. They are not much interested in the university standards of critical distance, comparative study, or historical objectivity in approaching Jewish sources. They want to study Judaism because it is their own, because they love it, because they feel at home, or want to feel at home, with their traditions.

From a broader historical perspective, one might say that this generation is reacting, along with many other young people, to a breach that deeply underlies the entire Western academic enterprise, but one quite alien to Jewish tradition. I refer to the bifurcation between sage and scholar, between the quest for wisdom and the pursuit of knowledge that so characterizes the academy as we know it. The combined Greek and Semitic paradigm that underlay Western intellectual life, including that of Judaism until modernity, knew no such distinction. The absorption of teachings caused one to grow in wisdom, reaching toward the ideal of intellectual and moral perfection, defined in various ways within the traditions. It was the *yeshiva* or house of study, alongside the Christian monastery and the Islamic *madrasa*, that preserved and promulgated the life of learning for well over a thousand years. The Renaissance humanist, even if a layman, was a continuer of this tradition, one who sought to be edified and made wise by his studies. It was partially a tragic by-product of the struggle of universities and scholars to free themselves from the yoke of ecclesiastical control (a struggle with which we surely in part sympathize) that led to the divorce of "sage" from "scholar" in the Western academic mind. The scholar was now to be responsible only to his own *ecclesia*, the temple of learning with its high altar of objectivity, approachable only through a sort of critical self-distancing that would ultimately de-legitimate the personal quest for wisdom in the university context. Thus, in the late twentieth century we were to see thousands of the finest and most searching young minds turn away from the university for the *ashram*, the *zendo*, or the *yeshiva* in search of that which the university dared not allow.

This quest for learning in the context of intense personal commitment does not fall entirely on deaf ears within the contemporary academic community. Partly under the influence of existentialism and some more recent currents of European thought—the names of Camus and Foucault immediately come to mind—the academy is engaged in its own critique of objectivity as its highest standard. The revolutions of the late 1960s, in which the campus became a crucible of commitment to social change, also contributed much to the urgency of this debate. These Jewish students, while in some ways ultraconservative in their views, belong in some ways also to this post-modernist critique of the academy and its vaunted claims for the exclusive legitimacy of detached and antiseptically objective study.

The coming of this intensely committed Judaism to the campus is not without its problems. Yale University found that out the hard way a couple of years ago when four highly Orthodox students sued against the university's policy of unisex dormitories, claiming that living in such dorms violated their Jewish standards of modesty. This was an extreme example (a horrifying one, by the way, to Orthodox students just a tad to the "left" of these) of a general tendency of many committed Jews toward some degree of social and residential segregation. Understandably, they need to eat in the kosher dining hall or Hillel facility. Avoiding general campus activities, from classes to football games, on the Sabbath and holidays is also a general norm. But some also want to live by themselves, having a suite or a dorm section that is entirely Sabbath-observant, for example. When viewed by the university in the context of other ethnic and racial groups choosing to self-segregate, this desire is seen as problematic.

Reaching deeper than the issue of social segregation, however, is the question of Judaism and its relationship to sources of knowledge outside the tradition, the value of secular studies, and the degree to which committed Jews find legitimacy in other religious traditions that they will inevitably encounter on campus. We know that liberal Jews have long been in the forefront of struggles for equal justice in this society and that Jews ever since Horace Kallen in the early twentieth century have been among the promulgators of a multicultural vision for America. But how does all this fit in with Judaism itself? Are there elements within the tradition that will pull the most committed in this generation away from the liberalism and multiculturalism that are so identified with Jews in the American academy? These questions need some careful examination.

Let it first be said that there are no monolithic answers to such questions, nor is there any single spokesperson who can give "the" universally accepted Jewish view. Attitudes change depending on time, place, and personal predilection, and not always in the direction of linear progress. Take the legitimacy of philosophy and philosophic reasoning, for example. Great Jewish thinkers beginning with Saadia Gaon in tenth century Baghdad have spoken positively about rational deductions from sense experience and syllogistic reasoning as legitimate forms of knowledge. The greatest of Jewish philosophers Moses Maimonides, writing in twelfth century Egypt, treated Plato (mainly as known from neo-Platonic sources) and especially Aristotle with the greatest respect. But later commentators on Maimonides had to explain Aristotle's wisdom by claiming that it had come to him via the Egyptians, who had stolen it from Moses. It was not conceivable, in this increasingly naive view, that such great wisdom existed outside the Torah. I have seen reference in a nineteenth century Hasidic source to "that uncircumcised Philistine Aristotle, may his name be blotted out!" Here we see openness to the outside world of knowledge diminishing, rather than increasing, over the centuries.

In general it is fair to say that the most open-minded and universalistic views on the legitimacy and value of studies outside Torah are to be found in the medieval sources composed in Spain, southern France, and the Moslem lands. Their traditions continued in such places as Amsterdam and became very much the "mainstream" of Judaism as it was taught in post-emancipation Germany and later in America. A stricter and more exclusivist view, one that saw no worth in studies outside of Torah, since all wisdom is contained within it, grew stronger under the influence of Kabbalah, the Jewish mystical tradition. Based on the old rabbinic reading of "you shall utter it [i.e., study the Torah] day and night (Joshua 1:8)," it was claimed that the faithful Torah scholar should have no time left for studies outside the realm of Torah. From medieval Germany, then the post-medieval Near East, this view spread to Eastern Europe and became the dominant view in the highly isolated and often threatened *shtetl* communities of Russia and Poland. Interestingly the supra-rationalist *yeshiva* world shared this attitude with the more mystical and sometimes credulous *hasidim*. A few great intellects within these communities stood up to this trend, especially with regard to the value of mathematics and a degree of scientific approach, even to Jewish sources themselves. These included Rabbi Elijah, the Gaon of Vilna, in the late eighteenth century and Rabbi Meir Leibush Malbim in mid-nineteeth century Romania. Even today, when students from the ultra-Orthodox *yeshiva* world want to undertake secular learning, they quote the views of these authorities.

Judaism has always been a householders' tradition as opposed to a monastic one. As such, it has generally respected its adherents' right to earn a livelihood and has sought to avoid putting unnecessary barriers—beyond such basics as ethical business conduct and Sabbath observance—in the way of that effort. Thus, legal loopholes were found in the cases of Jews who wound up in the business of selling non-kosher meat (to non-Jews, of course) or even in dealing in religious objects and trinkets of other traditions. These rather extreme precedents may be used today in allowing the *yeshiva* student to study computer programming or other vital skills. A *yid darf makhn a lebn*, as they say in Yiddish: "A Jew has to earn a living!"

Jews in the university, even the most observant, are generally far beyond the need for such technical legitimation of their intellectual activity. Still, there is a group who seek severe bifurcation between their studies in such realms as the natural and social sciences and their personal religious views of such issues as creation, evolution, the human soul, and so forth. Scientific and religious thinking, so the claim goes, are quite separate in their methods as well as their goals. "This is where I earn my livelihood," some will say, "while the world of traditional Torah Judaism is where I live my personal and spiritual life." Such Jews may participate fully in the world of scientific, medical, or psychological research. Aside from not showing up at the laboratory on Saturdays (and in extreme medical cases even that might be justified), their work will in no way betray their Jewish commitment. But at home on the Sabbath they will happily live in the world of Maimonides, who still believed in the four elements of Aristotle, or study treatises on body, soul, and the birth process that still rely on Galen.

Those committed to such radical separation of the Jewish from the "secular" intellectual pursuit generally are concentrated in the sciences, economics, and these days, especially in the field of computer studies. In such areas as clinical psychology, sociology, history, and the humanities it is a bit harder to slice things up this way. These inevitably touch sooner or later on the phenomenon of religion itself, offering their own modes of understanding religious behavior, truth claims, and the nature of faith commitments. It is harder to say that one views religion one way during the workday and in an entirely different way once that day is finished. The same is true within the recently much-expanded field of Judaic Studies. Once exposed to the critical/historical methods of text study and to the influences of various historic factors on the growth of Judaism, it becomes quite difficult to put the "jinni" of naive faith back in the bottle, as it were. Scholars and students in these areas tend to be more open to creative and developing syntheses between Judaism and contemporary academic trends. Their study of Jewish sources themselves or their discussions in campus chapel settings often revolve around such attempts at integration. The thinking and study in such settings, at its best, often ignores denominational lines, embracing everyone from the centrist Orthodox to the highly committed Reform or Reconstructionist Jewish seeker.

While the legitimacy of secular studies is mostly taken for granted within these groups, the question of Judaism's truth-claims and their relationship to the legitimacy of other religions is a much more difficult and unresolved issue. Essentially, it may be said that there is a great struggle taking place in our age (its origins can be dated to the Israeli victory in the six-day war of 1967) for the soul of Judaism, one revolving around an understanding of certain biblical, rabbinic, and medieval sources. The sharp edges of this struggle are much more apparent in Israel than in North America, but insofar as many of our students travel to Israel and study there, they too are exposed to the issues at stake and to various opinions about them. The struggle is taking place mostly within Orthodoxy, where the critical/historical perspective on Judaism's development is by no means taken for granted.

Non-Orthodox movements long ago resolved these issues in favor of developmental/evolutionary models, but those old resolutions (and the lukewarm Judaism often resulting from them!) somehow no longer satisfy the needs of a large group of younger Jews. One school of thought in the current conflict (and there are countless shadings within each of these) sees Judaism as a universal religion. Its most important moral claim is that every man and woman is fashioned in the image of God. Our shared human task is to protect and glorify that image; religion is a way of participating in that universally shared task. Human wisdom is universal, reaching back to Adam and Eve (formally, at least, the biblical story is treated as though literally true), who knew without instruction how to live fully in the presence of God. Some of this ancient wisdom, a wisdom embedded in the natural world itself, was passed on by the wise of each generation of Adam's descendants, from Shem and Enosh through Noah and his children, until it reached Abraham. Abraham looked into his own self and into the world about him, discovered the presence of God, and lived the first complete religious life since the expulsion from Eden. He was able to pass this way of life on to his descendants, who took it with them as they descended into Egyptian bondage. After generations of suffering in Egypt had deepened and refined their faith, God decided to call upon them to be His "kingdom of priests," to bring the divine message to all of humanity. "You shall love the Lord your God" and "Love your neighbor as yourself" are teachings that reach far beyond the bounds of the small historic Jewish people. Torah revealed truths that would benefit all, along with certain ritual prescriptions that would keep Jewry distinctive through history, so that we might bear God's message for humanity. Suffering and persecution have long kept Israel from this prophetic role, but the goal has not changed. The study of Torah is about the moral refinement of human behavior. Jewish suffering through the ages, while not to be justified or explained away, does add to the moral refinement and passion of Israel. Jews, the Jewish people, and now the Jewish state as well, exist as moral beacons and must conduct themselves according to the highest moral standards. The teachings of Torah need to be offered anew to the world. In order to do this, Jews need to study and be engaged with every aspect of contemporary culture in order to imbue and integrate contemporary life with the teachings of Judaism. This is the very work of redemption; to engage in it is to bring messiah a step closer. The establishment of the Jewish State has some undefined role in the redemptive process, but there is still a great deal more to be done.

A second school is much more pessimistic about humanity's early origins. All of God's attempts to create moral human beings, from Adam and Eve through Cain, the generation of the Flood, and the Tower of Babel, ended in dismal failure. Putting all those aside, God began anew with Abraham. Moral conduct is too much to expect of all humanity, but one elite family was created to become and remain the beacon of proper living through history. Those not able to live up to the family's highest moral standards (Ishmael, Esau) were cast aside. Righteous Jacob suffered at the hands of his violent brother Esau, and history is bound to repeat itself. "The deeds of the forefathers are a signpost for their offspring"—the ancient enmity/ jealousy of Esau for Jacob remains unabated. According to this school of thought, Esau's offspring (Christians) as well as Ishmael's (Muslims) are bound to hate Jews. That's just the way the world is, eternally and unchangingly. The Jewish people, the only ones willing to receive God's Law at Mount Sinai, became forever His chosen people. Because we and we alone were present at that all-time transformative event, we have a power of religious insight greater than that of non-Jews. "You shall love the Lord your God" and "Love your neighbor as yourself" are the essential constitutive rules of the religious commonwealth called Jewry. To expect such conduct of all humans is naive. The salvation of the non-Jewish world is not the chief concern of Jews. Our primary task through history is to continue to exist, because the corporate community of Israel is the sole bearer of God's truth in undiluted form. While lesser and somewhat compromised forms of Judaism's wisdom exist in Christianity and Islam, Jews must remain separate from others throughout history, even though this penchant for separateness will increase the inevitable persecution to which we are subject. The wickedness of the nations knows no bounds, as the holocaust confirms. The attempt of pre-war European Jewry to assimilate was mocked by history. God has begun to redeem Israel by restoring us to our Holy Land. The culmination of this process, brought about by our further repentance and faithfulness, will be the advent of messiah. He comes to bring peace to all people and nations, which will then recognize Israel's truth and role in history. The return to Zion, and especially to the holy city of Jerusalem, indicate that redemption is nearly at hand.

These two versions of classical Judaism, both derived from the same body of texts, interpretations, and historical experiences, lead in very different directions. The former, rooted in the views of Maimonides and the eighteenth century enlightener Moses Mendelsohn, was taught with various nuances by such American Jewish luminaries as Rabbis Joseph Soloveitchik and Abraham Joshua Heschel; in Israel it was philosopher Yeshayahu Leibovitz who most embodied a certain radical version of it, and it is now taught by such moderate religious figures as David Hartman and Avi Ravitsky. The latter, darker vision, reinforced by the holocaust and by the ongoing struggle of Israel for survival, was taught by Rabbi Zvi Yehudah Kook and the settler movement, and in its most extreme form by Rabbi Meir Kahana and Baruch Goldstein. A secularized version of it became the nationalist ideology of Menahem Begin and the Israeli right wing. It is the theology believed by most of the Sephardic or Eastern Jews in Israel and by those closest to both *shtetl* and holocaust memories.

Each of these approaches (and again I warn the reader that this typology does not truly reflect the complex and nuanced spectrum of views) has a strong basis within the tradition. If Maimonides can be marshaled by one group, Judah Halevi and nearly the entire mystical tradition can be claimed by the other. The Judaism that comes to the American campus is mostly of the former, more universalist, variety. But that is not to say that seeds of the exclusivist tradition are not present as well.

Religious exclusivism, after all, has a long history within Judaism. When the Psalmist proclaimed:

> The idols of the nations are silver and gold,
> The work of human hands.
> Eyes have they, but they see not;
> Ears have they, but they hear not;
> Neither do they speak from their throats (Ps. 115:4-7),

he was putting forth an idealized Israelite view of the religions against whose backdrop Israel's monotheistic faith first developed. The religion of ancient Israel saw itself as a revolutionary development. Like all revolutions, it minced no words in denouncing all that had come before. Of course we now realize how very much Biblical religion was based upon prior models and inherited existing religious forms, verbal images, and so forth. Nevertheless, Judaism retained the prophets' crusading attitude toward what it considered "idolatry," the worship of gods by means of graven images. Graeco-Roman religion was thus condemned by the Jewish authorities of late antiquity who saw it as epitomizing the immorality and hedonism they had come to associate with idolatrous religion.

When Christianity conquered the Roman Empire, the surviving Jews took a somewhat different view of things. This was a biblically-derived religion, they realized, and one that preached a morality not terribly different from their own. They referred to it as *minut*, "sectarianism", meaning that Christians were following the sect of Jesus rather than accepting what they saw as the "mainstream" of Pharisaic/rabbinic interpretation of scripture. Without the formality of conversion (remember Paul's denial of the need for circumcision), the followers of the new religion remained gentiles, but their religion was that of sectarianism rather than idolatry. Of course by then the "sect" had become by far the larger and more powerful of the two Biblical-successor religions, but that made no difference in the eyes of the minority.

Later Jewish authorities wavered somewhat in their view of Christianity. The prominence of images in the medieval church was confusing to the Jews and led some (particularly those living in Muslim lands!) to think that perhaps this was idolatry after all. Islam, on the other hand, was thought of by the rabbis as an ideal religion for non-Jews, pure in its monotheism and even stricter than Judaism in its prohibition of images.

Non-Western religions are still viewed with concern by Jewish authorities, for whom contact with them is almost entirely new. Abstract and contemplative forms of religion are easiest for Judaism to accept, but certain forms of popular devotion in which images, altars, and offerings play a role look too much like the religions of the ancient Near East to leave the Jewish mind entirely comfortable. The veneration of human beings, when it veers close to worship, is also unnerving to Jews, though one must say that it has recently become a wide-spread phenomenon within Judaism's own Lubavitch Hasidic movement as well.

Jews have never been in a position to tell others what is or is not a proper religion for them. As we are taught to bless God for the diversity among people, so, too, do we offer our blessings for the many ways in which the Divine Presence is perceived and celebrated throughout the world. But when we ask of our tradition what it is that religion is to teach, our answer is quite unequivocal: "One God and every person God's image!" Therefore love each person, treat each person as holy, as reflecting the greatness of God.

The core of Jewish teaching lies in the ten commandments. According to the early rabbis, all the commandments of our Torah may be derived from these ten. But some go even farther, saying that all the commandments derive from the first two of the ten commandments, those we heard spoken "in God's own voice." The first of the ten commandments, by our count, reads: "I am the Lord your God who brought you out of the Land of Egypt, out of the house of bondage." It is knowledge of the one God (and acting on that knowledge) that liberates us from all the many forms of slavery and degradation to which humans are subject. The second commandment is the prohibition of idolatry. Why should that prohibition be so prominent in our teachings? Rabbi Abraham Joshua Heschel explained it this way: "You shall make no statue or graven image" is not because God has no image. God in fact does have an image: YOU! Each of us humans is the image of God, and we must spend our entire lives forming that image, using soul and body as one to become what we most essentially are: God's image on earth. And we must help one another to fulfill that task, removing all the many barriers that keep people from realizing themselves as God's image. To take anything less than your entire self, than a full living, breathing human being, and to make of it the image of God—that is idolatry.

Here we see Judaism with its most humanistic face. If it is this universalist reading of the tradition that today's more learned and committed Jews are bringing with them to the campus, the North American academy may yet be enriched by an encounter with the teachings of Judaism, as it already so long has been by the presence of Jews themselves.

As religiously committed Jews become a more open presence within the academy, they will have to face a new series of challenges that they have hardly noticed until now. Will they be willing to join with religiously sensitive types from other traditions (mostly Christian, but increasingly also Muslim, Buddhist, and Hindu) to legitimize religious points of view within the academic community? Generally Jews (mostly secular Jews) have insisted that religious neutrality within the academy can only be protected by the academy's purely secular self-definition. But there are some limits to this position. Might people of faith band together, for example, to see that religious poetry is appreciated in its true faith-bound context? Or to see that religious experience is not entirely "explained away" or dismissed as folly in context of various psychological and sociological explanations of religious phenomena? Or to understand that religious difference may be a real cause of strife and intergroup conflict, rather than serving as a mere stand-in for differences of class, ethnic, or other interests?

In these and other related areas, religious Jews may become important partners in a community of religiously committed academics that seeks to lend new perspectives to the shared academic enterprise. But openness to participation in such a broader coalition requires full affirmation of the first of the two perspectives on Judaism described above. It also means an abandoning of the sense of isolation from the broader society and a sharing of responsibility for shaping it—something quite new to religious Jews in the diaspora context. These will come only with time and a building of trust, replacing a deep distrust and alienation that were many centuries in the making.

11. From Diversity to Pluralism: The Roman Catholic Challenge and the Roman Catholic Opportunity

JOHN W. HEALEY

It is not uncommon for those of a courageously optimistic bent to redefine "challenges" as "opportunities." At this moment in Roman Catholic history, however, those who see religious pluralism as a "challenge" and those who see it as an "opportunity" are likely to have very different concerns about the future of Catholic higher education and even conflicting agenda.

Few, if any, Catholic educators would regret the increasing religious diversity on their campuses. Nor would they be likely to treat this diversity with anything but respect. Despite the often misunderstood axiom, "outside the church no salvation," Roman Catholicism leans much more towards "inclusivism"—which Diana Eck describes as "an understanding of diverse traditions as approximating, approaching or partially realizing the Truth given fully in one's own tradition"—rather than towards the "exclusivism" of some evangelical Christian churches. In twentieth century theology, the Roman Catholic Karl Rahner, with his theory of "anonymous Christians," might even be regarded as the prime spokesperson for inclusivism.

"Inclusivism" may pose serious obstacles to interreligious dialogue, especially when it seems to be what the philosopher Sidney Hook once dismissed as "baptism by redefinition," but, as Diana Eck also points out, "To some extent all religious people are inclusivists, insofar as we use our own particular religious language—God, Jesus Christ, the Holy Spirit, the Buddha, Vishnu—and struggle with the limits and meaning of that language. As long as we hold the religious insights of our particular traditions, cast in our particular languages, to be in some sense universal, we cannot avoid speaking in an inclusivist way."[1]

So far so good: Catholics can be comfortable with inclusivism. But genuine "pluralism" is another matter when dialogue involves not only hearing "the other" in the other's terms and interpretative framework but also requires at least the openness to self-redefinition.

But quite apart from the serious theological problems Catholics and other Christians might see in a move from inclusivism to a genuine pluralism, this move itself is, at this moment, not likely to be very high on the agenda of most Catholic colleges and universities. While many secular institutions—certainly many of those represented at the Wellesley conference on "EDUCATION as *Transformation*"—are concerned to recover, in a new context, the spiritual values of their own religious foundations, Catholic colleges are especially concerned to maintain their

Catholic tradition, and the energies of their administrators are likely to be dedicated largely to explaining how they are "Catholic," and how they will stay "Catholic," whatever the evident and increasing diversity of their student populations and of all American society.

This overriding concern to maintain the Catholicity of institutions is partially due to an awakening on the part of Catholics that their colleges and universities are in danger of losing the religious heritage these institutions were founded to preserve. For many Roman Catholics, studies such as George Marsden's *The Soul of the American University: From Protestant Establishment to Established Non-Belief* and, more recently, James Burtchaell's *The Dying of the Light: The Disengagement of Colleges and Universities from Their Christian Churches* have become "cautionary tales," warning that Roman Catholic institutions are in danger of sliding down the slippery slope already transgressed by Yale and Brown and Wellesley and many other originally religious colleges.[2]

This is the "challenge" which currently preoccupies many Catholic educators. The issue also divides the larger Catholic community—including its bishops—as the community looks for ways to implement a Roman document, *Ex corde ecclesiae* (*From the Heart of the Church*), which has defined just what it means for a college or university to be Catholic. The Roman document, many years in preparation, defines an ideal which Catholic college administrators find very acceptable but leaves to regional church authorities the determination of how the ideal will be implemented, subject finally to Roman approval. The norms proposed for the United States are currently being debated and have been the occasion of great controversy in the Catholic community, with some Catholic college presidents even proposing that, if the currently proposed norms were implemented, especially the norm that Catholic faculty in theology must receive a "mandate" from the local bishop, the college's trustees would be forced to say that their colleges were not officially "Catholic." For those thus opposed to the norms implementing *Ex corde ecclesiae*, what is at stake in the debate is academic freedom and the nature of the American university.

Not all Catholic educators are equally concerned with this alleged threat to academic freedom. Some see it as a reasonable way to self-preservation. For others the controversies over the implementation of *Ex corde ecclesiae* and the anxieties over the future of Catholic colleges are really indications of larger divisions within Roman Catholicism. These divisions are summarized even in the title of Ralph McInerney's *What Went Wrong With Vatican II: The Catholic Crisis Explained.* McInerny is a philosopher who has had a distinguished scholarly career at Notre Dame. His charge is that theologians "stole the council" which held such promise for Roman Catholicism in the sixties. Their "thievery" consisted in their claiming for themselves a right to define Catholicism, which rightly belongs only to the church's "magisterium," i.e., to those officially appointed to teach in the church, principally the pope and the bishops in union with him.[3] Whatever the merits of McInerny's charge, his work is, at the very least, an indication of the resistance likely to meet any new moves to religious pluralism. This is, in short, not an entirely favorable time for taking the risk of self-redefinition which genuine dialogue requires.

One might also summarize the tensions currently affecting Roman Catholicism by comparing the Vatican Council's decree, "The Relation of the Church to Non-Christian Religions" (or, as the decree is known from its first Latin words, "Nostra Aetate") with subsequent Roman hesitation on where dialogue leads. This decree, originally intended as a statement on the church's relationship to the Jewish people, was expanded during the Council's deliberations to a statement condemning anti-semitism "in any form whatsoever," and acknowledging the church's roots in the covenant with Abraham, but also to an affirmation of distinctive religious values in Islam, Buddhism, and Hinduism. Diana Eck is certainly correct in reading "Nostra Aetate" as "inclusivist." The document is explicit in declaring the church's duty "to proclaim without fail Christ who is the way, the truth and the life.... In him, in whom God reconciled all things to himself...men find the fullness of their religious life." One cannot criticize the document for being inclusivist (and Diana Eck does not criticize it for that) since it is a statement of the Church's faith made by the Church's bishops to the Catholic community. As an internal affirmation of the Church's faith, it is not meant to be "dialogical" but "doxological" —i.e., a praising of God for God's gifts bestowed on the community.

But, for all its inclusivism, the decree, "Nostra Aetate," has, in fact, functioned in Roman Catholicism as an opening to dialogue with other religious traditions. Permanent ecclesiastical bodies have been formed to continue conversations with non-Christians and even with "non-believers." There have been moments of setback—e.g., Pope John Paul's criticism of Buddhism in his book, *Crossing the Threshold of Hope*; the Vatican's declaration on the church's (non-) responsibility for the Shoah; Vatican warnings about the surely pluralist meditations of Anthony DeMello, etc.—but since the close of the Second Vatican Council (1965), interreligious dialogue has become pervasive in Roman Catholicism.

Interreligious dialogue has not, however, had the impact one might expect on the American Catholic college campus. There has been increasing recognition of diversity and increasing signs of respect for diversity. Some colleges have, for example, invited non-Catholics and non-Christians to offer prayers at presidential inaugurations and, in a few cases, have invited non-Catholic clergy to preach at major Catholic ceremonies such as The Mass of the Holy Spirit, which traditionally begins the academic year. Courses in Judaism, Buddhism, and Islam have been added to the curriculum and are often taught by adherents to those traditions. Many colleges also offer the students opportunities to worship in their own traditions, but most of these moves have been intended as respectful attention to diversity rather than a move towards pluralism.

There are several reasons why the colleges have been slow to move towards genuine dialogue and genuine pluralism. One is surely the basic resistance to self-redefinition in Roman Catholicism, as in every deeply traditional religion. Especially when "Catholic identity" seems threatened, as it now does seem threatened on many campuses, interreligious dialogue will seem to be a distraction from the colleges' immediate concerns. When one is struggling to define Catholicism, one will hardly be eager to discuss how it might be redefined by a dialogue with Buddhism. And for those scholars such as Ralph McInerny who believe that Catholicism has already been illegitimately redefined, further ventures in interreligious dialogue will be approached with caution or even suspicion that "Catholic identity" is being further diluted.

But that there will be a move towards more interreligious dialogue is inevitable, especially as the colleges' faculty, even in theology, and the student bodies increasingly reflect the new religious diversity of American society. Despite some stereotypes of Roman Catholicism, concern for "the salvation of the unbeliever" is a long-standing Catholic concern, going back as far as the Middle Ages and especially in later Scholastic efforts to come to terms with the discovery in America of whole populations to whom the Christian gospel had never been preached. In this theological tradition, Karl Rahner's inclusivist "anonymous Christianity" is only the latest answer to a very old question.

Roman Catholicism also has its heroes of interreligous dialogue: the Jesuit Matteo Ricci, who became a Mandarin and entered into dialogue with Buddhists in sixteenth century China; Roberto de Nobili, another Jesuit, who took on the ways of a sannyasi in sixteenth century India; and, more recently, Dom Bede Griffiths, who founded a Christian ashram in India, and Thomas Merton in the United States, whose dialogue with Daisetz Suzuki opened an extensive Christian dialogue with Zen Buddhism, continued now in the work of Robert Kennedy, S.J., *Zen Spirit, Christian Spirit: The Place of Zen in Christian Life,* and at an even more theoretical level by the Episcopal priest John Keenan in his book, *The Meaning of Christ: A Mahayana Theology,* and in his later *Mahayana Reading of the Gospel of Mark,* and Leo Lefebure in his *The Buddha and the Christ.* Ewert Cousins has also dealt with interreligious dialogue extensively and systematically in his *Christ of the 21st Century.*[4]

There is also an especially important affinity between the Roman Catholic mystical tradition, some forms of Buddhism, and Vedanta Hinduism. This affinity has been studied in detail by works such as Paul Mommaers's *Mysticism: Buddhist and Christian* and Francis X. Clooney, S.J.'s *Theology after Vendanta: An Essay in Comparative Theology* and Clooney's recent *Hindu Wisdom for all God's Children.*[5]

There is, of course, an even greater affinity between Roman Catholicism and the monotheistic traditions of Judaism and Islam. There has so far been relatively little dialogue between Catholicism and Islam in the United States, but that will surely increase as the number of Muslim students grows on Catholic campuses and as Christian-Muslim dialogue increases throughout the world. Jewish-Christian dialogue, on the other hand, has been extensive in the United States ever since the Vatican Council.

Jews and Catholic Christians approach "dialogue" with different interests, reflecting differences in the two traditions. For Jewish participants, the issue of the Vatican's recognition of the State of Israel was once a major issue and Christian responsibility in the Holocaust is still a major and neuralgic issue. Catholics, on the other hand, are more inclined to raise what they would think of as crucial theological issues—e.g., the issue of the Sinai Covenant and its permanence, the continuing religious validity of Judaism, and the Messiaship of Jesus in the economy of salvation.

While Jews and Christians have not found it easy to discuss these theological issues together, considerable progress on these questions has been made within Roman Catholic scholarship, especially in Catholic scriptural studies such as John Meier's *A Marginal Jew* and John Dominic Crossan's *The Historical Jesus: The Life of a Mediterranean Jewish Peasant*.[6] (Crossan's "Jesus" and the Jesus Seminar have in fact been criticized by Catholics and others for describing an "insufficiently Jewish" Jesus.) It is indeed safe to say, while there may be scholarly disagreements about the varieties of Second Temple Judaism and about the exact location of Jesus in this context, Jesus was "Jewish" is beyond question in contemporary Catholic scholarship. With Jesus's Jewishness thus established, and increasingly recognized also in the Jewish community, attention has shifted somewhat more to Paul and his role in the establishment of early Christianity. Here, too, scholarship has opened new opportunities for discussion about history, if not about doctrine; for example, in the work of the Jewish scholar, Alan Segal, *Paul the Convert: The Apostolate and Apostasy of Saul the Pharisee*.[7] Finally, on the doctrinal issue of "supersessionism" (the replacement of God's covenant with Israel by the "new covenant in Christ") there have been subtle but very significant changes in Catholicism with even the official *Catholic Catechism* affirming the permanence of God's covenant with Israel. Given these developments, it might not be too optimistic to say that a genuine Jewish-Christian dialogue, which Jacob Neusner has said never yet took place, could now begin.

These, and many similar developments in scholarship, show the new potential for the dialogue between Catholicism and the world's religious traditions and the possibility of a move beyond "inclusivism" to genuine pluralism—the "opportunity" of the present moment. How this movement might be played out on the Catholic college campus is suggested by a document which had nothing to do with interreligious dialogue but is widely taken—and by more conservative Catholics sometimes criticized—as the Magna Carta of contemporary Catholic higher education.

In 1967 a group of Catholic scholars, most of them clergy but also some lay administrators, adopted a statement on "The Nature of the Contemporary Catholic University." This statement, known as the Land O'Lakes Statement from the place where it was adopted, declares that "The Catholic University today must be a full university in the full modern sense of the word, with a strong commitment to and concern for academic excellence." The statement also declares that "to perform its teaching and research function effectively the Catholic University must have a true autonomy and academic freedom in the face of authority of whatever kind, lay or clerical, external to the academic community itself. At the same time, "The Catholic University adds to the basic idea of a modern university distinctive characteristics which round out and fulfill that idea.... The Catholic University must be an institution, a community of learners or a community of scholars, in which Catholicism is perceptibly present and effectively operative...first of all and distinctively by a group of scholars in all branches of theology."

The Land O'Lakes Statement does not advert at all to the urgency of interreligious dialogue, which was just beginning in Catholicism in the years just after the Second Vatican Council. The statement does however describe the task of the theological faculty in a way that is surely open to dialogue: "The theological faculty must engage directly in exploring the depths of Christian tradition and the total religious heritage of the world, in order to come to the best possible intellectual understanding of religion and revelation, of man (sic) in all his varied relationships to God."

In describing what undergraduate education ought to be in the Catholic University, Land O'Lakes affirms the obligation of the university to establish a community in which the student will be able "to express his Christianity in a variety of ways and live it experientially and experimentally in liturgical functions, Christian service and conversations with the faculty."[8]

The Land O'Lakes Statement reflects not only the primarily male character of the institutions represented by its signers—coeducation was accepted somewhat reluctantly by Catholic colleges in the '70s and thereafter—but also the almost exclusively Catholic character of their student bodies. With the new diversity of all American education, including especially urban Catholic colleges and universities, one may ask whether the same educational values which urged that Catholic students be enabled "to express (their) Christianity in a variety of ways and live it experientially and experimentally" should not be extended also to Jewish, Muslim, Buddhist, Hindu, and Sikh students.

On many campuses this last question has already been answered. Several Catholic colleges have moved to provide these opportunities, especially to Jewish and Muslim students. Some have added clergy of other traditions to their campus ministry staffs and, given the basic Catholic reverence for religion as such and especially the ecumenism of post-Vatican II Catholicism, one may assume that all religious traditions will be respected on the Catholic campus, even on the most religiously conservative.

What is less likely to occur on the Catholic campus is the conscious decision to recognize religious diversity as not just a fact, however respectfully to be regarded, but as an opportunity to acknowledge non-Catholic religious traditions as having a positive value from which Catholics might learn religiously and which ought to be honored not only as approximations to Catholic truth (i.e., "inclusively") but as truly diverse traditions to be valued in themselves and in their own right. This next move—in effect, to genuine pluralism—will be more difficult, not only because Catholicism shares the bias of every religion towards "inclusivism" (Diana Eck is surely right on that) but because Catholicism has its own special dread of "relativism" and its own bias towards integral defense of "the faith once delivered to the apostles."

This tension between an open and a less open (not too easily to be written off as just "closed") Catholicism is also reflected in the current dispute between those holding "Land O'Lakes" as a Magna Carta and those seeing "From the Heart of the Church" as a necessary reaffirmation of genuine Catholicism.

How this tension will be resolved in the short run, and even more in the long run, is uncertain. For many reasons, however, one may expect, and hope, that Catholic colleges and universities will foster the pluralism that is already implicit in ongoing interreligious dialogue and interreligious scholarship. Although a certain defensiveness has marked Catholicism since the Enlightenment and notably in the early years of this century, Catholic theology has also been marked by a willingness to question its own assumptions. (The *Summa Theologiae* of Aquinas consists entirely of questions and very early on asks *utrum Deus sit*—"whether God is.") Theology has classically been defined as "faith seeking understanding" (*fides quaerens intellectum*) but someone has remarked that, to the extent religion is attended to in the modern university, theology might better be described as "understanding seeking faith." In such a questioning world, "pluralism," with all its risks of self-redefinition, is likely to have the upper hand.

The willingness of Catholic theologians to ask questions is, of course, always matched in Roman Catholicism by watchfulness on the part of Church authority lest "Catholic truth" be distorted or diluted. (This ecclesiastical vigilance is currently reflected in the demand that Catholic theologians have a "mandate" from the bishop.) At times this vigilance has led to premature and even unjust condemnation. (Catholics have their own list of proscribed theologians, including Aquinas, who were subsequently rehabilitated by the Church.) But, in the long run, the dialectic between the probing work and the risk-taking of individual theologians and the inevitable conservatism of Church authority may be the particular Roman Catholic contribution to the emergence of a genuine religious pluralism. A religious tradition is more than the invention of scholars. Its symbols hold together whole communities over centuries. It has sometimes been subject to several reinterpretations and has survived through them all. It nourishes holy ones, bodhisattvas, hasids, and saints, who may not read the tradition critically but whose goodness is not to be written off as irrelevant. It is, therefore, well that religious change come slowly, or, at least, carefully, and that religious self-definition be undertaken with full awareness of the seriousness of the questions being asked. Bishops and popes, when they function at their best, and best of all when they are scholars themselves, remind the rest of us what is at stake in the dialogue, and it may well be a service to the larger dialogue if "the Catholic voice" retains its own distinctive timbre in interreligious conversation in the American university.

But change from mere diversity to genuine pluralism will surely come. Just too many people are involved in what the Roman Catholic theologian, John Dunne, has called "passing over"—i.e., "a shifting of standpoint, a going over to the standpoint of another culture, another way of life, another religion"—for this change not to come. "The holy man of our time, it seems, is not a figure like Gotama or Jesus or Mohammed, a man who could found a world religion, but a figure like Gandhi, a man who passes over by sympathetic understanding from his own religion to other religions and comes back again with new insight to his own."

Lest Dunne should seem to be espousing a pure relativism or a "common denominator" world religion, it should be noted that he stresses also "the coming back" with new insight to one's own religion. He does not, however, describe the "coming back" as an obligation laid upon oneself beforehand, as if the sympathetic entering into another tradition were only a pretense which would be withdrawn if the engagement with the other tradition became serious. Rather, "the experiment with truth," which is another way of describing "passing over," begins as an "autobiographical" venture, a journey of the self to the strange world of another tradition. If genuine faith is truly an engagement of oneself, a real self-commitment—rather than a superficial commitment to the ideology of a tradition —it makes sense that "a Christian would begin and end with Christianity, a Jew with Judaism, a Buddhist with Buddhism." But the self will be changed by this journey as it is changed by every journey and "comes home" with new insight even into its own tradition and into its own "self." Such is the real challenge, and, happily, the real opportunity, as we undertake the new journey from diversity to pluralism.

ENDNOTES

1. Diana Eck, *Encountering God: A Spiritual Journey from Bozeman to Banaras* (Boston: Beacon Press, 1993), 180.
2. See George Marsden, *The Soul of the American University: From Protestant Establishment to Established Non-Belief* (n.p.: Oxford University Press, 1994); and James Burtchaell, *The Dying of the Light: The Disengagement of Colleges and Universities from their Christian Churches* (n.p.: Eerdmans, 1998).
3. Ralph McInerny, *What Went Wrong with Vatican II: The Catholic Crisis Explained* (n.p.: Sophia Institute Press, 1998)
4. See Robert Kennedy, S.J., *Zen Spirit, Christian Spirit: The Place of Zen in Christian Life* (n.p.: Continuum, 1996); John Keenan, *The Meaning of Christ: A Mahayana Theology* (n.p.: Orbis, 1989); John Keenan, *Mahayana Reading of the Gospel of Mark* (n.p.: Orbis, 1995); Leo Lefebure, *The Buddha and the Christ* (n.p.: Orbis, 1993); and Ewert Cousins, *Christ of the 21st Century* (n.p.: Element, 1992).
5. See Paul Mommaers, *Mysticism: Buddhist and Christian* (n.p.: Crossroad, 1995); Francis X. Clooney, S.J., *Theology after Vendanta: An Essay in Comparative*

Theology (n.p., 1993); and Francis X. Clooney, S.J., *Hindu Wisdom for all God's Children* (n.p.: Orbis, 1998)

6. See John Meier, *A Marginal Jew* (n.p.: Doubleday, 1991); and John Dominic Crossan, *The Historical Jesus: The Life of a Mediterranean Jewish Peasant* (n.p.: Harper Collins, 1991).

7. See Alan Segal, *Paul the Convert: The Apostolate and Apostasy of Saul the Pharisee* (n.p.: Yale University Press, 1990).

8. Neil G. McCluskey, S.J., *The Catholic University* (n.p.: Notre Dame Press, 1970).

9. John Dunne, *The Way of all the Earth: Experiments in Truth and Religion* (n.p.: Macmillan, 1972), ix.

12. Buddhism as a Pluralistic Tradition

Ji Hyang Sunim

Buddhism contains within it a multitude of traditions. Through understanding what Buddhism is and what teaching has been given in relation to its internal pluralism, we can better discern Buddhism's relationship to religious pluralism.[1] In all the three vehicles (Theravadan, Mahayana, and Vajrayana) and myriad forms of practice across continents and ages, there are certain principles that stand out:

> that the Buddha taught the Four Noble Truths, that he sought the liberation of persons from self-clinging and consequent suffering, that he sought their awakening to a penetrating wisdom and unconditional love free from such clinging.[2]

The elements of wisdom and compassion are found in every lineage and encourage a wide field of vision. The means for carrying these values into clear action are contained within the precepts, which are vows taken by Buddhist monks and many other Buddhist practitioners. The first five are simple: not to take life, not to take things not given, not to give way to lust, not to lie, not to take intoxicants to induce heedlessness.

The following precepts are also geared toward an ethics of "spiritual development and social harmony,"[3] in more subtle form:

> I vow not to talk about the faults of others
> I vow not to praise myself and put down others.
> I vow not to be covetous and to be generous.
> I vow not to give way to anger and to be harmonious.
> I vow not to slander the three jewels (Buddha, Dharma, Sangha).[4]

Through precepts, we learn that awakening is based upon the practice of tolerance and compassionate relationship in moment-to-moment life. The temple rules, used by Chinese and Korean monasteries as a standard for monastic life, also reflect these values: "If in this lifetime you do not open your mind, you cannot digest even one drop of water."[5] Mindfulness requires that one be completely open and present to what is, without any agenda.

The Doctrine of Skillful Means

The Doctrine of Skillful Means describes the infinite mediums through which original nature finds expression in this world. Originally introduced in the *Astasahasrika-prajna paramita Sutra*, the Doctrine of Skillful Means is a key element in the development of Buddhism's internal tolerance and dialogue across time. The doctrine teaches that the Dharma (Buddhist teaching) has a fluid expression, taking infinite and variegated form, just as water appears as an ocean, or drops of rain.

"Skillful means" are the diverse and often subtle activities through which Bodhissatvas progress on their path and elicit the wisdom of enlightenment (*prajna-paramita*) in others. In *Vimalakirti* and *Avatamsaka Sutras*, the concept is expanded and much further developed: "skillful means" includes the infinite scope of activities and methods through which Buddhas and Bodhissatvas communicate Dharma in the precise ways appropriate to all living beings. "Skillful means," in such texts, is an incredibly vast, incomprehensible mystery, for the methods that Buddhas and Bodhissatvas employ to reach beings are as diverse as beings themselves, and are operative through all space and time.[6]

The *Avatamsaka Sutra* employs strong teaching and poetic imagery, elaborating upon the Doctrine of Skillful Means to directly reflect an awareness of pluralism, as in the following instances:

> [The Bodhissatvas whose] compassion and pity extends to all—they know the mind of every sentient being, and expound to them in accord with their predilections, infinite, boundless, enlightening teachings.[7]

> Just as the great clouds rain water of one flavor, yet there are innumerable differences according to where it rains, in the same way Buddha appearing in the world rains water of teaching of one flavor of clear compassion, yet his sermons are infinitely variegated according to the needs of the situation."[8]

> Just as the ocean water flows under the continents and islands, so that all who drill for water find it, yet the ocean does not form any notion of itself giving out water, in the same way the water of Buddha's ocean of knowledge flows into the minds of all sentient beings, so that if they examine things and practice ways of entering truth, they will find knowledge, pure and clear, with lucid understanding— yet the knowledge of Buddha is equal, nondual, without discrimination; but according to the differences in sentient beings' mental patterns, the knowledge they obtain is not the same.[9]

> In this world there are four quadrillion such names to express the Four Holy Truths, in accord with the mentalities of beings, to cause them all to be harmonized and pacified...[And] just as in this world...there are four quadrillion names to express the Four Holy Truths, so in all the worlds to the east—hundreds of thousands of billions, countlessly, innumerably, boundlessly, incomparably, incalculably, unspeakably, inconceivably, immeasurably, inexplicably many worlds, in each there are an equal number of names to express the Four Holy Truths, to cause all the sentient beings there to be harmonized and pacified in accordance with their mentalities. And just as this is so of the worlds to the east, so it is with all the infinite worlds in the ten directions."[10]

Taken in context against the backdrop of an incredibly diverse Buddhist tradition, we can conclude that there is not a single correct practice, but a vast treasury of wisdom. John Makransky writes, "Skillful means in such texts, as the infinite self-communication of undivided and unlimited enlightened awareness, is as vast a mystery as the Judeo-Christian God."[11]

And yet, the broad perspective and infinite compassion of this pluralism does not weigh all practices and traditions alike. Tradition also includes Buddha's advice to the Kalamas, not to rely on spiritual authority but to know within oneself whether teachings are clear:

After the Kalamas had hosted a succession of spiritual teachers they became confused. When the Buddha arrived and heard of this he said, "You may be puzzled, Kalamas, and in doubt, and your doubt has arisen about what should be doubted. Do not believe me either. If you want to know spiritual truth, you must investigate it this way: Do not, O Kalamas, be satisfied with hearsay or tradition, with legends or what is written in great scriptures, with conjecture or logic, or with liking a view or disliking it, or saying, 'This comes from a great master or teacher.' But look in yourselves. When you know in yourselves what teachings are unprofitable, blameworthy, condemned by the wise, when adopted and put into effect lead to harm and suffering, you should abandon them. If they lead to falsehood and greed, to thievery or obsession, to the increase of hatred or delusion, abandon them. Again, O Kalamas, do not be satisfied with hearsay or tradition, or any teachings, however they may come to you. Only when you know in yourself when things are wholesome, blameless, commended by the wise, and when adopted and practiced lead to welfare and happiness, should you practice them. When they lead to virtue, honesty, loving- kindness, clarity and freedom, then you must follow these."[12]

Taking the Doctrine of Skillful Means together with the teaching given to the Kalamas, we have a legacy of dynamic dialogue, the openness of compassion balanced with critical wisdom. If these teachings have historically been interpreted as a key to internal pluralism, they also open the door of religious pluralism. If the form of spiritual insight is infinitely adaptable, these forms must exist within other faith traditions.

An increased capacity to hear and revere Buddhist perspectives that had previously seemed alien from our own may also help us enter more seriously than in the past into dialogue with other religions and cultural traditions of our time. Perhaps some of the "four quadrillion names" of the Four Noble Truths can only be heard if we learn the mindfulness that permits echoes of the trans-historical Buddha's voice to be heard in the words of non-Buddhists.[13]

In this spirit, we follow in the footsteps of Zen Master Joju, who said, "Even with a seven-year-old child, if he is superior to me, I shall follow him and beg for his teaching. Even with a hundred-year-old man, if he has something to learn, I will follow him and teach him." [14]

PLURALISM IN HIGHER EDUCATION

To bring a vibrant exchange of religious ideas and traditions onto a college campus does honor to higher education and complements its deficiencies. For undergraduates away from home, facing the freedoms of college life, there is the incalculable benefit of ethical teaching, including, for example, precepts which provide structure and compassionate direction.

The difficulty of actually living a deeply spiritual life on contemporary American campuses is a key challenge. And yet,

precisely finding the time and space to carve out a spiritual life and practice in the context of learning in an intensive way...and in the context of a new social environment (for many students, drugs, sex, and other new circumstances differentiate college from high school when they lived with their parents) is vitally important. Not only creating a mind that can analyze issues, but (developing) a mind that can cultivate equanimity and compassion is surely a crucial part of growing up.[15]

Professor Robert Thurman also spoke to the necessity of integrating spiritual practice with higher education:

> Because liberal arts education should...be reserved for that time of seeking about life's values and reviewing one's own religious faith and learning about those of others and using every possible means to pull together an integrated motivation and optimism about life, and to know the range of one's own mind...there could be and should be encouragement of spirituality in the sense of making people self-consciously aware of how the mind works, learning how to calm it and learning how to focus..., and learning how to balance their body." [16]

Higher education needs to balance knowledge with the "not knowing" of spiritual growth. Knowledge fills the mind with information; spiritual growth creates the space for that information to become wisdom. In the words of the Tao te Ching,

> Thirty spokes share the wheel's hub;
> It is the center hole that makes it useful. [17]

By creating this space within, we are able to respond to life with greater clarity, energy and resiliency.

Out of America's religious diversity there is a growing use for chaplaincies particular to various faith traditions. This need runs up against two administrative constraints: money and space. As religious life programs at College's like Wellesley are primarily funded by older alumnae, whose classes did not mirror today's religious diversity, religions such as Buddhism—which are new to campus and do not have infrastructure—run up against budget shortfalls. In the same way, many of the chapels which dot American campuses were specifically bequeathed to the Protestant chaplaincy; almost all of them have a Protestant legacy. So, how to make resources available for the necessary work of pluralistic campus ministry is an abiding challenge.

Yet, it is a worthy challenge. Interfaith dialogue takes on an added richness against the backdrop of higher education. Teaching and learning based upon the inner tradition of each member of a religious life team resonates simultaneously in the intellect and in the deepest core of who we are; it is truly transformational. This entering into conversation can model conflict resolution for the larger campus community and nourish community life overall.

EXPERIENCE WITH PLURALISM

My personal path mirrors that passage described earlier, of internal pluralism paving the way for religious pluralism. In the course of my early work as director at Cambridge Zen Center, I regularly visited Carlos, a sangha member who had AIDS. Carlos' practice was a mix of Korean Zen chanting, Japanese Pure Land recitations, and Tibetan imagery. We practiced these various forms together. At first, I was uncomfortable with these disparate practices, and my discomfort kept me from practicing wholeheartedly. However, when I gave myself completely to the act of chanting in English, Korean, or Japanese, practice resulted in clarity and energy. Carlos was nourished by all of these practices, without any distinction. His gift to me was an openness to the authenticity and spiritual beauty of other practice forms.

At Cambridge Zen Center and in my work in the community, I was able to get to know Japanese Zen priests, Tibetan lamas, Cambodian monks. Through these encounters, I developed friendships, and a certain amount of curiosity. What did the Dharma look like from a Tibetan or Vipassana point of view? Out of this, I arranged a breakfast for representatives from area Buddhist groups to come together in a spirit of friendship, to share teachings from our various traditions and collaborate in areas of mutual interest. Our traditions had been coexisting in the Boston area for many years without such dialogue; this breakfast opened our eyes to the "four quadrillion names" of the Four Noble Truths. I gained a deeper appreciation of my own tradition through this intimate experience of other traditions.

Within a few months, we discovered many other groups we had not known existed. What was once an occasional breakfast grew into the "Buddhist Coalition of New England." We created a newsletter to share the wealth of information regarding visiting teachers and events. After a year, we held our first community liturgy, a richly diverse celebration of practice incorporating ritual and teaching from all of our traditions.

At the meditation which prepared us for this celebration, held in a neighborhood Baptist church, there were four Buddhas: one for each direction, for the corners of the earth. The Buddhas were Tibetan, Korean, Thai, and Chinese, seated facing in. We various Americans formed a circle around them, also seated. Around us, the quiet church was sheltering us: its worn oak floors and luminous variegated glass a prayer. The memory of this event sustains me in this pluralistic work even now. I offer it to the Buddhas of the four directions.

Through this work with the Buddhist Coalition, and intensive meditation practice, I began to see my work more in widening circles of relationship. In that context, I felt appreciation for the places which had nourished me, and an instinct to give something back. Opening the mail upon returning from retreat, I received a brochure from Wellesley College, my alma mater. A new chaplaincy model was being set forth, a religious life team that reflected this interconnectedness in their ways of working with each other. Under the guidance of the dean of Religious and Spiritual Life, Victor Kazanjian, there was even a group of Buddhist students listed! This was an indication that the college as an institution was experiencing new growth, a creativity which was exciting and provocative. I arranged to meet with Dean Kazanjian. Out of these beginnings grew the Wellesley Buddhist Community and my appointment as advisor to Buddhist Students at Wellesley.

The outstanding quality of this endeavor was, through and through, the exploring of relatedness in our work together. How could we support each other? How could we truly enter into dialogue? It is easy to be open to and present with students of one's tradition; in that relationship, we bring out the Buddha-nature within each other. There is a connection in giving and receiving the teaching that runs very deep, to the original root of what we are. However, this coming together as chaplains of various faiths is more challenging. We do not have a common language of prayer or a shared understanding of what prayer might mean. In our individual work, the other chaplains manifest as "other," separate from our ministry, or outside of it. Our treasured connections to meditation, to Christ, to the Koran, or to Jewish tradition are foreign to each other. Of these original connections we construct boundaries, through which we wall ourselves off from actually encountering each other. Knowledge alone cannot bridge that gap. What we are most deeply called to do is to return to the deepest, pure elements of our faith and of our ministry: listening, openness, trust.

This work inexorably calls us to know ourselves better. How can we be present without any agenda, no matter how subtle or well intended? Can we perceive the impulse to impose our belief upon someone else, and without acting on it, let it go? How can we open our hearts to each other, along with the frustration, joy and other elements of heaven and hell that arise in this work?

Finding the trust to establish such a connection, our own faith is revealed to us anew. There are common themes in our stories: the struggle to establish a spiritual life in an academic setting, the balance between being available to students and creating space for our own growth, the ordinariness of spiritual life as it manifests when we choreograph a potluck lunch together and together break bread.

Then, how do we trust the independence of each person's experience within this interdependence? How do I hear pain or anger expressed without trying to "make things better," and forcing a closure? Listening, it becomes clear that others can benefit from simply being with loss, grief, and anger. Also, they benefit in ways which are outside my experience.

The relationships we develop are the seeds of luminous multifaith services, and also the sustaining ground through which the service takes hold and grows. One planning session especially stands out in my memory, in which we chose the theme, "Weaving together our lives and learning." Discussing the ways that our traditions spoke to that theme, we learned that in Muslim tradition, a carpet is always made with a thread out of place, to illustrate the imperfection of all human things before the perfection of God.

In Buddhist tradition, we borrow the image of Indra's net, which originates with Hinduism. Imagine a net: the vertical threads of which are representing time, the horizontal threads representing space. At each place where these threads meet, there is a crystal, which not only reflects each crystal, but every reflection of every other crystal. In that way, we believe, we are composed of reflections of each other.

These discussions came to fruition in a multifaith service that spoke simultaneously to the theme of weaving through the process of composing a liturgy, its liturgical content, and prayer. Taking up the discrete strands of our experience, it created a single cloth of many colors. Elements of the liturgy included African dance and a harp solo juxtaposed, a choral performance of Psalm 121, Jewish and Christian rounds, and a spiritual. Singing, "Joyful, joyful, we adore thee," as we recessed, I experienced the hymn's joy and wonder in their first intensity.

Out of this comes a dialogue which provokes us into deeper relationship and a new prayer. Within this dialogue we find rich creativity, seeing our practice anew in relation to others, seeing our own practice through others' eyes. At Wellesley, we chaplains worked extensively together as a religious life team; through this work we put each other, and ourselves, through dynamic changes.

Sounding our bell chant at a crowded baccalaureate service, I focused upon the breath, which led me out of anxiety into spaciousness and creativity. As I finished, Rabbi Ilene Lerner Bogosian began chanting from the Book of Genesis, "The Lord's breath hovered upon the waters." The bell chant and reading, in proximity to one another, took on a rare and deep connection.

ENDNOTES

I would like to acknowledge the work and the help of John Makransky.

1. In this context, to adopt Professor Diana Eck's definition as found in *On Common Ground*, pluralism is "the recognition and engagement of cultural and religious diversity in the context of creating a common society."
2. John Makransky, "Historical Consciousness as an Offering to the Trans-Historical Buddha," *Buddhist Theology: Critical Reflections of Contemporary Buddhist Scholars*, ed. Roger Jackson and John Makransky (n.p., Curzon Press, 1999), 15.
3. Karma Lekshe Tsomo, *Sisters In Solitude* (Albany: SUNY Press, 1996), xii.
4. Kwan Um School of Zen, *Precepts Information* (Cumberland, RI: Primary Point Press, 1999).
5. Zen Master Seung Sahn, trans. "Temple Rules," *Chanting and Temple Rules* (Cumberland, R.I.: Primary Point Press, 1996), 51.
6. Makransky, 6–7.
7. Thomas Cleary, trans., *The Flower Ornament Scripture* (Boston: Shambhala, 1993), 437.
8. Cleary, 976.
9. Ibid. 999.
10. Ibid, 276, 281.
11. Makransky, 8.
12. Jack Kornfield, *A Path with Heart* (New York: Bantam Books, 1993), 160.
13. Makransky, 20.
14. Joshu, *Radical Zen*, trans. Yoel Hoffman (Brookline: Autumn Press, 1978), 7.
15. Duncan Ryoken Williams, letter to Ji Hyang Sunim, Jan.25, 1999.
16. Robert Thurman, from remarks at the EDUCATION as *Transformation* National Gathering, Wellesley College, Wellesley, Mass., September 27, 1998.

17. Gia-fu Feng and Jane English, trans. *Tao Te Ching* (New York: Vintage Books, 1989), 13.

13.   Pluralism, Awareness, and Mastery of the Mind: A Sikh Imperative for Education

GURUCHARAN SINGH KHALSA

In Sikh Dharma, education is central. The word "Sikh" means student. "Dharma" can be translated as "action and thought taken with awareness." So a practitioner of Sikh Dharma is a student of how to live with full awareness. Education for a Sikh is education of the whole person from conception throughout the entire life. It gives equal weight to body, mind, and soul. It realizes that knowledge without awareness, values, and character cannot become wisdom. It recognizes that truth is not something that can be captured in words or a belief. Education about truth should lead not to a fixed belief but to the power to be believable, to quiet and command the mind and to act with invincible integrity regardless of the circumstances. The encounter with the question of truth is used to build character and personal discipline to master the mind.

The task to educate people with intelligence, integrity, awareness, and spirit is as relevant today as it was during the time of the ten Sikh Gurus who founded this tradition (1469–1708). In fact, we are faced with a crucial need for those attitudes and approaches to education and the spirit so we can survive and excel in the near future.

Few people doubt the need to profoundly change our approach to education in our institutions in order to cope with the rapid shift to a global, interconnected, information-based world. In the next few decades we will need to face the following types of challenges:

- Information doubles every few years now and will only accelerate.
- Learning must be constant throughout the lifespan.
- Increased exposure to every religious, political and philosophical tradition will demand a new level of personal choice and understanding.
- Students will gain education in particular skills as much from outside traditional educational institutions as from within them.

All of these trends and forces of change are coming to a major crossroad. Education must shift and produce a person more suited to thrive in a world of change and unrelenting standards of excellence.[1] We need people who can sort through vast bodies of information and know what is worthwhile. We need people who can act with clarity and integrity under great pressure and little time. We need people who have a secure sense of their own identity and values. And we need people who can consciously refine their own senses and mind to match their analytic ability with perception that is both subtle and intuitive.

The estimates of growing information density, population growth, and other measures of change point toward 2012 A.D. as a culmination and point of major transition—a kind of phase shift in the pressures on the mind and the demands on our awareness. By that point the way we used knowledge in the past, the way we learned and held that knowledge, and the way we have defined ourselves in terms of things, possessions, and people will no longer work. We must learn, as part of education itself, how to find a center of neutrality and awareness within our self. Learning, leadership, and balance will originate from that point within, not from what we learn outside our self. Many individuals will come to higher education with extensive information resources. They will need wisdom not more information, character not just personality, intelligence not just intellect, pluralism not just tolerance, and a way to tap and integrate the spirit as an aspect of experience and education.

Education for thousands of years has dealt with the problems of scarcity. A primary goal was to find, accumulate, and make accessible information. Now and in the future education will deal with the problems of abundance: how to limit content to relevant ideas; how to fine tune information into knowledge that we can immediately apply and use wisely in unfamiliar contexts. And we will need to deal with the psychological impact of effectively unlimited information availability for the average person.[2] The mind itself can become unstable from the very conditions created by the success of information technology, globalization of communication and travel, and population survival rates.

It is in this context that we should understand and deal with the issues of diversity and pluralism. Pluralism is best approached as part of this larger context of information overload, the reactions our mind has to that overload, the ability to hold multiple and paradoxical views, and the need to develop our relationship to our mind to match the demands of global connexity.[3] Pluralism framed as a *problem* about fairness or communication between varied religious or ethnic traditions is an outdated framework. That framing comes from a cultural and educational history that emphasizes the past instead of the future, objectification rather than participation, and problems over solutions. Pluralism and its current challenges should be viewed as a *resource*. It is a ground on which we can develop solutions to the larger challenge of polyvalent beliefs, information overload, and the need for dialogue at all levels of education, business, and life.

From the beginning of the Sikh tradition the need to cultivate and conquer the mind itself was emphasized. The founder, Guru Nanak, declared an oft quoted phrase:

Man Jeetai, Jag Jeet
"If you conquer your mind, you conquer the world."[4]

This implies that: (1) You see and engage the world through your own mind, so its state is critical to what can happen; (2) When there is a problem first take responsibility and check your own projections and internal state; (3) You need a personal and practical discipline to relate to your mind. Good education lies as much in training the mental state of the student as in learning content, problems, and solution strategies.

In the same tradition there are many stories that make it clear that intellect alone is not important.

> Sochai soch na hova-ee jay sochee lakh vaar
> "By thinking, thinking a hundred thousand times, you can reach no knowledge of God at all."[5]

It is even a source of problems because we can create clever, even useful, categories and become attached to them. Then we act from those categories out of intellectual reflex rather than from a flexible intelligence that can drop or change those categories. We create knotty problems and die from hardening of the categories. We need to maintain cognitive flexibility so the mind is our servant and not the master of our actions.

It is deeply ingrained in Sikh education that a sign of a matured and refined mind is the ability to sense the whole and to see beyond the surface differences of people and things. A motto of Sikh Dharma is

> "If you can't see God in All, you can't see God at All."[6]

A core value and practice is to respect the spiritual equality of men and women, rich and poor, low caste and high, and of all traditions of religious practice. The touchstone is always actions of kindness, compassion, fearlessness, integrity, service, and humility before vastness and God.

In this new era we must start with the mind itself and our ability to bring it to an appropriate state to solve the problems we confront. We see three keys to our future educational success: a neutral mind, a conscious relationship to the mind, and the capacity to experience and share spiritual awareness. Opposing these factors for success are impediments: old attitudes, production of industrial minds in an information age, and reliance on techological-cures without an equal development of people. We will examine the nature of the mind and particularly the neutral mind and its implications for education. In this new light, we may better understand the opportunity and challenge of pluralism and the discussion of spirit in education.

THE CYCLE OF THE MIND AND THE ENCOUNTER OF PLURALISM

Pluralism is an encounter with "the other," the stranger, and the unknown. It is also the opportunity to practice a state of mind that can hold in contrast two or more views simultaneously. Education of the future must help each student master this state of mind and its potentials. They need the ability to apply the mind to hold the dynamic tension inherent in a polarity or a paradox until they can fully process the situation. When the mind is trained to process thoughts well, the student will either reach a judgment about how to act, or expand the scope and complexity of the self, or gain an insight as features of uniqueness and creative awareness emerge from the situation. A powerful education must train the student to refine a neutral mind and to consciously direct their mental state.

The education process often fails to train students in the skills needed to take the stance of the neutral mind. Instead the student learns to detach from emotions rather than refine them, to objectify rather than identify, and to represent a position rather than sustain the creative ambiguity of a true dialogue with multiple views. This comes from a long tradition[7] that cultivates good judgment by opposing subjectivity with objectivity, by opposing emotionality with rationality, and by preferring observation over participation.

I am not suggesting that the skills associated with the "objective stance" are not useful and appropriate for many things. I am suggesting that what is needed is the development of the neutral mind and that neutral and objective minds are different creatures.

Pluralism approached with the objective stance does not lead to interactions that create emotional integration or that interconnect conceptually diverse viewpoints about spirit, life, and knowledge. Just recall the failed experiments in ethnic integration in many classrooms. Contiguity and respectful language led to neither familiarity nor cooperation. It was much more effective if cross-ethnic teams were formed to take on projects. Then the students shared a mutual goal, communicated in order to complete a task, had to learn social and emotional coping skills, and had experiences that broke old stereotypes in a new context. Participation and the experience of a neutral mind triggered learning and transformation and tolerance.

THE THREE MINDS

Let's look a little closer at the concept of the "Neutral Mind" and the cycle of the three minds. We feel that the mind has a great deal of structure and individuality. This is discussed in some detail in the authors' book: *The Mind: Its Projections and Multiple Facets.* For the present discussion, however, we only need to look at a model of three personal minds and their interactive cycle.

The three personal minds are simply called: negative, positive, and neutral minds. Each of these produces a mode of mind. Each is characterized by how it handles thoughts, how it relates to the other two minds, and how it activates corresponding neurochemical systems and pathways. Here is a table that contrasts the three minds and their corresponding modes.

Personal Minds	Negative Mind	Positive Mind	Neutral Mind
Traits	Receptive Mode; Fast, protective, Moves away from pain, innovates new tactics; listens to problems; initiates new need or direction; uses norepinephrine related systems, lower pathways, and right prefrontal cortex	Active Mode; Expansive, pragmatic, action-oriented Moves toward pleasure, goals, tasks; invents pathways, procedures; Gives contrasts to negative mind thoughts; dopamine related systems, middle and upper pathways, and left prefrontal cortex	Observant Mode; Expresses purpose and identity; assesses and judges; Embraces thoughts and feelings from both negative and positive minds; compares frames, contexts; serotonin and similar systems, upper pathways, cingulate and bilateral frontal cortical and pituitary- pineal axis.

Each of us has and uses all three personal minds. They are natural functions that compose the functional experience of our mind. But each person differs in how developed each mind is and in what combination we use these minds in different situations. Ideally we work to develop all three minds regardless of our initial tendencies.

THE GENIUS CYCLE

If you study the three minds and how they operate in creative people and in breakthrough thinking, there are certain simple patterns that stand out. A central one is the "genius cycle." Every thought, key theme, or core emotion goes through a robust cycle of all three minds. Students trained to use this cycle engage "the other" easily and in a natural way. This cycle opens the way to meaningful experience and communication.

First is the negative mind process, then positive mind, then neutral mind. The negative mind acts as a receptive amplifier. The senses are wide open. Pains and problems are magnified. Risk taking is increased. New directions and dreaming flow freely. It often has a direction without a plan. It creates movement away from a problem without a clear vision of the final goal and path to it. If a student processed a thought with only this part of the mind, it is a bit like grabbing at anything that is not an "X," where X was the perceived problem.

An atmosphere of pluralism ruled by this mind alone would have strong boundaries. It would be clear how each group could behave without hurting anyone or violating any territory. There would also be a lack of depth in the engagement of each other across groups. There are many stated and unstated rules that moderate interactions to be neutral or at least not confrontational. It is enough to avoid any problem and create some new behaviors that adapt to the proximity of the new groups.

In the genius cycle, the negative mind passes the thought or feeling on to the positive mind. This mind has an active mode. It does two key things. First it provides a contrast to the negative mind's propositions and perceptions. Second it searches for a way to act on the idea. It is a practical doer. As much as the receptive mode of the negative mind may dream and try something new, the active mode of the positive mind will focus everything toward accomplishing a goal or task. It is very telic.

An atmosphere of pluralism ruled by this mind alone is utilitarian. It is marked by cooperative tasks and a perception of "the other" in terms of how they help or hinder your important goals of the moment. The problems and pains that are very real to "the other" are often under-represented or simply ignored as irrelevant unless they somehow block progress toward a goal.

In the genius cycle, positive mind and the negative mind pass on the thoughts to the neutral mind. The neutral mind assesses the input from negative and positive mind simultaneously. It is the observant mode of the mind. It applies equal amounts of insight, intuition, and investigation. It checks the propositions and impulses from the other two minds with the real purpose. It aligns goals to purpose and tactics to strategy. It seeks confirmation and feedback. It does not react to intensity as a singular measure for need or truth. It searches for what is unique and what is the central identity in the concept or action. It decides or sends the assessed feeling or thought back to the negative mind. It creates security, clarity, and commitment based on identity, purpose, and values.

When the three personal minds work together in a rapid cycle, with each thought or theme, it becomes a cycle of learning and refinement: Receptive Mode/Negative Mind ⇒ Active Mode/Positive Mind ⇒ Observant Mode/Neutral Mind. The chart below illustrates this. The three subdivisions under each mode are further elaborations of the minds' process.

The neutral mind assesses and completes the cycle with a decision or it sends the feelings/thoughts back to the negative mind to search again for facts, perceptions, and problems. This prevents premature closure and incomplete solutions. It also prevents premature stereotyping. It asks for an appropriate level of detail to inform a decision. The negative mind re-opens the case. It amplifies sensations and data and searches for new directions and things left out during the first cycle. Then the positive mind both expands on the new data and contrasts it with paths of action. Each small action or path of action provides new constraints and potentials that are needed for a realistic evaluation. All this goes once again to the neutral mind in the observant mode. Each cycle refines the thoughts and feelings.

Most people recognize this cycle among their own patterns of thinking. There is an occasional objection to including intuition in the neutral mind equal to objective assessment and numerical metrics. Studies of real decision-making, especially when individuals are under pressure or in environments high in information-density, show that intuition is critical to top performance. Intuition increases both in frequency of use and in accuracy as someone becomes more of an expert in some area. It is especially critical in places where there is a lack of full data or a pressure to act in an area with many unknowns. Intuition then uses simplicity, mental heuristics, and direct perception to guide actions.[8] If the genius cycle of the three minds is fully developed and robust, the actions taken will seem spontaneous and will help you to quickly adjust to changing conditions.

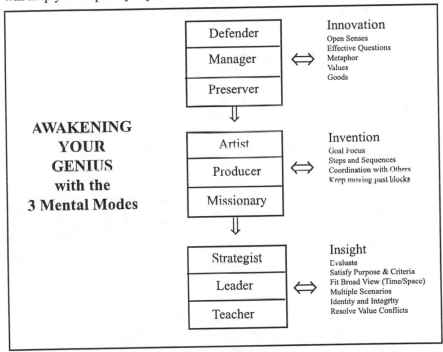

An atmosphere of pluralism ruled by the neutral mind and by the genius cycle of the three minds is experiential, open, and constantly changing. It is a learning environment that embodies certain values: openness, learning through engagement, embracing the unknown, direct clear communication of your self not just your position, and dialogue to refine perception and express your purpose and identity. The use of the neutral mind in a group engages people in conversations and projects that fulfill important objectives (learning a subject, helping a targeted group, making a profit, improving a topiary, etc). Along the way they learn about each other. They learn by actions that evoke knowledge in applied contexts. If the study of each other is focused only on abstract beliefs or viewpoints, then the neutral mind process will invite contrasts, questions of the process itself, and awareness of the personal state of mind of each person involved.

When students bring different spiritual, religious, and ethnic experiences into the educational arena, they will utilize those differences in a way that conforms with the dominant mode of the mind as we have outlined. The teacher, the narrative in the classroom, the beliefs embedded in the learning community and the state of the individual mind create the space and constraints in which learning can occur.

With a dominant negative mind we recognize diversity. With a dominant positive mind we cultivate pluralism. With a dominant neutral mind we express identity in a conscious community of spirit. In this sense, we move beyond pluralism to something more. Something as real in the heart and spirit as in the head. To reach that state we need to combine the neutral mind with responsibility for our personal awareness and with a narrative that expresses experiences of the spirit.

Neutral Mind: the Undiscovered Territory

Education of the future must use and develop the neutral mind. It is the undiscovered territory. In the schemas of the three minds, the neutral mind is the key. In times when business and learning are slower, we can make do with the contrasts shown by the negative and positive minds. We can look at pros and cons and be detached. We can make mistakes and have time to correct them.

As we enter this next millennium, we do not have this luxury. Each decision is tied to an increasingly complex and interconnected world. A single decision can lead to a cascade of unexpected consequences—a Chernobyl or a hedge fund collapse. We need several of the key capacities that only come with the neutral mind:

- ability to savor paradox and polarity
- sensitivity to wholeness and part/whole relationships
- rapid learning
- experience multiple states/thoughts simultaneously
- openness and personal security that anchor a refined sense of self
- resilience under stress and change
- continuous creation of new frameworks, categories, and perspectives
- applied intuition

Each of these capacities has obvious advantages and applications to an education that values a combination of intellect, intelligence, and intuition.

Less obvious is what we need to develop the neutral mind, especially in an educational context. The things we need to do become clear if you remember that the human being, with its body mind and spirit, is at the center of any educational effort.

We need a language. We need a language that admits metaphors beyond simple polarity. We need a language that allows emergence, transcendence, and new experience. We need language in the classroom that lets us capture implicit, ineffable, and cross-sensory experience and communicate it in some way to others. Huston Smith, a brilliant scholar of religious traditions and philosophy, warned that we have let ourselves be drawn unconsciously into a way of speaking about experience that cannot handle transcendence. Our emphasis on reaching a singular conclusion, needing certainty, operationalizing our concepts and resolving dilemmas has robbed us of the benefit of simply chewing on a question. There is value in holding certain questions without necessarily resolving them: Questions like, What is truth? Why do I exist? What is the experience of beauty? What is moral and ethical? What is it like to have a known, conscious relationship to the unknowable? How do I experience persons if I assume they are infinitely different from me and infinitely the same at the same time? What is it like to be aware of one of my assumptions or beliefs and suspend it for a moment?

The great value of such questions and language that invites such questions is to make my sense of self greater, to deepen my heart, to increase my capacity to hold an ambiguity and move to a new level of question.

The neutral mind has a kind of "diagonal language," a language partial to inviting multiple levels of feelings and thoughts. A diagonal language might speak about the polarities mentioned in the first section with questions like these:

Are you being subjective, objective, or neutral?
Are you attached, detached, or non-attached?
Do you like it, hate it, or love it?
Do you feel trapped, free, or committed?
Are you rational, irrational, or aware?
Do you want to observe, participate, or witness and give feedback?
Do you belong, are you a stranger, or are you awakening our relationship?
Should we focus on the past, the future, or how the present choice creates
      the past and future in the self?

The neutral mind speaks of each polarity but always has a place beyond the dichotomy. It is a mannered language that tolerates the discomfort and tensions inherent in a dynamic polarity and paradox.

The place to find this language is in the direct experience of students. When the "spirit" touches the heart and a student tries to express it, all the diagonal elements are there. We ought to affirm the catalytic power of a spiritual moment for creative thought and let that moment be part of the discussion about how we understand everything from equations and chemistry to art and philosophy.

To develop this neutral mind we need to reframe and guide the instinctive emotions that arise as the negative and positive minds work, especially when you

sense of consequence for immediate actions. This is one reason it is so effective in lowering the impact of stress.

Besides all these benefits, you can use meditation in a group to attune members of the group to each other, create rapport and open the discussion of common experiences. You cannot overestimate the value of this. Our normal range of experience and engagement of others is severely restricted by the social norms and expectations accompanying any gathering. Meditation, viewed and used as a technique, allows members of the group to speak openly, to take responsibility for their own views, to stay open and communicate directly and to make each person aware of their own state.

Meditation in this context is a tool for the mind, fertilizer for deeply held feelings, and a language of experience to tap intelligence, intuition, and implicit knowledge. There are literally thousands of specific meditation techniques. You can select a spectrum of techniques to use for different purposes. You can select those that use the universals of breath, attention, and posture. Meditation has been used by almost every spiritual tradition. But, as a technique, it precedes all of them. Meditation is between you, your mind, and your senses. It is a way to balance the interaction of your conscious and unconscious processes.

Meditation will become essential to education. We will need to shift gears smoothly and effectively to learn well, to sift through information and find wisdom, and to modulate and use our higher emotions. It should be thought of as a resource and a technique, not only as a subject in some department. The deluge of ideas, beliefs, information, and people that we will all be exposed to requires a conscious relationship to the mind. Meditation is the premier way to accomplish that.

Tapping the Hidden Intelligence, Your Body

Shared experience, even vicariously shared, is the superglue of pluralism. Experience itself is not flat. It has levels, structures, subtlety, and quality. Sharing hate or fanaticism or even strong advocacy for a humane cause without the neutral mind is not effective. It is ineffective because that experience is not truly shared. Shared experience requires the ability to hold multiple thoughts, to be nonattached even to your own commitments, and to engage in real dialogue, not simple proclamations of a position.

The body, which is central to our ability to share profoundly, is often forgotten in these discussions. The body is in fact a hidden intelligence. There is striking evidence for the use of somatic experience as a base to structure the primary metaphors in our language.[13] Those first fundamental connections of feelings and thought mediated through the structure of the body form the base for the universal sharing of a range of emotions and concepts regardless of the language of our culture. We start with this, then add many other resources to our cognitive capacity as we grow older. But somatic intelligence grows and refines throughout life.

We now know from research that small changes in breathing, the tonus of the autonomic system, and hormones all affect how we think and how we process feelings. We are deeply embodied creatures.[14] Our thought and our ability to be flexible and creative in that thought are not an abstract problem even if we can perform abstractions. How well crafted those abstractions may be, how distorted and how flexible we may be with them, depends greatly on the basic structures in our body and on the immediate state of the body.

When everything is slow, stress is low, and demand is spread over time, the condition of the body is less critical. As we enter the age of high demands and chaotic speeds of change, the immediate balance of energy in the body becomes more critical and its effects on thought and performance more apparent. Just look to areas of high performance, such as top athletes. A slight change in breathing or posture decides the game. Or watch the top chess players and the subtle shifts in breathing and posture that accompany clear decisions or stress.

We can no longer separate thought to a rarefied mental realm and the body to an earthly prison. The body responds to our emotions and fears even when we are not consciously aware of them. Our mind responds to the tensions and flows of the body automatically. This inescapable entanglement shapes the dynamic underpinnings of our decisions, our perception, and our ability to be open and understanding of new ideas and people.

This is one reason that in meditation traditions, exercises and the use of regulated breathing are an integral part of the meditation techniques. In fact, for traditions like Kundalini Yoga and Meditation, body motion, breathing, and posture are integrated throughout the meditation techniques. That tradition was aimed at rulers, sages, healers and householders—ordinary people who were not monks and removed from the world. The separation of meditation from exercises for the body is exaggerated by our western tendency to split body and mind, emotion and intelligence, spirit and passion. Exercising the body to shift its pattern is an integral part of meditation to shift the gears of the mind.

To reach and sustain the neutral mind, first break the body's pattern of tension and energy. When that energy is released it is free to be used in thought and to generate alternative emotional states. The body is open for understanding and so is the mind. Once the basic body state is open, then meditation by directed attention of breathing can establish a new condition. That condition a"ows new perceptions, a new state of mind, and new decisions.

Instead of trying to eliminate the body and the influence of a person to reach objectivity, we need to refine the body and identify and command the state of the mind. Then we can sense new emotions and experience, we can use the neutral mind to create an experiential ground for pluralism that goes past the limits of purely intellectual discussion.

In a neutral mind state it is easy to hold multiple emotions in the body simultaneously. It is easy to use the tension from paradoxical viewpoints as leverage to invite insight, emergence of a greater perspective, and cultivation of practical sensitivity beyond our immediate historical experience.

Sharing the Spirit—Catching It in the Act of Opening Mind and Heart

The culmination of all this is simply sharing the spirit in each of us in a way that promotes understanding and enhances learning and creativity in education. The neutral mind, meditation, the mind cycle, the body's intelligence, and diagonal language must come together in a practical way. Here is an actual example of an experience we had in a class of students from MIT and Harvard.

The topic of the day was "the impact of technology on human fulfillment and excellence." After some initial discussion and rousing debates, I noticed one student with a dreamy look on his face. He had been quiet so far. I inquired, "It seems like you have a thought or a dream going on. Would you like to share your feelings?" At first he hesitated as the group carefully watched. I said, "There is no better way to hear the subtle voice of the unconscious or the inspired voice of a muse than to speak out regardless of how personal or peripatetic the thought seems. Jump in!"

Jump in he did. He was from Costa Rica. He shared a dreamlike image that caught his mind. In the image he was walking back and forth from the plush jungle to a porch where he used a cell phone and a satellite uplink to a T-1 line to the Internet. He described his feelings, the conflict between how he valued nature and its ability to enwrap him, to give him place, and the speed of technology and how it lifted him past any context, country, or time.

We did a basic meditation as a group to be calm and open to insights about the core feelings and thoughts we each had around this subject. The meditation was to sit still and slow the breath to less than four times a minute as we concentrated at the brow point. After 11 minutes we stopped and simply noted our thoughts.

Several students shared images and ideas that came up. A few expressed "spiritual" feelings since they sensed some conflicts with the influence of the information ecologies we are creating and the values they enjoyed most—privacy, independence, uniqueness, and a sense of belonging. We had many traditions represented in the group—Christian, Sikh, Buddhist, Jewish, atheist, and Hindu. But we talked in terms of our direct experience, not from a belief or history.

Then we did a second meditation. We interlaced the fingers of both hands and held the hands comfortably at the level of the solar plexus. We closed the eyes and focused through the brow point. We breathed in slowly through rounded lips. Then we held the breath in. Then we released the breath slowly through the nose. The time for each segment of the breath was 10 seconds. On the inhale and exhale we imagined the topic and how we would experience various technology changes—how it would help, hinder, change, extend, and narrow us as humans. As we held the breath we consciously picked images or statements from other students and became them. We imagined the experience literally through the eyes of the other.

Then, with the exhale, we immediately returned to experience through our own eyes.

This meditation evoked many comparisons, insights and opportunities for students to comment on the imagination of others about themselves. It proved creative and opened students to clearer perception of other opinions and beliefs in the class.

One student summed up the interaction in this close paraphrase: "It was like swinging from one pole to another. On one pole I became quiet and all the things I heard got calm and silent. On the other I was active and had a flood of feelings and images. But best of all, I felt extremely alert and had a strong sense of my own self. It is as if I could handle anything from this place in myself that was still and aware. I never got lost and was never anxious, scared, or scattered. Whether this is the touch of spirit or just my mind tamed I could use this a lot."

THE FINAL CHALLENGE

The challenge of pluralism is a challenge of how we master the mind and how we invite a conversation of the spirit that is creative, open, and useful. It may seem that the problem is how to share values or to learn and respect the many historical traditions of religion. The problem is to find ways to evoke and share experiences that tap core values and the spirit in each individual. We can find those experiences easily if we turn our attention inward and invite them into the dialogue and process of educational inquiry.

The unavoidable confluence of every belief and perspective demands that we inquire about "the other" and test our traditional beliefs against our experience with contrasting views. It is from that experience that we must speak. The quality and scope of that experience will depend on how well we have refined and used our three minds.

As educators we must move beyond mere information to knowledge, and from knowledge to wisdom. We need to develop each student's ability to recognize and manage a clear mind. Along with this we need to consider the need to encourage daily or at least frequent disciplines to refine the three minds. The encounter with pluralism is an opportunity to take the student beyond personality habits into the roots of their character. This is an imperative for future education; to evoke wisdom expressed through character by a clear and neutral mind.

ENDNOTES

1. Howard Gardner, *The Disciplined Mind: What all Students Should Understand* (New York City: Simon and Schuster, 1999).

2. Keith Devlin, *Infosense: Turning Information into Knowledge* (New York: W.H. Freeman and Company, 1999).

realities created by advances in science and technology and by the greater numbers of human beings who are migrating from one country to another and from one
region to another.[7]

This growing interdependence between human beings and their societies is
yet to be fully acknowledged by all human groups and their leaders. In saying this,
I should hasten to add that the Muslim population of the United States of America
is not a monolithic body of believers.[8] Rather, it is divided into three main groups
with different attitudes toward religion. They can be divided into what I described
in zoological metaphors elsewhere as the *grasshoppers*, the *oysters,* and the *owls*.[9]

A METAPHORICAL ANALYSIS

The *grasshopper Muslim* is a cultural Muslim who embraces completely—
emotionally and intellectually—the philosophy of secular humanism and is willing to dissolve into the American ocean of names and faces, into a melting pot
defined strictly in non-religious terms. These cultural Muslims have no qualms
about the much-discussed problems of church and state. They are more afraid of
religious authorities than of the politician who imposes taxes on them and passes
laws deciding how they live their lives.[10]

Opposed to them are the *oyster Muslims*, who are perturbed by the changes
taking place in their social and material world. Buffeted here and there by the
forces of social change that could threaten their way of life, while enjoying fully
all the creature comforts of American life, these American Muslims feel that the
separation of church and state is beginning to pose a problem for their spiritual
sense of well-being and that the moral order undergirded by religious sensibilities
is collapsing all around them. Unwilling to go anywhere else in the world, and no
longer assured of an opportunity for *hijrah*, that is relocation, to a community
somewhere in the American West that would offer them an Islamic environment,
these Americans see in the life of social isolation the only way out of their religious predicament.

To this second type of Muslim, the separation of church and state can be more
meaningful if the emerging social and spiritual problems of Americans are dealt
with more effectively through public policy-making processes that are not without
religious inspiration. In a way, *oyster Muslims* share the same philosophical and
theological premise with most self-declared religious fundamentalists now living
in democratic, pluralistic societies. Their religious freedoms are guaranteed but
they have to live with and share public spaces with members of a society whose
moralities and lifestyles are definitely unacceptable to them. No longer able to
count on mechanical majority based on religious hegemony, because of the internal splits within their own faith communities, these *oysters* bemoan the state of
affairs while pledging their loyalty and fidelity to the political institutions of the
post-Enlightenment era.[11]

The third group of American Muslims is the *owls*. Although the sociology of birds in the Muslim world places this creature at the top of any list of the most undesirable feathered pets, this metaphor of the *owl* is deliberately chosen because this is the bird of wisdom in the Euro-American world. Those Muslims I group under this category are the ones who try to strike a balance between the other two groups identified above. Not willing to dissolve in the ocean of names and faces and equally determined not to help build walls of religious apartheid in the name of territorial/religious imperatives, this group of American Muslims supports the existing order for reasons different from those of their co-religionists.

Unlike the *oysters* who wish to maintain their membership in the larger society without having what they perceive and believe to be "perilous encounters" with others too depraved for close encounter or comfort, the *owls* see themselves as individual believers with the necessary moral compass to interact without being contaminated by those who would be avoided desperately by their *oyster* co-religionists. They do not avoid the company of their cultural Muslim brothers and sisters who are Muslim in name only, nor are they necessarily unsympathetic to the moral and spiritual predicament of their *oyster* co-religionists. This body of Muslims, in my view, is the most sensitive to the realities of internal pluralism within the Muslim community.[12]

Dialogue between and among faith communities or between racial and ethnic/cultural communities cannot take place without the genuine acknowledgement of others who live within one's social and religious universe. Since no religious, ethnic, or racial group is co terminus with the entire physical universe, and since no significant human group is without subgroups, it makes good sociological and political sense for the promoters of dialogue and the defenders of religious and political pluralism to remind members of their own faith community that the beginning of dialogue is the recognition and the acknowledgement of what I have called elsewhere the processes of "islandization" in all human groups. To put it another way, one should say that the dialogical process could become more enriching if the same degree of tolerance shown to persons with whom one differs fundamentally within one's professed faith community can be stretched a little bit to extend one's spiritual embrace to include other humans.

American Muslims and Perceived Constraints to Religious Pluralism

One cannot complete the picture of the relationship between American Muslims and religious pluralism in American society today unless one examines five concerns that are perceived by Muslims to limit and inhibit their openness to religious pluralism: (1) the question of libertarianism, which allows for social and sexual behavior deemed reprehensible by Muslims; (2) that brand of materialism that keeps the fires of human greed at the boiling point in the field of interpersonal relations; (3) the question of education, the contents of the curriculum, and the representativeness of school text books dealing with sensitive matters such as the portrayal of minorities and ethnic groups; (4) the question of excessive individualism, which threatens the social solidarity of the family and the Muslim meeting place (*jama'at*); and (5) the excessive consumerism that has made Americans into some of the most gluttonous and most indebted persons in the world. Fearful of these threats to their survival as a community and seriously concerned about the socialization of their children in American public schools, it has been noted that American Muslims may feel less threatened by American sectarianism than by American libertarianism.

With respect to the first concern, we can say that the competition between the Religious Right and the secular fundamentalists in American society has made the principles of libertarianism a major battleground.[13] American Muslims overwhelmingly tend to side with the conservative forces whose constant refrain is that the forces of immorality are seizing control of the public square and that something must be done to limit the activities and practices of those whom they believe to be "immoral and depraved." This mantra of spiritual discontent is heard most often when the issues of pornography and homosexuality enter the discourse.

The second concern that occupies the attention of American Muslims is the brand of materialism that they believe encourages excessive acquisitiveness. Although Muslims constantly remind each other about getting their portion of this world—and they amplify such notions in their daily prayers as suggested in several *Hadith* sayings of the Holy Prophet Muhammad—there is universal condemnation of greed. The Quran urges Muslims to avoid greediness and to give alms (*sadaqah*). Most importantly, Islam teaches its adherents to pay *zakat*, an obligatory tax that Muslim jurists (*fuqaha*) over the years have computed at between two-and-a-half and five per cent of one's personal assets. Furthermore, the Islamic tradition of inheritance sternly and systematically discourages accumulation from generation to generation through inheritance. This history of abhorrence of greed in Muslim societies has been brought over by the immigrant Muslims. The same notions have been internalized by native-born American Muslims, who are now equally offended by signs of excessive greed among their neighbors.[15]

The third concern relates to the issue of educating the young among the Muslim population. Because of the rampant use of drugs in many American schools and college campuses, Muslim parents are equally worried about the nature and quality of education given to their young ones. Here again, one sees why American Muslims point to the limits of pluralism. Like their Jewish neighbors who strongly resist any imposition of church teachings in the public-school system, American Muslims wish to keep their children from the triple problems of religious indoctrination, drugs, and sexual promiscuity. With respect to school vouchers, Muslims would certainly embrace the Republican call for such measures designed to allow parents choice for their children's education. It should be noted, however, that when Governor Pete Wilson and his supporters in California tried to pass what was widely described as the "anti-immigrant Proposition 168," American Muslims in California voted overwhelmingly against it. As we can see, Ameri-

can Muslims are caught in the web of moral dilemmas just as the rest of the politically conscious and morally concerned members of American society are.

The Council on Islamic Education, based in southern California, has made
significant strides in the area of American religious pluralism. Single-handedly, it
has championed the efforts to have Muslims favorably portrayed in American textbooks. Over the last five years, this body, which has an impressive Muslim and
non-Muslim advisory board, has been able to initiate a dialogue between the Muslim community, particularly those living in California, and textbook publishers.
Much has happened since the initial attempt at contact was made. A review of
some publications on the market for California schools indicates that the concerns
of Muslims and other ethnic and religious minorities in that part of the U.S.A.
have been acknowledged and appropriate textbook changes have been made. The
challenge facing Muslims is whether they can replicate the successes of their Californian co-religionists in this exercise of their rights as citizens within an educational system where books serve as mirrors of local interest.[16]

The fourth concern revolves around the issue of individualism and the balance between it and social/community interest. Living in a minority community
anywhere has its limitations. Much more serious is that situation where the minority group could any time become the target of harassment and attack by the majority. American Muslims have, in recent years, witnessed many attacks. Mosques
and Islamic centers have been violated and, at times, burned down by hostile forces.
Like Jewish synagogues that also face similar hazards, Islamic centers and mosques
are the first symbols to be desecrated by anti-Muslim and anti-Islamic forces in the
U.S.A.

American Muslims have seen the mosques (*masjid*) and the Islamic centers as
a haven for families and the socialization agency for the young. For this and other
related reasons, when those who fit the description of *grasshoppers* assert too
much independence and avoid the *masjid*, becoming what some scholars have
called "Eid Muslims," then the problem of personal versus group interest rises to
the surface. Many Muslim families blame the excessive individualism that libertarianism offers to receptive Muslims for moral and spiritual dilemmas they now
face.

The idea of marrying outside the group has become the major source of family upheaval among many of these immigrants. The young men and women whose
parents married each other on the basis of arranged marriages are now reaching
puberty and dreaming about romantic love in the manner of their American non-
Muslim counterparts. The linkage between romantic love and the exercise of individual freedom in matters of choosing a partner and carving a niche for oneself
within the American social system will remain a thorny point for the Muslim body
religious.

The last concern is with excessive consumerism in American society. American Muslims remind their neighbors every year that Muslims are fasting for 29 or
30 days, depending on lunar sightings. This annual ritual is a pivotal point for

Muslims concerned about the eating habits of their society and the rigorous demands of Islam. Though there are various Muslim responses to the eating and consuming aspect of American culture, the fact remains that all Muslims, except the *grasshoppers*, fast for three important reasons. First, there is the tradition of not eating too much, of not becoming gluttonous. Here I believe the three Abrahamic religions converge on the idea of encouraging the faithful not to be overindulgent.

Second, the food proscription of Islam limits the consumption pattern of the believer. In the special case of American Muslims, those who follow the *halal* diet see fewer food choices available to them in eateries than their more voracious neighbors who, to the dismay of Muslims, seem to consume swine as easily as they imbibe alcohol. The *oysters* have been consistent in keeping themselves away from such temptations by maintaining a direct line between their kitchens and the *halal* food stores operating in their neighborhoods.

The third way in which American Muslims deal with the question of excessive consumerism is to avoid indebtedness. This attitude is most evident among those we call *oysters* (and some *owls*), who do not allow their propensity to consume to drown them in a sea of indebtedness. The same attitude propels these Muslims to prefer rentals to mortgages. All this is done in the name of avoiding usurious lending and borrowing (*riba*).

AMERICAN MUSLIMS AND THE CHALLENGES OF RELIGIOUS PLURALISM ON CAMPUS

The growing diversification of the American population has resulted in the transformation of the religious, ethnic, and racial composition of the society. This transformation is reflected on college campuses. To promote greater interfaith dialogue on college campuses, there must be institutional support for this dialogical process. For the Muslim students on American college campuses the creation of the Muslim Student Association (MSA) in 1963 has provided an important vehicle by which their aims, objectives, and dreams could be transformed into reality. The MSA network across the United States of America is vast and its outreach efforts touch both the American and Canadian campuses. If there is going to develop any meaningful dialogue between Muslims and other members of the world religious community on American and Canadian campuses, it looks as if it is going to depend heavily on the work of the leaders and members of the Muslim Student Association who have the network and the reservoir of energies to mobilize Muslims on a large number of campuses. With more than one hundred chapters across the United States of America, this body of Muslim students can lend institutional support to efforts at dialogue.

Although it enjoys autonomous existence, the MSA is associated with the Islamic Society of North America (ISNA). ISNA has, over the last several years, encouraged dialogue with members of other faith communities. This author has participated in such proceedings in various capacities over the years. Over the last 10 years, interreligious dialogue between MSA and ISNA leaders and members of other faith communities has been strongly encouraged. The dialogue has taken place mostly with Catholic and Protestant groups. Dialogue with Jews has been slow in coming but, since the thaw in the relations between Palestinians and Israelis, the climate has changed somewhat but no significant breakthrough has taken place so far. This is largely due to the poor performance by the major national Muslim and Jewish organizations.[17]

The failure of these major national groups to engage in any serious and meaningful dialogue has hampered the efforts of young people operating on college campuses. Being the products of their larger communities, and fearful of reprisals from their elders in national organizations, MSA leaders and their counterparts in the Hillel centers across the nation, in many cases hardly exchange glances outside the classes.

Although the Muslim presence on campuses has increased over the last 30 years, the problem of ethnic fragmentation within the Muslim community remains an obstacle to interfaith dialogue. Because of this growing diversity it is becoming increasingly clear that on many college campuses Muslim student leaders must first develop strategies of coping with such ethnic diversity inside and outside the Muslim community. The recognition of this heterogeneity has compelled Muslims and non-Muslims alike to appreciate the principles of internal and external pluralism.

Internal pluralism is important for these young Muslims in the sense that it forces many of them to shed some Old World prejudices derived from their parents and grandparents in order to live with and accommodate fellow Muslims from different *madhabi* and *tariqian* backgrounds. This is very much the case where the Shia students are many and Sunni Muslim students need their cooperation in addressing religious and cultural issues with university and college administrations.

On the one hand, there is the sociological reality of a mixed Muslim student body with representatives hailing from Africa, Asia, and the United States of America. On the other hand, there is the campus environment that impresses upon the students the fact that many of their peers do not accept the hegemony of one truth claim over the other. Finding themselves in the midst of such intellectual debates and controversies, these Muslims are forced by their university atmosphere to form a united front. Their sense of solidarity is heightened by any acts of hostility waged against Muslims on campus.

The third point to raise here, with respect to the challenges facing American Muslim students on American campuses, is that the increase in the number of native-born Muslims on college and university campuses has also led to a new phenomenon. This is the creation of a new type of Muslim student organization that caters almost exclusively to native-born American Muslims.

This process started in California and it is beginning to attract attention elsewhere. In the Californian context where it originated the rationale given by the student leaders is that they needed an organization that focused exclusively on American problems.[18] These young Muslims have agendas that are radically different from the older MSA students who are mainly graduate students working on their Masters and doctoral degrees.[19] The students who form such bodies usually call themselves a name that clearly differentiates them from the better known MSA.[20] They sometimes choose a name that underscores their cultural identity as Muslims. The state of California does not give monies to religiously based organizations. For this and other related reasons, students at the University of California-Los Angeles chose to give their organization a cultural Muslim name that would enable them to draw the same benefits that other culturally-based groups receive from university authorities.

The fundamental difference between these students and the other Muslims who are non-citizens is their greater awareness of the need for interfaith dialogue among Americans. This is not to be taken as unanimity of opinion among all native-born American Muslims. As pointed out above, the Muslim community is not monolithic. There are certainly many young *oyster Muslims,* for example, who have received socialization at the hands of *oyster* parents. These *oyster Muslims* tend to gravitate toward the older and more established MSA. An increase in their numbers would certainly affect the future of interreligious dialogue between Muslims and non-Muslims.

American Muslim students on campuses across the country have a strong interest in the adequacy of the food services of their universities and colleges to meet special dietary requirements. Because of the growing sensitivity among college and university administrators, many colleges and universities are beginning to take initiatives in response to Muslim student needs. The first order of business in this respect is the provision of *halal* or *kosher* food to Muslim students. This accommodation of Muslim students at the various college cafeterias is not only the result of cultural awareness among university personnel, but it is also the result of Muslim students' demand for culinary changes on the dining table of the college cafeteria.

This process of accommodation is more advanced on some campuses than others. For example, evidence available from Syracuse University and the University of Hartford suggests that administrators in these two institutions have responded more favorably to their Muslim students than their counterparts elsewhere have. Where these favorable responses occurred on many campuses before, it was largely because of the high percentage of foreign Muslim students whose governments paid huge sums of money to maintain their wards in these halls of higher learning of America. One may wonder whether this sensitivity was based on expediency or principles. Despite how one may view this action of college and university administrators in the past, there is compelling evidence that both the Muslim student leaders and the university authorities are now beginning to base their actions more on their adherence to the principles of internal and external pluralism.

There are many issues that preoccupy the Muslim students, among them the impact of global affairs. Being drawn from around the Muslim world, these young men and women have generally focused on matters relating to their countries of origin or to places where solidarity with fellow Muslims is strongest. Over the last 20 years, the publications of the Muslim Student Association have addressed themselves to the Palestinian Question, the Kashmiri Question, the Somalia Problem, the Lebanese Crisis, the Afghan Issue and, recently, the Kosovo Question.[21] Of these, the most controversial issue has been the Palestinian Question. On the other issues, Muslim students have not faced serious opposition from their fellow compatriots. On the Palestinian Question, however, the MSA leaders and members share physical space with Jewish groups that are vehemently pro-Israel. The confrontations between Jewish groups and Arab/Muslim students have provided the greatest test cases for pluralism on the college campuses. The continuing crisis in the Middle East has not helped matters on various campuses.

The most recent confrontational incident took place on the campus of Georgetown University on the occasion of the 50th anniversary celebration of the state of Israel.[22] The Jewish and Arab/Muslim students found themselves at loggerheads on this issue and their division was reinforced by the fact that the national Jewish and Muslim organizations joined the fray. What happened at Georgetown, however, was not an isolated incident as a thorough examination of college newspapers across the country will indicate.[23] These confrontations, which posed serious challenges to interfaith dialogue on campus, will not disappear overnight for they are inextricably linked to the future of talks between Israelis and Arabs in the Middle East.

ENDNOTES

This paper draws heavily from my analysis, "Seeking the Religious Roots of Pluralism in the United States of America: A Muslim Perspective," *Journal of Ecumenical Studies*, vol. 34, no. 3 (Summer 1997): 402–418.

1. For a recent study of Muslim students on campuses in the Eastern seaboard of the United States of America, see Mohamed S. Omeish, "Muslim Students' Perceptions of Prejudice and Discrimination in American Academia. Challenges, Issues and Obstacles and Implications for Educators, Administrators, and University Officials" (Ph.D. diss., George Washington University, 1998).
2. See also my study, *Islam in the United States of America* (Chicago, Ill.: ABC International, 1999).
3. This Islamic view of human beings and their role in the universe is based on the creation story in the second chapter of the Quran. It is restated in many other sections of the Muslim holy book. For discussion of this view, see Jaafar Sheikh Idries, "Is Man the Vicegerent of God?" *Journal of Islamic Studies* 1 (January 1990): 99–110; Seyyed Hossein Nasr, *Man and Nature: The Spiritual Crisis of Modern Man* (London: Unwin Paperbacks, 1976); Bilal Phillips, *The Purpose of Creation* (Shajah, United Arab Emirates: Daral al-Fatah, 1995); and Khurshid Ahmad, "Man and the Future of Civilization: An Islamic Perspective," *Encounters*, 1, no. 1 (1995): 39–55.

4. For discussion of the quranic view on ethnicity and race among human beings, see my "Islam and the Race Question," in *Islam: Its Relevance Today,* eds. Sulayman S. Nyang and Henry Thompson (Barrytown, N.Y.: Unification Theological Seminary, 1991); "Scriptural Faith and Ethnicity: Some Lessons from the Islamic Experience," in *Abrahamic Faiths, Ethnicity and Ethnic Conflicts* eds. Paul Peachey, George F. Maclean and John Kromkowski (Washington, D.C.: The Council for Research in Values and Philosophy, 1997), 237–252.

5. This *hadith* is reported in many books of sayings attributed to Prophet Muhammad.

6. On the question of Muslim relations with the People of the Book (*Ahl al-Kitab*), see the following: Sulayman S. Nyang, "Challenges Facing Christian-Muslim Dialogue in the United States," in *Christian-Muslim Encounters* eds. Yvonne Y. Haddad and Wadi Haddad (Gainesville, FL: University Press of Florida, 1995); Gary M. Bretton-Granaloor and Andrea L. Weiss, *Shalom/Salaam: A Resource for Jewish-Muslim Dialogue* (New York: United American Hebrew Congregations Press, 1993); Marilyn Robinson Waldman, ed., *Muslims and Christians, Muslims and Jews: A Common Past, A Hopeful Future* (Columbus, Ohio: The Islamic Foundation of Central Ohio, the Catholic Diocese of Columbus, and Congregation Tifereth Israel, 1992); and Byron L. Haines and Frank L. Cooley, eds., *Christians and Muslims Together: An Exploration by Presbyterians* (Philadelphia: Geneva Press, 1987).

7. For discussion of the question of Muslims who live as a minority under non-Muslim rule and on many other issues relating to Jewish-Christian-Muslim relations in the contemporary world, see Muzammil H. Siddiqui, "Muslims in Non-Muslim Society," *Islamic Horizons* (May-June 1986): 22. See also George B. Grose and Benjamin J. Hubbard, eds., *The Abraham Connection: A Jew, Christian, and Muslim in Dialogue, Academy for Judaic, Christian, and Islamic Studies* (Notre Dame, Ind.: Cross Roads Books, 1994); Tamara Sonn, ed., *Islam and the Question of Minorities* (Atlanta, Ga.: Scholars Press, 1996); Jorgen Nielsen, *Muslims in Western Europe* (Edinburgh: Edinburgh University Press, 1995); and Gerd Nonneman, Tim Niblock, and Bogdan Szajkowski, eds., *Muslim Communities in the New Europe* (Reading, England: Ithaca Press, 1996).

8. For Muslim views on the issue of assimilation and adjustment by Muslims to American cultural and political life, see Ismail al-Faruqi, "Islam and Other Faiths," in *The Challenges of Islam* ed. Althaf Gauhar (London: The Islamic Council of Europe, 1978); "Islamic Ideals in North America," in *Muslim Community in North America* eds. Earle Waugh, Baha Abu-lnban, and Rejiuln B. Oureshi (Edmonton, Alb.: University of Alberta Press, 1983); Ilyas Ba-Yunus, *Muslims in North America: Problems and Prospects* (Indianapolis, Ind.: Muslim Student Association, 1974); and Muzamil Siddiqui, "Muslims in Non-Muslim Society," *Islamic Horizons* (May/June 1986).

9. The three zoological-metaphor categories respond differently to the issue of assimilation in American society. The group called *grasshoppers* does not even think about this issue of continuity or discontinuity in the history of nonsettlement in areas outside Darul Islam. For this group of Muslims secular considerations are overriding. This is, however, not the case with the group called *oysters*. Their attitude is that settlement here is temporary and that the brevity of life makes it imperative for one to seize the time by doing missions *(da'wa)* among non-Muslims. The myth of return is most widespread among people in this category. The third group, the *owls*, takes the position that Muslims must assimilate, but they must not be assimilated to the extent of losing their Islamic authenticity. Given this breakdown, one sees parallels in patterns of adjustment to American society between the Muslims and other religious groups in the U.S.A.

10. These zoological metaphors, together with many others, were developed over the last 10 to 15 years during my cross-country lectures to Muslim community organizations, Muslim Student Association chapters, and local, national, and international interfaith conferences.

11. These Muslims have been called "Eid Muslims," "Salt-water Muslims," and many other terms specific to local Muslim communities. The zoological metaphor is used to avoid any negative categorization that may suggest some degree of self-righteousness.

12. This idea can be called "internal pluralism." It complements and reinforces the more widely acknowledged idea of "external pluralism." In the particular case of Islam, the idea of internal pluralism was legitimized in the mutual acceptance that developed among the four legal schools of thought *(madhhabs)*. In the twentieth century, Shaykh Mahmud Shaltut of al-Azhar and Shaykh Hassan al-Banna of the al-Ikhwan al-Muslimoon have been credited with widening the circle of internal pluralism by inviting Sunni Muslims to include the Jafari school as part of the totality of Islamic jurisprudence. See Larry Poston, *Islamic Dawah in the West: Muslim Missionary Activity and the Dynamics of Conversion to Islam* (New York: Oxford University Press, 1992), 80; and Kate Zebiri, *Mahmud Shaltut and Islamic Modernism* (Oxford and New York: Oxford University Press, 1993), 24–26.

13. For discussion of secularization and its impact on human rights, interfaith dialogue, and the struggle for freedom around the world, see the following texts: Robert L. Phillips and Duane L.Cady, *Humanitarian Intervention: Just Wars vs. Pacifism* (Lanham, Md.: Rowan and Littlefield, 1996); Terry Nardin, ed., *The Ethics of War and Peace: Religious and Secular Perspectives* (Princeton, N.J.: Princeton University Press, 1996); Abdullahi Ahmed an-Naim and Francis Deng, eds., *Human Rights in Africa* (Washington, D.C.: Brookings Institution, 1990); Heiner Bielefeldt, "Secular Human Rights: Challenge and Opportunity to Christians and Muslims," *Islam and Christian-Muslim Relations*,

7 (October 1996): 311–325; Ken Booth, "Human Wrongs and International Relations," *International Affairs* 71 (January 1995): 103–126.

14. For discussion of the debate between the Christian Right and the defenders of First Amendment rights, see the following works: Clyde Wilcox, *God's Warriors: The Christian Right in Twentieth-Century America* (Baltimore, Md.: John Hopkins University Press, 1992); and Michael Cromartie, ed., *No Longer Exiles: The Religious New Right in American Politics* (Washington, D.C.: Ethics and Public Policy Center, 1993).

15. On the Muslim view on economic issues and consumerism, see Mohsin S. Khan and Abbas Mirakhor, eds., *Theoretical Studies in Islamic Banking and Finance* (Houston, Tex.: Institute for Research and Islamic Studies, 1987); M. 'Umar Chapra, "The Economic System of Islam: A Discussion of Its Goals and Nature," pts. 1–3, *Islamic Quarterly* 14 (January-March, April-June, July-September 1970): 3–18, 91–96, 143–156; Muhammad Abdul-Rauf, "The Islamic Doctrine of Economics and Contemporary Economic Thought," in *Capitalism and Socialism: A Theological Inquiry,* ed. Michael Novak (Washington, D.C.: American Enterprise Institute for Public Policy Research, 1979), 129–149. See also Timur Kuran, "Fundamentalism and the Economy" and "The Economic Impact of Islamic Fundamentalism," in *Fundamentalism and the State,* Marty and Appleby, (n.p.) 289–301 and 302–341, respectively.

16. The Council on Islamic Education has made some important gains in educating publishers and school officials in California about the need for greater sensitivity to the educational needs of Muslim students in the school system. Its efforts at Muslim representation in the textbook debate have captured the attention of the *Wall Street Journal* (October 5, 1990; May 1, 1991), *San Francisco Examiner* (March 31, 1990), *Los Angeles Times* (September 20, 1992; October 3, 1992; February 27, 1997), *Los Angeles Times Magazine* (September 29, 1991), *Washington Post* (October 24, 1993), *Hartford Courant* (October 3, 1993), and other publications. For a sample of Muslim views on textbooks used in American schools, see Susan L. Douglas, *Strategies and Structures for Presenting World History with Islam and Muslim History as a Case Study* (Beltsville, Md.: Amana Publications, 1994).

17. For sample opinions on this and related issues, see *Islamic Horizons* (Southern California: Message International), *The Minaret,* and several other minor national Muslim publications. A recent study of Arab Muslims and the problems of finance in American society sheds some light on the nature of this problem. See J. W. Wright, Jr., *Discrimination, Immigration, and the Economics of Being Arab and Believing in Islam in America* (Ph.D. diss., Loughborough University, 1995).

18. Scholars interested in this phenomenon can search the back issues of the *Muslim Journal, Islamic Horizons, AMC Report, Pakistan Links, The Minaret* (Southern California), and the Bell & Howell Index.

19. This new trend was initiated by young Muslim leaders like Muhammad Khan and his colleagues in California. The idea has received the attention of other students on other campuses such as George Washington University. Recently, Muhammad Khan, at the invitation of the Muslim student organizations of the Greater Washington area, came to teach them how to integrate more fully and effectively within the American political and social mainstream.

20. The efforts of Muslim national and international organizations to woo and win these young men and women in the colleges and universities can be seen in the propaganda work of the Hizb Tahrir, an organization whose vision is radically different from the mainstream Muslim groups. See also note 1 above.

21. See, for example, M. Tariq Quraishis, "Lebanon: The Victim of U.S.-Israeli Collusion," and M. Mobin Shorish, "Dissent of the Muslims: Soviet Central Asia in the 1980's," in *al-Ittihad*, vol. 19, No. 2 (April-June 1982/ *Jumadah II-Shaban* 1402): 3–30.

22. The ideological conflicts between certain Jewish and Muslim organizations in the United States and Canada over the question of Israel sometimes interfere with the possible development of healthy relations as fellow Americans and Canadians. Witness the campus controversy at Georgetown University in April 1998, when the Pro-Palestinian faction of the student body clashed with Zionist students on the celebration of the 50th anniversary of Israel. See the *Washington Times* and the *Washington Post* of the day.

23. For the latest controversy involving Jewish and Muslim organizations on-and off-campus, see the *Los Angeles Times* editorial, news reports, and letters to the editor on the aborted appointment of Mr. Salam al-Marayati, executive director of the California-based Muslim Public Affairs Council, to the Congressionally-commissioned body on terrorism. Mr. al-Marayati was originally nominated to the committee by Congressman Richard Gephardt but, under strong pressure from certain Jewish organizations, he withdrew the nomination. *See Los Angeles Times* editorial, "A Loss of Diversity," of July 12, 1999, see also letters to the editor published on July 16, 1999.

15. A Hindu Perspective on Moving from Religious Diversity to Religious Pluralism

ANANTANAND RAMBACHAN

It is necessary to begin our discussion with a clarification of the distinction between "religious diversity" and "religious pluralism." In her well-known work, *Encountering God: A Spiritual Journey from Bozeman to Banaras*, Diana Eck provides a helpful interpretation of the meaning of these terms.[1] Religious diversity, for Eck, refers to the fact of different religious traditions existing together. Diversity, however, is compatible with isolationism within the same community, ignorance, and fear. People of different traditions may be detached from and indifferent to each other. Pluralism, on the other hand, is the antithesis of indifference. It requires one to seek out, know, and build relationships with the neighbor of another faith. As Eck describes it,

> Religious pluralism requires active positive engagement with the claims of religion and the facts of religious diversity. It involves not the mere recognition of the different religious traditions and the insuring of their legitimate rights, but the active effort to understand difference and commonality through dialogue.[2]

If we pursue Eck's distinction, we may argue that the movement from diversity to pluralism is motivated, in part, by the discovery that God is known outside the boundaries of our own religious communities and is not limited by our theological claims. The British Methodist missionary, Kenneth Cracknell, tells a revealing story of going out to Nigeria in 1962. He was venturing, he thought, to the "darkest Africa," taking God to the heathen. Cracknell started living among the Igbo people and learning the Igbo language. It was not long before he discovered that his theology was inadequate to the truth of God because the Igbo language "was already full of God." "What is your name?" Cracknell inquired of a tribal member. "Chinyere." "What does Chinyere mean?" "It means the grace of God, the gift of God."[3]

A pluralist who has discovered and understood the reality of God in the world's religions cannot make the facile claim that other religions are desperate human efforts to know God while one's own religion is the definitive instance of God reaching out, finding, and revealing Godself to us. Any serious encounter with people of other traditions enables us to see an intimacy with and awareness of the divine which may challenge our most cherished theological assumptions. As a group of Christian theologians recently reflected, the "conviction that God as creator of all is present and active in the plurality of religions makes it inconceivable to us that God's saving activity could be confined to any one continent, cultural type, or groups of people."[4]

The movement from mere religious diversity to religious pluralism is inspired by the understanding that God is not an object or commodity to be possessed exclusively or controlled by any single tradition and that God or the absolute exceeds all human efforts to define and describe. The tradition of Hinduism is rich in resources for religious pluralism.[5] Hinduism is firmly rooted in the view that the universe has its source and being in an ultimate reality which the Upaniṣads refer to as brahman (the limitless). As the father in the Chāndogya Upaniṣad (6.4.2) instructs his son:

> "In the beginning, son, this world was simply what is existent—one only, without a second. Now on this point some do say: 'In the beginning this world was simply what is non-existent—one only without a second. And from what is non-existent was born what is existent.' But, son, how can that possibly be?" he continued. "How can what is existent be born from what is non-existent? On the contrary, son, in the beginning this world was simply what is existent—one only, without a second."[6]

The nature of brahman transcends all limited human efforts to fully define and describe as we would do the objects of our world. Human languages have evolved to represent our finite objects and experiences, but the infinite eludes the clutches of our words. The Taittirīya Upaniṣad (2.9.1) speaks of brahman as "that from which words, along with the mind, turn back, having failed to grasp." The Kena Upaniṣad (2:3) expresses the impossibility of exhaustively comprehending the infinite as an object of one's mind. It delights in the language of paradox.

> It is known to him to whom It is unknown; he does not know It to whom It is known. It is unknown to those who know well, and known to those who do not know.

The Hindu teacher Ramakrishna (1836–1902) loved to tell the story of two sons who were sent by their father to learn about brahman. After a few years, they returned from their teacher's home and bowed before their father. Wanting to ascertain how much they had learnt, the father questioned the older of his two sons. "My child," he said, "you have studied all the scriptures. Now tell me, what is the nature of brahman?" The boy began to explain the nature of the absolute by reciting various texts from the Vedas. The father did not say anything to him. The younger child was then asked the same question. He stood silent with eyes cast down. Not a word was spoken by him. His father was pleased and said to him, "My child, you have understood a little of brahman. What it is cannot be expressed in words."

The point of such texts and stories is not to demean human language or to negate its value, but to remind us of its limits and of our limits in relation to God. It is a central Hindu conviction that our words, at some fundamental level, are inadequate and that the ultimate is always more than we could define, describe, or understand with our finite minds. A God whose nature and essence could be entirely captured in our words or who could be contained within the boundaries of the human mind would not be the absolute proclaimed in our traditions. The recognition of the intrinsic human limitation in attaining or formulating a complete knowledge of God means that no intellectual, theological, or iconic representation is full or final. Each struggles to grasp and express that which is ultimately inexpressible and each attempt reflects and is influenced by the cultural and historical conditions under which it occurs.

If it is impossible to capture the limitless within the boundaries of our religion or to define it comprehensively through the limited language of our theology, we must be open to the possibility of meaningful insights from others which may open our understanding to the inexhaustible and multi-faceted nature of the divine. The centrality of the absolute in our traditions and our acknowledgment of the limits of human understanding and language provide a powerful justification for a pluralistic outlook and for meeting one another in a spirit of humility and reverence. If our theologies cannot limit the limitless, we can learn from and be enriched by the ways in which others have experienced and apprehended the absolute. Religious arrogance is the consequence of thinking and concluding that one has a privileged relationship with and understanding of the absolute. It is also the consequence of limiting the absolute to one's own community, the pages of one's sacred text, or the walls of one's place of worship. Since we cannot, in reality, limit the absolute, we impose limits on our own knowledge and experience.

My own religious life, as a Hindu, has been and continues to be immensely enriched and stirred by my encounters with the practitioners of other traditions. I think of myself as a fellow traveler on a vast highway who has discovered that he is surrounded by other travelers moving in the same direction. These travelers have stories full of wisdom, profound experiences, and unanticipated insights to share with me. I have benefited immeasurably from the opportunity to converse and interact with some of these pilgrims and I know that my spiritual poverty would be much greater without the wealth I continuously receive from people of other traditions and from their experiences of God. My failure to learn more is the consequence only of my own inattentiveness and self-absorption.

Unless our understanding of the absolute is specifically tribal, ethnic, or national in nature, we hold it to be the source, support, and destiny of all beings. Where the absolute is understood as a personal God, God is known as the creator of all beings and not just of a specific group. In the Bhagavadgītā, (9:17), Krishna speaks of God as the father and mother of the universe and the grandparent as well.[7] Our understanding of the absolute is such that it would be contradictory to propose that it could be anything other than one. If we admit the reality of two or more absolutes, we proclaim ourselves to be polytheists. Hinduism is clear in its belief that the object of quest and worship in the world's religions is the same, although we could speak in different and even contradictory ways about the same reality. This is the point of the often-quoted text from the Ṛg Veda text (1.64.46), "One is the Truth, the sages speak of it differently." With reference to the diversity of worship, there is a famous text from the Bhagavadgītā, (4:11), "Howsoever people approach Me, even so do I welcome them, for the paths people take from every side are Mine."

Writing from a Hindu standpoint therefore, God is clearly "our" God. Yet, while we recognize that our God may be called by many names and imagined in diverse forms, we choose one name and form as the center of our lives. This is referred to, in Sanskrit, as the *iṣṭadeva*, or the God of one's choice. The doctrine of the *iṣṭadeva* does not mean, as is often naively assumed, that Hinduism advocates a belief in a plurality of Gods. The oneness of God, along with the plurality of God's names, forms, and expressions, is deeply ingrained in the Hindu outlook. The *iṣṭadeva* doctrine signifies that from the many names, forms and manifestations of One, a person chooses one which frames his or her life and becomes the focus for the religious quest. There is a special commitment to one's choice along with the recognition that others have chosen differently and that God may be honored and celebrated under many names and forms. To celebrate the divine under one name and form does not imply the exclusion of its celebration under other names and forms. The *iṣṭadeva* concept also reminds us that there is an element of cultural creation in our respective ideas about God and that we need always to be humbly aware of the distinction between our ideas of God and the transcendental reality which these ideas symbolize and to which they point.

The doctrine of the *iṣṭadeva* is also a reminder of our human diversity and of the significance of this in the nature of our religious lives. At the very heart of one's religious life, as well as in any other dimension of one's life, is the reality of one's distinctive human nature (*svabhāva*). While the significance of human difference and diversity for our religious lives is acknowledged in other traditions, the Hindu tradition has recognized and affirmed human diversity in the doctrine of the *mārgas* or approved paths. A *mārga* is the primary, but not exclusive, mode though which the spiritual life is pursued and expressed and four major *mārgas*, corresponding to different types of human beings, are recognized. For the reflective, there is the *jñāna mārga*, a way which puts the emphasis on thought and introspection. The emotionally expressive person pursues the way of devotion (*bhakti mārga*), the activist pursues the path of work (*karma mārga*) and the contemplative practices the path of meditation (*yoga mārga*). The idea of different *mārgas* has enabled many Hindus to think of the world's religions in complementary and not exclusive ways. Conversations between different *mārgas* can broaden and enrich the particular emphasis of each one. Historically, for example, the encounter with Christianity has stimulated many Hindus into an awareness of the social dimensions of religion, while the encounter with Hinduism has inspired the quest in many Christians to rediscover the contemplative and meditative traditions of Christianity. Those of us who have been involved in interreligious encounters know the ways in which exposure to people of other traditions deepens and challenges our understanding of our own traditions.

There are obviously excellent resources within the Hindu tradition for religious pluralism in the sense defined by Eck and some of these have been highlighted above. Hindu approaches to religious pluralism, however, are not without problems. The Hindu approach is often criticized, with justification, for failing to distinguish between one revelation and another. This approach has resulted in a tendency to overlook differences, to see these as largely semantic in nature or to relegate differences to what are regarded as the non-essential aspects of religion. Such scant regard for differences is often frustrating to those who engage in inter-religious dialogue with Hindus.

Let us take, for example, the famous Ṛg Veda text cited above, "One is the Truth, the sages speak of it differently." This text is often employed to explain away doctrinal differences as merely semantic ones. But does the text suggest that the different ways in which we speak about the absolute are insignificant? Does the text imply that all ways of speaking about the absolute are equally valid and true? Does the text say that the way one speaks about the absolute makes no difference? Surely, the ways in which we think and speak about the absolute not only reveal our understanding of its nature, but this is also the basis for what we think the religious life is all about. How we think about the absolute determines how we live our lives. If we think that the absolute is vengeful, we are likely to justify anger and vengeance. If we think that love and compassion are the most important attributes of the Ultimate, we are more likely to live out these values in our relationship with others.

The point of the Ṛg Veda text is not to gloss over doctrinal differences, although this is what is usually emphasized in its use in Hindu dialogue with other religions. It offers a far richer insight for religious pluralism. The text may be read as a comment on the limitations and finitude of all human language in relation to the Absolute. In trying to describe the indescribable, human language will be multiple since the Absolute exceeds all descriptions. Doctrine and discourse are not redundant and differences are not unimportant. We must, however, in humility, hesitate to absolutize any discourse about the divine and not confuse language symbols for the reality to which they point. Such wisdom is surely precious in our mutual dialogue.

While religious pluralism encourages active engagement with the other, the unique claims of the other have to be taken seriously and a relationship of trust must allow mutual questioning and disagreement. Communities where differences are real, but where they are minimized or downplayed, are more likely to suffer violent and traumatic upheavals when, in times of tension and conflict, such differences become prominent. Communities, on the other hand, which engage each other in a deep search for mutual understanding and which acknowledge difference and cultivate respect are less likely to explode in conflict. Such communities will not be suddenly confronted with the reality of difference and are less likely to cite difference as a basis for hostility towards the other.

While there are Hindu pluralists who do not distinguish one revelation from another, there are others who argue that while all traditions point to the absolute, this does not imply that each one is true to it. One of the best contemporary examples of this approach is Mahatma Gandhi, who justified the necessity for a variety of religious traditions, but who was critical of specific doctrines and practices. He felt that no single religion could embody the whole truth and that each tradition reflected the errors and frailty of the human condition. The Hindu tradition was not free from weaknesses and imperfections and its principal sin, in Gandhi's view, was its tolerance of untouchability. This recognition of the possibility of error ought to lead to an openness to change and growth, and the encounter with the other could be a significant stimulus to such transformation.

> I came to the conclusion long ago, after prayerful search and study and discussion with as many people as I could meet, that all religions were true, and also that all had some error in them, and whilst I hold my own, I should hold others as dear as Hinduism.... So we can only pray, if we are Hindus, that not a Christian should become a Hindu, or, if we are Moslems that not a Hindu or a Christian should become a Moslem, nor should we even secretly pray that anyone should be converted, but our inmost prayer should be that a Hindu should be a better Hindu, a Moslem a better Moslem and a Christian a better Christian.... I broaden my Hinduism by loving other religions as my own.[8]

Our modern era is witness to a new vitality and resurgence among the world's religions. This is directly related to the ending of colonialism, during which the religions of black, brown, and yellow populations were perceived as pagan, superstitious, and idolatrous. Colonial empires sought to morally justify their enterprises of exploitation by claiming that they were "civilizing" missions, drawing heathens to truth. The world's religions have emerged from colonial subjugation with a renewed sense of purpose and universal relevance. They are anxious and ready to help shape our world.

We live in a world which is radically and self-consciously plural and, for all that we can see, determined to stay so. Western societies are rapidly becoming religiously plural. We are, at the same time, growing in awareness of our interrelatedness and the recognition that the major problems confronting our civilization can only be effectively resolved by new cooperative relationships that transcend old boundaries. The threats to our planet have helped us to discover, more than anything else in recent times, our interdependence and need for each other. Our problems can no longer be easily bracketed as Asian, Latin American, European, or North American. They are global in character and will be solved through global collaboration or not at all. New political and economic structures will and are evolving, but the success of these will depend upon the ability of people from diverse religious backgrounds to work and live together. Our hopes for a just and peaceful world will only be realized together and not individually. W. C. Smith, in a seminal work, musters a powerful argument to demonstrate why such cooperation is imperative.

> My own view is that the task of constructing even the minimum degree of world fellowship that will be necessary for man to survive at all is far too great to be accomplished on any other than a religious basis. From no other source than his faith, I believe, can man muster the energy, devotion, vision, resolution, the capacity to survive disappointment, that will be necessary—that are necessary—for the challenge.[9]

If Smith is indeed correct, then one of the vital tasks of education today is not merely to inform us about others in a detached and abstract way, but also to help us build bridges of understanding, loyalty, and trust across the frontiers of our religious diversity. There are many ways in which institutions of higher learning may approach this task, but the one which I want to emphasize is making the study of world religions a part of the required curriculum. In spite of the acknowledged significance of religious diversity in our present times and the challenges of life in a global village, no institution of higher learning in the United States or Europe, with the exception of the Harvard Divinity School in its M.Div. program, has made the study of world religions an integral part of its curriculum.[10] The study of world religions is yet to be seen as fundamental to the enterprise of theology. Where, for various reasons, it is not possible to offer separate courses on specific traditions, conventional theological and other courses could be creatively taught in a dialogical manner by incorporating perspectives from other traditions.

I recognize that church-affiliated institutions of higher learning face particular problems in this regard. There may be vigorous opposition to bringing the study of world religions to the center of the curriculum. It will and has been legitimately argued that students come with very little knowledge of their own Christian traditions. This need has to be met, but ought not to be seen as exclusive of the other. One of the most frequent and gratifying comments I receive from my students is that the encounter with Hinduism has awakened a new and deeper interest in the roots of their own spiritual heritage. Knowledge of another helps us to better understand ourselves. Many students have discovered that in seeing reality through the eyes of Hindus, Buddhists, or Muslims, they also see themselves with greater clarity. Their own experiences confirm what Max Muller once said, "The one who knows one religion, knows none." In any event, students with religious commitments are already struggling with the meaning of their faiths in relation to the faiths and claims of others whom they are encountering in a variety of daily situations. Religious diversity is one of the most important characteristics of the present day context in which they live their lives and poses some of the most difficult and challenging questions about which they must think. Educational institutions can respond by ensuring that such thinking occurs in the context of meaningful encounters with the other. Opportunities must be provided, not just for helping students to understand diversity and difference, but for developing the capacity for loving, living, and cooperating with others who are different. The others whom we are challenged to love, live, and cooperate with today include people of other faiths.

ENDNOTES

1. Diana Eck, *Encountering God: A Spiritual Journey from Bozeman to Banaras* (Boston: Beacon Press, 1993).
2. Ibid., 192.

argue that words of such intimacy are not well suited for settling ultimately the issues of a Christian theology of religions.

Such exegetical and hermeneutical moves have their legitimacy and can contribute to theological sensitivity among believers. Yet, there is no denying that those who affirm the Christian claims to unique and exclusive salvation have striking biblical warrants for their stances. On reflection, however, theologians through the ages have felt the need to soften or question such a stance. Our own time has intensified that need to an urgency as so many of the deadly conflicts of the world are intertwined with religious claims and counterclaims. There is not only that intensification. There is also, especially in the West, what I like to call a democratization, as a renewal of spirituality gives more authority to experience—that experience which makes it obvious that the zero-sum paradigm just does not apply.

Let me continue to speak from within my own tradition and add a perspective that might be helpful. (Yes, I like that word, for it is not a pretentious word like "true" or "unique" or "absolute" or "only"—it may in itself be helpful for our topic.) Christianity has its roots in Judaism. The language, its symbol-systems, and its thought patterns are those of Israel, their Scriptures and their interpretation in the time of Jesus. The Christian Bible includes the Bible of the Jews, our ambiguous bond with the people of Israel. Thus we Christians read also in our Bible the exclusive claim: "You shall have no other gods beside/before me" (Exodus 20:2). That commandment on Sinai is one of the ten that constitute Israel as a people, a distinct people among the nations. One of its prophets envisaged the time when "nation shall not lift up sword against nation, neither shall they learn war any more; but they shall sit every man under his vine and under his fig tree, and none shall make them afraid; for the mouth of the LORD of hosts has spoken. For all the peoples walk each in the names of its god, and we will walk in the name of the LORD our God for ever and ever" (Micah 4:3–5).

Here is a vision of the world—the world redeemed. And yet it is a plural world. Humanity is a community of communities. In its understanding and obedience to the exclusivist commandment "No gods beside/before me," Israel never came to believe that everybody should become a Jew in order to stand right before God. But they did believe that somehow God needed them in their uniqueness and distinctiveness for his plan for the redemption of the world "to be a light to the Gentiles."

This is a pluralistic model worth pondering in a religiously plural world. Especially since the Enlightenment, such a model has been severely criticized as "tribal" in contrast to a Christianity that overcame such particularism by its universalism. But the time has come for asking if it is not just the universal claims that developed in Christianity—especially since the Constantinian era—that have engendered the crusades and the pogroms and the colonialisms—political as well as cultural and religious.

Come to think of it, Jesus also used that language about "the light to the Gentiles." In the beginning of the Sermon on the Mount we read, "Let your light so shine before people that they see your good deeds and praise your Father who is in heaven." It does not say, "See your good deeds and become Christian." Here is the language of a witnessing minority as in the famous imagery, "You are the salt of the earth." For I guess one does not want the world to become a salt mine.

My point is this: perhaps we Christians should lift up that self-understanding of being Christian and being the Church which is in continuity with our Jewish inheritance. Is it not enough to be a new "minority," a distinct people, yet this time not constituted by ethnicity but with members from many nations who are drawn together by Jesus Christ our Lord and Savior? Yet, this is no less particular a community than is the Jewish people although our particularity has another shape. Such an understanding has its warrant in our Bible in both the Old and the New Testaments. It allows for more than tolerance, more than reluctant recognition of the actual pluralism that surrounds us relentlessly.

In short, it allows me to sing my song to Jesus with abandon and that without speaking negatively about others. Actually, such self-understanding adds a third rule to the two basic ones for inter religious relations. The first is, of course: Let the other define herself. For what one community says about the other is too often a breach of the biblical commandment "Thou shall not bear false witness against your neighbor." One does not necessarily intend it to be so, but it easily turns out that way.

The second rule is: compare equal to equal—not the ideal image of your own with the actual image of other, nor the actual of your own with the worst of other. That is a safe but cheap way to "win." We all have skeletons in our historical and contemporary closets, and sometimes we are on different timetables.

The perspective I have tried to lift up from my own tradition and experience—I leave it to others to speak for other traditions—adds a third rule: The practice of Holy Envy. By that odd term I mean the capacity of finding in the other faiths some things that are meaningful, beautiful, and which tell me something important about God—but they are not mine. I should let them stand—in my garden they would be cut-flowers.

When I sit way back in a synagogue on Yom Kippur as the Kol Nidre is sung, I must say with John Wesley, "My heart is strangely moved." It is not my song, nor should it be. But I am intensely conscious of being in the presence of God.

To be enriched without claiming that "we have it too," or without thinking that we honor the other by "stealing" her spiritual treasures, that is Holy Envy. Without something of that we cannot overcome the streak of condescension that so easily clings to tolerance. For it tends to let me claim to be so great that I can stand all those unenlightened others. Without Holy Envy I find it difficult to move Beyond Tolerance. Was that not one of the themes for the transformation we are about?

PART THREE

Taking it Home:
The Transformational Process
in Action

17. Quaker to the Core, Welcoming All

Douglas C. Bennett

Transformative purpose is essential to all we do at Earlham. "We have no small or ordinary missions at Earlham. We do not merely seek to give those who come better skills or improved capabilities.... We seek to transform lives, and we will be satisfied with nothing less." These are words from the inauguration speech I gave in the spring of 1998, during my first year at Earlham. It is not simply my hopes for the college that they express. They emerged out of several months of conversations with faculty, students, staff, alumni, and others discerning a broadly shared set of aspirations for Earlham. Quoting the Quaker philosopher and mystic Rufus Jones, I said, our aim, for those who come to Earlham, is to "quicken *the central aims and ideals by which they are henceforth to live.*"

At Earlham, we believe that conscientious seeking for the truth will strengthen the intellectual and moral integrity out of which people act and make them more aware of the significance of the consequences of what they do, for themselves and for others. We believe further—and know that this is less widely accepted in the academy—that truth seeking should involve both intellect *and* spirit, and that the conversation between intellect and spirit can be unusually fruitful. We believe that drawing together into a learning community those who are eager to explore and inquire, a learning community that accords fundamental respect to all members, will lead all to grow and deepen their capabilities. And we believe that making the community more diverse, bringing together those from varied backgrounds and cultures, will extend and amplify what each of us can learn from others and from ourselves.

Because transformation is important to us, because the conversation between intellect and spirit is important to us, and because building a plural learning community is important to us, we were intrigued at Earlham to receive a call to attend the national gathering on "EDUCATION as *Transformation*: Religious Pluralism, Spirituality and Higher Education" at Wellesley in September 1998. The conference invited us to explore matters of importance to us: the role of spirituality at colleges and universities; the relationship of spirituality to teaching and learning; and the impact of religious diversity on higher education.

We were at sea with one aspect of the call to the gathering, however: an underlying assumption that religion and spirituality had faded from the academy over the past several decades and the related claim that institutions of higher education had severed their relationships with religious denominations. "As the movement toward religious liberty grew in this country, and the demand for separation of church and state increased," the concept paper for the conference asserted, "religion began to disappear from the educational process and our colleges and universities gradually became secular institutions."

The faith and practice of Friends at Earlham also supports our creating a plural community, in religious or other terms. There is "that of God" in every person, not just within those who are drawn to Quaker beliefs. We strive to accord unreserved respect to all individuals. And silent worship allows each to pray or seek God in his or her own manner.

But can we remain true to our Quaker foundations and also welcome all who come to seek the truth in our learning community? Could we write a statement that both reassured us that this was possible and also provided guidance for making this so?

THE FINAL STATEMENT

Here is the full statement we wrote. Following it, I will provide a few notes about the work of drafting the statement, and about what it does and does not say.

RELIGIOUS LIFE AT EARLHAM COLLEGE

Earlham is a crossroads college. We are a meeting place of different cultures, different academic disciplines, and differing perspectives. We are also a meeting place for differing religious beliefs and practices. Religious life at Earlham is constituted by four overlapping communities.

A Quaker Community. Earlham is a Quaker college rooted in principles derived from the teachings of the Religious Society of Friends; we try to respect every individual, to be truthful and act with integrity, to pursue peace and justice, to seek consensus in making decisions, to live simply. For Quakers, these principles are religiously based in Friends' faith and practice and grounded in worship. For all people at Earlham, Quaker and other-than-Quaker, believer and non-believer, these principles are not merely exhortations. They are the standards by which we try to live. To assure that there is always a living Quaker presence at Earlham, we actively recruit Quaker faculty, staff, and students as an important part of our religiously diverse campus.

A Multi-Faith Community. Earlham College is made up of people of various faiths and religious practices and people of no religious faith. We recognize that there should be times for Catholics to be together with Catholics, Muslims with Muslims, Quakers with Quakers, Jews with Jews, Bahá'ís with Bahá'ís, and so on. We are committed therefore, to making it as easy as possible for students, faculty, and staff to celebrate their own holy days, hold their own retreats, and say their own prayers together. Whenever possible we provide special places for these observances—for example, Beit Kehillah, Stout Meetinghouse, and Interfaith House. We believe there must be occasions and places where each religious group feels itself to be the norm, where most of the participants are literate in the practices in a unique faith tradition. We do not impose our particular religious practices on others; at the same time, we welcome friends and visitors at all our activities. We facilitate participation of Earlham students in religious communities beyond the campus, and welcome our neighbors to religious practices and celebrations on campus.

A Rational Community. As a college of liberal arts and sciences, Earlham expects its students and faculty to develop their intellects to the greatest extent possible. Through our curriculum and through many activities outside the classroom, we seek to strengthen the disciplines of reason and the interconnections among them. We are a college committed to the view that the intellect can most fruitfully develop in an environment where there are also plentiful opportunities for spiritual seeking and religious life. We hope the possibility of spiritual wonderment, of awe, is never absent from our classrooms, our laboratories, our libraries. We do not ask members of the community to relate intellect and spirit in any particular way, but we do intend to create many opportunities for making the connection. We are a crossroads of the intellect and the spirit.

A Community of Dialogue. Our goal is to become good guests and good hosts within our various religious traditions. We want to become good students of one another's cultures and practices. Over the course of a year we hope our concerts, lectures, and other public events and celebrations represent the full religious pluralism of the Earlham College community. While we recognize the need for each group to spend time apart from others, we also recognize the need to get to know each other better, to enrich our lives by learning from people whose religious practices differ from ours and people who do not identify themselves with an historical religious community. Just as we discourage unwelcome proselytizing, we discourage continuous isolation within religious enclaves. Dialogue can sometimes be painful; the legacies of intolerance run through all our religious histories. Respectful dialogue, nevertheless, is the first step in modeling a peaceful world, in making new friends, in deepening our spiritual lives.

approved by the Earlham College Faculty: April, 1999
approved by the Earlham Board of Trustees: June, 1999

WRITING THE STATEMENT

Gordon Thompson, Professor of English and a Jew, wrote a powerful first draft. Its virtue was to frame the statement around four overlapping or simultaneous conceptions of our community. Earlham is a Quaker community, *and* a multi-faith community, *and* a rational community, *and* a community of dialogue. We aspire to be each of these as fully as we can—and all at the same time. While we rewrote the paragraphs that expressed each of these aspects of community, some several times, this basic framing of our statement remained unchanged from this very first draft.

How could we express the welcome we mean to extend to those from a wide variety of faiths? We quickly agreed on the key idea to be expressed: that each religious group should have occasions when it feels entirely at home, and perhaps spaces on campus as well. Others might be welcome to the worship or celebration or ritual, but these others should feel like visitors. Even as a strongly Quaker institution, Earlham should not be a place where only the Quakers feel at home. "We believe there must be occasions and places where each religious group feels itself to be the norm," we wrote.

Any college must make a fundamental commitment to intellect and reason. Our statement needed to make that clear as well. The difference between Earlham and colleges or universities that have severed their connection with religion is not that Earlham is *less* committed to reason, but that it is *also* committed to seeking the truth through religious or spiritual disciplines.

Having the commitment to truth seeking via both intellect and spirit makes it incumbent upon us to encourage dialogue between the two. "Earlham is a crossroads of the intellect and the spirit," we wrote, drawing on an image from my inaugural speech. And because we are a multi-faith community, welcoming practitioners from a wide array of religious practices, we also feel it is important to encourage dialogue among these various religious traditions. At the Wellesley conference, Krister Stendhal, an emeritus professor at Harvard Divinity School, spoke of the goal of such inter faith dialogue as stimulating "holy envy." In coming to appreciate the strengths of other religions, we will each be pushed to better understand our own practice and faith.

In Gordon Thompson's initial draft, the opening sentence of the first section (the section on our being a Quaker community) said that "Earlham is Quaker to the core." The sentence quickly felt important not only to several of us on the committee but also to many members of the faculty as well. Nevertheless, it was the sentence that drew the most flak, and in the final draft we allowed it to disappear. For some, our being "Quaker to the core" was an essential aspect of what allowed us to be welcoming to all seekers of the truth. But for others, the words "Quaker to the core" crowded out the idea that Earlham could also be a college that was welcoming to those who are other than Quaker. To make sure that the broad welcome was as full and clear as it could be, we decided to drop the phrase and make our full grounding in Quakerism clear in other ways.

SOME ISSUES FOR THE FUTURE

Now that the faculty and the board of trustees have approved the statement, here are some issues we will be addressing.

First, we need to live up to the statement. In drafting it, we were not trying to make new policy, only to state as clearly as we could what our intentions already were. But in drafting it we also realized that we were not fully living up to all that this policy asks of us. We are using the statement to improve our practice.

There are practical difficulties, of course. As a small college, we cannot afford to hire a campus minister or chaplain for each religious group on campus. And we cannot look for much contributed assistance from the community that surrounds us because its religious pluralism is more limited than that of the campus. We *will* make what provision we can. Muslim students would like a dedicated prayer room on campus. With space being scarce, can we find that? Can we help new members of the faculty make connection with students from the same religion? Can we schedule speakers and plan events to provide occasions for the full array of religious traditions and practices among us? Can we help those who take religious initiative to feel appreciated, not just tolerated?

Second, we are engaging in dialogue with some Quakers about the statement because it is not the statement that they would have had us write. There is considerable diversity *within* Quakerism on matters of belief and practice. Some Friends are Christocentric (as were George Fox and the first Quakers) while others have become more universalistic in their beliefs. Earlham is affiliated with two Yearly

Meetings (regional organizational entities) that are on the Christocentric end of that spectrum. Among Christocentric Friends (even within our two Yearly Meetings), some are more evangelical than others. For many evangelical Friends, the saving grace of Jesus Christ is the exclusive route to salvation. I expect that many such Friends would incline towards a statement that says Earlham is Quaker and Christocentric to the core, in a manner that accepts but does not encourage those of other beliefs. They would have us sponsor activities and occasions that are Christian, allowing those from other religions to make do for themselves, on or off campus. Earlham would be "home" only to those who look to Jesus Christ for salvation.

My response to Friends who incline to this view is that Earlham is a college, not a religious community. Our mission as a college is learning and truth seeking, not fidelity to particular established beliefs. If we are admitting students who are not Quakers (as we have, joyfully, for more than a century), we have to nurture their seeking as fully as possible. If beliefs are true, they will flourish in an environment of conscientious seeking.

A third and exciting challenge will be to use this statement of pluralism as encouragement for other kinds of pluralism in our community. Earlham aspires to be a college more diverse in race and ethnicity. We have made modest progress towards this goal over the past few decades, but we have much more progress we need to make. A genuinely expressed and experienced welcome to those from other-than-Quaker religious groups will help make Earlham a more plausible option for African American or Hispanic students. (There is disappointingly little racial pluralism within North American Quakerism.) The statement on religious pluralism emphasizes dialogue, valuing one another, and creating an environment where all can feel at home. We will need these same orientations—groundwork to something akin to holy envy—in making our community more racially diverse.

18. Deep Calls to Deep: Spirituality and Diversity at Goshen College

SHIRLEY HERSHEY SHOWALTER

Deep calls to deep
in the roar of your waterfalls;
all your waves and breakers
have swept over me.

Psalm 42:7

Near the Charles River stands Wellesley College, and near the Elkhart River, Goshen College. The two rivers are almost 1000 miles apart and share no waves and breakers. Wellesley and Goshen have little contact. Yet, by different courses, the waters find the same ocean.

What is true of physical geography is also true often of spiritual geography: waters that begin miles apart and take drastically different courses eventually flow together. Goshen College is one of scores of institutions that today hears new forms of "deep" calling to "deep." The national conference on the campus of Wellesley College in the fall of 1998 celebrated the multiplicity and complexity of these forms. The EDUCATION as *Transformation* Project continues to explore them.

The forms of spirit shaping my own life, Goshen College, and all of higher education, can all be seen as different kinds of rivers. Sometimes the rivers are turbulent, but I believe that education today is moving, and must move, through many rivulets of information and on through larger rivers of knowledge to reach an ocean of wisdom. Here is my story, and the Goshen College story, as a tale of three rivers.

THE SUSQUEHANNA RIVER

My soul has grown deep like the rivers.

—*Langston Hughes*

The creek that bordered the back acres of the dairy farm of my childhood flowed into the Susquehanna River, a name that I liked to roll around on my tongue. The only river's name that tasted better in my mouth was "Monongahela." I seldom saw the Susquehanna because my family rarely traveled beyond the roads that connected us to neighboring towns. In addition to the hundred acres of land I roamed freely, there were only two other places I really knew well: school and church. The school was public. The church was private and communal, a plain structure full of plain people. The Mennonites who had come from southern Germany and Switzerland to Pennsylvania in the eighteenth century had sought freedom to practice their pacifist Christian beliefs. By the 1950s Mennonites had cultivated the same land for as many as ten generations. Spirit lived in one place. Knowledge lived in another.

My membership in a religious subculture may have heightened the gulf between these two worlds in my life. Yet in some ways, paradoxically, it also overcame some of the separation. My teachers and my classmates confronted my religion every time they looked at me. I did not wear my religion on my sleeve; I wore it on my head—as a white cap called a "prayer covering."

My elementary school years were divided into the "pre-covering" years of grades 1–5 and the watershed year in the sixth grade when I joined the church. Until then, I would have given my left arm to be a Brownie and wear a uniform to school instead of the covering. And if some kind genie would have allowed me one wish, I would have asked for a television set to materialize in our living room. I wanted to sing its jingles on the playground and, more importantly, I loved its stories and drama. I wanted desperately to be part of the American mainstream—to fit in.

Nevertheless, when the whole community gathered to call the youth into the fold through revival meetings, I joined the church, pulled my hair back into a bun, put on the white cap, and, a day later, walked back into my public school. Dressing in what my church called a "nonconformed" way, I wore my "covering" the way a Jewish boy wears a yarmulke or a nun wears a habit. Consequently, I sometimes had to face social isolation at school (teasing, standing along the wall instead of participating in dances), and to face it at an age when my desire to conform socially was strongest. Fortunately, there were many friends and teachers who saw past the "covering" to the person. Even more, the community at home, the extended family, and the church were very strong.

Thirty-nine years later, I am still a Mennonite. Most of my church has changed its understanding of how to demonstrate a transformed spirit, and so have I. However, everything I believe and practice within the academy today was shaped early by the experience of growing up different in America's age of conformity, the 1950s. I learned I could survive difference and that the experience of being different could even make me stronger. Today when I stand in the airport and see distinctive religious garb, whether it is Hari Krishnan, Amish, Hassidic, or Muslim, I feel a special affinity for the person underneath the cloth. I also empathize strongly with people of color who must fight to be seen as individuals and do not have the option of taking off "the veil," as W.E.B. DuBois termed it.[1]

One who has lived under a veil, even temporarily, forms a "double consciousness,"[2] viewing the world from the "two-ness"[3] of being neither one thing nor the other. In high school, still wearing a "covering," I was too intellectual for my Mennonite friends and too Mennonite for my intellectual friends.

The Susquehanna is the river of my childhood and therefore the river of difference. It flows through my spirit today, over solid bedrock, whether its exterior surfaces are unified or not.

THE ELKHART RIVER

There's a spot in Indiana
where the leafy maple grows.
'Tis our dear and glorious Parkside,
where the Elkhart River flows.
—*Goshen College "Alma Mater," 1911*

The ten years from 1966, when I left my Pennsylvania home, to 1976, when I arrived in Goshen, Indiana, was a decade of great social and spiritual unrest in America. These were my college, high school teaching, and graduate school years. Among the important decisions I made, none was more critical than the choice of college. One of my high school teachers encouraged me to apply to Wellesley, another recommended Duquesne, and another Bob Jones. But I focused on only one college: Eastern Mennonite, in Harrisonburg, Virginia. After enrolling there, I was surrounded by Mennonites who liberated me from the stigma of difference and invited me into more spiritual and activist forms of nonconformity. We participated in demonstrations against the Vietnam War, and I felt my faith and my education coming together.

Once Eastern Mennonite handed me a diploma, I taught English at Harrisonburg High School and gained a strong sense of the courage that passionately committed teaching would require. I found tears coming in the fall of 1971 when I introduced myself to my students and said, "I am a member of a church that has said for 500 years that it is right to love and wrong to kill." After all, I was back in public school. This time I came without a visible covering on my head, but still willing to be different. During those two years I wrote one article called "The Sins of the Fathers." It described my attempt to heal the gap between black and white students in the classroom.

In 1972 my husband Stuart and I entered graduate school at Austin, Texas. In Texas my life was largely unconnected to the church. I spent more Sunday mornings playing softball with students and faculty in the American Civilization Department than attending church. There was no Mennonite congregation in Austin, and I was not terribly sad about that. I studied religion as part of American intellectual history. What little religion I practiced was private. I did not hide the fact that I was Mennonite. But I did not wear my religion either on my sleeve or on my head. I wanted to encounter the secular world on its own terms, to compete and excel in a place removed from family and church.

My Mennonite mother worried about me. She sensed that the geographical distance was also religious distance. She asked me pointed questions about going to church. I found ways to answer without further offending her. One night I was walking toward campus under cover of some large live oak trees. Suddenly, I felt suffused by a warm, powerful presence. I instantly had a name for it: "God," I breathed, "you love me and I love you!" What surprised me even more than the electrifying power of this revelation was that it came to me as a renegade Mennonite on the campus of a research university. What I had claimed with my heart long ago had been branded, unannounced and unbidden on my spirit as I was intensely focused on my mind. Later, I read *Pilgrim at Tinker Creek*, and in Annie Dillard's riveting description of standing before the "tree with lights" I recognized my own experience: "I had been my whole life a bell and never knew it until at that moment I was lifted and struck."[4] The experience stayed with me privately for years. When it was time to decide where to go after graduate school, I was ready to say "yes" to Goshen College, the oldest of the Mennonite Church colleges, a national liberal arts college with just over one thousand students.

My less-than-enthusiastic graduate adviser told me that Goshen was a place I should "write my way out of." Instead, Goshen wrote its way into my life. Here, "where the Elkhart River flows," is where I learned about spirituality and diversity in education. At first, however, I did not call it that. I called it SST.

SST, or Study-Service Term, an international service-learning program, is the cornerstone of the Goshen College curriculum. Established in 1968, the program is one of the few educational experiments of the 1960s that has continued and expanded rather than faltered and declined. "Everyone overseas!" was the cry when the program started.[5] The call initiated a new general education requirement, and each generation of students since then has heeded it. More than one hundred Goshen faculty members have served as leaders of groups of 12-23 students. More than six thousand students have left the small city of Goshen to travel to 15 different countries, among them the current destinations of Costa Rica, the Dominican Republic, Indonesia, China, Eastern Germany, and Cote d'Ivoire. Students typically spend six weeks learning language and culture in classrooms and host family homes, as arranged by the GC faculty member. Then they leave the capital city for a service-learning experience, often in a village, arriving with no more than two other students and frequently alone. They are responsible to someone in the village for doing work projects and to the GC faculty member for writing journals of reflection on their experiences, tied to the academic work of the previous six weeks. The shorthand way to describe the program is a mini-Peace Corps with an intensive cultural studies introduction; but while those categories are accurate, they are not sufficient.[6]

One cannot understand either Goshen College or SST without understanding some of the distinctive elements of Mennonite theology: peace, service, community, nonconformity, and discipleship. Mennonites have emphasized orthopraxy over orthodoxy. Therefore, when they began their first colleges over a century ago, they embraced applied learning from the beginning, choosing the motto "Culture for Service."[7] While mottoes connecting the liberal arts with noble social purposes were characteristic of higher education in the last century, they sound quaint to most academics today. However, because Goshen's ties to its church remained strong, the connection between applied learning, a spiritual base, and social good also persisted. Practical idealism has characterized the Mennonite Church. There-fore, it has flourished at Goshen College as well.

The relationship works in the other direction also. Because the college has discovered programs that built upon the work of the church (SST was made pos-sible because many members of the pacifist faculty had been involved in relief programs abroad following World War II), faculty have continued the pattern of nonconformity in higher education. Purely cognitive models of learning did not have power to explain what faculty learned as they accompanied students into experiences of cultural immersion in foreign lands. Therefore, the Enlightenment-based and modernist-enhanced emphasis upon pure reason and objectivism never overwhelmed an alternative Mennonite model that words alone cannot fully de-scribe. Herein lies a lesson for the academy. Spirituality cannot be contained in the material forms by which we so often try to measure our work. If we seriously want to practice spirituality as we teach and do research, we will encounter the diffi-culty faced by the poet, the mystic, and the activist: we will encounter the limits of language. At the same time, we will also learn new precision as we listen and as we question. We will look at the "tree with lights" and feel the river as it flows through us. We will know the truth more deeply than we ever knew it before. And as a result, all our cognitive learning will be enhanced.

Wilbur Birky, director of international education at Goshen College since 1994, has proposed an educational model that in current parlance could be called "em-bodiment." In traditional Christian language its name is "incarnation."[8] Menno-nites, whose spiritual ancestors were a persecuted people who spent generations in the sixteenth through eighteenth centuries wandering across Europe to till the soil for rulers who would allow some freedom for an outcast but pacifist belief, reso-nate in a particular way with this description of the founder of their faith:

> Let us propose the Incarnation as an act of divine imagination rooted in a profound realization that even God could not know and understand the human condition without entering into it, to experience it in the body. That was a true cross-cultural experience. So a description of at least the early parts of Jesus' incarnation applies aptly to the SST experience: it is to give up one's customary place of comfort, to become as a child, to learn a new language and eat in new ways, to be received into a new family, to work in the mundane "carpenter's shop," to attend the local house of worship, to question and be questioned, to experience frustration and success, and to learn to serve in the very "thick" of life.[9]

SST, therefore, takes students and faculty to a very deep place within their own religious tradition while it exposes them to other world religions and to other forms of Christian faith. Over and over again, the people in other countries, many of them "poor," teach our students what it means to be rich in spirit. Especially when the students come back from the villages, their voices choke as they try to describe how their host "fathers" or "mothers" prayed for them. They tell stories of being offered the best food, the best bed, the best gift, often by people who have almost nothing themselves.

For the year 1981–1982 my husband and I were co-directors of Goshen's SST program in Haiti. The contrast of material poverty and spiritual vitality made the reversal of these characteristics in American culture very vivid. Everywhere we went in Port-au-Prince we saw brightly painted tributes to God—in as many names as possible. They decorated the camions (vans and trucks) overflowing with people and their few possessions, including chickens and goats. Because the animist religion Voudou pervades the island, the Holy Spirit takes an important place in the worship of both Catholics and Protestants. Syncretism becomes not only a concept but also a practice to observe in everyday life. Under such conditions, students think much more about spiritual matters than they otherwise might. Their own belief systems are challenged as they see pluralism take different forms.

Haiti also provides a case study of all kinds of American and French Christian missions. Some are culturally sensitive, socially constructive forces. Others seem to increase dependence and feed on fears. Students do not always agree on which ones do the most good or the most harm. But agreement is not the point. Thinking and feeling—going deeper into new forms of knowing—these are the purposes of this kind of education. In their journals the students express how challenging they find cross-cultural immersion to be. Here is an excerpt from one such journal written in 1997. The student, David Roth, had just been on a field trip into Haiti from his SST base in the Dominican Republic:

> Going to bed tonight tired, but a good tired that has come from thoroughly extending myself in every intellectual, emotional and physical way.... I pushed so hard to soak up every word from every speaker, pushed my brain constantly for three days, examining, connecting, critiquing ideas presented to me.... And I've never learned so much in three days, never. I think my life/views/opinions have been altered permanently in some areas—like thinking about poverty, and about dependence/service issues, and about entering a culture you have little knowledge of. And it feels good to be spent. The rush I got from all the input has given me so much to ponder in a long-term sense.[10]

This journal entry, written at white heat, moves from exhaustion to exhilaration to reflective wonder. It narrates compressed stages of culture shock and illustrates why our alumni tell us so simply and so often, "SST changed my life." If a good liberal arts education can be measured by its intellectual and spiritual impact years later, this Goshen program has passed the test.

When I co-led that SST unit in Haiti, I was 33 years old. While we were there, my husband got an attractive job offer from a public research university. He said, "No"—mainly because of how much learning we experienced and witnessed by being SST leaders.

When we volunteered to lead SST again, it was to open the first unit in Cote d'Ivoire, West Africa. We went in the summer of 1993, when I was 45. By then I was more experienced as a teacher and writer and also better prepared to probe the process which produced the results that had so impressed me as a younger professor 12 years earlier. I had some new language and new practices I was willing to try. The new language was the idiom of poetry, of the spiritual life, and of science as used by Simone Weil, Thomas Merton, Albert Einstein, and many others. "Deep" had called to "deep" in my intellectual and spiritual life, and I was beginning to hear messages from distant places, faiths, and disciplines. All the sounds, all the voices, were helping me to understand the profundity of the Goshen College motto, "Culture for Service."

In 1989 I read, for the first time, Parker Palmer's book, *To Know as We Are Known*. Palmer awakened me to a new reality: that the divisions I had experienced between learning and spirit early in my life could find paradoxical resolution not only through intense experiences like SST but also in other ways. I needed and wanted to share what I was learning with other colleagues in the academy. I began a search for kindred voices in many disciplines as well as voices from the past. In 1994 I found a lost voice. Evelyn Underhill—writer, novelist, poet, and expert on mysticism—is well known in spiritual disciplines, but her educational ideas have languished. Although she was the first woman asked to give a series of lectures on religion at Oxford University (in 1921), she has not received the kind of renewed scholarly interest her work deserves. Her work predates by more than 70 years the reform movements celebrated in the present book.

The book with Underhill's 1921 Oxford lectures is called *The Life of the Spirit and the Life of Today*. She attacked boldly: "the best that most education does for our children is only what the devil did for Christ. It takes them up to the top of a high mountain and shows them all the kingdoms of this world.... It is a splendid vision, but unfortunately, fugitive."[11] She admitted that her own proposals would "sound fantastic" to her contemporaries,[12] and there is little evidence that they ever influenced education at Oxford. She believed that the medieval mind, a spiritual mind, was closer to the best psychological wisdom of her day than was the materialistic "roaring twenties" culture around her. She advocated molding young minds in the direction of God, helping them to explore the "psychology of religious experience" by appealing to the "mental qualities of wonder, curiosity and exploration which draw so many boys and girls to physical science."[13]

Underhill seriously advocated prayer both on behalf of the student and as a subject whose "nature and difficulties" should be taught.[14] But prayer should always be accompanied by expectations of work because "the spiritual life is only valued by those on whom it makes genuine demands."[15] She connected these ideas to practices of spiritual formation:

> Our aim should be to induce, in a wholesome way, that sense of the spiritual in daily experience which the old writers called the consciousness of the presence of God. The monastic training in spirituality, slowly evolved under pressure of experience, nearly always did this. It has bequeathed to us a funded wisdom of which we make little use; and this, reinterpreted in the light of psychological knowledge, might I believe cast a great deal of light on the fundamental problems of spiritual education. We could if we chose take many hints from it, as regards the disciplining of attention, the correct use of suggestion, the teaching of meditation, the sublimation and direction to an assigned end of the natural impulse to reverie; above all, the education of the moral life. For character-building as understood by these old specialists was the most practical of arts.[16]

On SST in Africa we did not instruct our students in monastic practices, but we did encourage them to observe carefully and to think of attention paid to other people and to the new landscape as a form of prayer. One of the students in the group, a biology major, paid so much attention that she spent the next three years writing poems out of the 13 weeks she spent on SST. Her M.F.A. thesis includes this poem:

> First Signs: Landing in Cote d'Ivoire
>
> The crescent moon tore a hole in the sky,
> and through it rushed streams of hot breath.
> I heard their rustle, the prickling in my throat
> as my pulse rose to greet them, the blood
> repeating its only name. Yes, perhaps
> God does speak the body's anxious language.
> Perhaps this ripe smell and the salt
> that's slipped to my skin can seal our wordless
> covenant: the call, my instinctive response.[17]

Lenae Nofziger was taken to Africa by Goshen College and asked to pay attention. We never explicitly used the word "incarnation" to describe our goals. Yet in this poem she turns naturally to familiar religious language—"God," "covenant," "call"—and combines them with less common images of raw physicality—"tore," "prickling," "ripe smell," "salt," and "skin."

The Elkhart River, in the form of "streams of hot breath," flowed through her on the other side of the world. Consequently, she gives us language for education of the spirit as experienced in the body.

THE CHARLES RIVER

> *I hear today for the first, the river in the tree.*
>
> *—Emily Dickinson*

After 20 years of teaching at Goshen College, I was called in 1996 to be its fourteenth president. Several months later I was sitting on the patio of the Wellesley College president's house, looking over Lake Waban on its way to the Charles River. President Diana Chapman Walsh was describing her interest in spirituality and the pluralism on the Wellesley campus. We had been brought together at the suggestion of our mutual friend, Parker Palmer, who by that time had inspired thousands of other educators through various speeches, books, and projects.

Our two campuses were ready for their next stage of evolution. We had the honor and the responsibility of drawing forth from our respective learning communities the kind of spirituality and diversity they need and the world needs. I listened to President Walsh describe the work of Victor Kazanjian, Wellesley dean of religious and spiritual life (and now senior adviser to the EDUCATION as *Transformation* Project), in facilitating intercultural and interreligious dialogue. The goal was to go beyond tolerance to deeper understanding and appreciation. The streams feeding the Charles contained all the world religions, including perhaps the largest religion in America—spiritual indifference. How could Wellesley deepen the spot in the river where all these channels could come together freely and forcefully? Here was a president willing, even eager, to ask the question and invite the rest of the academy to participate.

As I listened to my more experienced colleague, I marveled that we could be speaking the same language and yet have such different tasks. Goshen College also attracts students from many different Christian faiths and many world religions as well as students who are committed to no religion. But it is owned by the Mennonite Church. More than 60 percent of the students are Mennonite. So are more than 90 percent of the faculty and one hundred percent of the board. We frankly privilege Mennonite faith. In fact, our mission statement refers to the college as a "ministry" of the church whose purpose is to create "servant leaders for the church and the world."

I will use in my speeches, and I will personally claim, Christocentric language that would be offensive coming from President Walsh on her campus. Likewise, her words would be considered inadequately Christian in the Goshen setting. Can Goshen and Wellesley be part of the same movement in the larger academic world without either one compromising its forms of spirituality? I believe the answer is yes. True diversity in the academy does not dictate uniformity. It gathers up the many models, asking each to be as true to its tradition as possible while also engaging other voices both inside and outside its community.

The best contribution Goshen College can make to American higher education is to be Mennonite to the core. Increasingly, to do so is to be multicultural. It certainly does not mean being exclusively Swiss-German American in ethnicity and one or two generations removed from an agrarian subculture. Today, even the Mennonites along the Susquehanna are more diverse than that.

Goshen's pluralism, however, though larger than it has been in the past, will not be as broad as that of most campuses. It will continue to be bounded by the Mennonite understanding of the Christian faith. We aspire to be to Mennonites what Notre Dame is to Catholics worldwide—a symbol for combining the mission of the academy and the mission of the church in such a way so as to create in each an excellence impossible without the other. If we can serve our own church well and distinctively, we will as a result serve the rest of the academy also.

Let me conclude by describing some of the ways that Goshen will be discovering its own spirituality and diversity in the next few years:

1. Next year the theme for our faculty retreat, several all-school convocations, student senate discussions, and other settings, will be: "What does it mean to be an Anabaptist/Mennonite College: Can We Be Both Clearly Committed and Inclusive?" Among the resources will be this essay, others in this book, and about 50 more speeches and essays written by Goshen faculty and administrators in the last decade. I expect the conversation to be lively and far from univocal. I expect us to agree on common ground and to become stronger in the process. We may even produce our own version of a document like the one Earlham President

Doug Bennett shares in this volume.

2. We will explore ways to bring the wisdom of the elders into the residential life of our community. SST has taught us how valuable such wisdom is in other parts of the world. As I write this, some 60 retired Goshen faculty are about to arrive at a reception here in the president's house. I will ask them, "How would you like to contribute to the spiritual lives of our students? What are your concerns for them? What would you like to teach them outside the classroom? What would you like to hear from them? What stories would you like to tell?"

3. Faculty will continue to meet in voluntary small groups. Last year our academic dean Paul Keim led 24 faculty members in a weekly discussion group—one chapter at a time—of Parker Palmer's *The Courage to Teach*. If they are to live "divided no more,"[18] they need the chance to tell and to listen to each other's spirits.

4. I will continue to teach a course I have taught twice since becoming president— The Literature of Spiritual Reflection and Social Action. This course is part of our Uncommon Honors Program.

5. We will institute an all-school community service day in the fall to correspond to our Martin Luther King study day in January. In addition to the six weeks of service we require on SST, we will develop new ties to our local community.

6. We will continue to build a technology infrastructure that is guided by our larger purposes. One of these structures is Mennonite.net, a web-based connection for our church worldwide that will allow our students and faculty a platform for innovative communication and educational outreach.

There is more—much more. But these activities are representative of the spiritual base and its role in stimulating diversity within and beyond our campus. We mean to stay connected also to the *Transformation* Project. We want to be one of the sparks that creates a fire within the academy. As Alexander Solzhenitsyn said in his 1978 "Sermon to America":

> We have placed too much hope in politics and social reforms, only to find out that we were being deprived of our most precious possession: our spiritual life....All the celebrated technological achievements of progress, including the conquest of outer space, do not redeem the 20th century's moral poverty. We need a spiritual blaze.[19]

Wellesley President Walsh used the same metaphor in a recent speech: "If we subscribe to Yeats's oft-quoted insight that true education is not the filling of a pail but the igniting of a flame—then surely we want faculty who are themselves on fire with a passion for their work."[20]

We want and need such faculty. We shall draw them out by bursting into blaze ourselves: "What we have loved, others will love; and we will teach them how."[21] When we know and love our own spirits, and when we have found a home in some tradition, we will find joy in exercising what Catholics call the "charism" of that tradition—the particular river of faith which takes us to the ocean without which life has no meaning.

The word "spirit" means breath, life force. Like a river, it has to keep moving. In my life the spirit has moved through many rivers. It has gone from the particular to the universal and back again to the particular, like waves. I feel the bedrock of the Susquehanna, the Goshen "alma mater" singing within the Elkhart River, and the powerful Charles far away. As we draw nearer to each other, we are drawing nearer to the ocean, and to the mystery pulling us inexorably toward the Deep:

> We shall not cease from exploration,
> And the end of all our exploring
> Will be to arrive where we started
> And know the place for the first time.[22]

ENDNOTES

1. W.E.B. DuBois, *The Souls of Black Folk* (Greenwich, Conn.: Fawcett Publications, 1903, 1961), v.
2. Ibid., 16.
3. Ibid., 17.
4. Annie Dillard, *Pilgrim at Tinker Creek* (New York: Harper & Row, 1974), 34.
5. Allan O. Pfinister, "Everyone Overseas! Goshen College Pioneers," *International, Educational, and Cultural Exchange* 8:2 (Washington, D.C.: U.S. Advisory Commission Staff, Department of State, 1972): 1.
6. Schlabach writes, "At the risk of making a false dichotomy, it seems fair to say that Goshen's SST resulted more from the kind of church that sponsored the college than from the college itself." Theron F. Schlabach "Goshen College and Its Church Relations: History and Reflections," in *Models for Christian Higher Education: Strategies for Survival and Success in the Twenty-First Century,* eds. Richard T. Hughes and William B. Adrian, (Grand Rapids: William B. Eerdmans, 1997), 209.
7. Susan Fisher Miller, *Culture for Service: A History of Goshen College 1894–1994* (Goshen, Ind.: Goshen College, 1994), 44.
8. Birky was not the first nor only Mennonite to use this term as applied to a Mennonite philosophy of education. See Rodney J. Sawatsky, "What Can the Mennonite Model Contribute to Christian Higher Education," in *Models for Christian Higher Education: Strategies for Success in the Twenty-First Century,* eds. Richard T. Hughes and William B. Avery (Grand Rapids, Mich.: Eerdmans, 1997), 187.
9. Wilbur Birky, "SST: Vision, History, and Ethos," *SST Leaders' Manual* (Goshen: Goshen College, 1998–99), 2. Emphasis in original.
10. David Roth, as quoted by Keith Graber Miller "A One-Armed Embrace of Postmodernity: International Education and Church-Related Colleges," *Talking Out of Place: Professing in the Postmodern Academy,* eds. Stephan R. Haynes and Corrie E. Norman, (forthcoming, 2000).
11. Evelyn Underhill, *The Life of the Spirit and the Life of Today* (Harrisburg, Penn.: Morehouse Publishing, 1922), 184.
12. Ibid., 188.
13. Ibid., 190.
14. Ibid., 192.
15. Ibid., 196.

16. Ibid., 195–6.
17. Lenae Nofziger, "A Red Flap of Moon" (master's thesis, Eastern Washington University, 1992), 2.
18. Parker Palmer, *The Courage to Teach: Exploring the Inner Landscapes of a Teacher's Life* (San Francisco: Jossey-Bass, 1998), 163–183.
19. Solzhenitsyn, as quoted by George Gallup in "Seeking Spiritual Renewal," *Philadelphia Inquirer*, Sunday, 25 December 1994, Commentary.
20. Diana Chapman Walsh, "The Academic Calling: Changing Commitments and Complexities" (unpublished speech, American Association of Higher Education, Seventh Annual Conference on Faculty Roles and Rewards, San Diego, California, January 22,1999), 2. For another use of the same metaphor see Laurant A. Parks Daloz, Cheryl H. Keen, James P. Keen and Sharon Parks Daloz, *Common Fire: Lives of Commitment in a Complex World* (Boston: Beacon Press, 1996).
21. William Wordsworth, *The Prelude* (London: Oxford University Press, 1933), 241.
22. T. S. Eliot, "Little Gidding," *The Four Quartets in Collected Poems 1909–1962* (New York: Harcourt, Brace & World, Inc., 1942), 208.

19. Appreciative Engagement of Diversity: E Pluribus Unum and the EDUCATION as Transformation Project

James P. Keen

In 1996, my spouse Cheryl Keen and I joined our co-authors Laurent Parks Daloz and Sharon Daloz Parks in publishing *Common Fire: Leading Lives of Commitment in a Complex World*. This book is the result of more than a decade's research into how people develop and sustain commitments to working on behalf of the common good, defined to include the whole human family. Our most salient finding was the importance of enlarging encounters across thresholds of difference, so that someone or some group that had previously been part of "they" became part of a wider, reconstructed sense of "we."[1] From our research we are convinced that promoting encounters that help people learn to sustain relationships which reach across boundaries of irreducible difference should be among the most important aims of contemporary higher education.

The EDUCATION as *Transformation* initiative speaks powerfully to this need and responds concretely with innovative practices. The work of Victor Kazanjian as dean of religious and spiritual life at Wellesley College, fostering dialogue, sharing, and engagement across a number of the world's major religions by Wellesley students is but one example. Another is the extraordinary interactions and commitments I've witnessed in the nurturing context of the E Pluribus Unum program, bringing together Catholics, Protestants, and Jews to explore how their own traditions can support collaboration on issues of social justice and prospects of community service. In both these activities young people learn to find ground on which they can work together even when they may differ on particulars. No one is pressured to compromise their own religious identity in pursuit of some false homogenization. Rather, they discover, in the appreciative encounter of irreducible difference, that they have in common a basis from which to generate collaboration for the common good.

My vantage point as scholar-in-residence at the E Pluribus Unum (EPU) conference for the past two summers has afforded me an opportunity to gather reflections of participants on how interreligious dialogue and sharing connects for them with community service and issues of social justice.

By way of introduction, the E Pluribus Unum conference is a collaboration among The Washington Institute for Jewish Leadership and Values, The National Council of Churches, and The National Federation for Catholic Youth Ministry. The conference is financed by grants from several sources, including but not limited to, The Lilly Endowment, The Righteous Persons Foundation, and the Ford

Foundation. EPU brings together, in a Washington, D.C. venue, 60 recent high school graduates, who come from a national pool and will be going to all corners of the United States for college.

These 60 students are selected to represent equally: Catholics, Protestants (and other non-Catholic Christians), and Jews. The purposes of the conference are to afford each group an opportunity to learn more about their own traditions, particularly how these support community service and interreligious collaboration on issues of social justice. In addition, each of the three groups receives an introduction to the religious beliefs and practices of the other two groups and to the diversities which exist within each of the three groups. Formal study at the conference is augmented by a powerful group experience ignited by the challenge the conference puts to its participants at the outset, to spend three weeks building a community among themselves that recognizes, celebrates, and engages their diversity—a powerful, and some might say, utopian challenge, but one that the participants, in spite of some misunderstandings, some tough moments, and some very real conflicts, rise to meet with energy and grace. It's as though a generation that's been told all their lives that they're going to have to learn to live in a diverse world are finally getting to learn the walk that enlivens that talk.

In the summer of 1998, my second with the program, I had the opportunity to spend a number of hours in conversation with a group of participants from the 1997 conference who were able to reflect not only upon what they'd learned the previous summer at EPU but on how they felt EPU had affected them as they proceeded to go to college. In the following pages I will share some highlights from these conversations followed by a few interpretive reflections of my own. I began by asking a version of William Perry's time honored, open-ended question for interviewing young adults.[2] My question was, "Reflecting back over the past year, what stands out for you now about E Pluribus Unum?" Their first response named the direct experience of diversity within community the key aspect of EPU. As one of them put it, "That Jews and Christians can come together in community and share the experience of working together for the Common Good, even when specifics differ, gives me hope for the future."

The eight other students supported this statement, talking about the power that the intensive experience held for them. They also spoke of the EPU network of support that had remained real for them—mostly through lively e-mail correspondence because the group was dispersed on various college campuses. A key theme that emerged as we talked was the importance they placed on learning the practice of interreligious dialogue that is central to the EPU mission. Following their lead, I focused the group's attention on this area. What did they learn? How has it affected them?

First, all agreed that EPU had taught them much about "how to listen across difference." Several of them spoke of becoming "more self-reflective in the process of listening and talking," and finding themselves "reacting less defensively when encountering difference." Another reported getting "to comfort across difference more quickly" which makes him "better at working across boundaries." When I noted that bridging boundaries more quickly can sometimes come as a result of failing to acknowledge real differences, they countered that they felt that the increased ease they were reporting came along with a capacity to "ask better and deeper questions" and to be "more analytical around difference." I was impressed with their understanding that this kind of dialogue is hard work and the sense they conveyed that each of them had gotten a lot better at dialogue as a result of their EPU experience.

As they reflected further on the impact of interreligious dialogue as it affects how they think about themselves, one student observed, "My thoughts and faith are more my own." Another added, "I can incorporate belief into my actual self—when I talk, it's me, rather than what I'm supposed to believe." These statements appear to signal that these students have experienced a shift in locus of control from external to internal—a shift that Fowler associates with the transition from conventional to post-conventional faith development.[3] There is further confirmation of a shift to post-conventional thinking reflected in statements such as "I've learned to become more cautious about becoming prematurely sure," and "I've become comfortable about being unsure and living with the questions." Both of these statements remind me of what Perry described as tentative-wholeheartedness, which he associated with advanced intellectual and ethical development for college students,[4] quite an accomplishment among a group that had just completed the freshman year!

Another student added, "Faith has come alive for me." When I probed, it became clear that he meant that the world and people had become real for him in both a religious and a social sense. Another student, reflecting on the values of dialogue across difference on his understanding of his own religion, stated, "Through dialogue with Jews I gained a whole new appreciation of Christianity," testimony that upholds Diana Eck's contention that in order to understand one's own religion it is helpful to learn about another.

In a subsequent conversation, I returned to the theme that had emerged in our first encounter, this time asking the group if they could draw for me a direct connection between the two key elements of EPU, interreligious dialogue and social justice. That the group was clearly able to articulate such a connection is evidenced by some of their statements, including:

> What we discovered last summer was the three different faith traditions each teach that you should go out and do community service and social justice. When we discovered that working for social justice and the common good is something we definitely had in common—and could all work together for—we all discovered that going out and making a difference is something that's common in all our religions."

The same student later added, "Before last summer I'd have been against working collaboratively. I would have worked only to support [my religion's] organizations."

A second student added depth:

Last year we looked at the religious texts from our various backgrounds and what our faith in general has to say about the quest for social justice. When you realize they're so similar and so right on track, you realize how much bigger a group of people you have and if you can agree that you're going to work for the common good from different faith backgrounds it's a very empowering thing. You're not alone in your concern about social justice.

A third said:

It's like you're trying to get the bigger picture. It's like you're trying to put together this puzzle, you have your faith and you're trying to figure out what the puzzle is from that one little view. And, in actuality, it takes all these little pieces together to make this giant mural and for you to see what you have to do. EPU gave this window to see the entire thing.

A fourth student stated:

I feel it has a lot to do with expanding how many people you include in your circle and when you get to talk with people of other faiths I personally feel you begin to realize that even though you have different practices of worship and different rituals, and different names for things, you all have an abiding faith. I feel that brings people closer together. And when you expand your definition of people you have something in common with, then you feel much more committed to the common good.

In sum, these nine students were clear that pursuing the EPU goals of interreligious dialogue, community service, and the quest for social justice had become a priority for each of them during the first year in college. Each of them had ranged from *somewhat* to *very active* in working on these issues after EPU. All now felt that the second year's experience, working across their own differences in enacting their collaborative project, had further clarified for them how to be "servant leaders" on their own campuses. For some, interreligious collaboration could be focused around engaging together and, in some cases, initiating service projects. For others, engaging in community service opened opportunities for dialogue across difference.

Consistent for this group, as they talked of their experience and their hopes with respect to their college campuses, was the nexus of service to the community in pursuit of social justice, of interreligious dialogue connected to an emerging sense of the common good, of leading by example, through service and from within the group—putting "practicing before preaching"—as one of them said it, and of engaging differences through careful listening and self-reflection.

My own reflections on this set of conversations take several tacks. First, these students make a clear connection between interreligious dialogue and community service. Several students led their own campus religious organization to join with other religious groups in community service initiatives. In planning and carrying out these initiatives, opportunities for dialogue about their faith traditions arose naturally. In at least one instance the beginning point was a dialogue between two faith groups in which the question emerged of something they could do to respond to homeless people on the borders of their campuses. Hence, it appears that the connection can move in either the direction of dialogue to service or from service to dialogue.

Second, while productive encounters across thresholds of difference often occur naturally, it would be naive to suggest that such encounters are inevitably productive of the kinds of insights and outcomes reflected in the quotations above. On the contrary, the most common responses to such encounters are discomfort and retreat into stereotyping. Most of us have seen or heard ample testimony regarding the balkanization of ethnic, cultural, religious, and other identity groups on our campuses. Unfortunately, the culture of high school and college is often one of seeking identity within cliques and with that often comes simplistic dismissal of difference through the caricature of type casting. Because productive encounters across difference often involve a reconfiguration of one's own sense of identity, they require effort and commitment. Encountering beliefs, practices, and, above all, truth claims which differ from and challenge one's own requires significant self reflection to move past the point of suspicion and into the realm of appreciation. For most adolescents and young adults, in most situations, it's easier to go with the flow of "in group, out group" identification.

Nevertheless, tremendous potential exists for productive encounters across boundaries of diversity. Curiosity and what Alfred North Whitehead called "romance" promotes attraction toward engaging difference. But even when one is attracted to the boundary, the problem of moving from "romance" (where achieving common ground might be seen as easy and the assumption reigns that "we're all really the same under the skin") to what Whitehead terms "precision" (where we have to come to terms with variations of cultural experience and religious belief that cannot be collapsed into different shades of sameness, but demand their own vivid colorations) can be tricky. If, in the blush of romance, one carries naive assumptions that differences are superficial and we're all "really the same" across such boundaries, the result can be a sense of betrayal when differences basic to the identity of those across the boundary continue to persist. Such a sense of betrayal can lead to retreat and reinforce stereotyping. Transforming "romance" into "precision" requires hard work and is much more likely to occur in contexts which name the problem and support young people in stepping up to the challenge of learning to appreciate the differences that make for diversity.

Third, this is the point at which initiatives on college campuses like the reconfiguration of the chaplaincy at Wellesley and short-term intensive learning programs like EPU can play a critical role as mentoring environments. Such programs provide inviting opportunities for participation, dialogue, and reflection. They also specify that the journey from "romance" to "precision" will require commitment, time, patience, and work. In particular, they balance sharing of particularity—no one must compromise their religious or cultural identity—with a norm of appreciative encounter: you actually may understand your own particularity more clearly and deeply when you've become precise in your understanding of how another, possibly several others, are irreducibly different from you in ways that constitute their own identities.

Finally, we need more initiatives like these. Short-term intensive programs like EPU serve as models of excellent preparation for engaging diversity in the cause of community service and social justice both in the college years and throughout life. Moreover, the EPU model could be adapted to bringing together student leaders in interreligious dialogue and collaboration from several campuses for further exploration and training on how to fulfill the potential of the centers of religious and spiritual life now emerging on their campuses.

The EDUCATION as *Transformation* Project should proceed in its reconstruction of campus ministries as centers of religious and spiritual life that support identity, and engage and celebrate diversity and collaboration on community service. By doing so, EDUCATION as *Transformation* can transform campus ministries into what may become the epicenter of educational purpose for colleges and universities dedicated to graduating young adults ready to engage a world of complexity and diversity.

ENDNOTES

1. Laurent Parks Daloz, Cheryl Keen, James P. Keen, and Sharon Daloz Parks, *Common Fire: Leading Lives of Commitment in a Complex World* (Boston: Beacon Press, 1996).
2. William G. Perry, *Intellectual Development in the College Years: A Scheme* (New York: Holt, Rinehart & Winston, 1967).
3. James Fowler, *Stages of Faith* (San Francisco: Harper & Row, 1981).
4. Perry, op. cit.
5. Diana Eck, keynote address at "EDUCATION as *Transformation*" Conference, Wellesley College, September 1998.
6. Of course, these quotations above do not constitute conclusive evidence that gains in intellectual, ethical, and faith development have taken place for these students, nor do we have evidence that even if such gains have taken place that they were necessarily initiated by the EPU experience.

20. Beyond Tolerance: From Mono-religious to Multi-religious Life at Wellesley College

VICTOR H. KAZANJIAN, JR. AND THE STUDENTS OF THE
WELLESLEY COLLEGE MULTI-FAITH COUNCIL

In the center of the hundred-year old Protestant Christian chapel, Jackie, a senior who is the Jewish representative on the multi-faith student council at Wellesley College, moves to the front of the stage on which women from Bahá'í, Buddhist, Christian, Hindu, Jain, Jewish, Muslim, Sikh, Unitarian Universalist, and Wiccan traditions are gathered. "It hurts me when people think that Jews are racist," she says. The silence that follows is excruciating. Those who are gathered to watch this performance-piece on religious pluralism that reflects the experience of these women begin to squirm. Slowly but confidently, Desiree, a senior who is of African descent and the Christian representative on the council, steps towards Jackie. She gently touches her on the shoulder and says, "But Jackie, some Jews are racist!" Jackie pulls away sharply and then responds, "And some Christians, too!" The tension builds. Simi, who is Sikh, turns to Anindita, who is Hindu, and shouts, "And Hindus!" "That's right!" adds Yasmeen, the Muslim representative. Suddenly, conflict consumes the group.[1]

It had taken us six years to reach the point where this multi-faith group of students could risk a public presentation like this; six years of slowly building a foundation of trust and understanding; six years of creating a new model for engaging the growing religious diversity within the Wellesley College community. In the fall of 1998, at the EDUCATION as *Transformation* national gathering, the Multi-faith Student Council at Wellesley College was ready to share their story with others. In the context of a multi-faith celebration on the second day of the gathering, students from the council presented a performance piece called "Beyond Tolerance" which uses drama, music, song, dance and ritual to tell the story of the encounters that these students had with each other over a three year period as they worked towards building a multi faith community. The essential message of the piece is that it is possible for people of different religious traditions to celebrate the uniqueness of their own tradition while also seeing the beauty and truth of other religions. This is the essence of religious pluralism.

The impact of this performance-piece in the context of the spiritual celebration at the national gathering was obvious. All of the speeches and panel discussions on religious pluralism and spirituality which had formed the basis of the national gathering up to that point became embodied in these students. No longer was religious pluralism simply a concept, but rather religious pluralism was Colby, Antonia, Desiree, Anindita, Lisa, Jackie, Yasmeen, Simi, Allaire and Sarah. Like everyone else, I watched with a sense of wonder and awe as these students brought to life not just the possibility of pluralism, but the reality of it. As I listened to the comments of participants afterwards, so visibly moved by the experience, I was heartened to see that people were as inspired by these remarkable women as I certainly am. But I was also concerned that those observing this performance were unaware of the time-consuming, complicated process that had led up to the creation of this moment. Without this history, there is no way to understand how religious pluralism had emerged at Wellesley.

This essay is an attempt to fill in that missing context and to offer something of the story of the journey that we have shared at Wellesley College; a journey from mono-religious to multi-religious community which has taken us beyond tolerance. This has been a profoundly relational process. It is the joint creation of the chaplains, advisors and students who over a six year period have devoted themselves to exploring the uncharted territory of that which lies beyond tolerance and towards interdependence. And so I want to begin by acknowledging each of them as my co-authors in this process. I have listed their names at the conclusion of this essay. These words are as much theirs as mine.

A JOURNEY BEGINS

The "Beyond Tolerance" performance-piece begins with ten women moving onto the stage to the rhythm of traditional Native African drumming and song. Each stands alone. Then when all of the students have taken their places, they begin to speak one at a time. (The words at the beginning of each section represent the "script" written and performed by the students in "Beyond Tolerance" at the national gathering.)

Colby:	*I am Bahá'í.*
Antonia:	*I am Buddhist.*
Desiree:	*I am Christian.*
Anindita:	*I am Hindu.*
Lisa:	*I am Jain.*
Jackie:	*I am Jewish*
Yasmeen:	*I am Muslim.*
Simi:	*I am Sikh.*
Allaire:	*I am Unitarian Universalist.*
Sarah:	*I am Wiccan*
Colby:	*I believe in the progressive revelation of all prophets.*
Antonia:	*I follow the path of Buddha.*
Desiree:	*Jesus is my Savior.*
Anindita:	*I worship Durga, Lakshmi, Saraswati, Krishna, Shiva.*
Lisa:	*I follow the teachings of Mahavirswami and the 23 other Thirthankars.*
Jackie:	*I follow the teachings of the Torah.*
Yasmeen:	*I believe there is no God but Allah, and the Prophet Mohammed, may peace be upon him, is His messenger and prophet.*
Simi:	*I believe in one God. Waheguru and the 10 Gurus are my teachers.*

Allaire;	*I seek my own truth drawing from the wisdom of all traditions.*
Sarah:	*The Goddess is my Mother.*
Colby:	*To be Bahá'í is to practice the oneness of humanity.*
Antonia:	*To be Buddhist is to live mindfully in the present.*
Desiree:	*To be Christian is to follow Christ's example of love and justice.*
Anindita:	*To be Hindu is to see unity in many aspects of God.*
Lisa:	*To be Jain is to try to reach an inner peace and to let the soul become free from attachments .*
Jackie:	*To be Jewish is be part of a community.*
Yasmeen:	*To be Muslim means being in submission to the will of Allah.*
Simi:	*To be Sikh is to stand up for what is right and true.*
Allaire:	*To be a Unitarian Universalist is to be constantly questioning.*
Sarah:	*To be Wiccan is to be in attunement with nature.*

In 1992 the president and trustees of Wellesley College made the rather startling decision that, in seeking to better prepare students for leadership in the world, they would reexamine the role of religious life and spirituality in Wellesley's educational experience. After nearly a century of shedding the constraints placed upon academic institutions by their religious founders, this was an unusual step, to say the least, for a secular, liberal arts institution. At a time when most academic institutions, confused by a mono-religious and mono-cultural institutional history and a multi-religious, multi-cultural contemporary community, were abandoning even the rather harmless service of providing religious support for students, Wellesley's efforts seemed unusual. In addition, to suggest that spirituality, even free from its institutional religious context, plays an essential role in a college's basic educational mission, was certain to be seen as antithetical to secular education. This, however, is precisely what Wellesley College set out to do by creating a multi-faith religious and spiritual life program under the direction of a new position of dean of religious and spiritual life.

The goal of the proposed program was to develop a pluralistic multi-faith community in which all particular expressions of religious faith were celebrated and in which dialogue about common moral and ethical principles was nurtured. This goal challenged the common practice of many colleges and universities, which assumes that the religious and spiritual life of a diverse educational community can adequately be served by a program in which there is still one dominant religious tradition (usually Protestant Christian), around whom everyone else must orient themselves. Wellesley was interested in dismantling its old Protestant Christian-dominated structures and creating a program which reflected the principles of religious pluralism and multi-culturalism while honoring its history as well. To do this, Wellesley created the position of dean of religious and spiritual life. The dean was to create and oversee a program that nurtured people of all religious traditions and spiritual practices and begin a process of exploring areas of spirituality and education with faculty, students and staff. The position of dean was designed specifically not to represent any one religious tradition on campus. In this way, the dean would not function as a chaplain in a particular tradition, but as an administrator and spiritual leader for the whole college.

I arrived at Wellesley in February of 1993, with a professional background as an Episcopal priest and community organizer. My work prior to Wellesley centered mostly around social change and, in particular, conflict resolution and economic justice in diverse communities in San Francisco, the South Bronx, and Boston. This vocational work was a reflection of my personal background and particularly the influence of my two grandfathers. My paternal grandfather, Varastad Kazanjian, passed on to me the gift of difference in my Armenian identity, and a belief in the necessity of community. My maternal grandfather, Harold Case, former president of Boston University along with with his dear friend and colleague Howard Thurman, dean of Marsh Chapel at Boston University, taught me to see the beauty and truth in people of all religions, races and cultures. Now at the age of 33, I found myself with the unique opportunity to give concrete form to a vision of a global spiritual community of which I had heard Dr. Thurman speak so often when I was a child; a vision of the wholeness of the human community in which one could celebrate the particularity of one's own experience without diminishing the beauty of anothers', and thereby glimpse a more complete image of the divine.

In the twenty or so years before 1993, religious life at Wellesley College was led by a full-time college chaplain who was the Protestant Christian chaplain, a part-time Hillel director/Jewish chaplain, and a part-time Roman Catholic Christian chaplain. (Prior to this time, it had been the responsibility of the president, the faculty and local clergy to provide religious and spiritual leadership for the College.) In 1990, in her final act as college chaplain, Connie Chandler Ward put forth the analysis that religious life at the College would no longer be well served by a model which was centered around a Protestant Christian college chaplain and recommended that a non-religion-specific dean be hired to create a new model. My initial work as Wellesley's first dean of religious and spiritual life was to enter into dialogue with people from various religious traditions on campus, some organized into groups and some not, in order to learn about their needs and about their vision for how religious and spiritual life might be a more integrated element of the educational experience on campus. In addition, I met with faculty, trustees, alumnae, staff and students, some of whom identified with religious groups and many who did not, in order to get a sense of the larger community in which this program was to be created.

Time and time again, the message that I heard from people of all religious and spiritual traditions, as well as those outside of religious traditions, was that the current model was obsolete and ineffective. As with many efforts in inter-religious cooperation, Wellesley had fallen prey to the belief that in order to bring people of different traditions together, one had to find a common, neutral context in which everyone felt comfortable and in which no one was offended. The result was the stripping of all particularistic experience from community rituals and programs, leaving a kind of universalistic mush in which no one's unique perspective was reflected. The paradox, of course, was that even with this universalizing tendency, the ethos of the college remained Protestant Christian, in part because the official religious leader of the college was the Protestant chaplain (her rather remarkable work in serving the whole community regardless of religion not withstanding.) The non-Christians still felt as though they were outsiders in a community where Christianity remained normative and the Christians felt as though their tradition had been lost in the attempts to universalize.

During the discussions about recreating religious life at Wellesley, the college had considered doing away with the religious life program altogether. But a coalition of students, administrators and trustees persuaded the president and the board that the spiritual well-being of members of the Wellesley community was an integral part of Wellesley's original mission and remained an essential ingredient in its contemporary goals of educating women who will make a difference in the world.

There are many people who helped to make this original idea of a multi-faith community a reality at Wellesley. In 1992, then President Nan Keohane, Dean of Students Molly Campbell, and Associate Dean of Students Joanne Murray, carried the vision in its early stages. Current Dean of Students Geneva Walker Johnson and many other alumnae, faculty, staff and trustees have been vital to the development of this program. But it is safe to say that the arrival of Diana Chapman Walsh as president of Wellesley, six months after my arrival in 1993, transformed the process completely. As is evident by her introduction to this volume, President Walsh effortlessly articulates a vision for higher education that necessitates pluralism and includes spirituality. She continues to be an inspiration for me and a leader in the movement towards a more holistic educational process, not only at Wellesley, but also across the nation.

TELLING OUR STORIES, SPEAKING OUR TRUTHS

Colby:	*I have so many memories as a child...of monthly holy day fasts,*
Antonia:	*of pouring sweet tea over the baby Buddha on Hanamatsuri,*
Desiree:	*of stories of the life of Jesus at bedtime,*
Anindita:	*of my mother doing Lakshmi puja every Thursday,*
Lisa:	*of talking to my guru about all kinds of religious questions,*
Jackie:	*of lighting Shabbat candles,*
Yasmeen:	*of going to Makkah with my parents and praying in the Great Mosque,*
Simi:	*of singing Shabads in Gurdwara,*
Allaire:	*of reading poems about the beauty of nature,*
Sarah:	*of doing rituals with my family on the full moon.*

My experience in conflict resolution and diversity training taught me that the most creative encounters between people of different identities begins with the sharing of their stories. But even before bringing people together to speak their stories and listen to the stories of others, it is necessary that each religious community have a sense of its own identity and place at the college. Although beginning by strengthening the particular in order to achieve pluralism seems to be counter-intuitive, it is a crucial first step. Only when religious groups feel as though they have a well-established home for the celebration and practice of their traditions are they likely to engage in the work of building multi-faith community. At Wellesley, the first step in this process was to create a team of chaplains and religious advisors who would take up the task of nurturing their particular religious communities while engaging as a team in exploring new dimensions of inter-religious dialogue.

The vision of a multi-faith team of advisors, led by a dean, called for thoughtful consideration not only of the current needs of the Wellesley College community, but also its future needs. The diversity that is transforming America is transforming her colleges and universities as well. Students from Muslim, Hindu, Buddhist and many other traditions comprise a growing and significant part of student, and often faculty and staff, populations. At a residential college like Wellesley, the dormitory has become the first place where the impact of this growing diversity is being felt. Students of different religious traditions and practices are thrown together and expected to figure out how to create a common life. In some cases, students from religious communities that are literally at war with each other are asked to be roommates, without any clear advise on how to engage the situation. In addition, issues of religious food restrictions and holy day work prohibitions are becoming an increasing source of conflict and confusion in academic communities. The needs of these "newcomer" communities have outstripped the capacities of staff or faculty members who have in the past volunteered their time as religious advisors to these communities. The need for a team of professional advisors who would provide support to their own religious communities and also be a resource to the whole community on issues of religious difference was becoming poignantly clear.

My belief was that for this envisioned group of religious advisors to adequately explore the movement from a mono-religious to a multi-religious community, they needed to live the questions and the conflict. Therefore, it was necessary to have on-campus advisors whose job descriptions indicated that a portion of their time be spent on multi-faith work. The notion that people can navigate the treacherous waters of inter-religious cooperation in their spare time is absurd. The work of inter-religious dialogue and multi-faith community-building requires specific skills and enormous effort. Creating a team of religious advisors who are part of the College's administrative staff and who devote professional time to multi-religious work, has been essential to the development of our program. This enabled us to function as a team, meeting regularly for conversation/reflection/study and program planning, and to engage in professional training in conflict resolution and cross-cultural dialogue. Further, this reinforced that the religious advisors, as part of the student services division, were accountable to the educational mission of the College.

When I arrived at Wellesley, only the position of Hillel director/Jewish chaplain was solidly in place and she, Rabbi Ilene Lerner Bogosian, had been an integral part of the search process for a dean of religious and spiritual life. Through conversations with members of each religious and spiritual group on campus, it was determined that additional advisors were immediately necessary for the Buddhist, Hindu, Muslim, Protestant Christian, Roman Catholic Christian and Unitarian Universalist communities. The College agreed to seek funds for these positions through an annual appeal to alumnae, modeled after the very successful fundraising which supports Wellesley Hillel. While this effort was being established, the College agreed to make funds available to establish these positions. In developing the structure for each religious group on campus we drew heavily from Hillel's experience. It was decided that each religious tradition would have an advisory board of alumnae, faculty, staff and students. Each board would then work with the dean to support the life of their community. Representatives from each advisory board also served on a multi-faith advisory group to the dean. Eventually this group took up the task of overseeing the annual fundraising process for the religious and spiritual life program. To have peaceful and productive inter-religious dialogue is a formidable task, but many people warned us that to try raising money together was simply foolhardy. They were wrong. The work of this group continues to be one of the most inspiring aspects of our work together.

It is significant to note that one of the defining moments in the early development of this program came when Wellesley Hillel not only voted to support the multi-faith model and the new, and, as of yet, untested religious life structure, but agreed to fold its very successful fundraising program into the collaborative multi-faith fundraising effort to raise the funds necessary for the support of all religious groups. There have been many moments when people showed great courage in their willingness to pursue the dream of a pluralistic religious community at Wellesley, but none was more significant than this moment. Hillel had a lot to lose and very little to gain (at least financially) from this effort and yet the alumnae board unanimously voted to not only be a partner in the process but to provide leadership for this effort. It is a moment I will always remember.

For the past six years, members of the Religious Life Team have, through their deep commitment to nurturing the lives of their own communities and engaging in inter-religious dialogue, brought to fruition a multi-faith vision of a community committed to religious pluralism. At the same time that the Religious Life Team of advisors and chaplains was beginning their work, the student Multi-faith Council, formally the Interfaith Council, came together in a new way. The purpose of the council was to explore the possibility of religious pluralism through a process of dialogue among student representatives from as many different religious and spiritual groups as possible.

In 1993, 14 of the 16 student religious groups active on Wellesley's campus were Christian (the other two were Jewish and Muslim). And yet the Wellesley

College community included students from Baha'i, Buddhist, Hindu, Jain, Native African, Native American, Shinto, Sikh, Taoist, Unitarian Universalist, Wiccan and Zoroastrian traditions, as well as a host of spiritual seekers who did not define their practice within the context of institutional religion. At that time, the student Interfaith Council was made up of representatives of all official student religious groups on campus. The obvious problem was that the makeup of the group was therefore 7/8ths Christian. It was clear that if we were to explore the possibility of a multi-faith community in which each religious and spiritual tradition was equally valued and had equal voice, the structure of the council needed to be changed. To do this we needed to get beyond proportional representation.

Does the fact that there are fifteen hundred Christians and two Jains at Wellesley College give Christians a right to a privileged voice? In seeking religious pluralism, the answer must be NO! One analogy is to think of this work as more like the United States Senate than the House of Representatives. Two representatives from each state/religious community, regardless of population, are necessary for there to be a balanced dialogue. Initially it was necessary for me to spend a great deal of time working with the Christian community to help them understand that, in the work of religious pluralism, they are one religious community and that the fragmentation of Christianity into denominations was not an excuse for multiple representation. (There is at least as much diversity among Buddhists, Hindus Jews, Muslims etc., and yet we most often treat each of them as singular religious communities in inter-religious initiatives.) Applying this principle meant the transforming of the old Interfaith Council made up of 14 Christian representatives (Congregational, Episcopal, Evangelical, Lutheran, Intervarsity Christian Fellowship, Campus Crusade for Christ, etc.), a Jewish representative and a Muslim representative, into a Multi-faith Council with two representatives from each of the religious groups represented in the Wellesley College community (Bahá'í, Buddhist, Christian, Hindu, Jain, Jewish, Muslim, Native African, Native American, Shinto, Sikh, Taoist, Unitarian Universalist, Wiccan and Zoroastrian).

It is important to note that in a pluralistic model, where people from each religious group are encouraged to bring the fullness of their tradition to the dialogue, religious exclusivists have a voice. I am fond of saying that ours is not a program based on a group of like-minded religious folks holding hands and singing unity songs. In the course of the past six years we have had students on the multi-faith council and participating in the religious life programs from various traditions, including Christianity, Judaism, and Islam, who self-describe as conservative, orthodox, evangelical and fundamentalist. I am a pluralist and a Christian, and although I may disagree profoundly with those who believe in exclusivist principles, I am also committed to their right to speak and practice their faith (as long as it does not violate the rights of others).[2] Only if we can live this conflict in an intentional way can we discover creative ways to transform it.

As soon as the Religious Life Team and Multi-faith Council began to meet, the work took off. We began by listening to the stories of each tradition and not just the stories from holy books or the official doctrine, but also personal stories about what it was like for each person to live their lives as a Buddhist or Jew or Muslim. During these sessions we adopted several principles of dialogue which guided our discussions:

- Speak from your experience as a person within a tradition and not on behalf of the tradition as a whole;
- To ensure equity of voice, it is critical that each member has the opportunity to speak their story and listen to the stories of others;
- To create a safe space in which to share stories we must recognize and re- spect each other's perspectives as authentic. We need not agree with, or even fully understand someone else's story, in order to respect it. At the same time safety does not mean unanimity or avoiding conflict. Conflict is an essential part of this process;
- If someone says something that you do not understand, ask her to elaborate;
- If someone says something to which you have a strong reaction, share it when it happens;
- All questions are valid and necessary;
- Answer questions posed to you to the best of your ability, but it is equally acceptable to say, "I don't know;" and,
- Asking and answering questions is a way of both learning about others and being drawn deeper into one's own tradition.

The Religious Life Team and Multi-faith Council used a variety of different designs for their work. Our intent was that our meetings would be less about busi- ness and more about encounter. At both the weekly meetings, and fall, winter and spring retreats, there was always time set aside for members to share a teaching from their tradition. Meetings also always included time for being with each other in reflection, meditation or prayer, each according to their own tradition, or wit- nessing each other's forms of worship or practice. During one year we divided the year into segments and studied each of the religions represented in the groups. During another year we read and discussed several books and articles on religious and spiritual themes. The student Multi-faith Council developed learning "games" such as:

1. *Two Truths and a Lie*, in which each group member presents three things about their religious tradition to the group, two of which are true and one of which is not. The group then tries to guess which is untrue.
2. *1 Minute Drill*, in which group members, in pairs, attempt to find out as much as they can about their partner's religious tradition.
3. *Everything You've Always Wanted to Know About My Religion But Were Afraid to Ask*, a question and answer period dedicated to questions that

are hard to ask about someone else's religious tradition. Questions are sometimes submitted on cards anonymously and after a while asked directly.

4. *Multi-faith Pictionary*, in which groups try and guess which religion is being represented by the drawing of clues on newsprint.

5. *Prejudices and Stereotypes*, an exercise in which the group lists as many stereotypes as they can think of for each tradition and discusses how stereotypes and prejudices emerge.

6. *Children's Story Hour*, group members tell stories about their religion that they learned as children.

In addition, members of each group brought in religious symbols/items important to them from their religious tradition, and shared rituals and their meanings with the group. It was this last exercise of sharing rituals with each other that gave us an idea for bringing the rest of the community into this learning process.

FLOWER SUNDAY—TRANSFORMING COMMUNITY RITUALS AT WELLESLEY

Colby:	*I remember learning about the teachings of Bahá'u'lláh*
Antonia:	*about the teaching of the Buddha*
Desiree:	*about the teachings from the Bible*
Anindita:	*about the teachings from the Gita*
Lisa:	*about the teachings from the Agam Sutra*
Jackie:	*about the teachings from the Torah*
Yasmeen:	*about the teachings from the Qur'an*
Simi:	*about the teachings from the Guru Granth Sahib*
Allaire:	*about the teachings of past Unitarian Universalists*
Sarah:	*about the lessons of all living things*
Colby:	*and I remember dancing for peace*
Antonia:	*chanting the Bell Chant*
Desiree:	*singing hymns*
Anindita:	*singing bhajans*
Lisa:	*and doing samaik and pratikaman.*
Jackie:	*I remember praying during the Shabbat service*
Yasmeen:	*the call to prayer*
Simi:	*chanting Waheguru at religious camp*
Allaire:	*exchanging flowers to celebrate community*
Sarah:	*and dancing around the May pole.*

The Religious Life Team and student Multi-faith Council have over the years offered a series of discussion and educational programs to the broader college community. The structure and themes of these programs ranged from lectures on different religious traditions to dorm-based discussions on whether it is possible to be religious and a scholar. But to draw members of the community into a deeper experience of religious pluralism, we focused our work on creating new forms of community ritual.

Wellesley College has a long tradition of community rituals, most of which originated from its Protestant Christian past. As the community changed, becoming more culturally and religiously diverse, most of these rituals were abandoned. The ones that remained, Flower Sunday (a beginning of the year community gathering on the theme of friendship) and Baccalaureate (a spiritual celebration the day before commencement), had become hopelessly watered down and poorly attended. As the Religious Life Team and student Multi-faith Council explored ways to invite the broader college community to experience the work of religious pluralism, it seemed that these rituals might be useful.

To begin this process it was necessary for us to set aside the structure of these rituals, which were based on Protestant Christian liturgical forms, and create new structures into which each group could offer something from their own tradition with integrity. We needed to get beyond the feeling that non-Christian traditions were being graciously included in a Christian experience, to a place where we were creating something totally new out of the authentic offerings from each tradition. At first, and to some degree to this day, questions remain about just what we are doing when we gather for these multi-faith community celebrations. Is it worship? When the Buddhist chaplain offers the bell chant as a call to gather, what does that mean for the non-Buddhists? Are those gathered simply spectators at a performance, or actual participants in religious ritual? Good questions, the answers to which we are still living out.

In creating these rituals, we are careful not to ask people to participate in a devotional practice from a religion other than their own, but rather to experience the various forms of song, dance, and spoken word from diverse traditions, not as spectators at an event, but as recipients of a gift. The challenge of creating such a ritual celebration is to make it participatory rather than spectatory, worship rather than performance, something relevant to the broadest possible gathering and yet with offerings from particular traditions. Our multi-faith celebrations occur six times during the year, four times for students and twice for alumnae. They are held in the chapel, which we acknowledge is a space originally constructed for a particular tradition but which we are now using for a pluralistic purpose. (This was only possible once space was made available to meet the needs of particular religious groups, including a Muslim prayer room, Buddhist and Hindu mediation rooms, and a small multi-faith chapel now used by 14 different religions.) These rituals have grown and changed over the six years. They have become alive again and a part of the Wellesley experience. More than 1300 students gather for the Flower Sunday celebration of friendship to the sound of African drumming, Buddhist chanting, Hindu dancing, Christian singing, a reading and reflection on the Torah, the Qur'an, and much more. And as President Walsh or Dean Walker-Johnson rises to lead the gathering in a responsive reading or meditation/prayer, it now feels familiar and welcome, even to those students who are not part of any religious tradition.

MOVING BEYOND TOLERANCE

Colby:	*I remember...being told that my religion was a cult;*
Antonia:	*cringing during the pledge of allegiance, "One Nation under God;"*
Desiree:	*being made fun of for carrying my rosary beads;*
Anindita:	*being laughed at for saying that cows are sacred;*
Lisa:	*people criticizing me for being vegetarian and letting my religion control what I eat;*
Jackie:	*being called a Satanist for wearing the Jewish Star;*
Yasmeen:	*a teacher at high school asking me, "Isn't the veil a little too much?"*
Simi:	*my brother's turban being ripped off on a school bus;*
Allaire:	*my friend telling me that Unitarian Universalism wasn't a real religion;*
Sarah:	*my grandmother saying she looked up Pagan in the dictionary and it meant I had no religion;*
Antonia:	*I feel angry when people think Buddhism is something you can just take up, like it's a fad.*
Desiree:	*I get so mad when I'm told that I can't be a real scholar and a Christian.*
Lisa:	*It angers me when people think Jainism is no longer an active religion.*
Colby:	*I hate it when people use religion to oppress others.*
Sarah:	*It makes me mad when people say my pentacle is a sign of Satan.*
Yasmeen:	*How long do I have to put up with hearing that all Muslims are terrorists?*
Simi:	*It infuriates me when people stare at Sikh men and women because they don't shave, because they don't cut their hair, because they wear turbans on their heads.*
Allaire:	*It frustrates me when people think UU is a Christian denomination.*
Anindita:	*It upsets me when Hinduism is exoticized and I see people wearing "body dots" and t-shirts with Hindu deities on them.*
Jackie:	*It hurts me when people think that Jews are racist.*
Desiree:	*But Jackie, some Jew's are racist.*
Jackie:	*And some Christians too.*
Simi:	*And Hindus!*
Yasmeen:	*That's right!*

The group is consumed by conflict, then by a rigid silence.

Perhaps the most profound lesson that institutions such as Wellesley are learning from their experiments with religious pluralism is that tolerance is not the goal that we should seek in forming a pluralistic community. However, in the face of a world punctuated by acts of intolerance, one might ask how tolerance could possibly be an unworthy goal for which to strive.

Throughout history, tolerance has been the goal towards which forward thinking people have worked in seeking to respond to conflict between diverse peoples, while intolerance has led to the massive destruction of life on all corners of the planet. At a time when tolerance has often been replaced by overt acts of hate in communities around the world, a little tolerance seems a worthy goal. History teaches us otherwise.

Tolerance as the ultimate goal has not and will not lead us to the healthy, peaceful, just society we seek. Tolerance is conflict arrested. It is a great harness applied to the destructive forces of ignorance, fear and prejudice. It provides a wall between warring parties. At best it is a glass wall where protected people can see one another going about living parallel lives. Nonetheless it is still a wall dividing us from each another. As such, tolerance is not a basis for healthy human relationship nor will it ever lead to true community, for tolerance does not allow for learning, growth or transformation, but rather ultimately keeps people in a state of suspended ignorance and conflict.

In many societies tolerance has historically been either democratically legislated or forced upon people by less democratic means. In both cases, the result has been far short of achieving any sense of healthy, interdependent community. During the past several years, we have seen the results of forced tolerance in the horrific ethnic conflict that has followed the unraveling of the former Soviet Union and the former Yugoslavia. Long-standing inter-ethnic conflict was suspended by the imposition of a forced states of tolerance under the guise of nationalistic common identity. But as we have now learned, the conflict did not go away. It stayed festering until the walls of tolerance were taken down, unleashing the fear, frustration and rage that had grown beneath the relatively calm surface afforded by tolerance.

The racial Balkanization of America holds the same lessons as the ethnic fragmentation of the Balkans. Tolerance forced or legislated does not lead to mutual understanding, societal transformation and community. In the United States, tolerance, although democratically legislated, has had a similar effect on our society. Legislated tolerance forms the basis of our civil rights laws today, institutionalizing in our society the principle that particular expressions of gender, race, religion, physical ability and sexual preference should be protected as individual freedoms. However, even with these democratically chosen principles of social tolerance in place, religious prejudice, xenophobia, racial, gender, and sexual orientation related violence continue to plague American society. Tolerance has not led to the formation of a healthy, interdependent community, but rather a country divided by walls of tolerance, only occasionally crossed and usually for destructive purposes. Tolerance has not protected us from acts of hate but rather cast us in a frozen state of societal fragmentation and ignorance.

As the students of the Multi-faith Council and the advisors and chaplains on the Religious Life Team began to search for ways to deepen their understanding of religious pluralism, they found it necessary to explore the places of conflict amongst themselves and between the religious traditions which they represent. As we began to explore areas of difference and conflict, the level of fear and apprehension grew in the groups. "If we disagree," group members asked, "if we really disagree will we still be able to function as a team?" If not, we agreed, then our work will have little or no meaning to the world. And so to this day, we are still exploring the role of conflict in our work. Perhaps the most powerful reflection of the process was the creation of the Beyond Tolerance Workshop, a training program on dealing with religious difference in which students offer a performance-piece that tells the story of their encounters with each other across lines of religious difference, and then lead participants in a discussion about issues of religious difference, inter-religious conflict and multi-faith community building.

The process of creating the Beyond Tolerance Workshop began by asking the students of the Multi-faith Council to enter into a structured dialogue around these issues. Over a weekend retreat, the members of the Multi-faith Council broke into pairs where each partner was from a different religious or spiritual community. Partners interviewed each other using a series of questions, which are included below. It was important that everyone answer the same questions, but they were also meant to stimulate discussion between partners and to raise additional questions for discussion. After each segment of questions, the group reconvened and each person reported to the whole group significant learnings from the work with their partner.

The answers to these questions, and the stories that were shared between partners and within the group, then became the text for the script of the beyond tolerance performance-piece.

BEYOND TOLERANCE PARTNER INTERVIEWS:

Group members divide into pairs with a partner from a different religious or spiritual tradition. Partners take turns interviewing each other and writing down the answers to each question to share with the whole group later.

Part I–Defining Ourselves

1. With what religious or spiritual tradition or traditions do you most identify?
2. Is there a particular leader/prophet/teacher whom you follow or who is important in your faith?
3. Is there a particular text that has meaning for you?
4. Are there symbols in your tradition which are important to you? What do they mean?
5. What does it mean for you to be a _____(your religion/s?)
6. What memories do you have of practicing or learning about your faith?
7. Could you tell me two or three things about your tradition that would help me understand why it is important for you?
8. What is difficult for you about being _____ (your religion/s?)
9. What do people from other religious traditions not understand about

you as a _____(your religion/s?)

10. What do others say or do that upsets you?

The group then reconvenes and each person reports what they learned from their partner in answer to each question and shares any reactions to the process itself.

Part II–Sharing Our Stories

Group members return to discussion with their partners.

If you wanted to show your partner or have your partner experience some aspect of what being a _____ (your religion/s) means to you, what would you do? Imagine using as many different forms of expression as possible including, but not limited to, stories, songs, dances, prayers, or rituals. Choose several of these forms of expression and use them to show your partner some aspect of what your religion means to you.

The group then reconvenes and shares the ideas that were generated with the whole group.

Part III Encountering Each Other

Again, group members return to work with the same partner.

1. What differences do you see between people of different religious traditions?
2. How does your tradition view other traditions?
3. What tensions do you feel exist between people of your religious tradition and people of other religious traditions?
4. What stereotypes and prejudices do people hold about your religious tradition?
5. What stereotypes and prejudices do people in your religious tradition have about other religious traditions?
6. What gets in the way of people from your religious tradition being able to work in a multi-faith group?
7. What questions would you like to ask your partner as a person of a different religious tradition?

Other possible questions include:

How does your tradition/practice affect your daily life?
When you pray/meditate/reflect, what do you think about?
What is your connection to others in your faith?
Do you ever have questions or doubts about some aspect of your tradition?
What is the meaning behind your rituals?
What stories and songs are part of your religion?
What does your religion do for you?

Why do you practice religion?
Do you experience a divine force or presence?

The group then reconvenes and each individual shares the answers of his or her partner to the questions. Also, the group discusses what it felt like to enter this process. What are the reactions to asking and answering these questions? Was there a particular moment that was significant or inspirational? Was there a moment that was uncomfortable? This is a deep process and it is important to express what it feels like to engage in this work and to maintain connections within the group throughout the experience.

Part IV–Closing Ritual

It is important to periodically pause and acknowledge the importance and complexity of this kind of work. The student Multi-faith Council has developed a ritual closing for our retreats in which we honor the beauty and truth of each other's experience. We begin by passing a bowl of warm water around the circle, dipping our hands in it and allowing them to be dried by the person next to us. Then the partners of different religious traditions who have worked closely together in considering the above questions pair up once again, face to face, and offer the following statement. The final word is never scripted, always spontaneous. (In the sample dialogue below, examples from the Beyond Tolerance performance piece at the national gathering are given.)

Colby to Simi:
 I am Bahá'i. You are Sikh and in your eyes I see _____. (Aliveness)
Simi to Colby:
 I am Sikh. You are Bahá'i. In your eyes I see_____. (Commitment)
Yasmeen to Anindita:
 I am Muslim. You are Hindu. In your eyes I see _____. (Beauty)
Anindita to Yasmen:
 I am Hindu. You are Muslim. In your eyes I see _____. (Faithfulness)
Antonia to Allaire:
 I am Buddhist. You are Unitarian Universalist. In your eyes I see_____.
 (Hope)
Allaire to Antonia:
 I am Unitarian Universalist. You are Buddhist. In your eyes I see _____.
 (Contentment)
Lisa to Sarah:
 I am Jain. You are Wiccan. In your eyes I see _____. (Passion)
Sarah to Lisa:
 I am Wiccan. You are Jain. In your eyes I see_____. (Reverence)
Desiree to Jackie:
 I am Christian. You are Jewish. In your eyes I see _____. (Such Love)
Jackie to Desiree:
 I am Jewish. You are Christian. In your eyes I see_____. (Spirit)

In his concluding remarks at the 1998 national gathering, Vincent Harding offered the following reflections in reference to the Beyond Tolerance multi-faith celebration. He said,

> I have a feeling, and I am taking this home with me, that at the multi-faith celebration offered by the students yesterday, we were visiting the future, and the future was visiting us. And as I go home, I am promising myself that I want to be faithful to that vision all the rest of my life.[3]

I feel profoundly blessed to have been a part of this experience and to have been in the company of so many loving, courageous and deeply spiritual people who have been a part of the religious life program at Wellesley. In closing I would like to offer you their names as a way of honoring the sacred work in which they have been and continue to be engaged.

Those members of the Religious Life Team who participated in this project include: Ilene Lerner Bogosian, Rabbi and Hillel director; Cheryl Chip, assistant to the dean; John Culloty, Catholic chaplain; Mary Foulke, Protestant chaplain; Laura Hawes, Buddhist community advisor; Fatimah Iliasu, Muslim advisor; Ji Hyang Sunim, Buddhist community advisor; Gerdes Fleurant, advisor for Native African traditions; Erika Jefferson, Protestant chaplain; Sue Koehler, Catholic chaplain; Katie Krauss, Muslim advisor; Kathe Lewis, assistant to the dean; Nurya Love Lindberg, Unitarian Universalist Chaplain; Judith LoGerfo, associate Catholic chaplain; Stephanie Nichols, Unitarian Universalist Chaplain; Idrisa Pandit, Muslim advisor; Vincent Poirier, Catholic chaplain; Karin Tanenholtz, Unitarian Universalist chaplain; Neelima Shukla-Bhatt, Hindu advisor; Patricia Walton, Protestant Christian chaplain. The student members of the multi-council from 1993–1999 include:

Baha'i: Goly Anvary, Nahz Anvary, Seema Anvary, Crissy Caceres, Colby Lenz, Risa Robinson, Elizabeth Walker

Buddhist: Antonia Bennett, Maura Ginty, Thuy Le, Suzanne Negoro, Bergen Nelson, Mabel Tso

Christian: Therese Anne Collette, Elizabeth Cote, Gwen Davis, Anna Hubbard, Amanda Freeman, Margaret Kowalsky, Jamie Levine, Stephanie Pierce, Kim Priori, Larissa Ranbom, Karin Rollins, Vera Tranlong, Heather Ure, Desiree Urquhart, Shannon Wright

Hindu: Anindita Basu, Renu Bazaz, Varsha Giridharan, Meghanna Hate, Rachana Khandelwal, Shreyasi Lahiri, Viji Natarajan, Supriya Patodia, Nidhi Singh, Priya Talwar

Jain: Kunjal Chaudhari, Lisa Shah

Jewish: Joanna Arch, Tara Feinberg, Stacie Garnett, Jackie Gran, Molly Kaplowitz, Stacey Palestrant, Carolyn Rabin, Lili Schwan-Rosenwald

Muslim: Anjum Ali, Nasrin Al-Dawoodi, Syeachia Dennis, Hina Ghory, Yasmeen Golzar, Asma Hasan, Samar Suehela Fatima Muzaffar, Sophia Queshri, Nadiyah Sayeed, Zeba Siddiqui, Manar Waheed

Native American: Risa Robinson

Sikh: Gagen Khera, Sat Katar Khalsa, Simran Malik

Taoist: Mabel Tso

Wiccan: Christine Brown, Kerry Masteller, Sarah Whedon

Unitarian Universalist: Allaire Diamond, Rachel Johnson, Jennifer Kiest, Eleanor Klieber, Linda Legeyt, Lisa Scanlon

Zoroastrian: Shaan Kandawalla, Rashna Mehta, Tanaz Petigara

ENDNOTES

1. The dialogue portions which appear in this essay are taken from the Beyond Tolerance Workshop which was written by the members of the student Multi-faith Council at Wellesley College (listed above).

2. The "Code of Conduct for Religious Organizations" at Wellesley College explains the responsibilities of religious groups active on the Wellesley College Campus. It can be accessed through the programs web page at www.Wellesley.edu/RelLife

3. Vincent Harding, "Concluding Remarks" National Gathering: EDUCATION as *Transformation*, Wellesley College, Wellesley, Ma., 1998

21.   The Possibility of Transformation:
25 Years Later

DONNA BIVENS

The EDUCATION as *Transformation* conference was held at a significant time for me. First of all, it was held at my alma mater in my twenty-fifth reunion year. Second, it was held during a time when the organization I work for, the Women's Theological Center, was concretizing its new mission: to nourish women's spiritual leadership and communities for liberation movements. These two occurrences in my own life converged to make the conference and my participation in it a time of synthesis and of new understandings about spirituality and education.

Just before a panel in which I was to respond to the comments of Parker Palmer was to begin, an old college friend, Jennifer, came up to me. I had not seen her since we graduated and it was all I could do not to burst into tears. I instantly recalled how close she, Elena (another friend we shared), and I had been. Here was someone I had known so well and loved dearly. And yet, as with all of the white women friends I had had at Wellesley, we had completely lost touch. It was so clarifying for me to begin a talk on spirituality and education with such a vivid reminder of the complexity and fragility of spiritual community across lines of race, class, and culture in the late twentieth century United States.

Our class had entered Wellesley in 1970. My own presence there was a direct consequence of the Freedom Movement of the '50s and '60s. I was part of the second largest class of African American students at Wellesley. For the most part, my spiritual life at Wellesley *was* the African American community there. Together we shared the new experience of substantial and diverse numbers of us having some direct access to the resources of elite white America.

"We" included the students, just about every Black employee at Wellesley, and significant numbers of Black Bostonians who reached out to us. So many worked overtime to create a spiritual shelter for us in our temporary home away from home. We supported each other through family crises and the confusion of growing up away from home. We sang gospel, spirituals, and contemporary message tunes in our choir. We cooked our favorite dishes and braided each other's hair. We explored the wide world together and did what we could to contribute to the liberation movement that was still so alive in African-America. Together we created the environment that made it possible for us to make our education a transformative experience for us. *That* was spiritual community.

But seeing Jennifer reminded me that my spiritual community had also extended beyond that base of support. Like me, Elena and Jennifer were a bit outside the "norm" in the Wellesley environment. Elena was Jewish, from the South, and was very devoted to her religion and heritage. She was a diligent student who had faced more than her share of personal tragedy, which had shaped her into a particularly grounded and deeply compassionate young woman. Jennifer was the daughter of international development workers. She was a devoted Christian with a vision of global social transformation that included ecology, feminism, and economic justice. I was a fairly sheltered young Black girl, openhearted because of how well I had been loved. I was temporarily estranged from the church for many reasons, which propelled me on a spiritual search before I had words for it. On a personal level, there was much to connect the three of us.

My last year at Wellesley, though, I fell into what was described to me by medical professionals as a depression. I did not know how to understand the despair I fell into in my senior year but now—twenty-five years of life later—I am convinced that it was in fact a profound spiritual crisis. It was during that time that Jennifer, Elena, and I grew apart. I retreated into the cocoon of the African-American community. Friends and mentors nursed me through that last year, helped me get my first job, and nudged me over the finish line that was graduation.

With the community I had around me, Wellesley made sense for the first three years. But as I faced my last year and the challenge of integrating my experience there into my life and my life into the world, the meaning came crashing down. This was not a failure of my personal relationships or community. It was my personal reaction to a crisis of the larger society and its spiritual fabric. It took me those full twenty-five years to come to a satisfying understanding of that crisis. That crisis was a blessing because it helped me to clarify my life's work and purpose. The conference 25 years later was a gift. In it I saw the fruits of my alma mater's efforts over twenty-five years to begin to address what it did not even know was missing in 1970.

In the early '70s the school and the society lacked adequate vision, process and structure(s) for providing and nurturing spiritual leadership in diverse new communities. Spiritual leadership flows from a People's deepest values and beliefs. Rosemary and Vincent Harding once described spiritual leadership, in referring to movement leader Ella Baker, as that which helps us to discover our best path, our deepest resources and meets us at the amazing springs of our own spirit. It is difficult enough to nurture in a homogenous community or society. At the Wellesley conference in 1998, many of us shared our efforts to understand how to nurture spiritual leadership by utilizing the level of expertise that already exists in academia for developing intellectual and problem-solving leadership in institutions of higher learning.

A SPIRITUAL FOUNDATION OF FREEDOM AND EQUALITY

A man named Henry Durant founded Wellesley with a clear and noble spiritual agenda for the education of young women. But those young women were for the most part privileged, white, and Protestant. The Freedom Movements of the 1950s and 1960s changed that for the school and the society at large. Before that, only exceptional individuals had the rare opportunity to experience vast boundary-spanning across race, class, culture and spiritual tradition. The Movement ushered in unprecedented meetings and new experiences of shared community, interaction, and direct confrontation for women as peers across difference.

As children of the movements of the '50s and '60s, we were all given a unique opportunity to test and uphold the Movement's spiritual foundation. As African Americans, we came with our own People's vision for our responsibility in upholding that foundation. That vision came out of our particular way and culture, history and understandings, as did those of others.

As a People, African Americans shared one of the longest and deepest commitments to freedom and equality in the history of the United States. Our history compelled us in unique ways to stand firm on those principles politically, and our culture supported us to do so spiritually.

Long after Wellesley, I began doing anti-racism education and training in my work at the Women's Theological Center. When I began, I did not know I carried an assumption that freedom and equality were the priority of all spiritual and moral people. Through my work there I came to an understanding of the possibility of other priorities (e.g. transcendence, dignity, service, righteousness, order or perfection). Those priorities (and others) became like lenses through which different Peoples saw others and each other. I also assumed for many years that there was a shared understanding of what various concepts meant. I learned to recognize the differences in understanding of any given concept again as experienced primarily through spiritual understanding and culture.

Only at the 1998 conference did I fully see the extent to which these assumptions and misperceptions were at the root of my crisis at Wellesley. In many ways, through the conference—and including reconnecting with Jennifer and, weeks later, with Elena—a restoration and healing were completed for me. The conference not only raised the issues of the inadequacies of our resources for providing spiritual leadership and community in higher education, it also offered an opportunity for spiritual leaders in higher education across the country to deepen the sharing and development of solutions.

On a personal level, when I reconnected with Jennifer and Elena, I saw the miracle of spiritual unfolding. Twenty-five years later, I was amazed by how much our lives had paralleled. Across differences of race and spiritual tradition, we *did* share a commitment to freedom and equality and shared many assumptions about what that meant that we had never talked about before.

Our lives took us to similar places: addressing the needs of our families and communities with limited financial and material resources. We led lives and chose work that in some way reflected our yearning for freedom and equality. Jennifer had lived and raised her family in Appalachia. Her work had been tending her family and community—sharing material and spiritual resources with the community that came with her family's privilege as an equal member of that community. Elena had taught children with learning disabilities, a passion that she had since college. And I had spent many years working at the WTC as a part of a community working on the theological education and then the spiritual leadership of women. Jennifer e-mailed me after our reunion:

> Reunion was refreshing and troubling to me. I was blown away, as I have been each time I go to reunion, by the collective power of that gathering of women— smart, capable and successful. But at the same time, coming from where I have been living all these years, I feel strongly the gap between social groups, between the haves and have-nots...how differently the world inhabited by people high on resources or low on them. I thought back in the 70's that we were collectively headed toward a qualitatively different future, one with more equity, appreciation of plurality, etc. Reunion left me wondering. Wishing that in the *next* twenty-five years, our class might make a different kind of difference.

As we shared, I knew that I had reconnected with a "soul sister." Without knowing where each had gone, we had begun in different ways to work toward the same gifts for the world. My reconnection with other Black women had a different quality but the same essence: there was some sense in me that though we had gone in many different directions we had a shared starting place and sense of purpose, an integrity as a group that was our inheritance. But more of a surprise was considering the possibility that *all* of us at Wellesley had been brought together in the early '70s for a purpose. We were each other's resource for realizing our visions in a way that all the differences between us may have made it difficult to realize. I responded to Jennifer:

> Seeing you was a big part of my coming to clarity. I still see and have in my life a few of my Black friends from Wellesley but had lost touch with all white friends. Reconnecting with you erases a sense of profound alienation I had from that wealthy white world because it made me have to remember that I also had some authentic and loving relationships that bridged differences even though I couldn't know that then...(T)his perspective has something to do with my changing perspective on the "haves and have-nots": they/we are more united than they/we seem or sometimes want to admit to themselves/ourselves. We all live in the "income gap" and racial divide as a species and however discrete and separate our groups are, we'll heal together or be lost together.

In our reunion gathering there was an abundance of material, spiritual, and intellectual resources to live our generation's deepest values. With great effort we could perhaps still build the vision, process, and structures to make that "different kind of difference." But maybe too much time had passed with too little honest and sustained sharing across difference for us to actualize this. Still the prospect left me supporting any and all efforts—like the EDUCATION as *Transformation* Project—to reduce such missed opportunities for future generations. To that end my work—like that of the friends-across-difference I made at Wellesley and a large part of the community and People I came from—was and continues to focus on issues of liberation and equality.

DEVELOPING SPIRITUAL LEADERSHIP

The work of making "a different kind of difference" is massive. It involves deeply integrating personal transformation with structural and systemic change in our society. It cannot be done without the development and support of enormous spiritual leadership resources in many individuals and communities throughout our society and our world.

At its heart, African American community has a gift for developing spiritual leadership. It was this gift that delivered me to Wellesley College from my basically all-Black upbringing. White America, as I experienced it, had a gift for what I have come to see as problem solving or, more recently, what Ron Heifetz calls adaptive leadership.

In traditional white institutions like Wellesley, the primary educational model was geared toward developing excellent problem-solving or adaptive leadership. Students were educated to take their place in society and to take on roles of leadership in which they managed and directed others to meet the challenges of that society. On the periphery, chapel or certain committed individuals nurtured spiritual leadership. But it was clear that the work of discovering one's spiritual bottom lines, one's path, and one's gift to society were primarily the responsibility of each individual and not so much the community at large. The vast majority of structural and institutional support went to preparing students to fill problem-solving/adaptive leadership roles and developing the skills and knowledge for them to do so.

In his book *Leadership without Easy Answers*, leadership development Harvard educator Ronald Heifetz confesses:

> Because we are not used to distinguishing between leadership and authority, the idea of leadership without authority is new and perplexing. As a result, the person without authority gets few relevant pointers from scholarship. Analysts have generally neglected the distinctive problems and opportunities of mobilizing work from positions of little or no authority.

I would extend this observation to mainstream institutions of higher learning. The art of teaching students to harness the leadership that comes from their deepest wellsprings has lagged behind the imparting of more technical or intellectual knowledge in traditional white institutions. It was assumed that the "authority" would be forthcoming to one with the appropriate expertise and position.

As a consequence of history in this country and African-derived culture, this was just the opposite in African America. As individuals, it was rare for African Americans to be able to have the luxury of being endowed by society with an authority that would legitimate our leadership. African American institutions—especially churches, extended families, and schools—were masterful in the art and technology of inspiring spiritual leadership. This was not a leadership of roles. It was expressed in action and expected not just of the few elites bound for leadership but of all.

"A different kind of difference" will require that educational institutions be better able to develop spiritual leadership and to integrate it with problem-solving leadership. Through conversation, reading, and personal reflection, I have begun to try to identify some of the differences between the two:

> Problem-solving leadership isolates and focuses on leadership in those individuals who stand at the head of "the masses" to lead or manage them. Spiritual leadership is found in everyone. It grows out of one's sense of belonging to, having a place in, and responsibility for a particular culture, history, and/or community/People.

> Problem-solving leaders are judged effective by how they identify, diagnose, and treat issues or problems while spiritual leadership focuses more on holding to intention, purpose, and values.

> Problem-solving leadership models focus on resilience, strategizing, and autonomy to maximize the power and influence of the individual leader. With spiritual leadership, each individual is a sample of the whole—a drop of its ocean, a ray of its sun. Its expression is an ecological endeavor—it is about the tending of the whole.

> Problem-solving leadership models see "the problem" as an attack at best and an invasion at worst. Spiritual leadership looks at "the problem" as a demand to expand our spiritual understanding and deepen our value system.

> Problem-solving leadership models often posit death or "assassination" as failure and the end of effectiveness. Spiritual leadership asks us to see beyond our limited existence.

> As problem-solving leaders we are challenged to perfect our performance in our role. Our spiritual leadership deepens our integrity and our commitment to and expression of our deepest values.

> Problem-solving leadership draws largely on our personal power, talents, and skills. Spiritual leadership is expressed in our development of what Freedom Movement leader Diane Nash termed "agapic energy"—the power of love of humankind and of creation, the force of love.

Spiritual leadership and problem-solving leadership complement each other. They go hand in hand as we work to be in the world in a way that we can be proud of. Young people—and all of us—face crisis when we do not have adequate structures to help us integrate our problem-solving abilities with our spiritual development as we take our place in the world. Our world grows more complex. We face more threats—many of our own creation—to our long-term survival. It is critical that we have more adequate support for developing spiritual leadership across difference to help us articulate, acknowledge, and learn from that difference.

TRANSFORMATION AS EDUCATION

A friend who directs a multi-ethnic African American youth organization was recently describing the difference between the youth who change their behavior and those who actually are transformed through the philosophy their organization imparts and the community it creates. It is a good reminder. Those who tend the spiritual needs of students create an environment for them to commit to their own transformation. It is not simply an individual transformation. It is the transformation of the whole that is the challenge, the transformational gift of a generation.

Changing behavior can be like a seasonal change of clothes. But true spiritual transformation encourages us to know our deepest values and to use our lives to live them. When I think of the "different kind of difference" Jennifer yearns for, it is this transformation that comes to mind. The education imparted in institutions of higher learning brings about transformation to be sure. But at the same time our deepest education comes in tracking our own and our community's transformation. How do we live our beliefs? And how do we inform each other across difference of the consequences of our living when modern life gives us so many opportunities to ignore our shared reality?

In the complexity of diverse communities it is easy to want to leave this learning to chance, to let it unfold as each individual sees fit. But the boldness of movements to promote spirituality in education is that they actually attempt to create environments that foster learning from our own transformation. They offer skills and resources to see beyond the obvious and to survive the pain of what we would rather not acknowledge. They also offer the courage to accept that we do not always know the answer or end up with perfection.

In our work at the Women's Theological Center (especially in doing anti-racism work), we often consider our work on four levels: personal, interpersonal, institutional, and cultural/ideological. While this model was created for understanding political or systemic transformation, it may also offer an outline of the work of spiritual leaders and those concerned with developing spiritual leadership. In fact, as I consider the myriad issues addressed at the conference and in the work of the EDUCATION as *Transformation* Project, this model does offer a picture of the scope of the work those interested in the intersection of spirituality, religious pluralism, and education are beginning to explore.

For those who nourish spiritual leadership in our institutions, perhaps the most obvious work is on the personal level. To develop their spiritual leadership, students need support and resources to make sense of their own particular life situation. This is perhaps the area where there are the most resources available. Spiritual leaders can offer support to understand each journey, to read the text of one's own life. There are many general and specific tools for contemplation, reflection, and transcendence to help face the challenges of growth.

On an interpersonal level, much of the work is about mediating differences, community building, and finding ways to help students get to know themselves, each other, and the mine field of relationship—especially across difference. Through ritual and liturgy, reflection on relationship, study of sacred texts, art and music, we offer students ways to deepen interpersonal relationships.

The less obvious work for spiritual leaders in general and on campus in particular is not in the area of the personal and interpersonal but in the area of systems and structures. We are often called to help students question, challenge and negotiate structures and institutions. This is the hard work that the '50s and '60s liberation movements began and it is in our inability to do it more effectively that I believe we have yet to make the different kind of difference.

In institutions—starting with the ones in which we receive our education—we need courage and support to really examine how and by whom decisions get made and who has access to resources. The degree to which spiritual leaders are willing to lead this discernment process varies but I do believe it is our work. If diversity is represented only tokenistically in terms of decision-making and re-source sharing, we support the status quo and not true transformation. If we have no process across power difference for being accountable to each other economi-cally and politically, we are hardly serious about human equality or liberation.

This part of the work does not get done in talking and reflecting. It is done in the living of our lives—the choices, compromises, and decisions we make around our own spiritual beliefs.

The cultural and ideological piece is equally pertinent to the work of spiritual leaders. This is the work of negotiating standards and norms and naming reality. It is extremely difficult, if not impossible, for institutions founded for and by a ho-mogeneous group to become truly diverse. For this to take place something essen-tial to the original identity must die. No one knows this better than those truly committed to spiritual life because so much of spiritual development involves dy-ing to who we *think* we are.

This is the growing edge for spiritual leaders on campus: to help young people to learn to accept equality and liberation and to find strength in it. Again, this cannot really be done until there is some true diversity because without that as a context you cannot really know the "different" individual.

I taught for many years in the Study/Action program at the Women's Theo-logical Center. Most years we would have one or two Korean women in a largely white group of women from the United States and I truly thought I was learning something about Korean Christian women. But it was only in the year when the group was half Korean and there was a Korean teacher on staff that the culture of the program was significantly transformed. Only then could I really begin to un-derstand some of what I thought I knew from previous years.

Perhaps we will never have such deep diversity in previously homogeneous mainstream institutions. But we will not have a different kind of difference until it is present at all levels in our institutions. The presence of such real difference not only allows us and our students to ask life-generating questions we never knew we had. It also teaches us who we really are, where we come from, and how to have some say in where we might go together.

With attacks on affirmative action and concepts of human equality and with so many policies and systems in place that continue to widen and deepen the in-come gap, the possibilities for freedom and equality won in the movements of the '50s and '60s seem dimmed. In fact, it is only when I ground myself in a spiritual understanding that I really believe the different kind of difference Jennifer yearns for is possible. But then that is where any real movement for human liberation is grounded: in the spiritual.

I recently heard Freedom Movement activist Anne Braden say that there were actually *more* white people actively committed to ideals of the Movement now than there were in the '50s and '60s. And yet, in many ways, the inequalities have grown and many have a sense that little has changed. If the earlier movements for liberation succeeded in igniting a commitment to *struggle* for freedom and equality, this leg of the movement is faced with the challenge to make it real. This calls for deep systemic changes in both individuals and institutions. Many seeds have been planted. Those who fear those changes rip them up, fearing that what they love will be destroyed or what they fear will be put upon them.

The main things we have to fight against to gain our liberation are expressions of fear that transformation is not possible. There are many ways to identify the enemy or problem: as consumer culture, or addiction; as unjust political and economic systems and policies; as evil. However we identify the problem, it becomes increasingly clear that the enemy is not simply out there. It is internal to us because it is systemic; it is ecological.

When I went to the EDUCATION as *Transformation* Conference, held in what I thought to be a most unlikely place (my alma mater), I saw more than 800 people from institutions across the country brought together to ask how we might begin to address our systemic reality. Like the coming together that had happened in my class 25 plus years before, this coming together did not assure that the transformation we yearned for would happen. But what possibilities!

22. Burn the Ark: Kindling the Sacred at the Heart of American Higher Education

Janet Cooper Nelson

In the world of conceptual art, works are created in response to a set of requirements or specifications. Stipulated by the patron or sponsor as the basis for a juried competition or imposed by the artist, the delineation of these modes and intentions is critical to the work's self-explication. In 1996, two large-scale American projects began to emerge less than 35 miles apart that may helpfully be labeled "conceptual art." This contemporary nomenclature labels a concept whose origins can be traced to sources as ancient as the inclusion of design specifications for an ark in God's surprising disclosure to Noah of a coming flood. This essay briefly surveys Providence, Rhode Island's *Waterfire*, a self-consciously conceptual art project, as the basis for proposing that "EDUCATION as *Transformation*" may also be best understood as art, a work of conceptual art whose mythic sources and design specifications continue to be articulated as it is being produced.

Providence, Rhode Island's current renaissance is exemplified in the media by Barnaby Evans' conceptual art installation *Waterfire*. The work itself emerged in stages, first in prototype as part of First Night and then triumphant in a design competition which especially noted its transformation of a set of vestigial granite stanchions, anchored to the bottom of the Providence River. It continues to expand and respond to its setting. A decade of redesign of the Downcity had disclosed the city's original river ways by placing car traffic along only one bank and creating an extended pedestrian way on the other. The old granite highway supports sat protruding from the river like an extra set of molars, or stone pilings for a long-vanished dock to which Noah's mythic ark had once tied up.

The power of Evans' installation in full flame obscures his solution to this straightforward problem but it is the foundation of the entire work. Those granite pylons and an elaborate system of floats and anchors secure more than 60 metal baskets of firewood along the sinews of the Downcity's canal-like river channels and tidal basin. Ignited at sundown and accompanied by the harmonies and dissonances of the ages, these fires summon, comfort, and honor a city that had forgotten that it was named after God. Unprepossessing in daylight, these baskets become the architecture for an urban liturgy, juxtaposing elemental forces of fire and water, interpreting them through ancient melody and memory, evoking campfires, Saracen circles, pyres, Diwali, resurrection vigils, hearths, and covens.

The discourse Evans's fires ignite is societal and personal, and it is becoming perennial. Conversations begin among the strollers and ripple outward into letters to the editor, sermons, therapist appointments, bedsides, and the blank books by which Evans invites the public to sign his work. Neither analysis nor fortnightly lighting diminish *Waterfire's* capacity although its mature form is different than its early light. It draws us—regulars, seasonals, even a handful of naysayers and cynics. This continuing voltage confirms Evans' exceptional capacity, but it is also predicated upon careful methodology. The careful articulation and accomplishment of design requirements infuse *Waterfire's* beauty with durability. Its mystery and popularity have sources, new and primordial. These foundations, informed and intentional, anchor Evans' dazzling accomplishment in its functional capacity to employ the essential granite of an earlier city in the transformational creation of a new one.

The contention that "EDUCATION as *Transformation's*" 1998 startling, singular, autumnal emergence on the academic landscape may best be understood as conceptual art may not at first be compelling enough to warrant the effort required to accomplish this. However, the present need for "EDUCATION as *Transformation*" to define and to articulate its structural capacity and intention within higher education requires a mode of exploration. The breadth of the vision that launched this project was an important element in its initial magnetism. But this strength also set the project at risk. It is easy to imagine the reduction of "EDUCATION as *Transformation*" to a remembered event, a kind of Woodstock, a one-time infusion of energy and hospitality, in brilliant weather, during the reign of a visionary college president.

Understood as conceptual art, the 1998 September, Wellesley-based, national gathering of "EDUCATION as *Transformation*" becomes the first public manifestation of a project begun in 1996, whose fruition and coherence continue to be exhibited and explored in each manifestation. The intelligibility of this coherence in these articulations, not replications, of the design proposal will become the project's signature and perhaps its legacy. The conceptual art model does require the articulation of design requirements but it allows for the project's renderings to accomplish this task in many forms, anticipating this initiative's potential for multiple sites and creators.

The three defining design ideas that animated the first public installation of "EDUCATION as *Transformation*" must now be articulated and examined for their adequacy as the signature of subsequent installations. A rudimentary statement of "EDUCATION as *Transformation's*" design specifications might be rendered as follows: a widening perception within the academy that the almost dogmatic secularism of American higher education is in need of, and will be positively transformed by, an infusion of spiritual energy and conviction; this transformation can and will occur on the landscapes of American higher education only to the extent that it is neither parochial nor dogmatic and is the collective work of the academy's many constituencies, including faculty, administration, trustees, students, and alumni/ae; and finally, that the burgeoning diversity of these constituencies, especially their religious and spiritual convictions, will both strengthen and complicate this needed process of transformation.

These signature principles of "EDUCATION as *Transformation*" now must respond to the challenges of being enacted within the context of higher education which poses several of its own particular design requirements: a normal, if peculiarly academic resistance to change; a complex, volatile, deeply political environment; and a pervasive and cherished academic conviction that each such institution is unique. These contextual constraints, like Evans' granite stanchions, require discrete examination. But these design requirements are also interactive, neither existing in isolation within their campus settings nor within the largest landscape of American higher education. A successful design structure for "EDUCATION as *Transformation*" must work to transform the broadest institutional contexts while being accessible, even inspirational, to individual educators whose vision may be the transformational energy their institutions will require.

These challenges are the analogs within the academy of the Providence River's granite pilings to which Evans' *Waterfire* is anchored. Evans' project cannot be equated with the solution of this design requirement. His work mines mythic sources and observes spiritual, environmental, and ethical principles. But the complexity of Evans' creative process never superseded its structural solutions. The academic community will test "EDUCATION as *Transformation*" no less rigorously. If a design proposal, including its mythic sources and spiritual, environmental, and ethical principles, can be coherently articulated then the academy may be able to engage its structural challenges—an inherent conservatism, a highly-politicized climate, and prized institutional idiosyncrasy—in a process of transformation and rescue itself from the very real threats of dogmatic ideology, compartmentalization, and professionalism. If "EDUCATION as *Transformation*" furthers this process, like *Waterfire*, it will earn an honored name.

A mythic spiritual foundation that may prove useful to this process is found in the story of Noah and the Flood recounted in Hebrew scripture. Consider the following excerpt:

> God said to Noah: An end of all flesh has come before me, for the earth is filled with wrongdoing through them; here, I am about to bring ruin upon them, along with the earth. Make yourself an Ark of gopher wood.... As for me, here, I am about to bring on the Deluge...all that is on earth will perish. But I will establish my covenant with you:... from all living things you are to bring two...to remain alive with you....
>
> The torrent was upon the earth for forty days and forty nights...all that were on firm ground, died. But God paid mind to Noah and all living things...that were with him in the Ark, and God brought a rushing-wind across the earth, so that the waters abated.... God spoke to Noah saying: Go out of the Ark...So Noah went out...according to their clans they went out of the Ark...Noah built a slaughter-site to YHWH...and offered up offerings upon the altar...and YHWH smelled the soothing savor and said... I will never curse the soil again on humankind's account.... My bow I set in the clouds so that it may serve as a sign of the covenant between me and the earth.... I will look at it, to call to mind the age-old covenant between God and all living beings—all flesh that is upon the earth.[1] (*Genesis* 6-8)

God forewarns doom and specifies actions for Noah to take to secure his family's safety and to rescue the animals. Noah's ark is constructed in response to divine design specifications, including dimensions and materials, e.g. gopher wood and pitch. God's instruction demands Noah's response but it also reveals a creative collaboration. The rescue of life which God purposes is coincident with God's determination to destroy life by flood, but is wholly contingent on Noah's response to God's directives. Understood as design requirements of a conceptual art project, Noah becomes the artist, God's warning of destruction with its enclosed plan for rescue is the foundational myth, and the defining environmental, spiritual, and ethical principles are articulated in the gathering and sustaining of such life as the ark can contain.

This narrative's richness and complexity offer real potential as foundational myth for "EDUCATION as *Transformation*." The flood of change that has thoroughly altered the landscape of higher education in the last decades is the most obvious first connection. Themes of devastation and rescue are central, although their facile appropriation might seem to equate massive academic change with catastrophic loss of life, which is offensive at best. Details of Noah's role in this narrative, especially the exercise of his choices, may be the most useful for these purposes. First among Noah's actions is his decision to build the ark and gather family and critters within it. Noah's choice reveals his conviction that the knowledge he has of impending devastation is credible and its source sacred. It is expressed primarily in creation not argument or refutation.

At the conclusion of the narrative the flood recedes, the ark rests, and again Noah acts to create. But his building of a "slaughter site" is baffling. The decision to sacrifice creatures, presumably critical to the replenishing of the environment, seems counter-intuitive and almost defiant of the Divine directive to rescue them. No textual precedent of *burnt* animal sacrifice exists in Genesis to support the contention that what Noah is enacting an antediluvian ritual. His source of dry wood for this sacrificial fire is almost as problematic as the ritual itself. Again the text is silent. But after nearly a year of flooding one is led quickly to the startling thought that the only source of the fuel for this fire is the ark itself. And finally, having enjoyed since childhood the reassurance that God's action of placing a heavenly rainbow confirmed that flood would never again destroy the earth, the text reveals that it is the good-smelling smoke of Noah's sacrifice that prompted the placing of the bow in the clouds, more a colorful string tied around a divine finger that reminds God not to pull the flood trigger.

Maintaining the focus on Noah's actions in this narrative permits a range of interpretative foundations for both the sweeping changes that have already occurred in the academy and those that continue to require transformational response. Initially, this flood/ark narrative seems to be about God's action and human reaction. But closer reading suggests that it is about shared task, human and sacred. It urges an understanding of this historical moment, when a flood of change has swept away the academy's curricular and social foundations, delivering most of our institutions to tasks and locations never imagined, as the product of both sacred and human agency. This conceptual move both clarifies and suggests. If, for example, the academy's contemporary *lingua franca* is compared to Noah's creatures then something remarkable happens aboard the ark. The voices that emerge after the flood speak a new tongue. Antediluvian vocabulary is inadequate, although ark-speak is awkward. Current campus discourse is ark-speak, a vocabulary created to speak about comprehensive change and loss, about uncertainty and vision. The sounds of new canons, feminism, multi-culturalism, globalization, minority recruitment and leadership, religious pluralism, sexual harassment and misconduct, bioethics, appropriate uses of technology, e.g., e-mail, websites, homepages, the Internet, and distance learning, nondiscrimination policies, community service, out-sourcing, hedged portfolios, financial aid, federal funding, indirect costs, soft-funding, lab start-up costs, and of course, post-modernism, refer to realities never known before the flood. The months aboard the ark are gestational and produce new words and understanding.

Unfortunately, the urgency of this discourse drowns most of what was said before. Strains familiar to prior generations, the academy's classical anthems are, at best, arcane or sentimental and, at worst, relics of affiliations to Protestant hegemony, white male privilege, upper middle class values, heterosexism, American imperialism, and environmental abuse. But the new music's arrival is so sudden and normative that almost all that had breath from the former era is drowned out, swept away. Perennial strands of teaching, learning, moral purpose, service and leadership continue. But their tunes sound wistful, bittersweet, reminiscent of songs that might have first been sung on the ark in the first days of rain. But in the long months of waiting for the flood to dissipate the words and tempo changed. Melodies and language for a new age began to emerge.

The hope that inspired the prayers of the sixties for "transformational flooding" in higher education was anchored to high moral purpose, ethical reflection, personal experience. An extension of that generation's suspicion of the military industrial complex and its critique of higher education began in disillusionment but moved to creativity. Disclosure of the connections between university-based research funding and the military-industrial complex heightened suspicion of broad societal and institutional co-optation, sensibilities that were intensified by America's deeply controversial engagement in Vietnam. Even the language of eighteenth-century individualism got nuanced to focus on privacy and autonomy as the highest goods, thereby relegating public life and all things corporate to the realm of tainted.

Beliefs and convictions were no longer referenced to the shared life of communities, but were claimed as radically personal, each the equal of all others: All personal emotional expression must be accorded equal value as a corrective to the era when there was only the privileged expression of the few. While this approach helpfully abrogates hierarchy and argument, it also encapsulates each person within a singular point of view. Deeply and profoundly free of each other, we are also free *from* each other, and free of the need and the possibility of subscribing to each other's realities. The unanticipated side effect of attributing structural sanctity to all individual conceptions of the good is more isolation and loneliness than we ever dreamed. We unwittingly doomed ourselves to endless conversations about community while making it a concept that may not exist in a post-modern world.

The structural change that these philosophical claims produced in universities and colleges was, on balance, more good than bad. Academic institutions self-consciously became the laboratories within which societal transformations were attempted. Creating a coherence of social structure and intellectual theory within the academy was the only protection available against self-accusation of hypocrisy. We stated boldly and enacted our conviction that truly transformational education could neither be taught nor learned within homogeneous, chauvinistic, insular communities. The gates must be thrown open and the world, with all of its issues and peoples, welcomed within. American scourges would require energetic and immediate attention. Racism's tangled roots, religious and cultural bias, and socioeconomic bigotry mocked higher education's rhetoric about meritocracy, rendering it hollow and cynical. Access to these gated communities, which were then not need-blind but rather where success was predetermined by class, gender, race, and orientation, had to be altered. Plans were made and implemented. Ark construction began. The demise of higher education as it had existed for generations was anticipated eagerly. Without spoken consciousness of the myth, we empathized with YHWH's justification for the flood "that the earth is filled with wrongdoing through them." We knew who "they" were. The change necessary to produce truly good institutions, while vast, was possible. Radicality was good and the academy, in the name of all that is good, would create it.

But this moment of educational radicality and creation is neither the first such occasion nor will it likely be the last. Consider this historical observation about the preceding century by the current president of Wellesley College, Diana Chapman Walsh:

> ...Institutions of higher learning did split off almost entirely from their religious roots, did split the head from the heart. This split occurred gradually and without much fanfare, first to accommodate science, later diversity. Both of these stories were played out against a wider socioeconomic backdrop of industrialization, cultural modernization, professionalization of American society.
>
> Out of those forces emerged our secular national culture, which gradually eclipsed religious and spiritual perspectives almost completely in the academy. Professional scholars felt acutely the need to be autonomous and free to pursue their casual chains wherever they might lead, to seek truth through confirmation rather than revelation. And those of us who have made our lives in the academy do treasure the refuge this pure sphere offers us. . . .
>
> But we paid dearly for our freedom.... The price was a great suspicion, not only of organized religion, but more broadly of the spiritual dimensions of teaching, learning, knowing, a great fear of granting that we have a place of knowing that comes directly from the heart and the soul—not instead of the intellect; we exist to nourish that, but in addition to the intellect in all its beauty and power.... The impulse toward great inclusion ironically spawned a new form of exclusivism,

conflating non-belief with academic freedom, substituting freedom from religion
for freedom of religion, and sweeping all things spiritual in its wake.[2]

The radicality of academic secularism which Chapman Walsh describes
emerged for the good purpose of ameliorating the effects of parochialism and dogmatism on intellectual inquiry. Its design, first at the urging of the scientific
community, was taken up again in the 1960s as a creative and urgent response to a
new allegation: "higher education" was inextricably linked to the process of accul-
turation to upper middle class, white, Protestant Christian, male sensibilities. So
embarrassing and indicting was this contention that academic faculties reacted
radically again. They worked to create distance in language, institutional culture,
and the methodology of their disciplines from anything that could be termed religious and spiritual. Individual institutional stories of these transformations are particularly instructional for observing the process of "airbrushing" that was employed
to produce the current visage of academic secularity. Once largely the creation of
the devout, the academy established new and important openness and minimal
pluralism. But it simultaneously lost any voice with which to demonstrate, to describe, or to discuss the religious and spiritual dimensions of its work or its community.

Seasons and time shift. It may be that the secularism which rescued us from
one form of dogmatism has become its own doctrinal box. The preferential juxta-
position of the secular against the sacred is now spoken of as though it proves the
presence of research-like dispassion. The delineation of the scholarly as secular
has become synonymous with the sacred and the spiritual being distortions of academic clear-sightedness. Maintenance of the distance between the scared and secular
is equated with the maintenance of academic integrity. But the parameters of these
spaces remain undefined save for the almost universal academic prohibition against
invoking or evoking the authority of the sacred in the academy in anything other
than personal terms. Clearly, our knowledge of the space between the sacred and
the secular needs more recognition of complexity. The irrational resistance to discourse about such exploration as authentic scholarly endeavor is the surest confirmation that these currents of opinion are not emanating from cool climes of rational objectivity. If they are an expression of belief, then the academy needs to create again the environment within which doctrine, even secularism, does not distort
the contours of learning. The political challenges of such creativity are vast.

The swirling currents of academic politics are both product and evidence of
massive change on campus. The doctrinal claims of Christianity no longer norm
academic discourse, but in their place treacherous currents of opinion and structural methodology dominate disciplinary and institutional conversation. These forces
are rarely discussed as topics themselves. But they wreak havoc, prompting the
swift ascent of people and priorities while causing others to plummet to obscurity.
Formed as ideas and ideologies, these forces surge and swirl around the academy's
ivy-covered traditions of erudition and stability. Architects and critics alike ride
these currents like surfers on an invisible ocean. This pastime, a truly odd sport,

garners most of the media's coverage of higher education and can be simultaneously perilous, silly, lucrative, and occasionally productive. The academic establishment eyes these developments with sadness, resignation, and disdain, sure that all that they have known as the academic enterprise is being swept away. From this perspective, scholarship's measured analysis, discourse, and civility are replaced with acrimonious dispute, egomania, entrepreneurialism, and identity politics.

Perhaps it is useful to suggest that this era in the academy resembles others that have preceded it and that have been considered briefly in this essay. The creation necessary to relieve the tensions will be yet another manifestation or articulation in a vast "EDUCATION as *Transformation*" conceptual art project. This suggestion provides perspective and locates the more immediate work of "EDUCATION as *Transformation*" within a broader historical context. This work will best be accomplished by returning to the mythic foundation of the Noah text for one final consideration. The details in the concluding segment of the flood story hold an important clue. Noah's action to create a "slaughter site," to choose several pure animals from among the rescued, and to offer burnt offering to YHWH startles. But the narrative reveals that so pleasant is the heaven-arriving smoke of this ritual that YHWH proposes an eternal covenant with humanity and chooses a dazzling symbol by which both heaven and earth will be reminded.

The rainbow promise of God may well bring comfort amid the floods of change in higher education, but for purposes of this essay I direct your attention to the collaboration that ensues between God and humanity, apparently inspired by Noah. The text does not reveal his thinking but we know that this is the first evidence in Genesis of animals offered as *burnt* sacrifice and that it is Noah's first act on dry ground. He is apparently creating new ritual. The smoke of this act recommends to YHWH some of humanity's better aspects and re-awakens a tenderness toward earth. However reassuring to us, the promise of the bow in the heavens seems primarily to remind YHWH that we are worth saving. It is Noah's action that prompts God's; a collaboration of the human and the divine is forged to secure a sacred promise to sustain life. Human proposal secures sacred blessing.

Noah's choices could certainly be reviewed by the Trustees of the Ark and determined to be risky, ill-advised, not in keeping with the fiduciary role of the Board. After ten months of keeping a whole range of animals alive, the wisdom of reaching dry land and choosing to kill any of them is certainly worthy of question. Beyond the question of the wisdom of this action, a second query emerges. Where did Noah find dry wood for his fire after all that rain? If the answer to this query is that the ark itself becomes the fuel, Noah's judgment seems questionable. To be sure the Noah/flood narrative is not one about reasonableness, human or divine. It is a story of extremes of every sort. But amid all the turmoil one structure, made with his own hands, the ark, had been a constant for Noah. The choice to burn it is extraordinary, even if it is the only dry wood. The picture of this moment is not that of a bonfire. But it is one of profound faith. The constructs and sources of safety of Noah's age are ignited, risked, burned, to create the liturgies of the new age. So powerful is this action that divine blessing ensues directly.

Although bonfires of change have consumed much of the past practice of the academy, it is not fire and destruction that this mythic foundation for "EDUCA-TION as *Transformation*" suggests. We are summoned instead to examine what it is we clutch tightly for security and definition in the world of the academy and to consider using it to fuel the fires of change. This is enormously risky work and we will need to be quite patient with one another. Survivors of the flood are necessarily relics from a prior era as well as architects of the new. Can we, should we, trust ourselves as products of an earlier educational era to articulate design principles for transformation that are adequate to the structural requirements of a new era?

Although our collective difficulties are not solved by conceptualizing "EDUCATION as *Transformation*" as art, the proposal does provide us an identity as an artists' collaborative that has recently begun to meet more regularly both to critique and to create. The reason we ever met one another in the context of "EDU-CATION as *Transformation*" is that we were those who recognized this concept and are committed to this idea in some form. Our collective difficulty has been that our attempts to exercise this perspective are often not endorsed and have even been actively or passively rejected. The sufferings and failings we have felt and observed cannot be minimized. It has been water in a dry place for us to discover one another and to come together if only for a day or so. But our task both at home, nationally, and even globally remains before us.

It is highly unlikely that from within or beyond the academy the idea of education as transformation will meet real opposition. Dismissal is far more likely. This initiative, which received broad initial interest from the academic community, could easily evaporate, another blip on the radar screen of educational chic and multi-culturalism. "EDUCATION as *Transformation's*" provision of a refuge for an array of interrelated issues attracted the beleaguered, provided validation, and officially launched a broad national discourse. Presidents, deans, faculty, chaplains, and students came in droves. This charmed infancy of the project offers some protection from the infamous razor of academic dismissal. But this breathing-room must neither be squandered nor expected to endure. Both at home and in the national initiative the challenge to articulate a clear broad purpose for "EDU-CATION as *Transformation*" remains essential. The withering judgment contained in the simple phrase, "It's not altogether clear what 'EDUCATION as *Transformation*' is about," is a threat with substance. Artists together, we must rally around our work.

The autumn gathering on a gorgeous New England campus in 1998 will remain dear, even defining. Our emergent concept, however, must be made of "sterner stuff," intelligible, available to those who never knew such a gathering occurred, and it must certainly not be celebrity culture. As conceptual art, "EDUCATION as *Transformation*" will draw its form from the collective energy, insight, and animation of its artists. It will be many centered, and needs to meet the installation requirements of widely varied academic settings. But if the fires of transformation can ignite the spiritual dimensions of academic institutions across the nation, then the synergy of these artists and their work will be more broadly seen. It is also possible that "EDUCATION as *Transformation*" will be primarily a date and place, a transforming recollection. Human sight alone cannot make the determination between these two possibilities. But Noah's example suggests that humanity's role in securing divine blessing is neither passive nor strictly speaking obedient. Our role toward the sacred must be propositional risk-taking. The fuel for the fires of such risk will be of the dearest sort, difficult to conceptualize, and harder still to risk. But the purpose and promise of the beauty that may yet emerge within America's communities of higher learning is beyond our telling and worth our finest effort. Over the shoulders of those who are born on the ark we glimpse not only the future but eternity. What is such vision worth?

ENDNOTES

1. *The Five Books of Moses,* Everett Fox, trans. *The Schocken Bible*: Volume I (London: Word Publishing, 1995), 35–42 excerpts.
2. Diana Chapman Walsh, "Welcoming address" National Gathering: EDUCATION as *Transformation*, Wellesley College, Wellesley, Ma., 1998

23. Building a Multi-faith Center at MIT

ROBERT M. RANDOLPH

This is the story of how the Religious Activities Center at the Massachusetts Institute of Technology was created. The Center represents the culmination of a process that began after World War II. The building is a modest reminder that religion plays a role in the education of young men and women at MIT, as it does elsewhere. It is also a reminder that a thoughtful plan well executed can bring results. In addition, the building, which is dedicated space for Muslims, Christians, and Jews, is a visual statement illustrating how the student community has changed since the post-World War II generation returned to the university. From this story I hope others can learn how they might create similar space.

THE POST-WORLD WAR II ERA

James R. Killian became the president of MIT in 1949. He was chosen because it was clear that he had the skills needed to lead the Institute in the halcyon years after the war. He had been exercising leadership in the absence of Karl Taylor Compton who was away fighting the war. Duke University recognized Killian's skills and asked him to become their president. The MIT Corporation responded by persuading Killian to stay at MIT.

Killian led MIT through difficult years. He was an unlikely candidate for a presidential post. He was not a scientist or an engineer. Instead, he was a graduate of the business program that would become the core of the Sloan School of Business. He did not have a graduate degree. The late Kenneth Wadleigh, former dean of the Graduate School, remembered that he was "viewed by many as a lightweight. They were wrong, but that was the way they felt at the beginning."

One of Killian's first tasks was to respond to what has come to be called *The Lewis Report*. Released in 1949, this lengthy report to the faculty reevaluated the MIT process of education, laid the foundations for a new School of Humanities and Social Sciences, and gave Killian the chance to put his stamp on the institution as no president has before or since.

Central to that report was the view that we should be able not only to create new science and to innovate technology but also to relate them to human values and aspirations; that we should have a certain responsibility for forecasting the impact of scientific and technical developments on society; and that we should learn how to manage the new technologies in a humane fashion.

For James Killian the legacy of the war and the powers it unleashed meant that people in the university needed spaces where they might reflect on what they were doing with their education. He envisioned a facility that "a distinguished physicist from Cambridge University who was to lecture to our community would find pleasant and satisfying as a place to present a formal address...where the London String Quartet could appropriately play. It should also be a place where a distinguished minister might hold religious services."[2] Such a building was to be "The Meetinghouse of MIT," words now etched in the arch at the entry to Kresge Auditorium. In addition, Killian also began to think of a small chapel where weddings, baptisms, and memorial services might be held.

Killian was a committed Unitarian whose broad church vision informed many of his actions. A Christian, he believed that the era demanded new attention to the things of the spirit and to a new set of questions. He intended to educate a "new man." Killian was responsible for building Kresge Auditorium and the MIT Chapel. They opened in 1956 and established new precedents because the spaces were designed to be used by each religious community on campus that wished to use them. During this same period, Brandeis University built three chapels, one each for Catholic, Protestant, and Jewish use. Harvard was rethinking the use of Memorial Church.

Hopes were high at MIT; there was even talk of creating the position, Dean of the Chapel. Ultimately, however, once the buildings were built, little else happened. President Killian had deferred other construction to build these two important structures, both of which created controversy within and without the MIT community.

The chapel was called the "Gas Can on the Charles" by those offended by its unconventional design. The wags noted that MIT was the only university in the country to build a chapel and then put a moat around it. The comment was uncharacteristically ill-informed given that the water around the MIT Chapel was, in fact, a reflecting pool designed to cast light into the sanctuary.

There were other setbacks. In his dedicatory address, Sebastian Kresge, the Presbyterian layman from Detroit who funded both buildings, tried to sell the virtues of abstinence from alcohol. This served to underscore for the audience the perils of religious extremes.

Killian's dreams for MIT and the education of the "new man" were not realized. Following the launch of Sputnik in 1957, Eisenhower invited Killian to come to Washington as his science advisor, the first to fill such a role. He embarked on a long career in helping to establish national science policy and in the founding of the Public Radio and Television network. One might argue that the Cold War took many casualties, not the least of which was Killian's program for religious life at MIT.

RELIGIOUS LIFE PROGRAMS

The period after World War II was a time when returning veterans changed the shape of American higher education. They came back from war idealistic, dreaming great dreams. This idealism informed the careers of many of those who became campus ministers and chaplains in the 1950s. Many members of that generation may also now, in fact, be in a position to help fund multi-faith programs and facilities.

There are those who might argue that the Civil Rights Movement and the Vietnam War protests marked a more appropriate cache of idealism. However, the rancor that dogged the war protests has in some places left a bitter legacy. As a matter of fact, some university administrators remember the role played by chaplains during the Vietnam era and, because of their strong, negative memories, defer efforts to deal with today's campus religious realities.

As the Cold War began to wane, MIT turned again to questions related to student life. Nineteen eighty ushered in a period of introspection and reorganization. As a reflection of the fact that MIT was changing in significant ways, the Office of the Dean of Students was reorganized. MIT had been coeducational since its founding, but it had remained predominantly male. The number of women was slowly increasing and by the end of the century the numbers would approach parity in the undergraduate community. The Institute recognized a subtle shift in student housing preferences. An article of faith during the 1970s was that students wanted coeducational housing. Therefore, MIT had developed many coeducational housing opportunities. However, a lot of women did not wish to live with men even if appropriate spaces were available. This was certainly true for large numbers of international women. Many Muslim women, for example, do not shake hands with men much less share even approximate living space.

Since 1956, women had been offered single sex housing in McCormick Hall (named after Katherine McCormick, a leader in the early feminist movement). With the growing number of women wishing single sex housing, McCormick was not adequate. Residential sororities and an independent living group had taken some of the pressure off the residential system but it was clear that more space for women was needed. The space then housing the chaplains was a prime target for conversion.

The number of minority students was also increasing, as was the international population. The Institute, for example, had a growing population of Muslim students. National and international conflicts with Iran and Iraq drove home the fact that there was much we did not understand about our student body.

The increasing number of Muslims on campus made it feasible to propose and provide a prayer room for this community. In an environment that prided itself on being organized around science and engineering, such attention to religious matters was unusual. At a time when serious conversations about diversity were beginning, it became increasingly clear that the greatest diversity on campus was among religious groups. On any given weekend, for example, the Catholic community brought together people from across the globe in a worship setting. Muslims gathered daily for prayers. Hillel was also multicultural.

During the 1980s, in addition to religious traditions from other countries, new homegrown religious groups had appeared on campus. Some stayed while others disappeared; those already here continued to grow. Hillel and the Lutheran-Epis-

tunities this presents is critical if the case for multi-faith space is to be made in a convincing fashion.

Second, *diversity that is not experienced is not real diversity.* If religious communities were operating in ghettos either by choice or because of institutional ignorance, an educational opportunity was being missed. What opportunities did Muslims and Jews have to even notice one another much less interact with one another? What about the opportunities of mainline Christian communities to interact with their counterparts in the para-church communities? The resistance to shared space was in fact most articulately raised by student Christian groups that did not want to risk being paired with other mainline religious bodies. Jews and Muslims welcomed the opportunity to be near the heart of the Institute and Kosher dining opened possibilities for both groups.

Third, we assumed at the outset that we would have conflict. We knew that having the Muslim Prayer Room and the Hillel Library next to each other meant that Jews might trip over shoes left in the hall leading to the library. We did not, however, expect such scenes as these: a cab driver rushing to pray inadvertently blocking the Rabbi's car as the Rabbi sought to catch a ferry taking him to Martha's Vineyard and his Sabbath responsibilities; student Christian groups hanging a large poster of Jesus where only they and the Jewish students could see it. What we did want to happen was that the community would recognize that the Prayer Room served the wider Boston/Cambridge community. What we discovered is that *conflicts represent opportunities for growth in understanding and that shared space means potential conflict.*

Fourth, we believed that ample space for preparing and serving meals would lead to shared religious and dining experiences that would ease tensions between groups that would otherwise seldom interact. In theory, both Muslims and Jews have dining needs that are different from the community at large *and shared dining opportunities are a possibility that will lead to fruitful interaction if we are wise enough to provide the resources needed.*

Finally, *those involved in developing shared space must understand at the outset that they might be learning as much as they are teaching. They must be conduits of information and insight to the larger community they serve.* It is well known that American higher education is an international enterprise, but few recognize what this means in religious terms.

We have made progress but we have a long way to go. Evidence of progress includes a recent Holy Cross Day when Episcopalians and Lutherans were displaying various forms of the cross while Jewish students were preparing their kosher supper and Muslims were taking off their shoes prior to prayer. Each group gingerly avoided interrupting those going to and from the other gatherings. These simple afternoon activities illustrate what we wanted to accomplish on our campus: we wanted people to recognize one another and respect differences in a context where genuine learning can occur.

This fall we will have a freshman seminar on the Abrahamic Faiths and MIT, which prides itself on training leaders for the new millennium, will begin to build a corps of young people who can understand and talk to one another about a range of religious matters. Given the human propensity for tolerating evil made all too real these last years in Africa and the Balkans, our intentions may seem to some too little too late.

One day, across a table where there is potential conflict, we believe that our students who become leaders of their respective communities may remember one another from their years in Cambridge. They may remember conversations over meals shared or words exchanged as they met their religious obligations. We believe that multi-faith space makes possible these dreams and that, in our time, this may be the best way to give peace a chance.

ENDNOTES

1. Paul Gray, *The Report of the President* (1979)
2. James R. Killian to R.M. Kimbull, 3 October 1950. Institute Archives AC 4, Box 32.

24. Notes from a Jewish Dean of Religious Life: On Moving from Religious Diversity to Religious Pluralism

SUSAN LAEMMLE

On the evening of April 14, 1999—the day after Yom Hashoah (Holocaust Remembrance Day), barely a week after Passover's conclusion and on the 13th day of counting the Omer toward Shavout (Pentacost)—I, Rabbi Susan Laemmle, dean of Religious Life at the University of Southern California, hosted a dinner for some 30 Muslim leaders. The guest list included dignitaries from local mosques and Islamic organizations as well as leaders of USC's three Muslim student groups. The vegetarian menu softened the likely requirement for halal meat, had meat been served, while also supporting my own pattern of avoiding non-kosher meat. The Imam who blessed the meal did so in a manner that comfortably included me and the other two non-Muslims present—an associate dean of Student Affairs and USC's executive vice-provost, to whom I report. By coincidence, or providence, all three of us are Jewish.

What my assistant and I refer to as "the Muslim dinner" probably represents the riskiest thing I have done in nearly three years as dean of Religious Life. Bringing together such an assembly of Muslims had been my own idea, not something suggested by others. In the weeks between setting the date and the event itself, there were many moments that led me to question my good sense and to accuse myself of overweening pride. Who, after all, was I to bring the Muslims together, especially when they increasingly revealed themselves to be every bit as contentious and complex a community as is my own Jewish one?

The history of USC's Muslim dinner goes back at least several years, back to a time before I took up my position as dean of Religious Life. Serving as director of the Hillel Jewish Center at USC, I was freshly returned from several years in Israel where I had been active in the peace movement in a more immediate manner than is possible here in the United States. Returning to Los Angeles with a deep yearning to continue working toward peace in the Middle East, I soon saw that my best contribution could come through bringing together Jews and Muslims on campus. And so I created a group called AMJID—Arabs, Muslims, and Jews in Dialogue—which offered participants a facilitated opportunity to learn about another religious civilization while forming personal relationships with fellow students who belonged to it.

I pause to notice the way in which I have taken the history of the Muslim dinner all the way back to my time in Israel, the way I have acknowledged that personal biography influenced my professional decision to mount a campus program. What will be made of such subjectivity, such blurring of realms which the academy, like American society as a whole, prefers to keep distinct? Two levels of answer come in reply to my self-posed question. On the meta-level comes the realization that it is precisely this sort of subjectivity that contributes to a vision of education as transformation. This is to say, a good part of what it means to make education a search for meaning as well as a source of knowledge depends upon academics, students, and professors alike bringing their whole selves into the educational encounter. The current state of fragmentation in higher education derives in no small part from the way in which individual teachers and learners are split into their intellectual, physical, psychological, and spiritual aspects.

Important as it may be to resist such fragmentation, it feels odd to be bringing my personal history and commitments into a serious essay—just as it felt awkward, and even frightening at times, to plan an event where the degree and complex quality of my personal investment rendered me particularly vulnerable. Clearly, I needed to remain self-aware from beginning to end; to keep touching base with my motives and my limitations as the process evolved.

And so I did, and continue doing, as the dinner's ripples spread. For the first time in USC's history, our roster of religious directors includes someone whose title is "Sheik." Where past advisors to the Muslim student groups have come and gone, Sadullah Khan's being supported by the Los Angeles Islamic Center enables him to be on campus at least half time. Negotiating his way with student leaders who cherish their autonomy, he is making himself invaluable in support of their interests and in representing Islam within the overall campus environment. The next step will be to garner sufficient Muslim support to open an office within the University Religious Center where groups have traditionally "paid their own way." As Sadullah works to galvanize such support, I, as dean of Religious Life, encourage but do not push, offer advice but take pains not to be in the lead or take over. We Jews call this way of operating *Tzimtzum*, taken from the Kabbalistic idea that God, as it were, pulled back from divine omnipresence and omnipotence when creating a world in which freedom could flourish.

In considering how religious diversity can evolve into religious pluralism, my dwelling at such length upon the Muslim dinner provides a concrete instance. There are others. My proudest achievement in three years as dean of Religious Life has been helping to create USC's first ever Hindu Student Organization. A short month after the dinner, we managed to launch the first viable Buddhist student group, there having apparently been overtures in the past which had been blessed by the chaplain but not massaged into actualization. Gradually, the "patent" for launching a new student group has become clear: find at least one strong student leader, put that person together with a member of the university faculty or staff or an outside clergyperson or community leader, and invest some of the Office of Religious Life's budget in advertising and food for an opening event which I, as dean, attend and bless. And then, stay loosely in touch with the group through their e-mail network to have a sense of how they are proceeding and especially to keep offering encouragement to the student leaders.

USC's Hindu Student Organization just completed its first full year, electing an impressive slate of officers for 1999-2000. Not coincidentally, this year's baccalaureate speaker—selected by me and confirmed by the president and provost—is a scholar of Hinduism and world religions whom I heard speak at one of the Hindu group's meetings. Needless to say, the students are proud to have their faith represented in the baccalaureate setting, a setting which still fits into a Judeo-Christian worship mode but which is being slowly stretched to accommodate the new religious reality.

It is that reality, the reality of multi-religious diversity, that spurs me on as dean of Religious Life, certainly. But my being Jewish, instead of Protestant as were my chaplain predecessors, plays a role. Like my personal investment in the Muslim dinner and my subjective experience within this very essay, the ways in which my being Jewish affect my functioning as dean need to be carefully monitored. There is no substitute for self-awareness and self-restraint when handling religious diversity and especially when moving beyond it to religious pluralism.

Let me, then, recount the history of our Hindu Student Organization, a history where my own Jewishness played a small but probably decisive role. New on the job as dean, I noticed that there wasn't a Hindu group on the roster of student organizations and placed the possibility of creating one on one of my many back burners. Then it happened that the university received an angry call from Hindu parents whose daughter had joined one of our many Christian groups, and their complaint eventually wound up on my desk—which is precisely where it belonged. After speaking with the angry parents by phone, I then spoke and met with their daughter as well as with the religious director whose group she was in. In the process, I learned that, rather than having been swept away from her roots at USC, the young lady had been on a Christian path since high school. Meeting with her enabled me to determine that her commitment was carefully considered, very solid, and fundamentally healthy. Still, as I said to the parents during our initial conversation, my heart ached for them in a way that only someone who belongs to another "minority religion" could feel. While respecting and indeed defending their daughter's right to shape her own religious world, I also registered deep inside what it would feel like to have one of my daughters leave Judaism.

This edge of personal investment enabled me to respond to the parents with particular empathy, but I took care that it not blind me to the student's sincere commitment to her new faith. Given Jewish history, spotted with instances of pressured conversion to Christianity, this was not easy. In order to be scrupulously fair, I needed to do what I keep needing to do to be an effective dean of Religious Life: digging deeper into my own Jewish wellsprings and also tapping into the sources of universal spiritual essence.

As my mother, who is 83, says about old age, "This is not for sissies." Considering that the United States is still primarily a Christian country, it has to be easier for a Christian to fill the university chaplain/dean of Religious Life slot. Considering numbers alone, a school like USC has far more Christian students and many more Christian religious groups than those of any other tradition. It must also be noted that Christian students and their groups are most likely to engage in proselytizing; most likely to, as we say, "push the envelope" in terms of campus presence and recruitment. Thus it is that a dean of Religious Life who is not Christian—even more, a dean who is Jewish—must keep steady watch on ancestral angers and suspicions while fulfilling the religious needs of both the Christian and non-Christian students: all this, while also managing to hold fast to personal integrity and religious identity.

Just barely managing such juggling when dealing with the Hindu parents and their Christian daughter, I emerged with the daughter grateful and the parents still, despite my best efforts, angry. While it would have been nice to gain their approval, my sense of professional accomplishment did not depend upon that. Indeed, it has become clear to me that being able to navigate the waters where family, religion, and student autonomy all swim virtually requires the peculiar mix of experience and education gained through a good seminary. As I quipped to the provost during the period of daily conversations with the Hindu parents, surely my USC salary for the entire year was being earned through that one encounter. There is simply no substitute during this and other delicate confrontations for being not only someone with graduate education, but someone who knows what it feels like (not just what it means) to take religion seriously.

My Jewish seriousness made the transfer in both Hindu and Christian directions. And yet, something was left wanting and that something is what energized my work toward creating our new Hindu Student Organization. With plenty of tasks to keep me busy, I nonetheless experienced a new urgency, an urgency that led me to move the Hindu project from its back burner. Once on a mid-level burner, the idea of creating a Hindu group hovered in my consciousness sufficiently that it enabled me to decode the signal emanating from the young woman who later became the Hindu Student Organization's founding president. Priya presented herself at the Religious Life table during the Activity Fair portion of summer orientation for new students. After surveying the listing of student groups in our Religious Opportunities at USC brochure, she let pass over her face a look of disappointment, perhaps even a look of pain.

Surely, it was the God who created us all, the God to whom all religions turn, who helped me to spot and understand that look. And it was my training as a teacher, as well as my experience as a parent, that helped me frame my understanding in a way that respected her privacy: "Are you finding the group in which you are interested listed in our brochure?" I inquired somewhat disingenuously, for she looked Indian. From that inquiry and her answer, it was only a matter of time until the organizing meeting of the USC Hindu Organization. Priya needed to matriculate and get settled, during which time she established contact with a distinguished engineering professor who had agreed to serve as advisor to Hindu

students. That professor had come to my attention through what began as a negative interaction: he wrote to the provost about the listing of religious occasions
distributed by the university, criticizing the list's exclusion/omission of Indian holidays. Very new on the job as dean, I was asked by the provost to handle the matter
and, thank God, I had the wit to remain undefensive when I spoke and then later
met with the professor. When the time came to form a Religious Life Advisory
Committee, I invited him to join the group. And so it is that a man whose religious-
ethnic background had clearly generated some feeling of alienation from the university—otherwise he would not have disputed the Provost's memo—moved from
the periphery to the center of campus religious life, taking his place as a contribut-
ing and valued member of a newly pluralistic religious reality.

Knitting back to the beginning of the Hindu story, we see that the protesting
parents have not been personally helped by the new Hindu Student Organization;
indeed, knowing of its existence might well increase their anger and sadness. I,
too, feel sorry that their daughter had to leave her ancestral fold in order to experience a sense of spiritual community and a sense of God's presence—not because I
prefer Hinduism to Christianity, but because I value the way in which religion can
be passed on from generation to generation within a family, binding that family
together and knitting it into a larger fabric. To continue the fabric metaphor, since
to my mind each of the world's religions forms a section of the universal quilt, it
seems best when each individual takes up their sewing in the square to which their
parents introduced them.

Of course, that way of handling things religious applies only when other things
are equal, which they often are not. In order that religious practice avoid becoming
sheer formalism and in order that it meet people's spiritual and moral needs, individuals must find a path that supports their own personal way of walking. I am
convinced that the multiplicity of religions must be God's will and that all paths
will eventually be revealed to be the same broad highway. However, at this point
in human evolution, particular paths suit particular people along their life's journey. Indeed, my experience with people of diverse religious commitments leads
me farther and farther in a resolutely pluralistic direction.

Being pluralistic may come more easily to a Jew than, say, a Christian. For the
Jewish People has always seen itself as one people among others, chosen for special responsibilities according to the traditional view, but also held to moral account in the same way, following Amos, as Edom and Moab and Egypt. Moreover,
the early rabbis bequeathed to us the oft-quoted assertion that "the righteous of all
the nations have a place in the world to come." It seems clear to me that when
one's respect for other religious traditions does not have to jockey with a belief
that those traditions cut their adherents off from salvation, genuine respect and
earnest pluralism are more easily achieved.

Nonetheless, even then many of us find that forging a theory and a practice of
religious pluralism presents a real challenge. In her wonderful book, *Encountering
God: A Spiritual Journey from Bozeman to Banaras,* Diana Eck draws a careful

and helpful distinction between exclusivism, inclusivism, and pluralism.[1] Eck reminds us that "while we speak of exclusivists, inclusivists, and pluralists as if they were entirely different groups of people...these ways of thinking about diversity may well be part of the ongoing dialogue within ourselves."[2] Where Eck's pluralistic stretch spans between her Christian commitment and her academically-based sympathy for Hinduism, my own stretch faces its toughest hurdle in relation to Christianity. Most of the Christian clergy and students with whom I work help me loosen my muscles. Their generosity of spirit, interest in Judaism, and self-awareness in relating to me strengthen my capacity to relate not just to them personally, but to Christianity as a faith system, with openness to its gifts. Now and then, however, there occurs an incident that freezes my progress and requires careful handling.

So it was that the director of one of our evangelical fellowship groups proudly brought to the December luncheon of our Religious Directors Association her response to my inviting people to share something about their winter holiday: a sheet of biblical sources on which she had based her final Bible study teaching of the semester. Imagine my unease when those sources turned out to include ones taken as pointing to Jewish resistance to acceptance of Jesus as Messiah. Carefully weighing my options both during the luncheon and after it, I managed to channel my tumultuous feelings in productive directions. I decided that taking on the issue with my young colleague, publicly or even privately, would risk skewing my relationship with her—given my standing as dean of Religious Life. Had I still been in my previous position as director of the Hillel Jewish Center, I almost certainly would have proceeded differently.

Being dean of Religious Life or University chaplain at a secular university means walking a delicate line between personal religious commitment and religious neutrality. Maintaining balance when crossing a mountain stream or even a bridge makes me very nervous, but it turns out that performing the religious balancing act has not been as difficult for me as anticipated. Early in my tenure, I made the important decision that I would go on moving around the university as "Rabbi Laemmle," rather than taking on as my preferred title the more prestigious and easily handled "Dean" or "Doctor." When once in a while I am asked about this way of proceeding, I reply by citing a desire that people bear in mind my being a member of the ordained clergy. Being fully honest, both with myself and others, I acknowledge that I also want people to bear in mind my being a Jew. A good part of that second, more emotionally-based, identification flows from the fact that, as far as I know, I am only the second Jew to have served as dean of Religious Life or chaplain at a major university. (Rabbi Michael Paley, also a former Hillel rabbi, served as Columbia University's chaplain during the '80s.) Moreover, my having been selected by USC after a national search represents an important breakthrough in the university's relationship to the Los Angeles Jewish community. All this is true and relevant to how I handle my job, but it is only half of the picture. The other half is continually being sketched in by my encounter with people and groups across the religious spectrum.

It comes naturally to invoke light imagery when talking about religion, for such imagery can convey both multiplicity and unity, both complexity and essentialism. To speak of "the religious spectrum" is to touch base with the diversity of the world's religious traditions, a diversity which now increasingly makes itself at home within the United States of America. Speaking thus also, even if indirectly, touches the edge of the garment within which divinity itself is clothed. Let me close by invoking verses from Psalm 104 that form part of the meditation recited by Jews when wrapping themselves in the Tallit prayer shawl: "Bless the Lord, O my soul! Lord my God, you are very great. You are robed in glory and majesty. You wrap yourself in light as in a garment. You spread out the heavens like a curtain."

ENDNOTES

1. Diana Eck, *Encountering God: A Spiritual Journey from Bozeman to Banaras* (Boston: Beacon Press, 1993), 166–199. See especially chapter 7, entitled "Is Our God Listening?"

2. Ibid., 170.

25. LINKS: Establishing Communities of Dialogue on Campuses

FREDERIC BRADFORD BURNHAM

The Episcopal Church Foundation and Trinity Church/Wall Street, in partnership with the EDUCATION as *Transformation* Project, is launching a telecommunications network designed specifically for college and university audiences called "LINKS: Connecting Head and Heart on Campus." Using the interactive capacities of the Internet and satellite communications, we will seek to establish intergenerational, interdisciplinary, interfaith communities of dialogue on college campuses all across the country.

LINKS broadcasts will ask hard questions about critical issues before our culture. For instance, economists and financiers might debate with international leaders from Asia the future of global capitalism and its impact on the quality of human life. Or religious leaders from the major faith traditions might share with one another their understandings of God at the new millennium. Or, students and faculty together might ponder the rise in violence among our youth.

The goal will be to foster dialogue across generations, disciplines, and faiths that have become increasingly isolated from each other during the twentieth century. By mixing and matching multiple ways of knowing and thinking, we anticipate that new and unexpected truths and relationships will emerge from the journey into complexity. In every case, members of the college audience will be able to engage in the live dialogue and interact with the broadcast panelists via phone, fax, and e-mail. Internet chatrooms will be established to keep the conversation and learning alive long after the broadcasts.

Ideally, the participants on each campus will be as diverse as the college community itself. Through mutual respect and open dialogue, these diverse communities will be able to explore the value of pluralism, the benefits of multiple ways of knowing, and the merits of cross-generational perspectives. Through these communities of dialogue we hope to break down the artificial boundaries which we have erected between the sciences and the humanities, between students and faculty, and between people of different religious traditions. We seek to model a new kind of public discourse in this country, a new pathway to truth, one that honors diverse ways of knowing and truly links the head and heart.

Throughout most of human history "head" and "heart" have been used as shorthand for two quite distinct ways of knowing. The head has been associated with analytical knowledge, the kind that breaks the world down into individual components and studies them separately.[1] The heart, on the other hand, has been associated with relational knowledge, a more intuitive kind of perception that is sensitive to the relationships and connections that exist among the component parts.

Traditionally, both ways of knowing were considered essential to a full and integrated understanding of reality. During the past three hundred years, however, the phenomenal utility of mathematical analysis has overshadowed the contributions of relational thought and led us to ascribe inordinate importance to scientific truth as opposed to humanistic or religious wisdom. Now all that is changing. Relational knowledge is staging a comeback all across the academic spectrum and a fuller appreciation of multiple ways of knowing is on the upswing.

WAYS OF KNOWING

The origin of these two ways of knowing is a fascinating story that takes us back to the ancient cultures of Greece and Israel. Their common starting point is one of the fundamental enigmas of early human experience. Mystified by a natural world that was full of continuous change and unpredictable calamity, ancient beings pondered whether there could be something permanent, something stable, underneath all that flux. The pre-Socratic philosophers of ancient Greece named that immutable "stuff" *physis* and they associated it with a changeless essence that makes it possible for a material element like water to go through physical transformations from solid to liquid to gas without losing its identity. Another group of ancient Greek philosophers followed a different path in the search for the *physis*. They reasoned that any material substance that was immutable must also be indivisible because to divide something was to change it. So the Greek word for indivisible, *a-tomos*, became a substitute for *physis*. And the concept of an atom was born.

In theory, then, the material world was made up of minuscule particles, so small in dimension that they could not be divided. All change in the natural world was explained as the relative motion of these immutable particles. Philosophically speaking, ancient atomism was quite a satisfactory explanation of the physical world. It accounted for all the flux in the world and preserved the assumption of permanence. Unfortunately, there was no empirical verification for the existence of these mythical atoms. So the atomic hypothesis lay fallow for almost two thousand years until it could be wed to mathematical analysis in the seventeenth century.

Meanwhile, across the Mediterranean, the ancient Israelites had been working out quite a different solution to the question of change and permanence. Confronted with the same daily experience of ceaseless change, the Israelites concluded that matter must be ephemeral. Therefore, they didn't look for a permanent substance in the physical world. Instead, they reasoned that only God could be immutable. But in what sense was God unchangeable? Certainly, not in a material sense. How, then, was God unalterable?

Well, the Israelites knew God as the God of the Covenant. Indeed, for them, it was God's steadfast commitment to the covenant relationship that would never change. God's faithfulness, God's steadfast love, God's *hesed* was the only permanence upon which humans could rely. In fact, the God of the covenant was a God whose nature was to enter into relationship. If, in turn, we humans were made in the image of that God, then we, too, were made to be in relationship. Remember, after creating Adam, God observed: "It is not good for Adam to be alone." So God created a companion. In Biblical terms, therefore, *to be* is not simply to be an independent, isolated material entity. *To be* is *to be with, to be in relationship with*. The Hebrew word, *A-dam*, which the Old Testament uses more than five hundred times as the generic term for human being, best captures the meaning of this alternative understanding of being.

Unfortunately, this relational ontology, which was thoroughly embedded in the story line of the Old Testament, never was given explicit philosophical expression. Consequently, when the Christian faith ventured forth into the sophisticated Hellenistic world, it lacked the learned language to compete with the philosophical legacy of Greece. Hence, the relational ontology of the Bible quickly succumbed to the more material understanding of *being* explicit in Greek thought. And Christianity gradually adopted the dualism of body and soul as a synthesis of Greek materialism and more transcendent Judeo-Christian notions of *being*.

So, we have two ancient understandings of being: *Atom* and *Adam*. Atomic ontology is the child of ancient Athens. It argues that *being* is material. It breaks the world down into discrete analyzable pieces. Adamic ontology is the child of ancient Jerusalem. It argues that *being* is relational. It perceives the world in terms of the relationships that bind the pieces together. These two views of *being* delineate at their roots the fundamental differences between the two most influential forces in Western civilization, science and religion. In fact, as we shall now see, the dominance of atomic thought in science over the past three centuries has contributed to the eclipse of relational ways of knowing and a loss of prestige for major religions.

The rise of modern science in the seventeenth century is intimately linked with the resurgence of atomism. Like other ancient schools of thought that were lost to the West in the Dark Ages, atomism was rediscovered by Europe during the Renaissance. Galileo was one of those who took the atomic hypothesis to heart. He found a way to wed atomism to mathematics and experiment and almost single-handedly launched modern science.

Here's how the story goes. Prior to Galileo, scientists had not applied mathematics to the real world because, as we have already seen, the natural world was viewed as the scene of change and flux, while math was understood to model the logic of law and order. Mathematics (i.e., geometry) was used instead to trace the perfect circular motion of the stars in the immutable heavenly realm. Flying in the face of centuries of philosophical tradition, Galileo had the audacity to break with that cosmological dualism and bring mathematics down to earth. He argued, prophetically, that the book of nature is written in the language of mathematics and its characters are circles, lines, and points. The fact was, however, that the language of mathematics could not fit the physical world until matter was broken down into atomic particles. Galileo had the intuitive brilliance to see that the atom could be a physical analogue of a geometrical point, which moved in straight lines, smooth curves, and perfect circles. This connection between material particles and geometrical points was the conceptual bridge that built modern science.

Once that theoretical link was established, the experimental confirmation of this powerful analytical tool was soon to follow. In fact, when Galileo rolled balls down inclined planes, dropped stones off the tower of Pisa, or plotted the path of cannon balls, he was operating within the same theoretical framework: they were all physical analogues of a geometrical point moving in simple mathematical patterns. Soon thereafter, when Newton analyzed the motion of the planets, he found that they, too, were—figuratively speaking—physical analogues of geometrical points. Then he broke the properties of light down into "corpuscles" and analyzed their geometrical motion. Next, Newton and his contemporaries reduced virtually every other natural force, including gravity, electricity, magnetism, and heat, to ethereal fluids filled with tiny physical particles which moved like geometrical points through space. The same model of reality led a century later to the development of the atomic chart that reduced the material world to approximately one hundred distinct chemical elements. A century after that, the same analytical way of knowing split the indivisible atom into a hundred additional elemental parts. In each and every one of these cases, physical analogues of geometrical points yielded to mathematical analysis and modern science marched onward.

It was only a matter of time before the atomic model crossed the boundary into social science. Late in the seventeenth century John Locke adapted Newton's atomic theory to the study of human culture and gave birth to the Enlightenment idea of individualism. The individual human being became, figuratively speaking, the social analogue of a geometrical point. Subsequently, even disciplines like economics (capitalism) and biology (Darwinian evolution) yielded to atomic analysis. All the world was fragmented into myriad parts. As William Blake lamented at the outset of this revolution: "Tis all in pieces...all coherence gone."

So the analytical way of knowing held sway and the power of science to reveal natural truth seemed limitless. Other ways of knowing paled by comparison. Indeed, some philosophers even questioned whether other kinds of knowing had any meaning at all. Atomism and individualism ruled Western culture.

During the course of the nineteenth century, however, the atomistic analysis of nature began to manifest limitations and relational models of reality began to reemerge. In the study of light the concept of a "wave" demonstrated greater explanatory power than particles in some instances. And in the science of electricity and magnetism the concept of a field actually replaced the particulate model. Both waves and fields are relational and not atomic models. Furthermore, by the turn of the twentieth century it became clear that light could behave like a particle one minute and a wave the next. It wasn't a particle or a wave, but both a particle and a wave. In other words, material beings could be both individual and communal, both Atomic and Adamic. The scientific community called this paradoxical property of reality complementarity. Both atomic and relational categories suddenly seemed equally critical to the understanding of the nature of light.

During the twentieth century other unexpected discoveries in physics have heightened the value of relational ways of knowing. For example, the EPR Paradox, perhaps the greatest enigma of contemporary science, is a classical example of the limitations of atomic analysis and the need to develop more sophisticated relational models of reality. The EPR Paradox is named after the three scientists who first told the curious tale: Einstein, Podolsky, and Rosen. Imagine an atomic accelerator in which two elementary particles, an electron and a positron, collide. In the head-on impact, the two original particles are annihilated. In their place appear two photons (packets of light) that fly off into space in opposite directions at the speed of light. These two photons are not quite identical. They are, as it were, fraternal twins. The axis of polarization of one is vertical, the other horizontal. Traveling at 186,000 miles per second, they are millions of miles apart within a matter of seconds. If a scientist were then to pass one of those photons through a magnetic field and alter its polarization, the other photon would change its polarization instantaneously, no matter how far apart they were. Now, that is remarkable! How can one photon know what is happening to the other photon? How can the message get from one photon to the other? Light is the fastest moving phenomenon in the universe. If each photon is moving away from the other at the speed of light, then the actual distance between them is increasing at twice the speed of light. So no signal could possibly get from one to the other. How then does one photon know instantaneously that its twin has been altered? It seems impossible. Yet it has been demonstrated to be true over and over again. How could that be?

Within the framework of the atomic view of reality, this experiment makes absolutely no sense at all. As long as we see the photons as individual isolated entities, the results of the experiment are unintelligible. But if we look at the phenomenon in relational terms, they begin to make more sense. Instead of seeing the photons as separate particles, consider them to be fraternal twins, born out of the same womb. Our knowledge of the extrasensory relationship between twins helps us begin to understand how photons might be related to one another in subtle ways even though they are far apart. Or look at it another way. Think of the photons as products of the same event in time. No matter how far that event spreads out into space, it is possible to perceive the photons as part of a spatial field where all the parts are integrally connected one with the other regardless of the distance between them. In each of these cases a relational analogy helps to make sense out of what would otherwise be total mystery.

The new science of chaos offers further confirmation of the relational character of reality. Back in the 1960s when Edward Lorenz, a meteorologist at MIT, was studying weather patterns, he discovered that tiny changes in weather systems could have very large effects over time. He was using the newly invented computer to help him analyze the life histories of complex systems like the weather. One day he input hundreds of variables based upon a model of a weather system and the computer executed the thousands of computations necessary to predict the future of the system. Let's say the result was a sunny day. He decided to run it again, but he inadvertently changed one variable, one variable out of hundreds, only a thousandth of a decimal point. This time, in effect, he got a snowstorm. A negligible change made a monumental difference in the outcome. He coined a phrase to illustrate this enigmatic result: The Butterfly Effect. The argument goes like this: If a butterfly flaps its wings in New York today, it could totally change the weather pattern in Tokyo two weeks from now. In other words, everything in reality is so sensitively interconnected, interdependent, interrelated that very small changes in local conditions can have huge consequences over time.

Such insights into the intricate relational character of reality are becoming commonplace. In a 1986 article on Chaos theory in *The Scientific American*, the authors, Crutchfield et al., offered the following illustration: If I were to roll a billiard ball across a smooth floor, in order to calculate precisely where that ball would be 15 seconds later, I would have to take into account the gravitational effect of an electron on the opposite side of our galaxy. Now, consider how small an electron is and how tiny its gravitational force would be. Then figure out how many light years away the other side of our galaxy is. Lastly, take into account the fact that the force of gravity varies inversely with the square of the distance. Then you can begin to get some idea of how infinitesimal the gravitational effect of that electron would be. Once you recognize how tenuous that connection is, then you can begin to appreciate how truly intricate and complex relationships really are in this incredible universe.

Henry Stapp, a theoretical physicist, summed up this new relational understanding of reality with the following proposition: "There is no longer any such thing as an individual, isolated entity called an elementary particle. An elementary particle is, instead, a set of relationships reaching out to other things." Focusing on those sets of relationships which make up reality, scientists have begun to call this new understanding of reality "non-locality." In other words, it is no longer possible to speak of an entity as occupying a particular location in space because it can only be fully understood in terms of its relationships with everything else, stretching all the way to an electron on the other side of our galaxy. To put it in striking terms: We are our relationships. Or as an African friend of mine once put it: "I am who we are."

These observations sound far more like the relational ontology of the Bible than the esoteric theories of modern science. In fact, they remind me of Jesus' words about the fundamental character of being human. See if the following paraphrase of Jesus' summary of the Law doesn't echo this new relational understanding of reality: "Love the Lord your God with all your heart and all your mind and all your soul. This is the first and great relationship. The second is like it. Love your neighbor as yourself. On these two relationships hang all the law and order of creation." Indeed, scientific and religious ways of knowing seem to have more in common now than they have for centuries.

Physics isn't the only discipline in which these relational insights are staging a comeback. They are equally bountiful in biology. For instance, the original Darwinian model of evolution was intrinsically atomistic. Individual, isolated organisms experienced random mutations that impacted their immediate descendants and no one else. Now the principle of non-locality is absolutely fundamental in biology. No contemporary biologist would try to understand an organism apart from its ecological environment. These kinds of relational insights have greatly heightened our awareness of the sensitivity of the environment. Two other movements have contributed substantially to the new understanding that relationships are fundamental. The insights of feminism concerning the web of life are profoundly significant. Likewise, the impact which global communication is having upon the relational intuition of the human psyche cannot be overlooked. From all directions we are slowly being nudged into a new consciousness of reality.

In the end, however, it is important to recognize that this is not an either/or proposition: either individuals or relationships. It is, instead, a both/and world we live in. Just as light is both particle and wave, so reality is both Atomic and Adamic, both individual and relational. And our ways of knowing should include both head and heart, both analytical and relational truths. That, of course, is precisely what we hope to accomplish through the LINKS program. Our goal is nothing short of an epistemological revolution within the academy.

These, then, are the considerations that have led the Episcopal Church Foundation and Trinity Institute to establish a partnership with EDUCATION as *Transformation* in order to create interdisciplinary, intergenerational, interfaith communities of dialogue on college campuses where the analytical and relational ways of knowing can share the same table and speak with mutual respect. If we can reconnect the metaphorical head and heart on campus we will have broken down the walls that divide the gifts of the human spirit and that diminish our capacity to appreciate the wondrous complexity of creation.

ENDNOTES

1. According to the OED, the word "analysis" means "to take to pieces; to separrate, distinguish, or ascertain the elements of anything complex, as a material collection, chemical component, light, sound, a miscellaneous list, account or statement, a sentence, phrase, word, conception, feeling, action, process."

26. Teacher Formation: Identity, Integrity, and the Heart of a Teacher

SALLY Z. HARE, MARCY JACKSON, AND RICK JACKSON

In our rush to reform education, we have forgotten a simple truth: reform will never be achieved by renewing appropriations, restructuring schools, rewriting curricula, and revising texts if we continue to demean and dishearten the human resource called the teacher on whom so much depends. Teachers must be better compensated, freed from bureaucratic harassment, given a role in academic governance, and provided with the best possible methods and materials. But none of that will transform education if we fail to cherish—and challenge—the human heart that is the source of good teaching....[1]

—Parker J. Palmer

[NOTE: under the guidance of Parker J. Palmer, PhD., the Fetzer Institute created the Courage to Teach program for the personal and professional renewal of teachers, counselors, and administrators in public schools. Piloting an approach to professional development called "teacher formation," this program is rooted in the belief that good teaching—and inspired student learning—flows from the identity and integrity of the teacher. The formation process invites educators to reclaim their own wholeness and vocational clarity, and makes connections between the renewal of a teacher's spirit, the retention of our best educators, and the revitalization of good teaching in public schools. College and university leaders are exploring ways in which teacher formation can contribute to good teaching in higher education as well.]

WHY IT TAKES COURAGE TO TEACH

For most educators, teaching is a calling inspired by a love for children, an ethic of service, and a desire to make a positive difference. Unfortunately, a growing body of evidence suggests that the difficult conditions in our public schools, the excessive demands on a teacher's time, and the heightened job pressures too often grind teachers down, distort their ideals of teaching, and erode their commitment to the profession.

Higher education, as well as K-12, is feeling the stress. State legislators are calling for reforms that faculty find demeaning and sometimes even threatening to academic freedom and integrity. Tenure has become highly controversial, and in a number of institutions no longer exists. Virtual colleges offer programs that seem to undermine the significance of the faculty-student relationship. Teachers across the country are opting for early retirement, private counseling, and the business world.

Good teachers speak simultaneously of the noble contributions in their work and the compromises they are often forced to accept if they are to meet the press of their professional obligations. These conditions have led many to call teaching an imperiled profession.

> I am at a decision-making point. I truly enjoy teaching, but I feel buffeted by the public assault on teachers; the strain of dealing with especially needy students; the day-in day-out structure of teaching; and my own personal development issues. At times I feel drained, uninspired, and just plain tired. I've considered leaving teaching and, in fact, have taken classes in preparation for a change in career. A major concern that has influenced my exploration has been around whom is taking care of the teacher? I see teachers giving so much and then running out of gas. What is needed to inspire them once again? How can they "feed their souls" and continue teaching with commitment and feeling? I know these reflections are as much about me as they are about my fellow teachers.

—High school teacher with 15-years' experience[1]

In higher education, teacher education programs are feeling the impact in lower numbers of entering students, in the loss of students of color, and in the eroding morale of their faculty and alumni. Teachers returning to graduate school are opting, in high numbers, for majors such as counseling and administration that will take them out of the classroom.

Many research studies also highlight the negative impact on students of teachers' detached or cynical attitudes. Too many are unavailable to students who need the support and involvement of caring adults—teachers who are willing to listen, to encourage, and to inspire. Representatives from teachers' organizations agree that this is too often the case, due to fear of misunderstandings, reprisals, and lack of parental and administrative support. Increasingly, public schools and the larger community are struggling with the difficulty of finding and keeping good teachers in the increasingly complex and demanding public education environment.

TEACHING: A PROFESSION UNDER DURESS

In spite of decades of reform initiatives, public schools remain "on the ropes" in too many communities around the country. Why do so many carefully planned efforts fail to achieve their well-intended outcomes? Why is it that so many initially successful reforms have difficulty enduring, often losing ground as their champions become depleted by overwhelming demands? Could it be that what is missing is what is most essential: sustained support for good teachers?

> I'm absolutely convinced that the amount of stress and complexity that teachers confront every day does not allow them to be in a healthy way.... Teachers need time for themselves. They don't get that. Teachers need reflection time. They don't get that. If people aren't at a comfortable place with who they are, they don't do a good job in the classroom.

—African American male middle school
principal, 20 years' experience[2]

Scant attention has been directed toward actually supporting teachers to revitalize their commitment to teaching by tapping inner resources and core beliefs. In *The Courage to Teach*, Parker Palmer suggests that teacher training and school reforms must follow a prior process of helping teachers explore *who they are and how they are*—aspects of personhood clearly present in good teachers. On the surface, this message is deceptively simple—that good teachers teach who they are. But the book's nationwide popularity indicates that Palmer's message has clearly touched a sensitive chord among large numbers of teachers, and that many feel they are in danger of losing sight of why they were drawn to teaching. Beyond teachers, other professionals—doctors, lawyers, ministers, community leaders—are drawn to the ideas in *The Courage to Teach*.

What kinds of support might inspire renewed commitment to creating spaces for engaged learning and trusting relationships in schools and strengthen the kinds of teacher-centered leadership necessary for good education today? What are ways we might create space for all our undergraduate and professional students to explore their personhood, to develop their identity and integrity? In *The Courage to Teach*, Parker Palmer writes:

> The question we most commonly ask is the "what" question—what subjects shall we teach? When the conversation goes a bit deeper, we ask the "how" question—what methods and techniques are required to teach well? Occasionally, when it goes deeper still, we ask the "why" question—for what purpose and to what ends do we teach? But seldom, if ever, do we ask the "who" question—who is the self that teaches? How does the quality of my selfhood form—or deform—the way I relate to my students, my subject, my colleagues, my world? How can educational institutions sustain and deepen the selfhood from which good teaching comes?[3]

The premise of *The Courage to Teach* is precisely that good teaching cannot be reduced to technique. Whether in the public school or college classroom, the core beliefs held by teachers—intellectually, emotionally, and spiritually—are essential to sustaining the personal courage necessary for teachers to create and sustain the transforming learning environments all students deserve.

The Courage to Teach Program

The Courage to Teach program was originally designed for K-12 teachers and administrators in public schools, educators on whom society depends for so much, but for whom we provide so little meaningful support. In the Courage to Teach program, the direct focus is neither on teaching techniques nor on the reform of school systems. Instead, it is on renewing that which is closest and most immediate to good teaching—the inner life of the teacher.

Parker Palmer piloted the Courage to Teach program with a group of K-12 teachers in Michigan from 1994-96. Following the extremely positive response to the pilot, four additional Courage to Teach programs were sponsored by the Fetzer Institute to test the model. These four groups—in coastal South Carolina, south-west Michigan, Baltimore-Washington D.C., and Washington state—completed their two-year programs in the summer of 1998.

Interest in the program came from higher education as well as public schools, and the coastal South Carolina site accepted university faculty and administrators in addition to K-12 educators. Whether from public schools or higher education, participants uniformly gave the highest marks for the program's impact on both their personal and professional lives. Since 1998, additional Courage to Teach groups have been launched in rural South Carolina; Dallas, Texas; and Kalamazoo, Michigan; Boston, Massachusetts; Fort Worth, Texas; Portland, Oregon; Austin, Texas; Chapel Hill, North Carolina; Baltimore, Maryland; and Seattle, Washington. Several institutions of higher education, including Lewis and Clark College and Bellarmine College, are also beginning Courage to Teach programs in the fall of 1999.

Due to the success of these initial programs, the Center for Teacher Formation was established in 1997 to develop and deepen the work of teacher formation, and expand the Courage to Teach program nationally. The center provides information, consultation, and program development assistance to schools, colleges, and communities that wish to initiate Courage to Teach programs. A primary mission of the center is to select and prepare facilitators for Courage to Teach programs.

How the Courage to Teach Program Impacts Public Education

An extensive outside evaluation of the Courage to Teach program was conducted in 1998. Through lengthy interviews and written surveys, participants were asked to reflect on how the Courage to Teach program impacted their intellectual, emotional, and spiritual lives; their in-school leadership roles; and their classroom practice and student relationships.

The evaluation report offered substantial positive evidence in all three areas. Participants found the program to be a profound experience that honored the complexity and dignity of teaching. They also cited numerous ways in which Courage to Teach program experiences not only contributed to classroom practices but also strengthened their resolve to build a more collegial school culture—a hallmark of effective schools. Central themes that emerged from the interviews were testimony to the program's effectiveness in renewing the teacher's faith in and long-term commitment to their students and their profession. These findings are especially impressive in the face of alarmingly high attrition rates of both veteran educators and those new to the profession.

In their seminal work on systemic education reform, *What's Worth Fighting for in Your School?*, leading educational authorities Michael Fullan and Andy Hargreaves write:

> Educational reform has failed time and time again. We believe that this is because reform has either ignored teachers or oversimplified what teaching is about. And teachers themselves have not taken the initiative to build the new conditions

necessary for reversing a trend that has overburdened schools with problems, and ironically added insult to injury by overloading them with fragmented, unworkable solutions. **Teachers have been too busy responding to the latest forays to steer a bold and imaginative course of their own.**[4] [Bold added.]

These authors identify six endemic problems—a synthesis of what is commonly known in the research field—which impede reform efforts. There is a clear connection between these six dilemmas and the potential benefits cited by the Courage to Teach program's outside evaluators.

1. Teacher overload: Due to numerous factors—socio-economic, cultural, media, high technology, and others—expectations placed on teachers are increasing exponentially. Particularly at restructured and/or restructuring schools, the demands on educators are often overwhelming, with the pace of constant change that pervades these schools taking a heavy toll. Teachers are expected to serve as advisors, develop new curriculums, interact with diverse parents and community members in new ways—and teach!

Fullan and Hargreaves note, "Innovations are not making the teacher's job more manageable. They are making it worse. Overload of expectations and fragmented solutions remain the number one problem."[5]

Many reform efforts begun in the 1990s are suffering from the effects of overwhelmed and depleted teachers. Too few ask how the increased pace and expectations in our schools impact teachers. Frequently, it is the most creative and responsible ones who burn out and leave the profession.

Again and again, Courage to Teach participants reported that the extended duration (two years of quarterly retreats) and humane pace of the program helped them to rediscover and reconnect with their calling, balance their lives, and harmonize their professional roles with a more grounded sense of self. Time for disciplined reflection led to choices to remain in the profession.

> I really care about kids and I've been told I've been an effective teacher.... But I think I would have quit. There's nothing else that I could have been given that would have been more valuable than the experience of the Courage to Teach.
>
> —Japanese-American female elementary
> teacher, 5-years' experience[6]

2. Teacher Isolation: Teaching has long been called the "private profession." Teachers are rarely provided with the time and means to collaborate and regularly support each other. The isolation of teachers is often made worse by dysfunctional school cultures that limit the access to new ideas, stifle creativity, and contribute to the accumulation of personal and institutional stress. And teacher isolation is exacerbated by the physical—so-called "egg-crate"—structure of most schools.

Numerous research studies note that a "culture of isolation" is a hallmark of struggling schools, whereas a "culture of collegiality" marks healthy schools. Research on schools that overcome isolation, and operate as collegial environments, demonstrates the powerful effects for student learning as well as teacher effectiveness and satisfaction.

Numerous research studies note that a "culture of isolation" is a hallmark of struggling schools, whereas a "culture of collegiality" marks healthy schools. Research on schools that overcome isolation, and operate as collegial environments, demonstrates that power effects for student learning as well as teacher effectiveness.

Higher education struggles with the same isolation as K-12, often physically separating the various disciplines, sometimes even by several miles. Faculty participating in the Courage to Teach program speak of the rare opportunity provided to talk with colleagues from across campus as well as with elementary and secondary school teachers.

> We give a lot of lip service to seamless education, but we don't even talk with each other. For the first time, I understand—and am even trying—interdisciplinary approaches in my classroom. And I have some sense of the students' experiences before they come to me and when they leave.
>
> —College English professor

The testimony of teachers in Courage to Teach programs clearly indicates that participation inspired renewed collegial practices in schools. The "interactive professionalism" Fullan and Hargreaves advocate as necessary to successful reforms . was created in the "trustworthy space" of Courage to Teach retreats. The pattern that emerged is one of teacher collegiality at program retreats leading to deeper interest in and leadership of wider professional engagements.

> Colleagues have asked about what we are doing and have been interested in learning more. Consequently, we have started a dialogue group that meets to discuss issues of personal and professional concern structured after ideas, concepts, and readings I have brought back from our CTT retreats.... The cumulative effect in our building alone feels great, but it hasn't stopped there. Teachers from other buildings in our district have expressed interest. As CTT expands its sphere of influence, revitalization will naturally occur. This program feeds the spirit.
>
> —White female high school teacher,
> 15-years' experience[7]

3. Groupthink: Fullan and Hargreaves advocate genuine collaboration, but wisely acknowledge that much of what happens in school reform practice too often involves what they call "contrived collegiality" and bandwagon thinking. They observe that groups tend to be more susceptible to fads than individuals and write,

> The unthinking self-suppression of one's own intuition and experiential knowledge is one of the major reasons why bandwagons and ill-conceived innovations flourish.... It is for this reason that **we see the individual as an undervalued source of reform**.... [Bold added.] So we must fight for collegiality, but not naively. We must protect and promote the individual too.[8]

Instead of another "outside-in" and/or "top-down" structural reform, the Courage to Teach program works from the "inside out." By carefully attending to individual teachers, an investment is made which yields greater personal responsibility and renewed creativity. Such fundamental results go well beyond the typical outcomes expected from "professional development" programs, and help produce the deep personal commitment that sustained change efforts require.

4. Untapped Competence and Neglected Incompetence: Fullan and Hargreaves assert that veteran teachers are grossly underutilized as resources of pedagogical craft and wisdom. There is an urgent need to keep effective veteran teachers in the profession: "Every time an old person dies, a library burns."[9] Likewise, every time a veteran teacher opens up to sharing their wisdom, a previously shuttered library opens.

Most teacher education and professional development approaches work to remediate flaws or omissions—either personal or structural—in education and instruction. It is a **deficiency model** of so-called self-improvement that fundamentally assumes that the original form of individual persons is defective, and in need of constant repair. The typical promotion and tenure process in higher education also does little to tap competence or address incompetence.

The *Courage to Teach* inverts this by saying to teachers, "Each of you bring powerful and unique gifts to your work." This creates a **proficiency model**, and the fundamental question becomes *how can you best infuse your teaching practice with your personhood?* The goal thus is one of identifying the innate and special aptitudes that uniquely inform and inspire each teacher's practice.

Isolation hides both competent and incompetent teachers. The Courage to Teach program surfaces vocational competence, as well as vocational misfits and/or incompetence, in a manner that requires and supports personal responsibility and choice making. The Courage to Teach evaluation is full of stories of teachers who made decisions to open their classrooms to colleagues and who begin to initiate new professional development activities. Many teachers also talk about having the courage to seek help or do things differently.

5. Narrowness in the Teacher's Role and the Need for Teacher-Leaders: Teaching has been called a flat career, with little room for advancement and variety. Over time, this often leads to reduced motivation, commitment, and effectiveness. Fullan and Hargreaves advocate fostering multifaceted teacher-leaders. They quote Roland Barth's powerful and compelling call to "uplift the chalk":

> To assert one's leadership as a teacher, often against forces of administrative resistance, takes commitment to an educational ideal. It also requires the energy to combat one's own inertia caused by habit and overwork. And it requires a certain kind of courage to step outside of the small prescribed circle of traditional "teacher tasks," to declare through our actions that we care about and take responsibility for more than the minimum, more than what goes on within the four walls of our classroom.[10]

Across the literature on school reform, researchers call for teachers to contribute to the essential dialogue about what our schools should be like. Elevating the professional voice of teachers may be the most fundamental thing necessary for sustained school improvement. Leadership by teachers should be practiced, valued, encouraged, and recognized. This practice must begin in teacher education programs, with leadership development an intentional goal of these programs.

The Courage to Teach program does this in a multitude of ways. The following story illustrates such teacher-leadership:

> Our plan was to raise some issues with the principal and invite conversation, which was something he never did. We [the CTT teachers] talked about it, we planned and then the five of us stood up and raised some issues. We empowered other people to ask questions. The principal had shut us down, but we opened him up.... We got started and we stayed until 6 PM. that night and we ended it by thanking him for the courage to listen to us. He left after that year. This year I got some feedback from someone that he said, "Our school was a challenge. I wish all principals could have the privilege of working with the staff because it made me grow as a principal. I learned so much and have never been supported and challenged in so many new ways."
>
> —African American female elementary
> teacher, 15 years' experience[11]

6. Poor Solutions and Failed Reform: Simply put, there are far more failed reform initiatives in education than successful ones. Fullan and Hargreaves write,

> "In short, the conditions for mobilizing teachers as a resource for reform don't exist.... However noble, sophisticated, or enlightened proposals for change and improvement might be, they come to nothing if teachers don't adopt them in their own classrooms...."[12]

In *The Meaning of Educational Change*, Michael Fullan asserts that reform and innovation are multidimensional processes involving 1) the use of revised or new materials, 2) the adoption of new teaching approaches, and 3) the alteration of beliefs about education. The last point becomes the thesis for his explanation of why school reform rarely works.[13]

Fullan holds that we rarely address the change in beliefs that accompany lasting reforms. Fundamental meanings must be clarified, examined, and affirmed. However, in schools many of these meanings are implicit, tangled, or buried under the commotion of less important things. Discovering and embracing the core beliefs people hold as individuals and as teachers is therefore the essential first-step in the process of reform.

Such discovery is the central purpose of teacher formation. The phrase, *we teach who we are*, is its most succinct affirmation. Gratitude for renewed discovery of core beliefs—of embracing teacher as a calling—was frequently voiced by teachers in the evaluation.

> It's given me a sense of destiny. I talk about destiny with kids at work in my teaching. It is a potent source—to know that their intention about the future is powerful. What you're thinking about does have power over what you experience. Courage to Teach reminds you of that. The idea of destiny entangles you in your life. I try to speak with kids about it, to get them creatively entangled into their lives.
>
> —White male high school teacher,
> 17-years' experience[14]

A "MOVEMENT MODEL" OF CHANGE

In the closing chapter of *The Courage to Teach*[15], Parker Palmer makes the case for a social movement model for revitalizing education. Dr. Palmer offers this question as key to enduring reform: *Is it possible to embody our best insights about teaching and learning in a social movement that might revitalize education?* The answer offered by the Courage to Teach program, and echoed by participants in the program evaluation, is a resounding yes.

At the heart of the movement model is the power of free and responsible choice—to teach with integrity. The wellspring for making this choice is in the heart of the teacher. It is in the teacher's heart where thinking, feeling, willing, and believing intersect, where identity is most truly rooted, and where an individual finds the courage to act in the world.

In the book's final chapter, titled "Divided No More—Teaching from a Heart of Hope," Parker Palmer distills the essential dynamics of a movement approach to educational change as follows:

Stage 1 Isolated individuals make an inward decision to choose integrity—to live *"divided no more"*—and find a center for their lives outside of institutions.

Stage 2 These individuals begin to discover one another and form *communities of congruence* that offer mutual support and opportunities to develop a shared vision.

Stage 3 These communities start *going public*, learning to convert their private concerns into the public issues they are, and receiving vital critiques in the process.

Stage 4 A system of *alternative rewards* emerges to sustain the movement's vision and put pressure for change on the standard institutional reward system.

This is a paradoxical approach to systemic change. It first requires individuals to summon the personal courage to reclaim teaching as a vocation—aside from whatever outside demands may be placed on them to "reform education." When teachers are motivated from a clarity of identity, integrity, and professional calling, they engage in inspired teaching that results in improved student learning outcomes, and ultimately, transformed schools.

It's the only way to revitalize public education. There are no more tricks or methods or resources to try. Down we go to the core of this thing we call education.

—African American female elementary teacher,
3-years' experience[16]

COURAGEOUS TEACHING

A teacher in a Courage to Teach program remarked, "If all you're going to have courage, you have to find it inside of yourself. No one stands at the school door and hands out courage."

In the Courage to Teach program, teachers come together as colleagues, steadfastly reclaiming their identity and integrity as teachers. Enormous potential for positive change is rediscovered. Such change can result in greater depth and vitality in student-teacher relationships, renewed collegial practices on campus, and outreach from colleges and universities to the public schools. Change may take these forms, and many more—all ways that serve students, education, and society truly and well.

[For more information about the Courage to Teach Program, please contact the Center for Teacher Formation at www.teacherformation.org]

ENDNOTES

1. Sam Intrator and Megan Scribner, *An Evaluation of the Courage to Teach Program* (Seattle, Wa.: Center for Teacher Formation, 1998), 1.
2. Ibid., 18.
3. Parker Palmer, *The Courage to Teach (San Francisco: Jossey-Bass Publishers, 1998)*, 4.
4. Michael Fullan and Andy Hargreaves, *What's Worth Fighting for in Your School?* (New York: Teachers College, 1996), xiii.
5. Ibid., 4.
6. Intrator and Scribner, *op. cit.*, 13.
7. Ibid., 14.
8. Fullan and Hargreaves, *op. cit.,* 7.
9. Ibid., 10.
10. Ibid., 11.
11. Intrator and Scribner, *op. cit.*, 26.
12. Fullan and Hargreaves, *op. cit.,* 13.
13. Michael Fullan, *The New Meaning of Educational Change* (New York: Teachers College Press, 1991).
14. Intrator and Scribner, *op. cit.*, 17.
15. Palmer, *op. cit.*, 163–183.
16. Intrator and Scribner, *op. cit.*, 13.

27. Teacher Education, Spiritual Transformation, & Child Advocacy

Carol L. Flake

What can teacher education institutions do to recruit and nurture the development of teachers who can and will create classroom environments that are sites for spiritual transformation? Do teachers even have the right to attend to spiritual development in classrooms given their role as citizens of the United States committed to being faithful to the American political contract and the spirit of the Constitution?[1]

I agree with David Purpel[2] that we are confronted with a moral and spiritual crisis in education, in our society, and in our world. Our role as citizens of a nation and a world at risk requires that we commit ourselves to education for transformation. All teaching is, in fact, about transformation since spiritual transformation begins the moment one soul experiences another soul and is changed. This soul-to-soul encounter occurs in all vital educational settings. It is only when we teachers are in touch with our own transformational processes that we can create learning environments which become the sites of positive transformation for others.

Pedagogical tensions invariably emerge when we teach for transformation. Once, when I was using guided imagery exercises to help teachers gain insights into what it means to be "the possible teacher" teaching in "the possible school," I was accused by a South Carolina state legislator of using "Satanistic" teaching practices. Most recently, when team teaching an Honors College course focusing on "living the mythic life," my co-teacher expressed his fear that I was "practicing therapy without a license."

There were times earlier in my life when I did not consciously recognize that I was teaching for transformation, but when I reflectively examine my years of practice as a teacher educator, I discover that transformational teaching strategies are woven throughout. Although many favorite transformational strategies have been modified or discarded as I have attempted to improve my practice, I have not allowed the inevitable pedagogical tensions make me lose sight of implementing a vision of education, generally, and teacher education, specifically, as transformational processes. In this chapter I share some of the variegated transformational strategies that comprise the complex fabric of my 24 years as a teacher educator and conclude with where I am now, with a focus on child advocacy, as we position ourselves on the edge of a new millennium with a mandate for educational, cultural, and global renewal.

Upon reading this chapter, a friend commented that "the paper strikes me as very conservative socially and politically." My response is that I have tried to be the "Master of Two Worlds," I have tried to see the vision from the top of the mountain and then to go back to live in the village.[3] In other words, since at least 1980, I have tried to live a spiritually transformative vision in a socially and politically conservative state.

AN EMPATHETIC APPROACH

Exiting graduate school in 1977 with a Ph.D. in child development and family relationships, I began to consider ways I might make a difference in the world. I wrote a textbook with two colleagues[4] in which we developed an empathetic approach to the study of child development and relationships. Designed for future parents, teachers, nurses, or other practitioners, and modeled on a similar strategy used by my major professors[5] in the field of family relations, our empathetic approach required that students identify their personal feelings and reactions to carefully crafted cases before attempting to experience emotional empathy with the people in the cases.

Once personal reactions were identified and emotional empathy was experienced, students were asked to achieve cognitive empathy and apply principles derived from theory and research to explain and predict the behavior of the children and adults in the case. Each examination in the course, designed for undergraduate students seeking teacher certification and entitled "The Young Child: Behavior and Development," was modeled on this empathetic approach to case analysis. Students were expected to internalize the "universal" behavioral principles they studied as they employed them to analyze cases in class, in papers, and on exams.

In the current postmodern moment and from a more globalcentric perspective gained in part through world travel, I have come to question the modern assumption that there are universal principles that can be identified to predict and explain human behavior and development or that we could or would wish to become objective in our interactions with children and their families. I would still argue, however, that the ability to attain through empathy a sense of deep, resonant connectedness with and compassion for children, adults, and even animals and the natural world is a necessary component of and catalyst for our spiritual transformation. I also agree with Ken Wilber[6] that, through developing the "eye of contemplation," we can access universally attainable spiritual depths not identifiable through modern "flatland" science.

A CURRICULUM FOR CARING

I discovered Urie Bronfenbrenner[7] and his relatively obtuse book in 1979. Bronfenbrenner's work built the case for a more ecological or holistic approach to the study of human behavior and development and precipitated a scientific revolution in American psychology. I told the teachers in my graduate classes that reading the book was like digging in a coal mine for buried diamonds. Digging through the coal is hard work, but when the diamonds are found they shine brightly and are worth the effort expended.

One of Bronfenbrenner's diamonds was his notion that we need a "curriculum for caring" in our schools. This curriculum would engage children in caring activities rather than teach about caring. Such a curriculum is an antidote for the alienation being experienced by our children and youth and for the resulting problems such as declining test scores, increases in school dropout rates, alcohol and drug abuse, empty sexuality, and violence.

In my course, "The Young Child: Applying Theory and Research," I insisted that graduate students, the majority of whom were teachers working on an M.Ed. or Ph.D., mine the Bronfenbrenner book for the diamonds found there. His descriptions of our children's sense of alienation and the importance of every child having at least one adult who is absolutely, irrationally crazy about him or her and the necessity of taking an ecological approach to the study of human behavior and development were critical in the evolution of my own understandings.

The major assignment in this course was for each teacher to design and implement a curriculum for caring in her own classroom. These caring curriculums spanned the age range from toddlerhood through fourth grade and focused on caring for self, for families, for pets, for classmates, for schools and homes, for community members, and for the natural environment.

More recently, Nel Noddings published a book entitled *The Challenge to Care in our Classrooms.*[8] Noddings bases her work on the cultural feminist notion that women and men who are involved in activities of caregiving are guided more by an ethic of caring than the ethic of justice described by Lawrence Kohlberg.[9] Noddings' work is much more readable and directly relevant to classroom practice than Bronfenbrenner's and I still use her book in a course for teachers focusing on advanced methods and materials in early childhood education classrooms. Caring for others in a truly compassionate and heart-centered manner is critical for those who wish to nurture young children and is also consistent with the practice of love for others advocated in spiritual texts throughout the world.[10]

LIVING THE MYTHIC LIFE

After having been reared in a Southern Baptist family with deep ties to the church, I became an atheist during my undergraduate years in college. Although I went to Wake Forest, at that time a Baptist College, the inquiry process that began as I took courses soon undermined the consensual reality of my family and my church. About 1980, however, I found myself in a period of major personal spiritual transformation. Certain strong intuitions of a larger spiritual reality began breaking through the scientific shell of objectivity that I had constructed around myself. For three years I participated in a Human Capacities Training Program, a "mystery school" developed by Jean Houston and her colleagues. Houston's model of the transformation of the psyche was at the foundation of the depth psychology that we studied and lived in the mystery school.[11]

Psychology, which is derived from the Greek word, *psyche*, at one time meant the study of the soul and the word itself implies spiritual transformation. Psyche means "soul" and "butterfly" in Greek and it is also the name of the beautiful young woman from Greek mythology who, through her deep, committed love for the God Eros, is transformed from a human into a Goddess. At one level of the psyche, according to Houston's formulations, an individual focuses on bodily-kinesthetic processes. This level is characterized by physical movements such as in dance, or Tai Chi, and rich sensory experiences. A person can live happily and hedonistically at the bodily-kinesthetic level and can even undergo spiritual transformation through such practices as hatha yoga.

Another level of the psyche involves a focus on personal psychological processes. Sometimes our personal psychological woundings are so great that we become immersed in them, blocking our transformation. At other times, our personal psychological wounds catalyze transformation. It is through restorying or remythologizing ourselves that we can consciously begin to transform. The symbolic mythic level, which is elaborated by Joseph Campbell,[12] allows us to mythologize our lives, to focus on a larger story, to undertake a vision quest. Developing our imagistic capabilities at all levels of the psyche and enhancing them at the symbolic mythic level can precipitate a spiritual transformation from our little local selves into a larger religious integral level in which we attain a great sense of caring and compassion and of deep unity with the earth and its people and animals and the larger mystery known by the 1001 names of God/dess.

The levels of the psyche are not developmental in nature. All levels are present in the adolescent and adult psyche, but the religious integral level may be latent. Spiritual transformation requires that we access the religious integral level and this can be facilitated through following one of the world's religious traditions available or through developing the "eye of contemplation" discussed by Ken Wilber.[13]

So, how does all this relate to teacher education and spiritual transformation? After studying with Houston and learning about the transformational "power of the myth,"[14] I began to use the mythological journey as a framework for various courses and programs.

In the mythological journey Campbell describes,[15] we first hear a "call" to adventure. I found that most preservice and inservice teachers had experienced a call to teach and this call had about it a numinous quality.[16] Teachers were called into teaching because they cared about children and wanted to make a difference in their lives. Often they became lost on the way, but their original call was clear. In Campbell's monomyth, once the hero (or hera, a feminine form from the Greek Goddess Hera) hears the call, he (or she) must "cross the threshold" into the world of adventure. The preservice teachers I worked with in our MAT program, designed to offer teacher certification at the graduate level, could easily identify with this station of the journey since they had often left high paying jobs to return to the university to accept their call to teach. The University of South Carolina's bureaucratic admissions process, complete with its "guardians of the threshold," allowed students to begin to identify with Campbell's description of the hero's journey.

Houston believes that by framing our personal journeys against the larger symbolic-mythic reality as described by Campbell, we can activate the entelechy, the "daimon"[17] that guides our spiritual unfolding in the same way that the tiny acorn is guided by its entelechy in a transformation into the mighty oak tree. I have used various myths at various times in my university courses that have focused on "living the mythic life," but one of my favorites for work with teachers is Dorothy and the Wizard of Oz.[18]

In my imagination, Dorothy's educational experience in Kansas paralleled her unhappy, monochromatic life. Her teacher was gruff and cranky like the neighbor that threatened her dog, Toto. When Dorothy imagined life over the rainbow, it was beautiful and she was called to enter this beautiful land of possibility. After a precipitous crossing of the threshold, Dorothy immediately began to gather "allies" who assisted her as she traveled the "road of trials" and confronted various "guardians of the threshold." She became "stuck in the belly of the whale" in the field of poppies and in the home of the Wicked Witch. Eventually, Dorothy's allies gained the heart, the brains, and the courage which they were seeking and which we all must seek in our journeys to achieve excellence as teachers. Dorothy's own wish was to "make the magic flight back" to Kansas. In Campbell's work, once we have attained the "boon" (the holy grail, the silver chalice, the golden fleece, or the vision of education or teaching certificate we are seeking) and have made the magic flight back to the world from which we left, we must become the "master of two worlds" and learn to live in the real world while never losing sight of our vision of what is possible.

I have learned that framing my personal journey against the heroic journey of transformation, the vision quest, that Campbell describes, allows me to become less attached to specific people or events that might otherwise serve to block my passage down my own particular "road of trials." I have learned that my allies can help me out when I am stuck in the belly of the whale. My own experiences and those of friends who have participated in Houston's ongoing Mystery Schools have validated the usefulness of Campbell's myth of the hero as a guide and an impetus for spiritual transformation.

At various times I have used Campbell's model of the hero's journey, of "living the mythic life" in different ways. Sometimes I have structured an entire course or certification program around the framework, asking students to create "professional growth portraits" utilizing an alternate sign system to report their personal and professional transformations at the completion of the course or program.[19] Sometimes I merely mention it in passing, in encouraging teachers to leave their personal castles of despair and to begin to help in greening the wasteland in which we find ourselves as we begin to awaken to this postmodern world. At other times,

I encourage teachers to read great biographies with children and to help them identify the trials that confront all great heros or heras as they live transformative lives.

Last year, an anthropology professor and I developed a course for our Honors College entitled "Culture, Myth, and Education." In this course, I discussed the cultural trance of our capitalistic, consumer-oriented, earth-destroying society and what it means to live a mythic life in a postmodern world. We watched movies such as "Blue," "White," "Red," and Ingmar Bergman's "Wild Strawberries," which allowed students to experience and share realities totally other. We read books chosen from a text set focusing on mythology and biographical narratives of transformation. Through individual conversations, I helped each student to identify a great myth or narrative which could serve as a framework for their own life's journey. Final projects for the course required that students analyze their personal journeys in terms of their chosen myth or narrative.

Because of the collaborative nature of team teaching, more pedagogical tensions emerged, or were made explicit, than in previous teaching experiences with "living the mythic life." An objective for co-teaching the course was that my colleague would learn more about the transformational work that Jean Houston does. His concerns about our ability to work with spiritual transformation at a large secular university have been noted. In fact, his concerns led me to seek a solution to the accusation he made that I was "practicing therapy without a license." I am still struggling with some of the issues, but authors such as bell hooks, Parker Palmer, and Jane Tompkins have convinced me I am on the right track as I continue to create transformational environments for students in higher education settings.[20]

A HOLISTIC VISION FOR EDUCATION

About 1990, I was still suffering the psychological wounds I experienced when a conservative member of the South Carolina legislature announced on a talk radio program in Charleston, South Carolina, that I was engaging in "Satanistic" teaching practices. I was shocked and deeply hurt by this accusation. Fortunately, about this time, I learned about an organization called the Global Alliance for Transforming Education (GATE). Phil Gang had assembled 80 international holistic educators in Chicago in June 1990, creating GATE and formulating an educational call for action.[21] At this point in my own spiritual transformation, I desperately needed some allies from mainstream educational settings! So, in 1991, when GATE met in Snowmass, Colorado, I joined the group to formulate a vision statement we called "Education 2000: A Holistic Perspective."

Ron Miller, a critical theorist and Montessori educator, drafted the original document and groups at the Snowmass conference revised and extended Ron's initial draft.[22] At the end of the week, I was asked to take the work submitted by the groups and edit a final document reflecting all that we had done. Later, I edited a book focusing on ways various holistic educators were grounding GATE's transformational vision of education in their own teaching practices.[22]

Ken Wilber argues that a holistic vision is still "flatland" when it comes to incorporating the spiritual dimensions of reality.[23] This may be true if we simply shift from an atomistic to a holistic description of the exteriors of things. Holistic education, as GATE envisioned it, includes those human depth dimensions that do account for a spiritual basis of reality. "Education 2000" continues to serve as a conceptual framework for my work. I will briefly summarize the 10 principles of holistic education here, editing the statements for the purpose of conserving space, and, in a later section on inquiry-based pedagogy, will describe how we at USC are currently applying them. The complete text of "Education 2000" may be found in Appendix A of *Holistic Education: Principles, Perspectives, and Practices*, which was designed for use as a college textbook or by individual teachers and parents. GATE has given permission to copy "Education 2000" freely.

Principle I. Educating for Human Development
The primary purpose of education is to facilitate the whole development of all learners. Rather than attempting to harness the abilities and dreams of the next generation to the capitalistic and consumer focus of our country's economic development, GATE's vision calls for a renewed emphasis on such human values as harmony, peace, cooperation, community, honesty, justice, equality, compassion, understanding, and love. We must treat our young people as human beings first and future workers secondarily. Only people who live full, healthy, meaningful lives can be truly productive.

Principle II. Honoring Students as Individuals
Schooling should be transformed so as to respect the individuality of every person We can build a true learning community in which people learn from each other's differences, are taught to value their own personal strengths, and are empowered to help one another. Our current practices of grading, assessment, and standardized testing serve more to assault the human spirit than to inform our teaching practices. Personalized assessments focusing on individual learning styles and unique patterns of intelligence are more affirming and useful in encouraging students to become inner directed.

Principle III. The Central Role of Experience
Learning is an active, multisensory engagement between an individual and the world, including the natural world, the social world, and the inner world. Experiential approaches are called for that immerse students in the wonders of life and nature and that connect them to the economic and social life of the community and to the inner world through the arts, honest dialogue, and times of quiet reflection.

Principle IV. Holistic Education
Holism is rooted in the assumption that the universe is an integrated whole in which everything is connected. Holistic education requires: a transformation of educational institutions and policies to result in holistic practices at all levels; multidisciplinary perspectives; a focus on whole human development, including physical, social, moral, aesthetic, creative, and spiritual aspects as well as intellectual and vocational aspects; and an affirmation of the inherent interdependence of evolving theory, research, and practice.

Principle V. New Role of Educators
Because teaching is a calling, requiring a blend of artistic sensitivity and scientifically grounded practice, educators must assume new roles which require

their own inner growth and creative awakening. Teachers must be attentive to the abilities and needs of individual students and require autonomy to design and implement appropriate and effective learning environments. Today's restructuring literature emphasizes accountability, placing the teacher at the service of administrators and policy makers. We believe, instead, that the educator is accountable, above all, to the young people who seek a meaningful understanding of the world they will someday inherit.

Principle VI. Freedom of Choice

Genuine education can only take place in an atmosphere of freedom. Freedom of inquiry, of expression, and of personal growth are all required. Whenever possible, students should be allowed authentic choices in their learning. Families should have access to a diverse range of educational options in the public school system and should have freedom to educate their children at home.

Principle VII. Educating for a Participatory Democracy

A democratic model of education empowers all citizens to take an active part in the affairs of their community and the planet. A democratic society hears disparate voices and addresses genuine human concerns. It is open to constructive change when social or cultural change is required. To promote the development of the skills and motivations necessary for life in a participatory democracy, the learning environment must embody such democratic values as empathy, an awareness of shared human needs, justice, and original, critical inquiry.

Principle VIII. Educating for Ethnic and Cultural Diversity and Global Citizenship

In the emerging global community, we are being brought into contact with diverse cultures and worldviews as never before in history. We must understand how diversity can cause conflict and experience methods of conflict resolution to establish conditions for peace. We propose that we commemorate, honor, and celebrate the traditions, ceremonies, and legacies of all peoples and envision a world without ethnic and cultural barriers. Since the world's religions and spiritual traditions have such enormous impact, global education encourages understanding and appreciation of them and of the universal values they proclaim, including the search for meaning, love, compassion, wisdom, truth, and harmony. Thus, education in this global age addresses what is most fully, most universally human in the young generations of all cultures.

Principle IX. Educating for Earth Literacy

We must rekindle a relationship between the human and the natural world that is nurturing, not exploitative. This is at the very core of our vision for the twenty-first century. Our children require a healthy planet on which to live and learn and grow. They need pure air and water and sunlight and fruitful soil and all the other living forms that comprise Earth's ecosystem. A sick planet does not support healthy children. Education for earth literacy must be rooted in a global and ecological perspective in order to cultivate in younger generations an appreciation for the profound interconnectedness of all life.

Principle X. Spirituality and Education

Just as the individual develops physically, emotionally, and intellectually, each person also develops spiritually. Spiritual experience and development manifest as a deep connection to self and others, a sense of meaning and purpose, an experience of the wholeness and interdependence of life, a respite from frenetic activity, pressure and over-stimulation, the fullness of creative experience, and a profound respect for the numinous Mystery of life. Drug and alcohol abuse, empty sexuality, crime and family breakdown all spring from a misguided search for connection, meaning, and mystery, and an escape from the pain of not having a genuine source of spiritual fulfillment.

INQUIRY-BASED PEDAGOGY

Critical inquiry is the foundation for a truly democratic society. Each learner in a culture of inquiry is honored as a unique, inquiring individual who is expected to participate in the development of a democratic learning community, taking personal responsibility for thinking, learning, and interacting in responsible, responsive ways.[24] Inquiry-based pedagogy is one transformational tool for nurturing the whole development of humans as conceptualized above in the principles of holistic education.

We have explored inquiry-based pedagogy for a number of years, in a variety of educational cultures, and have demonstrated that inquiry-based pedagogical practices are possible no matter what the socioeconomic status, ethnicity, or learning style of the learners. Preservice teachers have become researchers and reflective practitioners as they identify behavior management and curricular problems and improve practices in their clinical internship placements.[25] Children and their teachers have participated in a unique Center for Inquiry, a K-5 professional development school of choice, which serves as a clinical internship site for USC's preservice teacher education program. Undergraduate science majors have engaged in research-based learning in "critical connections courses" offered through USC's Honors College.[26] This section describes what happened when two cultures of inquiry were merged for part of a unique May Session course modeled on a holistic vision of education.

When, as part of the course, USC students visited the Center for Inquiry, we expected that the children's sense of wonder would inspire them and that their scientific knowledge would enrich the educational environment for the youngsters. We also hoped to recruit some of the undergraduate science majors into teaching. We were surprised when the sense of wonder and the knowledge base flowed both ways. The days' experience with third graders at the nearby "Hidden Pond" allowed USC students to see the possibilities inherent in their upcoming three week adventure on the rivers of South Carolina. The children had been walking to "Hidden Pond" for the entire year. Sometimes they would study the pond as biologists. Other times they would examine the pond through the eyes of a mathematician. On other occasions, the children would look at the pond through the eyes of an artist. In fact, as Thoreau found in his studies of Walden Pond, the learning possibilities are endless in a natural setting studied throughout the seasonal changes of the year. When one USC student asked how the field trip to "Hidden Pond" might be improved for the future, she expected an answer such as, "We could pick up trash." She was surprised when a third grader said, "We could pretend to be grass!"

The May Session course emphasized the cultural and environmental legacies of the rivers of South Carolina as undergraduates gained an awareness of what it means to live in harmony with the natural world. One class session, led by a religious studies professor and myself, focused on "Rivers as Metaphors for the Spiritual Journey." In this session, we discussed Hermann Hesse's book, *Siddhartha*, which describes the spiritual awareness gained from a lifetime of working on the river. We reviewed songs and hymns from sacred and secular traditions, including "Down by the Riverside" and "Old Man River." I asked students to form from clay a symbol representing what they expected to gain from their three-week adventure on the rivers of South Carolina. One young man modeled Atlas, on his knees, with the world on his shoulders. This young man said, "I feel like Atlas with the world on my shoulders. What I hope to gain is the strength to stand up and shoulder my part of the responsibility for the future of this planet."

USC students went camping for almost three weeks in the very hot South Carolina summer as they followed the state's rivers from the mountains to the sea. They paddled canoes on the rivers and swam in the ocean. One of USC's anthropology professors involved them in her excavation of a Native American site on a nearby river. They ate crawfish at the Gullah Festival in Beaufort, South Carolina, where they also studied the Gullah Culture, derived from African slaves. They studied the writings of plantation owners in a session focused on Southern literature and, finally, they examined what is happening as money-hungry developers attempt to capitalize on South Carolina's natural resources. Part of the experience included visiting the privately owned Dewees Island to learn about issues of environmental preservation and sustainable development that are being pioneered there.

USC students demonstrated their learning through field journals containing art, poetry, and photography; through reflective essays; and through a dramatic presentation. Learning celebrations held each Friday afternoon at a community building ritual at the Center for Inquiry allow for the demonstration of multiple ways of knowing. At the end of the three-week May session, the USC students presented a play at the learning celebration, sharing their knowledge of each of the cultures they had studied. One student was to be the slave driver, asking for volunteer "slaves" and cracking a whip to force the children to "pick" cotton. Later, this big football player confessed, "I was planning to be mean, but I couldn't do it with the little kids." This type of personal insight exemplifes the transformational experiences that occurred as three generations interacted.

When we all become learners and we all become teachers, what happens to those of us who are paid to be teachers? It is our job to provide structure, to serve as resource people, and to act as guides and mentors. In inquiry-based pedagogy, the learners ask questions and begin to answer their own questions through personal and social knowledge. As that personal and social knowledge reaches its limits, it is the job of the educator to provide for resource materials and people to expand and enhance the knowledge base. It is also the role of the educator to assure that the basic knowledge that society expects from an "educated" person is incorporated into the learning environment.

A CHILD ADVOCACY AGENDA

Child advocacy has always been an important focus in my family. My grandmother dearly loved her three children, nine grandchildren, and 13 great grandchildren. My mother was a teacher of first and second graders for 25 years. One of the ways to avoid the accusation of "practicing therapy without a license" is to remove the focus from the smaller, personal, local story and to focus on the larger story which, today, requires that we nurture our planet and the world's children. In addition to the children in my own family and community, my focus has expanded to include research in global child advocacy. Recently, I have asked graduate students to complete child advocacy projects that address a need that they identify in their interactions with children in educational and community settings.

Overpopulation, poverty, illiteracy, violence, and environmental degradation are affecting children, families, and communities all over the planet. What can be done to defuse these ticking bombs which may, in the long run, be as critical as nuclear disarmament to our children's future? Changing the traditional model of world development from a focus on economic growth to a focus on human development is one of the keys to defusing these ticking bombs. Studies from other cultures often provide lessons that allow us to prevent disaster in our own culture. Some lessons learned in India about the power of human ingenuity, inquiry-based pedagogy, child advocacy, and a holistic vision for human development are shared in the following paragraphs.

The Rishi Valley School, established in India by Krishnamurti, is situated on three hundred acres of land which had long been devastated through overutilization. It is seen as one hopeful note in a third world situation characterized by extreme overpopulation, poverty, and environmental degradation.[27] The main boarding school serves as the center of an extraordinary rural education outreach program characterized by inquiry-based pedagogy.

For the past 37 years, Mr. Naidu, one of the local people who gained an education and developed the skills of a naturalist, has been nourishing the land back to life with the help of the school children. The water table and vegetation have been restored due to their work. Children are planting 10,000 trees a year and are engaging in inquiry processes related to their lives, including the demographics and the biodiversity of their villages.

As the children engage in inquiry, they develop language, mathematical and earth literacy. Utilizing inquiry-based curriculum materials, the children ask questions about their villages and the biodiversity found there. How many pigs are there? How many goats? From the data gathered about the villages and the people, plants, and animals, the children construct charts and learn mathematics. They also learn to read and write for real reasons as they put on metric fairs and shadow puppet plays for the villagers and their school mates. They write reports and take those reports home for their parents to read. As a result, the literacy rate among villagers has increased dramatically from less than 20 percent to more than 60

Education and Training, ed. D. J. Waddington (Berlin: Springer-Verlag, 1995); and Stefka Eddins and Douglas Williams, "Strategies for Integrating Research Activities with an Established Curriculum," *Journal of Excellence on College Teaching* (in press).

28. Robert D. Kaplan, *The Ends of the Earth* (New York: Vintage Books, 1996).

28. A Walk in the Wilderness

Claudia Horwitz

I believe any kind of interfaith work is a wilderness experience because it draws us into new and messy places and because we usually don't know exactly where we're going. Crossing the boundaries of faith traditions and spiritual expression tests our ability to rest in a place of confusion and calls on us to deepen our comfort level with the unknown. With this come rewards we cannot begin to imagine at the outset. When Moses went up to the top of Mount Sinai, he had no idea he was going to walk away with the Ten Commandments. Siddhartha left his father's kingdom because he knew he was not seeing the world whole, but he never expected to find enlightenment and become the Buddha. And it was only after fasting for forty days and nights in the desert that Jesus was able to proclaim that "Man does not live on bread alone, but on every word that comes from the mouth of God" (Matt. 4:4).

Beverly Lanzetta, president of the Interfaith Theological Seminary in Tucson, Arizona, talks about interfaith work as an experiment which can bear paradox and, in fact, it must because there are multiple truths to learn. She believes that all of this is possible because we "inherit the collectivity of the human spiritual quest." In other words, Lanzetta believes that we have been activated to pursue one state of consciousness (often made manifest in the practice of one spiritual or religious tradition) but the others remain within us. And because of that, we can come to dwell in others' experience in an authentic way.[1]

So what does this walk in the wilderness require? You need to find fellow travelers, other people who want to be involved. You need an idea of why you are undertaking this voyage and what success looks like. You need to do some planning so you can determine what your first steps are. You need resources and you need skills. In other words, interfaith programming in higher education succeeds for the same reasons most other endeavors succeed: a circle of committed people, vision, first steps, resources, and skills.

A Circle of Committed People

"[We need] small groups gathering and creating help for us all. We need smaller groups now. That's all I can talk of and it's not nearly enough...Hope a new class of people will know what's necessary...It's these small groups of people who will lead in the eventual help...people who will be able to make the change to a higher place...Their small risk will become law."[2] Social philosopher Lewis Mumford uttered these words when he was nearing the end of his life. The truth is, good things happen because people make them happen. Small groups of individuals coming together on a regular basis for a common purpose are nothing new, nor do they belong only to one tradition. They have a great legacy in old and new forms that continue to thrive: in the Jewish *havurah*, Christian mission groups, Bible study, women's spirituality groups, 12-step programs, and many others. Change begins when small groups of people make commitments to each other, commitments that allow them to do something they would not do on their own. The group provides a space in which people can learn from the past, honor what is present, and envision a radically different future.

So, first you need to find a group of fellow travelers for this walk in the wilderness. You want to find others who share your ideas, your concerns, or your hopes. The best way to do this is through one-on-one conversations with people. Don't limit yourself to the obvious. Look for faculty, for students, for staff and administrators in unlikely places who might share your interest in interfaith work. Your effort will be stronger if you can link up with people from many different departments and offices on campus. Talk to housekeepers and math professors and athletes and librarians.

Eventually, you will notice that a potential group is forming. This will be your circle. The circle is a beautiful organizing principle. All people can be heard and seen. The circle, at its best, keeps people involved, motivated, and connected. It is a form which inspires union, democracy, and collaboration. And the circle can easily reshape itself when necessary into smaller units. Your circle will be the place you return to, a place where you share ideas, figure out next steps, teach each other, and get support for the next phase.

VISION

As a colleague once said, Martin Luther King did not stand up in front of the throngs of people gathered in Washington, D.C., and preach, "I have a strategic plan." It was about a dream, and all truly powerful efforts begin with the seed of a dream. This is the answer to the question, "Why do we do what we do?" or "What is it that we want to be different?" Visions are not pie-in-the-sky. Ronald Heifetz, director of the Leadership Education Project at Harvard University's John F. Kennedy School of Government, reminds us that "the word 'vision' refers to our capacity to see...the quality of any vision depends on its accuracy, not just on its appeal or on how imaginative it is."[3] Heifetz spells out three realities which must be faced: (1) core values and the gap between these values and actual behavior; (2) skills available and skills the situation requires; and (3) opportunities possible in the future.

The more people who have a hand in shaping a vision, the more staying power it will have. Collective thinking and honest dialogue in the visioning stage will help each person to clarify their hopes and intentions, and hopes and intentions are sacred aspects of collaborative work. Of course, this takes time. One common pitfall is cutting the visioning phase short or skipping it altogether. People of action are often eager to get to what some consider the "real work." We tend to forge ahead without stopping to figure out exactly where we are going. Using the process below will help us resist this temptation.

A SUGGESTED PROCESS FOR VISIONING

Note that each underlined tool below is described more fully in the "Tools for the Journey" section at the end of the article.

Meet at least once to get to know each other, without an agenda, if you aren't already familiar with one another. This might be a potluck dinner or brown bag lunch where folks do some storytelling about their faith or spiritual backgrounds. Try this activity called "faith stories." Have everybody pair up with someone they don't know well. Give them the following four questions and ask them to interview each other. Tell them that they have five minutes each, and encourage each person to be thorough and thoughtful in their answers. Ring a bell or chime when the first five-minute period is up and ask people to switch.

1. Did you practice a faith or spiritual tradition growing up? What highlights do you remember about it?
2. What has your relationship to faith or spiritual practice been over the past year or two?
3. What is inspirational to you?
4. When do you remember experiencing the presence of spirit or God in your life?

Come back together as a circle and ask people to reflect on what they said and heard.

When you're ready to dig into the visioning process, gather your circle in a comfortable setting, conducive to honest conversation and quiet reflection. Spend at least five minutes in silence together. If you or someone else feel comfortable leading everyone in a short meditation, you can try that. Then, frame in very general terms the ideas you have gathered to explore and ask everyone to freewrite or reflect on the following questions:

1. What are your greatest hopes for this work? What do you think is possible?
2. Do you have any fears about it? What are they?
3. What intentions do you have for this budding effort? What do you hope to gain?

Have everyone get into groups of three and share some of what emerged from their writing. Ask that everyone listen with reverence, and that each small group be prepared to share the main themes of their discussion. Come back to the large circle and have each group report out their main themes. Write them up somewhere that everyone can see them. Use the time remaining for discussion about where the overlap is. This is a good time to ask people, "What are you noticing?" Figure out another time to meet and continue the conversation.

In your next gathering, begin with a ritual. (You might ask one or two people to sign up for this ahead of time.) Then recap what happened at your previous meetings. Brainstorm possibilities for your vision as a circle. What do you want to see happen? What core values will you operate with? What opportunities have already presented themselves? Observe the priorities and common themes emerging and where there might be disagreement. Ask if a small group is willing to volunteer to put the main ideas into written form, which the whole circle can later review. This vision statement should reflect the areas where aspirations and hopes overlap.

First Steps

Once the vision becomes clear, you're ready to do some planning and get a sense of your first steps. The planning process you undertake should reflect the values that emerged during the visioning process. It will speak volumes about your future and your likelihood of success. Often we have a great idea and we are eager to just dig in and get going. Like visioning, planning is an opportunity to slow down, honor the process, and pay close attention to people's strengths and desires. You want to make sure that together you are designing tasks that are neither too small for people to forget them altogether, nor too large that they become overwhelming. (If someone is struggling with or avoiding a task they agreed to do, there is usually a good reason.)

Schedule time for planning and begin by reading your vision statement. Talk about the wording and decide what, if anything, needs to be changed. Next, pick an appropriate timeframe and break it down into manageable blocks. For example, maybe you'll look at two years, broken into six-month or semester blocks. Once you've chosen your timeframe, draw a large timeline that you can post on the wall and work with over time.

Determine your end goals. Ask the group, "In two years, where do we want to be?" Work backwards from there, brainstorming possible activity for each block of time. When it comes time to choose tasks—who is going to do what, and when—you might start this process with some one-on-one dialogue. Individuals can spend 10 minutes talking to one other person (again, remind people about listening with reverence) about what they'd most like to do. Then bring it back to a group conversation and make some decisions. These partner dialogues will enable people to articulate their strengths and desires, explore their level of commitment, and get to know each other better.

Taking it Slow

If you are fearful that you are "stuck" in the visioning phase and not digging into first steps quickly enough, don't worry. Sometimes the best ideas need time to germinate. I am part of a group of clergy and lay people from different faith traditions who want to start an interfaith monastery. It has been a long and luxurious process of discerning exactly what that means, what we want, and what we are willing to do.

Some of our community's most respected religious leaders had been considering this idea for quite a while. Over a year ago, I met with two of them—a Baptist minister who is a leader in the anti-death penalty movement and numerous other community activities, and a Catholic Sister who practices meditation and has been a social justice worker for three decades. Then there I was, raised Jewish, now with a regular meditation practice and ready to start yoga teacher training this fall. I suppose the three of us decided we were interfaith enough and put the call out to others who might want to join us. Many did, and many continue to. (In fact, the group's composition changes slightly each time we gather; does that sound familiar?) We had few preconceived ideas as to what the monastery would look like, how long it might take to get off of the ground, or who would do what. We decided to trust the group's wisdom and the power of relationships built over time.

So far, it has worked. We began meeting every two to three months, and now we meet monthly. We made the decision early on to begin with a half hour of silence, followed by an hour and a half of dialogue. We sit in silence and then we talk about what seems relevant: what the word "interfaith" actually means to each of us, what spiritual practices we each have in our lives, what kind of community we want to create. At one point, some land came up for sale and we scrambled to consider the possibility of buying it. After some conversations we realized that we were not ready to take that step, and that while eventually finding a place was certainly important, we didn't want the availability of that place to determine our timeline.

After more than a year, we are getting ready to "do" something. For many of us, this group has been a delicious contradiction to many of the other efforts we are involved in. Because there is no sense of immediacy, we are all more present to the will of the spirit, more open to how that guides us, now and in the future. We treat each other as truly sacred human beings, more so than any other group I've ever been a part of. I believe that our spiritual needs are clearly being fed, or by now we would have decided not to attend any more meetings, or to "move the process along." If we had rushed the visioning phase, I don't think we'd be as profoundly connected, as respectful, or as honest as we are. And I know that whatever direction this initiative takes, it will be the right one.

RESOURCES

I hold a fundamental belief about resources that some are necessary but a lot can be done with a little. Resources are anything and everything you can think of which will assist you in your work. For some this might be a photocopier or a fax machine. For others it might be a meeting space or access to a dean. First, take inventory of everything you have. Make a list together. Think about:—Funding that is already available to you. Be up front about this; it will add to the transparency of your project and help build trust. Often it is only the director, administrator, or student leader who knows the budget for a given project. If your circle includes people from many different departments, you may be surprised at the level of funding potentially available for your efforts. But you'll never know that if you don't talk about it.—Relationships. The networks and relationships of people in the group are vital. Create a large picture on the wall of who knows whom within your university or college. Think of this as a web or a map. You'll begin to see the breadth and depth of your connections.—Equipment and supplies.—Space, including all spaces you know of that might be useful in the future. Don't forget spaces off-campus.

Once your list feels complete, leave it on the wall in the space where you meet. Encourage people to add to it as your work together moves along. Think about what you need but don't have, and then brainstorm where or how you can get it.

Skills

Take inventory of the skills within your circle, much the way you did with resources. Have everyone write down on post-it notes what they know how to do, one skill per note. Remind people to include all kinds of skills, even the ones that might not seem immediately relevant. You might even get a list of skills out of a creative, career-planning book like *What Color is Your Parachute?* by Richard Bolles, to get people's minds going. Then ask everyone to put all their post-its on one large piece of paper so everyone can see all of them, and begin grouping the skills by theme. Make sure people spend time just looking and noticing what skills are present in the group. Sometimes just doing this brainstorming will spark program ideas or new action steps. Next, think about the planning you have already done as a circle. What additional skills will these ideas require? Who else do you know who might be able to help?

Interfaith work is still relatively new for many campuses and I believe the work will thrive as we invite more time and space for questioning, for doubt, for ambiguity. Common ground does not grow merely from the overlap of commonality. It sprouts slowly in the margins and around the edges, in the places easily overlooked by groups moving too quickly. It helps if we know how to honor individual strengths and create environments which call forth different perspectives. It is not always comfortable, leaning into difference, but the work of interfaith dialogue and action will be weak without it. It takes time and attention and a lot of patience.

For example, interfaith work often demands a willingness to move between the roles of participant and observer, particularly when worship or ritual is involved. This is a skill which can be easily learned. For example, if a group is sharing rituals from their faith traditions and someone begins to praise Jesus, I become an observer and I take that opportunity to learn more about their background and religious experience. If someone recites a prayer in Hebrew, non-Jews in the room might not be able to participate, but they can listen and perhaps understand more about Judaism.

Interfaith work also requires careful facilitation. When organizing groups around issues of religion, faith, and spirituality, it is particularly important that someone take responsibility for thinking about the entire group and creating a safe environment. A good facilitator draws out opinions and helps everyone to participate. Often this means using direct and open-ended questions. Calling attention to diverse perspectives is particularly important. Be on the lookout for what I call "the tyranny of the devout." Those who are most sure of and comfortable with their beliefs are often most likely to express them. Pay attention to those who don't seem as comfortable and help them find their voice in the group; they may need some extra support.

THE SKILL OF SILENCE

One of the most important skills for interfaith work is the ability to encourage and make space for silence. In the summers, I work with E Pluribus Unum, a leadership program for high school students that explores religion, social justice, and the common good. The first year I served as one of seven mentors, a diverse group with respect to religious and ethnic background. Our job was to help students reflect on their experiences with this intense, rather full program.

About halfway through the three-week program, we reached a somewhat predictable crisis point. As a result of a provocative speaker and subsequent conversation, issues of race had finally surfaced in a real way. Some of us were a bit surprised by the lack of general awareness among the white students in the group, too easily forgetting the students were only seniors in high school. (Actually, they had a much higher sensitivity than I did at that age.) As the staff members closest to the students, we felt it was our role to address this, and perhaps add something to the community dialogue that would bring the conversation to another level. But we couldn't figure out how to do it. Everything we thought of sounded too preachy, too righteous, or else too weak. Our conversation kept going around and around in circles. It seemed we needed to access our deeper wisdom, but how?

Finally, someone suggested that we take a few moments of silence for our own prayer and contemplation. Without any verbal agreement, we all decided to stay in the room together, and no one would say anything out loud until it appeared everyone was ready to convene. I closed my eyes, crossed my legs in the lotus position and began to focus on my breath. (Meditation is my best coping mechanism when things get hard, if the situation permits.) One of the Jewish mentors stood up, walked over to the window and began to engage in silent, standing prayer. Another mentor laid down on the floor, another sat facing the wall, head in hand. One of the Catholic mentors kneeled down in front of the chair she had been sitting on; I could just barely hear her Spanish words of prayer under her breath.

Without speaking or even looking at each other, we slowly made our way back to the circle. We sat and looked at each other in silence for a few moments. Someone spoke, then somebody else. The conversation flowed like water and within moments, it seemed, we had made a decision to do a mentor "fishbowl" on race. All seven of us would have a conversation about our own experiences and philosophy in the center of the room. The students would be asked to listen at first, then one by one we would leave the fishbowl and students who wanted to join the conversation would take our place. I don't recall exactly who came up with the idea, or how, but the rest of the planning was a piece of cake. And needless to say, the strategy worked as well as we'd hoped it would. It was a joint solution, born in the quiet, contemplative space we had created together.

THE ENERGY OF INTENTION

As the circle begins to take shape, spend time thinking about what energy will pulse through your efforts. Will your circle have an intentional, joyful energy because people are engaged and happy about what they are doing? Or will it have a tired energy because folks feel burned out and overworked? Think of a new endeavor as a unique opportunity to build a healthy foundation. You have a chance to model internally what folks are committed to externally. When you pay attention in this way, use the practices in the next section, "Tools for the Journey," you can expect: 1. Greater focus, because you have created opportunities for the circle to slow down and ground itself in purpose and meaning; 2. Stronger relationships, which include greater accountability, stronger communication around needs and expectations; 3. Effective teamwork based on appreciation, recognition, and evaluation of individual strengths and challenges; 4. Better crisis management, and an ability to face obstacles with more creativity and calm; and 5. Sustained commitment.

TOOLS FOR THE JOURNEY

In my work, I have found that I return to the same tools over and over again. Each one has become vital to me because each allows for clarity of mind, depth of spirit, and an open heart. These things make the difference between good projects and truly great ones, between scattered participation and sustained involvement.

FREEWRITING

Freewriting helps people express themselves, and it releases us from traditional notions of journaling. If a group is working together, freewriting is a way to remember how very different each person's perspective is. It's also inspiring to hear other people's writing. In freewriting, you write for a set amount of time (say five minutes) in stream of consciousness about a specific topic. Each person writes for him or herself, so punctuation, grammar, and sentence structure do not matter.

You want to invite folks to follow their stream of thought, not to edit, but to keep right on going, even if it seems there is nothing else left to write. As Natalie Goldberg says, "Go for the jugular," meaning go for the core of what you're thinking and feeling.

Writing is powerful because it allows us to tell stories (real and unreal), communicate feelings, voice worries, process experiences, work through challenges, and dream big dreams. With words and stories, we can sort through all of the ideas and messages floating in our heads and get down to the truth. To tell the truth is revolutionary and liberating because we can begin to teach people what we want them to know about us. Writing and storytelling can be tremendous tools for spiritual exploration, vocational discernment, and community building.

Note: Always give people a chance to opt out or find a different mode of expression. Literacy levels and learning disabilities vary widely, and some people just hate to write. Provide suggestions for other ways to reflect, perhaps through art or thought, so folks can opt out of writing without feeling self-conscious.

LISTENING WITH REVERENCE

Listening with reverence is an important building block in any sustainable relationship. The ability to listen well, with compassion, without responding, is a real gift. We often think that our response as a listener is vital. We have been taught to nod our heads in agreement, laugh in the appropriate places, tell our own stories to demonstrate our understanding, come up with solutions, and give great advice. In all of these cases, the usual result is that the person speaking does so for our benefit and not their own. The speaker becomes sensitive to our reactions and conscious of what impact their words are having and the focus subtly shifts. Listening with reverence, not reaction, gives the other person more space to tell their story without having to worry about how it will be received. The speaker actually becomes empowered to follow their own path rather than taking the direction offered.

RITUAL

Ritual is something—anything—that we do to draw special awareness to an event, a person, a time, or an idea. By focusing energy in a purposeful way, rituals allow us to recognize something we might not have otherwise paid much attention to. Ritual creates sacred space, allowing groups greater opportunities to build trust, unity, and safety. With ritual we can celebrate individual and group accomplishments, the power of community, common vision and goals, beginnings and endings. Rituals often involve the use of an object which becomes symbolic of the ritual itself. To mark the beginning of a three-day training, a group I worked with made a talking stick together. We walked outside and found the stick together.

Next, each participant tied a ribbon onto the stick as they named their goals and hopes for the training. The stick was used throughout the training whenever we wanted to bring a more intentional method of sharing to the circle.

SILENCE

Silence is a contemplative practice which has the potential to call forth a vast array of religious experience. And, in collective silence, each of us can find our own expression of God, our own words of prayer, our own acts of praise. Silence is an opening that encourages a different voice to emerge. This is the voice that we search for when we have to make a difficult decision, prepare for a life-changing event, or deal with great pain. Silence can enhance nonverbal communication, quiet our nerves and the endless chatter in our minds, and provide space to regain perspective. Silence is also a wonderful way to ritualize beginnings and endings. I have found silence to be a powerful tool when working with groups. If people can be silent together for more than just a minute or two, their bonds deepen in unpredictable ways. And the impact is felt long after the silence has been broken.

ENDNOTES

1. Beverly Lanzetta, "Interfaith Seminary: Training for Ministry in a Religiously Plural World," workshop at EDUCATION as *Transformation* Conference, Wellesley College, September 28, 1998.
2. Tonia Shoumatoff, "The Last Days of Lewis Mumford," *Lapis* 3, 61.
3. William C. Taylor, "The Leader of the Future," *Fast Company* 25 (June 1999), 132.

RESOURCES FOR FURTHER EXPLORATION

Baldwin, Christina. *Calling the Circle*. Newberg, Oreg.: Swan Rave, 1994. Extensive information and stories on creating circles in various contexts of work and community.

Carnes, Robin Deen and Sally Craig. *Sacred Circles: A Guide to Creating Your Own Women's Spirituality Group*. San Francisco: Harper San Francisco, 1998. Full of practical ideas and suggestions for starting your own circle, appropriate for many kinds of groups.

Goldberg, Natalie. *Writing Down the Bones: Freeing the Writer Within*. Boston: Shambhala, 1986. For people who want to explore their own talent for writing and/or use writing as a spiritual practice. Short essays on writing and exercises to try.

Horwitz, Claudia. *A Stone's Throw: Living the Act of Faith*. Durham, N.C.: stone circles, 1999. Resource for individuals and organizations who want to cultivate faith and spiritual practice as a vital part of social change work. Includes practical activities to do alone and with groups, worksheets, and stories of faith-based activists.

Kaner, Sam. *Facilitator's Guide to Participatory Decision-Making.* Gabriola Island, British Columbia: New Society Publishers, 1996. Clear and accessible guide to working with groups; indispensable resource for facilitators.

Peck, M. Scott. *The Different Drum: Community Making and Peace.* New York: Simon and Schuster, Inc., 1987. A look at community as an experience of self-awareness and profound connection. Includes a description of the classic stages of community building.

Shields, Katrina. *In the Tiger's Mouth: An Empowerment Guide for Social Action.* Philadelphia: New Society Publishers, 1994. Analysis and approaches for those working for change, including ways to cultivate individual and organizational support.

Spears, Larry. *Insights on Leadership: Service, Stewardship, Spirit, and Servant-Leadership.* New York: John Wiley and Sons, 1998. Collection of essays and articles from a variety of individuals on the concept of servant-leadership and possible applications.

Conclusion

VICTOR H. KAZANJIAN, JR. AND PETER L. LAURENCE

A t the close of the 1998 national gathering at Wellesley College, Vincent Harding, professor of religion and social transformation at the Iliff School of Theology, stepped to the podium to attempt to tie together the events of the previous two days.

> I think a very important meeting is taking place.... I feel that in a real sense I have come home by being at this gathering on transformation; and that you are my sisters and my brothers and have been for longer than either you or I could possibly know, and probably will be for even longer than that. And it is as a brother, not as a conference speaker, that I come to you at the close of this powerful and moving experience. And I come understanding my privilege, not as one of telling you how or what you should be doing to take all of this home, but I come simply suggesting to you what I am thinking about, feeling about, hoping about, as I go home from this place, and wondering if you might think, feel, and hope some of the same things or things different from this as we leave together.
>
> I was deeply moved by the various times we came in touch with our sister Diana Eck and when she said again and again that before we can celebrate diversity, we need to encounter it; not run from it, but encounter it, engage it, look it right in the eye.... I'm going back and invite you to go back seeing [this diversity]—seeing it, not being afraid to see it—and to recognize that seeing it is going to be difficult sometimes.... I'm going back trying to make sure that I encounter the painfulness, the demandingness of seeing diversity.... I want to go back remembering that diversity is not a style, that diversity is not an academic calling, but that diversity is the way of the universe itself. And I want to enter more deeply in every possible way into the path of the universe. So I will seek out my diverse brothers and sisters, because they will take me home. They will take me to the deepest levels of the river. They will take me to the deepest levels of God, because God is diversity, is truth, is my sister, is my brother. I'm going back, pondering these things, and I am so very glad that I could be here to be inspired again.[1]

As educators, scholars, teachers, administrators, and students, where do we go to get inspired again? As many of the authors have suggested, the answer appears to be two-fold: Inspiration waits for us in the world around us and in the world within us. This is what people at the national gathering spoke of over and over again. The antidote to the stagnation and fragmentation that too often infects our learning communities is to be found both within and without.

THE OUTWARD JOURNEY

The outward journey is something that we in higher education have been engaged in for quite some time. The cultural diversification of college and university campuses, like the cultural diversification of America, has presented us with the opportunity and challenge of seeing diversity as a resource for our learning rather than a barrier to it.

Too often, however, we have approached the diverse world around us as if we were standing too close to an impressionistic painting. All we see is a chaotic jumble of different colors and shapes, and in our initial discomfort we flee the apparent fragmentation, unaware of what awaits us if we were to take a few steps back and gaze at the magnificent beauty of all created things. Pluralism, as it has been discussed by the authors in this book, is a strategy to step back and engage the apparent chaos of diversity so that we can appreciate the beauty of many-ness.

In the past (and perhaps continuing in the present) most colleges and universities have approached diversity by using the practice of assimilation, not unlike that which has been at work in American society. The culture of our institutions, from their mono-religiously influenced founding to their current mono-culturally-influenced structure and curriculum, tends to approach diversity as a problem to be solved. Most often these problem-solving strategies have the effect of forcing people who are outside of the dominant institutional culture to adopt the language and etiquette of the normative culture through a series of rewards and enticements. The pressure to conform in order to succeed, which so many students, faculty and staff from non-dominant groups report as stifling and oppressive, is ironically precisely what scholars thought that they had gotten rid of when they loosed the chains of institutional religion from higher education a half century ago. But cultural exclusivism, like religious exclusivism, will always treat diversity as an enemy. And to go a step further, as Parker Palmer suggests, an intellectual exclusivism which bases its epistemology on objectivism and excludes all other dimensions of knowing, begins to look remarkably like the kind of religious fundamentalism which academics decry.

In as much as colleges and universities are microcosms of a diverse national and global human community, our institutions have a unique opportunity and responsibility to provide a context of learning which values diversity as a necessary component to education. Too often even the most progressive diversity initiatives and multi-cultural efforts leave religion out of the mix. How is it possible to be an educated person in this moment in history and not have an intellectual and a practical understanding of the role that religion plays in shaping the lives of individuals and societies? In the colleges and universities described in this book and in many other such institutions across the country, new models for incorporating religious diversity as one component of a global learning community are being developed. In each case these institutions have taken up issues of religion and spirituality as educational issues, important to the intellectual vitality of their communities. In this way, the struggle is no longer defined as educational institutions struggling to maintain their independence from religious institutions, but rather as educational institutions expanding their educational programs to incorporate a more complex understanding of teaching and learning so as to better educate the whole student for life and leadership in a diverse world.

THE INWARD JOURNEY

As has been evident in these essays, there is more to this movement towards a new vision of education as transformation than the external. Nearly everyone with whom we have worked in higher education readily speaks of being drawn into the profession of teacher/scholar by being inspired; inspired by a particular subject, or question, or by a particular teacher. Most of us can recount the very moment or moments that called us out onto our quest in the land of learning. Again and again, educators and students speak about the optimal learning experience as one in which there is a sense of wonder, awe, inspiration, freedom, or connection which leads to an inner awakening, a change in perspective, a transformation of the whole person.

Such is the power of education, if, and only if, teaching and learning is more than the amassing of information in order to gain mastery over some body of knowledge so as to reap the rewards of individual success. Participants at the national gathering began to consider how to develop an educational language to describe this experience of education as a transformational process. Many of the authors in this book have taken that discourse even further. Some have referred to this process as the spiritual dimension to education, but for others the term spiritual is too connected to a particular religious belief. In education as well as in business, science, economics and other areas of society, questions about spirituality and the inner life abound. Perhaps we might think about as spirituality as that which animates us, giving meaning, purpose and context to thought, word and action. The articles in this book have taken the next step in developing these questions and it is our hope that the discussions and debates are just beginning.

THE ONGOING WORK OF THE EDUCATION AS *TRANSFORMATION* PROJECT

Through ongoing training workshops, seminars and conferences; through a web site, email newsletters and electronic gatherings; through a variety of educational materials now available and being developed, the EDUCATION as *Transformation* Project is a catalyst for this dialogue and a support to the presidents, faculty, administrators, trustees and students who are interested in taking up these issues.

As the movement toward engaging religious pluralism and spirituality at colleges and universities moves forward, the project finds itself with many opportunities for new expression. One clear direction is the publication of resource materials like this book, to aid campuses in their desire to acknowledge religious diversity, work towards religious pluralism, and explore the role of spirituality in educational programs. The project will be a continuing source of such materials, compiled with the help of our advisors and colleagues throughout the country. One such project currently underway is the preparation of case studies describing ways in which some schools have created multi-faith spaces that welcome students of all religious backgrounds by converting existing mono-religious facilities or by engaging in new construction. Another is the development of an educational video entitled "Beyond Tolerance," which explores issues of religious difference and strategies of pluralism.

The project has also initiated a program of consultation with individual colleges and universities that are interested in forming multi-constituency teams for dialogue about their questions and concerns regarding religious pluralism and spirituality on their own campuses. Aspects of spirituality in education, such as overcoming institutional fragmentation and attending to the inner life of the teacher and student, are being increasingly addressed through workshops and seminars at conferences and at host campuses. We have already found that this work can lead to significant institutional change that better serves the needs of students, administrators, and faculty, and that brings the institution into alignment with its own educational mission.

How might strategies of pluralism and issues of spirituality provide connection, meaning and purpose in our educational institutions and programs? Perhaps you have found some answers and insights within the pages of this book, but ultimately it is only through our encounters with each other, across lines of difference, sharing our stories and experiences, searching for new and better ways to offer education in ways that liberate the mind and send the spirit soaring.

Contributors

Douglas C. Bennett is president and professor of politics at Earlham College in Richmond, Indiana. He was educated at Haverford College and Yale University. Previously, he held positions at Temple University, Reed College, and the American Council of Learned Societies. He is a member of the Religious Society of Friends (Quakers).

Donna Bivens has been a leader at the Women's Theological Center in Boston for 12 years. Together with the staff at WTC, Donna offers training, consultation and workshops for schools, social service agencies, religious institutions and other non-profits on anti-racism and anti-internalized racism. Among the rewards she has received are the DryLongSo Award for Community Change; the Community Service Award, and the Women of Justice Award from Network.

Frederic Bradford Burnham is director of Trinity Institute, a program for the continuing theological education of Episcopal clergy and laity sponsored by The Parish of Trinity Church, New York City. He was educated at Harvard University, the Episcopal Divinity School, Cambridge University, England, and the Johns Hopkins University, where he received a Ph.D. in the history of science.

Suheil Badi Bushrui holds the Baha'i Chair for World Peace in the Center for International Development and Conflict Management at the University of Maryland. He is a distinguished author, poet, critic, translator and media personality, well known in the United States, the Middle East and the Arab world, as well as in India and Africa.

Brad DrowningBear is the former spiritual life coordinator at the Haskell Indian Nations University in Lawrence, Kansas. He was born and raised in Seattle of a mother who is Yakama, Snohomish, Nez Perce, Wanapum, Danish and English, and a father from Oklahoma who is Cherokee and Irish.

Carol L. Flake holds the Moore Child Advocacy Distinguished Chair and is former chair of the Department of Instruction and Teacher Education at the University of South Carolina, where she has been a member of the faculty since 1976. Her doctorate is in child and family development and her masters degree is in religious studies with a focus on feminist theology.

Arthur Green is Philip W. Lown Professor of Jewish Thought at Brandeis University and former president of the Reconstructionist Rabbinical College. His most recent book, *These are the Words: A Vocabulary of Jewish Spiritual Life*, is published by Jewish Lights.

Sally Z. Hare currently holds the Singleton Endowed Professorship at Coastal Carolina University in Myrtle Beach, SC, where she directs the Center for Education and Community. She facilitated one of the pilot Courage to Teach programs.

John W. Healey is the former director of the Archbishop Hughes Institute on Religion and Culture at Fordham University. Prior to establishing the Institute, he served as vice president for planning and budget at Fordham and dean of the university's School of General Studies. He received his bachelors and masters degree in philosophy from St. Louis University and his doctorate in theology from the Gregorian University.

Claudia Horwitz is the founder of stone circles, a nonprofit that integrates faith, spiritual practice and social justice. She has ten years' experience in community organizing and youth leadership, and recently finished *A Stone's Throw: living the act of faith*, a resource for people committed to faith-based change.

Ji Hyang Sunim is a Buddhist nun in the Korean Chogye order, and abbot of Cambridge Zen Center. She has served as advisor to Buddhist students at Wellesley College, Buddhist chaplain at Harvard University, and is co-founder of the Buddhist Coalition of New England.

Marcy Jackson is co-director of the Center for Teacher Formation in Bainbridge Island, Washington. She is a faculty member of the Whidbey Institute, where she teaches and develops programs to sustain healthy families and promote reflective leadership. She holds M.S.W. and M.P.H. degrees from the University of Minnesota.

Rick Jackson is co-director of the Center for Teacher Formation in Bainbridge Island, Washington. He is vice-president of the YMCA of Greater Seattle, Board president of the Whidbey Institute, and consults with non-profits and foundations. He holds M.A.R. and M.Div. degrees from Yale University.

Victor H. Kazanjian, Jr. is the dean of religious and spiritual life and co-director of the Peace and Justice Studies Program at Wellesley College, as well as the co-founder and senior advisor of the EDUCATION as *Transformation* Project. He is the author of numerous articles and a frequent lecturer on issues of religious pluralism, spirituality, interreligious/intercultural dialogue and conflict resolution and principles of peacemaking and social justice.

Cheryl H. Keen is professor of self, society and culture at Antioch College and senior research fellow at the Bonner Foundation in Princeton, New Jersey. She is a co-author of *Common Fire: Leading Lives of Commitment in a Complex World* (Beacon Press, 1996).

James P. Keen is professor of social and global studies at Antioch College and senior research fellow at the Bonner Foundation in Princeton, New Jersey. He is a co-author of *Common Fire: Leading Lives of Commitment in a Complex World* (Beacon Press, 1996).

Gurucharan Singh Khalsa is president of Khalsa Consultants, Ins., an instructor at MIT, a chief minister in Sikh Dharma, and a psychotherapist. He does Mind/Body research in mediation and is an author, most recently of "The Mind: Its Projections and Multiple Facets" and "Breathwalk."

Susan Laemmle has served as dean of religious life at the University of Southern California since 1996 and was ordained as a rabbi by the Hebrew Union College-Jewish Institute of Religion, New York City, in 1987. She holds a BA (Summa Cum Laude) from USC, MA from Columbia University, and Ph.D. from UCLA in English literature.

Peter L. Laurence is director of the EDUCATION as *Transformation* Project, a national project on religious pluralism, spirituality and higher education located at Wellesley College. He has been a consultant to various national and international interfaith organizations for the past twenty years, and has served as chair of the board of the North American Interfaith Network and as a member of the Assembly for the Parliament of World Religions.

James Malarkey is professor and chair of humanities and general education of the McGregor School at Antioch University. He holds a Ph.D. in anthropology from the University of Texas at Austin, and is the author of "World Classics for World Citizenship" in the forthcoming book, *Teaching for Diversity, Unity and Human Values* (University of Maryland Press).

Patrick Morton is a research mathematician at Wellesley College, where he has taught since 1985. He received his Ph.D. from the University of Michigan in 1979, and is currently writing a book on the interplay between dreams and the creative process in mathematics.

Janet Cooper Nelson is chaplain of the university at Brown and a faculty member. She holds degrees from Wellesley College, Tufts University and Harvard Divinity School. American heterogeneity, the culture of higher education, and Christian social ethics hone her work as preacher, writer and consultant.

Andrés G. Niño is a clinical psychologist. He began research in the area of psychotherapy and spirituality at Harvard University in 1988, and has continued as a visiting scholar at the Wellesley College Centers for Research on Women. He is currently chair of a group of professionals studying the topic with the European Association for Psychotherapy.

Sulayman S. Nyang teaches in the Department of African Studies at Howard University, and has been there since 1972. During this time he has served twice as head of his department, has been a member of many academic boards and has written over one hundred scholarly articles and reviews.

Parker J. Palmer is a writer and traveling teacher who works independently on issues of education, community, spirituality and social change. He is a senior associate of the American Association for Higher Education and senior advisor to the Fetzer Institute.

Anantanand Rambachan is professor of religion and asian studies at St. Olaf College, where he has been teaching since 1985. He is the author of several books, chapters and numerous articles and reviews in scholarly journals.

Robert M. Randolph is senior associate dean in the Office of the Dean of Students and Undergraduate Education at M.I.T., where he has been since 1979. He has graduate degrees from Pepperdine University, Yale Divinity School, Brandeis University and Andover Newton Theological School.

David K. Scott is the chancellor of the University of Massachusetts at Amherst. He was educated at the University of Edinburugh and of Oxford, receiving his D.Phil in Nuclear Physics. He has worked as a scientist and educator at the University of Oxford, at Berkeley and at Michigan State, where he was provost and the John A. Hannah Distinguished Professor of Learning, Science and Society.

Shirley Hershey Showalter is a teacher, role model and leader at Goshen College, beginning her term as president on January 1, 1997. Since joining the college in 1976, she has taught in the English and history departments, eventually becoming a full professor and English department chair. In 1990, she won the Sears Roebuck Foundation "Teaching Excellence and Campus Leadership Award."

Krister Stendahl is Andrew W. Mellon Professor of Divinity Emeritus at Harvard University and Bishop Emeritus of Stockholm, Sweden. His writings center in Biblical studies, from which perspective he has addressed various issues of theology, history, the arts of ministry and contemporary problems in church and society.

Beverly Daniel Tatum is dean of the college and professor of psychology and education at Mt. Holyoke College. She is the author of *Why Are All the Black Kids Sitting Together in the Cafeteria? Other Conversations about Race* (Basic Books, 1997).

Diana Chapman Walsh is the twelfth president of Wellesley College. A leading expert in public health policy and the prevention of illness, she most recently was Florence Sprague Norman and Laura Smart Norman Professor at the Harvard School of Public Health, where she chaired the Department of Health and Social Behavior. Dr. Walsh has published extensively on topics related to the organization and financing of health care services, the conservation of health, the prevention and treatment of substance abuse, and the health effects of work.

Arthur G. Zajonc is a professor of physics at Amherst College and has been a visiting professor and research scientist at the Ecole Superieure in Paris, the Max Planck Institute for Quantum Optics, and the universities of Rochester, Innsbruck, and Hannover. He is general secretary of the Anthroposophical Society in America, president of the Lindisfarne Association, and a consultant to the Fetzer Institute.